Trading Places

TRADING PLACES

Colonization and Slavery in Eighteenth-Century French Culture

MADELEINE DOBIE

Cornell University Press

ITHACA AND LONDON

First published 2010 by Cornell University Press
First printing, Cornell Paperbacks, 2010

Printed in the United States of America

Library of Congress Cataloging-in-Publication Data

Dobie, Madeleine.
   Trading places : colonization and slavery in eighteenth-century French
culture / Madeleine Dobie.
      p. cm.
   Includes bibliographical references and index.
   ISBN 978-0-8014-4902-4 (cloth : alk. paper)
   ISBN 978-0-8014-7609-9 (pbk. : alk. paper)
      1. French literature—18th century—History and criticism.
2. Colonies in literature.   3. Slavery in literature.   4. Orientalism in
literature.   5. Colonization—Social aspects—France—History—18th
century.   6. Slavery—Social aspects—France—History—18th century.
7. Orientalism—France—History—18th century.   8. Material culture—
Social aspects—France—History—18th century.   9. France—Colonies—
History—18th century.   10. France—Intellectual life—18th century.
I. Title.
   PQ265.D63 2010
   840.9'3581—dc22
2010022630

Cornell University Press strives to use environmentally responsible
suppliers and materials to the fullest extent possible in the publishing
of its books. Such materials include vegetable-based, low-VOC inks
and acid-free papers that are recycled, totally chlorine-free, or partly
composed of nonwood fibers. For further information, visit our
website at www.cornellpress.cornell.edu.

Cloth printing   10 9 8 7 6 5 4 3 2 1

Paperback printing   10 9 8 7 6 5 4 3 2 1

For Norman, Donna,
and Milène Klein

This great colonial life: if people knew of its daily degradation they would speak less of it—they would not speak of it at all.

—RENÉ MARAN, *Batouala*

Contents

Preface

This book is about the cultural imprint of French colonization in the seventeenth and eighteenth centuries. It considers how the establishment of offshore colonies that produced valuable tropical commodities and relied on the labor of enslaved Africans registered in works of literature and philosophy and in the sphere of material culture. To be more precise, it explores the *absence* of representation of these colonial outposts over the period stretching from the inauguration of the colonial venture in the early sixteen hundreds to the closing decades of the eighteenth century.

In much current literary and historical scholarship, power is located in the production of discourse. In the case of colonial power, Edward Said's seminal book, *Orientalism,* has furnished an influential model for thinking about the interrelationships between power, knowledge, and representation. But relations of domination are not always mediated by discourse. They can also be grounded in silence, ignorance, and various modes of cultural censorship and repression. Taking a step back from the power-discourse model elaborated by Michel Foucault and later applied by Said, in this book I explore not only the corpus of representations generated by Old Regime French colonialism in the Americas and the Indian Ocean but also—and primarily—the resounding silence in which this expansion was enveloped.

A literary history of a "non-theme" or unactualized discourse might perhaps seem to be a rather strange endeavor. What I in fact examine in this book is not only the overall absence of representation but also the various detours and displacements by means of which silence spoke. Notably, I explore the complex relationship between the relative invisibility of the colonial world during a period that lasted until around 1770, and two related but far more prominent eighteenth-century thematics: fascination with "Oriental" culture, and the array of discourses devoted to the relationship between "civilized" Europeans and "primitive" societies exemplified by the indigenous peoples of the Americas. The first two parts of this book describe broad-based representational asymmetries between the limited representation of the colonial world, with its problematic dimensions of slavery and *métissage,* and the fascination invested in these two adjacent themes. It also examines specific texts and material objects in which, through processes of narrative digression or conceptual substitution, representation of the colonial world is transposed onto other geocultural contexts.

I argue that if the colonial world was sparsely represented, this was to a great extent because it was unrepresentable. During the Old Regime there was a strong cultural disincentive to portray colonial slavery, a system considered economically advantageous, but which raised moral questions. I also point to a number of other obstacles to representation, notably the absence of an established discursive framework for depicting the new diasporic environment of the colonial Americas.

Many academic studies published since the 1990s have merged the disciplines of literary analysis and social and cultural history. This book also attempts another, less familiar mode of interdisciplinarity by juxtaposing literature and material culture. This broadening of disciplinary perspective has seemed necessary for two reasons. One is that surveying a range of cultural media brings into focus patterns that are less obvious and harder to interpret when we focus only on literature or, only on foodstuffs or textiles. The second is that there is a propensity in both literary and historical scholarship to render colonial history as a web of discourses and representations. Since Old Regime French colonialism was in its core economic—since it generated far more commodities than representations—I have tried to bring cultural productions such as literature into dialogue with the material products of colonization and slavery.

In the introduction to *Orientalism,* Edward Said notes in passing that "the Orient is an integral part of European *material* civilization and culture" (2). He does not develop this point further, however, and instead proceeds to give an account of the relationship between Europe and the Orient that is grounded almost exclusively in the analysis of texts. Did Said mean that representational traditions cut across cultural platforms? That orientalism is manifested in objects such as furnishings and textiles as well as in texts? Perhaps. But I think that he may also have been getting at something further, and introducing an angle that on the whole is rather absent from *Orientalism,* which is that cultural traditions of the Muslim East materially penetrated European cultures. By this reading, material culture is understood both as a medium of exotic representation and as a site of contact and cultural transfer that is not reducible to the one-sided discursive economy of orientalism.

It is in this double sense that I examine material culture in this book. As the colonial world was not exotic in the eyes of eighteenth-century consumers—because there was no established figurative repertory for representing tropical environments or plantation societies—commodities derived from colonial sources, such as indigo, cotton, and mahogany, were often transformed into consumer goods manifesting an alluring Oriental facade. I explore this process of orientalization in two important spheres of material culture: furniture and textiles. But while I look at material objects as sites of representation, I also consider them as intersections between metropolitan and colonial histories and as potential vestiges of slave labor, one of the most fundamental but also one of the least tangible aspects of colonial experience.

This is a book about the colonial past, but also, and perhaps more significantly, it is about a somewhat neglected phase of French colonial history. Although since the late 1990s historians and social scientists have posited significant continuities between the colonial order and the contemporary era, particularly with regard to French perspectives on immigration, they have focused almost exclusively on the later French Empire in the Maghreb and sub-Saharan Africa. I argue that it is necessary to initiate longer genealogies and to consider how France's history of slavery, and historical disavowal of slavery, have shaped the ways in which identity and diversity are thought of in contemporary French politics and society. I suggest, in particular, that the repudiation of race that has been a distinctive feature of French social and political thought is rooted not only in the nation's republican tradition but also in France's complex relationship to its own history of racism, notably in the institutionalized form of colonial slavery.

This book could not have been written without the generous support of many colleagues and a number of institutions. I am thankful to Columbia University for a Junior Faculty Summer Fellowship that enabled me to conduct research in France in summer 2004, and for a research leave in 2005. During this sabbatical I had the good fortune to be a residential fellow at the National Humanities Center. I would like to thank the center's director, Geoffrey Harpham, and its able and assiduous staff for their assistance during my fellowship. In France I benefited from the research expertise of several colleagues. I am particularly indebted to Jacques de Cauna, who generously shared with me his knowledge of French colonial history and of the museums and archives of Bordeaux; Louis Bergès, director of the Regional Archives of the Gironde, who guided me to manuscript and published sources; Thierry Lefrançois, director of the Musée du nouveau monde of La Rochelle, an institution that has been in the vanguard of public exploration of the history of the French Atlantic; and Bernadette de Boysson, curator at the Musée des arts décoratifs de Bordeaux.

I owe a great debt to the colleagues who generously took the time to read and provide insightful feedback on various chapters. They include Vincent Debaene, Pierre Force, Phyllis Hunter, Dominique Jullien, Sylvie Lefèvre, Sara Melzer, Emmanuelle Saada, and two anonymous readers for Cornell University Press who made valuable suggestions for improvements. I have also benefited from the opportunity to share my work with participants in several workshops and seminars. These include the Institute for French Studies seminar of New York University, for which I thank Edward Berenson and Emmanuelle Saada. I also wish to express appreciation to the Warner Fund at the University Seminars at Columbia University for their help in publication. Material in this work was presented to the University Seminar in Eighteenth-Century European Culture. I am grateful to Bob Belknap, Director of the University Seminars, as well as to the members of the Eighteenth-Century Seminar, who participated in a helpful discussion of my ideas when this project was at a formative stage. I offer special thanks to the members of the Research Triangle French Studies seminar, including Keith Luria, Don Reid, Mary Sheriff, Philip Stewart, Anoush Terjanian, and Steve Vincent, and the Columbia French Department Writing Workshop, led by Vincent Debaene, for reading drafts of several chapters and offering constructive criticism.

I have presented parts of this book as lectures or at conferences and colloquia, and benefited from the valuable feedback generated by these presentations. I would like to express my thanks to Katharine Jensen, who invited me to present a preliminary overview to the French Department of Louisiana State University, and to Serge Gavronsky and Caryl Phillips, who invited me to speak at the Rockefeller Bellagio Center conference on "The Caribbean in New York and Paris." I presented a preliminary version of chapter two at the conference "Furnishing the Eighteenth Century," held at the William Andrews Clark Memorial Library and the J. Paul Getty Museum in Los Angeles in 2002 and wish to thank the two conference organizers, Kathryn Norberg and Dena Goodman, for inviting me to participate in this stimulating interdisciplinary exchange. I also express my gratitude to the furniture curators of the Getty, who gave us a memorable tour of their exceptional collection and materially changed the way in which I look at eighteenth-century furniture. A talk based on chapter seven was presented at a conference on the theme of literature and human rights organized by the graduate students of the Department of French and Italian of the University of California at Santa Barbara in 2008. I am grateful to Dominique Jullien and Pierre Bras for kindly inviting me to speak. Finally, part of chapter 6 was presented at the conference "Diderot Today" held at New York University in 2009. I thank the conference organizers, Lucien Nouis and Anne Deneys-Tunney, for the invitation to participate.

While working on this book I had fruitful discussions and e-mail exchanges with many colleagues. I am especially obliged to Serge Chassagne, Andrew Curran, Pierre Force, Dena Goodman, Dominique Jullien, Felicia McCarren, and Philip Stewart for their input on various aspects of my project. I have also been inspired over the last few years by lively discussions about French colonialism and its varied legacies with former and current graduate students, including Nayana Abeysinghe, Olivia Harrison, Ana Lazic, Mehammed Mack, Alexandra Perisic, Erin Twohig, and Toby Wikström, as well as by stimulating conversations on a wide range of intellectual topics with my colleagues in the Columbia French Department.

John Ackerman of Cornell University Press enthusiastically embraced this project from the first moment that it was presented to him and has been a lucid and extremely forbearing editor. I am deeply grateful both for his support and for his expert editorial advice. It has been a sheer pleasure to work with the manuscript editor for this book, Susan Specter, its copy editor, Marie Flaherty-Jones, and its indexer, Dave Prout. I am indebted to them all for their professionalism and meticulous attention to detail.

This book was written over several years, and at times during the most painful personal circumstances. Many friends and family members have helped sustain me during this time, but none more so than Norman and Donna Klein, who have provided not only emotional support but also innumerable hours of child care while I was busy writing. This book is for them, and for my incomparable daughter, Milène.

An earlier version of chapter 2 is published under the title "Orientalism, Colonialism, and Furniture in Eighteenth-Century France," in *Furnishing the Eighteenth Century: What Furniture Can Tell Us about the European and American Past* (Taylor and Francis, 2007). Material from chapter 6 appeared in "Going Global: Diderot, 1770–1784," *Diderot Studies* 31 (2009). I am grateful for the publishers' permission to reprint this material here.

Introduction
Trading Places

Writing about France's Caribbean colonies in his *Essai sur les mœurs* (*Essay on Universal History*) (1756–78), Voltaire touches on a fundamental contradiction. On the one hand he states that these islands are mere "dots on the map," and that their history is "lost in the history of the universe." On the other he notes that "these countries, which one can scarcely perceive on a globe, produce in France an annual circulation of sixty million in merchandise."[1] This book is about the contradiction inherent in these two observations. In it I propose that although the island colonies that France established in the Atlantic and Indian oceans in the middle of the seventeenth century had a significant and by some measures transformative impact on the nation's economy and material culture, their existence registered very little in cultural representations. Correspondingly I argue that these colonies have remained relatively peripheral to the writing of French history, including French colonial history.

It is often assumed that the leading figures of the French Enlightenment wrote extensively about France's overseas expansion and the regime of colonial slavery.[2] This is inaccurate. Despite their many contributions to the

---

1. Voltaire, *Essai sur les mœurs,* 2:380. The first edition of the *Essay* was published in 1756, but Voltaire continued to edit and make corrections until his death in 1778. The passage cited above was added in the 1770s. Please note that unless stated otherwise all translations in this book are my own.

2. In his study of the *lumières'* silence on colonial slavery, the historian Louis Sala-Molins recalls the intense skepticism with which colleagues and students greeted his claim that Montesquieu and even Rousseau did not write extensively about this topic. Sala-Molins, *Misères des lumières,* translated by John Conteh-Morgan as *Dark Side of the Light,* 72–73.

interrogation of political authority, their exploration of cultural difference, and their promotion of religious tolerance, until a turning point that occurred in the late 1760s, prominent thinkers such as Montesquieu, Voltaire, Rousseau, and even Diderot, for whom colonialism subsequently became a key concern, wrote little about the colonies or the system of slave labor that sustained them. When they did refer to slavery, it was predominantly in metaphorical terms, as a figure for human oppression in general, or with regard to other cultures and other historical periods. When Voltaire observes that the history of the Antilles was lost in the wider history of the universe, he is tacitly acknowledging that he and other French writers had not undertaken to write their history. I would add that if we can still be surprised by how little Voltaire and the other philosophes had to say on the subject of colonial slavery it is largely because the sugar islands of France's first colonial empire have remained peripheral to the principal narratives of French history.

This book explores the origins, modalities, and historiographical and ethical implications of the cultural invisibility of the colonial world in seventeenth- and eighteenth-century French culture. In readings of a broad range of literary and paraliterary texts, and through explorations of two key domains of material culture, textiles and furniture, it maps the principal ways in which the colonial world was—and was not—represented in prerevolutionary French culture.

With the exception of Quebec and Acadia (established, respectively, in 1604 and 1608), the territories of the first French colonial empire were plantation colonies devoted to the production of tropical commodities and maintained by a system of slave labor. Although the image of early French colonialism is bound up with the story of the French presence in Canada, the one French territory in which slavery was not prevalent, France's core overseas possessions lay in the Caribbean and in the Indian Ocean. They were the islands of Guadeloupe and Martinique (annexed in 1635); the western part of the island of Hispaniola, known then as Saint-Domingue and now as Haiti (first occupied by French settlers in the 1630s and officially annexed in 1697); French Guiana (established as a durable colony in 1664, following several earlier attempts); Louisiana (1699); and the Indian Ocean islands of Île Bourbon (1642) and Île de France (1715) (today La Réunion and Mauritius).[3] These colonies, which later came to be known as the *vieilles colonies,* primarily produced sugar, but at various junctures also yielded other tropical commodities including tobacco; coffee; cocoa; cotton; indigo; roucou (a rust-colored pigment); cochineal;

---

3. The Indian Ocean colonies were also relay points for French trade with India and Indonesia, and at times for the transfer of slaves from East Africa to the Antilles. See Vaughan, *Creating the Creole Island,* 78.

vanilla; spices; various tropical hardwoods; and decorative materials such as mother-of-pearl and tortoiseshell. These products were shipped to France and then either reexported to other European nations or transformed into consumer goods for domestic consumption or export.

The "circulation" of colonial merchandise (to borrow Voltaire's term) was an important source of revenue both for individual investors and for the state. Robert Louis Stein, a historian of the French sugar and slave trades, calculates that by the 1780s a full half of France's exports to other European countries was made up of colonial goods.[4] Commercial exchanges with the colonies also provided employment opportunities for many French workers—it has been estimated that one in eight French subjects earned a living in a manner connected with colonial trade—and they were an important source of raw materials for France's manufacturing industries.[5] Over time, imported tropical commodities transformed the tastes and consumption habits of French people of all social classes. Between 1700 and 1730, Kenneth Banks observes, "the tropical products of the French Americas passed from coveted luxuries to daily necessities."[6] Along the same lines, Stein notes that riots broke out in Paris in January 1792, not over the shortage of bread, but rather over the rising price of sugar.[7]

When French colonies were first established in the Caribbean in the 1630s, their principal crop was tobacco, and their workforce was composed primarily of indentured servants known as *engagés:* a contingent of peasants, manual workers, and destitute people who agreed, usually because of dire poverty, to bestow their labor for three years in return for passage to the Americas and the hope of one day becoming a freeholder.[8] In the late 1650s, sugar began to replace tobacco as the colonies' primary commercial crop.[9] With this transition, small plantations (known in French as *habitations*) were replaced by larger establishments, and the colonies' indentured workforce became inadequate.[10] To augment the supply of labor, France, following the lead of other European nations, entered the Atlantic slave trade. In the 1670s and 1680s, France launched two monopoly slave-trading companies: the Senegal Company (1673) and the Guinea Company (1685).[11] To facilitate their operations, it also seized Gorée (1677), an island off the coast of Senegal that

4. *French Slave Trade,* 197.
5. Cauna, *Au Temps des Îles à Sucre,* 12.
6. Banks, *Chasing Empire across the Sea,* 33.
7. *French Sugar Business,* ix.
8. On indentured servants, see Debien, *Les engagés pour les Antilles.*
9. Stein, *French Sugar Business,* 5–6.
10. The French term *habitation* roughly translates as plantation, but it has overtones that the English term lacks. By linking production with dwelling, it softens the image of the plantation, suggesting a familial community of planters and slaves engaged in a collective process of production.
11. See Banks, 24.

was to become one of the principal hubs of the slave trade in Africa. The monopoly companies, however, failed to supply slaves in sufficient numbers to meet the colonies' rising demands, and so, in 1716 slave trading was opened to merchants from five of France's Atlantic ports.[12]

When considered from the perspective of the United States, in which slavery and its social and economic legacies have carried enormous social and political resonance, the peripheral status of the history of slavery in French culture and historiography may seem surprising. This marginality might in fact lead us to conclude that the French colonies in the Americas were something of a colonial sideshow, a venture of minor importance when compared with the massive British, U.S., and Portuguese operations. Yet this was not the case. To put matters in perspective, let us consider statistics provided by Michel-Rolph Trouillot in his eloquent historiographical essay, *Silencing the Past.* Trouillot notes that during its history as a slaving nation, France imported three times as many slaves to the Americas as the British North American colonies and United States combined, and that the tiny island of Martinique alone imported more slaves than the United States.[13] Historians generally estimate that French vessels transported over a million Africans to the New World during the eighteenth century, a volume of trade that made France the third-leading supplier of slaves to the Americas after England and Portugal.[14]

But France was not only a major participant in the Atlantic slave trade. It was also the world leader in the trade in sugar, coffee, indigo, and a number of other tropical commodities. I think that it is often presumed that England controlled the wealthiest and most productive Caribbean colonies. Today we associate sugar with Barbados and Jamaica, whereas little is said about French Saint-Domingue. But in the mid-eighteenth century, France, not England, was the world's leading producer of sugar, as well as the dominant player in the global coffee market. By the 1780s Saint-Domingue alone produced close to one half of the sugar consumed in Europe and the Americas, as well as a substantial proportion of their cotton and indigo.[15] The reason for this dominant position was efficiency. According to William B. Cohen, French planters extracted 25 percent more sugar per acre than the planters of British Jamaica.[16] As a result, they were able to significantly undercut the prices of their British and Dutch competitors. Though French colonists chafed at the bit of the tight system of regulations imposed by the state, these controls ensured the efficacy of the system of production. Geared toward reexport to northern Europe, the

12. See Stein, *French Slave Trade,* 19–20.
13. Trouillot, *Silencing the Past,* 17.
14. Ibid., 20.
15. Geggus, *Haitian Revolutionary Studies,* 5.
16. *French Encounter with Africans,* 56.

French sugar business was a well-oiled machine, calibrated to keep prices low and consumption high.[17]

The colonies were economically important but not culturally visible. Why? One obvious answer to this question lies in the political and commercial regimes under which the colonies were administered from their founding in the mid-seventeenth century until the mid-1780s. The mercantilist principles that informed colonial policy emphasized the subordination of the colonies to the metropole, while keeping the colonial world at a certain remove. The colonies, it was held, existed to *serve* France. But what this meant, implicitly, was that they were not viewed as an integral part of France. A similar point could be made about the *Code noir* (*Black Code*), the body of legislation drawn up in 1685 to regulate the practice of colonial slavery. The preamble to the *Code noir* states that although the colonies were geographically remote, the power of Louis XIV was to be considered as present in them as in continental France. What the *Code noir* effectively established, however, was a regime of legal exception, a body of law that applied exclusively in the colonies, and that indeed could have no bearing in metropolitan France, where slavery was legally prohibited.

As Sue Peabody and Pierre Boulle have shown, over the course of the eighteenth century increasingly stringent laws were introduced to limit the rights of colonists to bring slaves to the metropole.[18] These laws had a positive side, to the extent that they afforded some slaves who were brought to France the opportunity to sue for their freedom. But they also had the effect of keeping slaves, and by extension slavery, out of sight and out of mind in safely distant "offshore" locations. Gradually these laws came to regulate and limit not only the presence of slaves in France but also, more insidiously, the presence of black people. A key example was the Police des noirs (Black Police), established by an edict of 1777 as a mechanism for documenting the presence of blacks in France. The primary objective of this measure was clearly to reduce the number of blacks entering the metropole. This effort seems to have been successful. The historian Léo Elisabeth has shown that whereas 1,098 arrivals of enslaved black individuals were registered with the admiralty of Bordeaux during the period before 1756, in the period from 1756 to 1786 when laws were more stringent, the number dropped to 102.[19] The limited presence of

17. See Stein, *French Sugar Business,* 94.
18. Peabody, *"There Are No Slaves in France"*; Boulle, *Race et esclavage.*
19. Cited in Eric Saugera, *Bordeaux, port négrier,* 291. This statistic reflects the number of blacks who were registered rather than the actual number of blacks in France in this period. Other data suggest that slave owners and free blacks sometimes evaded these controls.

enslaved and free blacks in France contrasted with the situation across the Channel, where planters regularly brought their slaves to the metropole to serve as domestic servants. Using the results of the census conducted at the time of the initiation of the Black Police, scholars including Boulle and Erick Noël have estimated that in the late 1770s there were no more than four to five thousand enslaved or free blacks living in France in an overall population of around 28 million.[20] In England there were perhaps three times as many in a population of around ten million. The presence of these colonial transplants is recorded in the many British family portraits that featured black domestic servants, as well as in the painter William Hogarth's well-known engravings of the "St. Giles Starlings": destitute black men who dwelled in the London slums.[21] The presence of black people in English society helped cultivate awareness of the features of colonial society, a consciousness that developed more slowly on the other side of the channel.[22]

But if the political and juridical culture of Old Regime French colonialism limited the visibility of the colonies and slavery, it did not produce this marginality. As the example of the Black Police suggests, policies and laws that held the colonies at a remove were symptoms of a deep-seated reluctance to allow colonial reality to penetrate metropolitan France. In his 2007 study of the literary imprint of French colonial slavery, Christopher L. Miller asks how "culture," in the sense of the production of texts, ideas, and discourses, accommodates "culture," meaning the cultivation of tropical commodities.[23] His answer: with a fairly clear conscience; and with indifference, irony, and inconsistency. I am not so sure. Though the silence surrounding a social phenomenon can certainly betoken indifference and even approval, it just as often reflects reluctance to confront or come to terms with a moral issue. Though silence clearly does not correlate with a strong ethical response (to this extent I agree with Miller), it often marks the boundary between confident acceptance and moral outcry.

Various kinds of evidence suggest that the low profile of the colonial world in French culture resulted, not from sheer ignorance or complete indifference, but rather from mechanisms of avoidance. A particularly telling pattern in this regard is the fact that until the late 1760s the colonies were represented most often and with greatest transparency in works whose authors, often participants in the colonial system, clearly felt very few qualms about slavery. By contrast, when a broader group of writers began to turn their attention to the

---

20. Boulle 196; Noël, *Être noir en France*, 95. On blacks in England, see Braidwood, *Black Poor and White Philanthropists*.

21. See Dabydeen, *Hogarth's Blacks*.

22. There were also more absentee planters living in England than in France. In eighteenth-century British parlance these planters were known as "nabobs"—an orientalist trope—and viewed as an ostentatious class of social climbers. The lower ratio of absenteeism in the French context was likely one of the factors that contributed to the efficiency of the system.

23. *French Atlantic Triangle*, 81.

colonies and slavery in the 1770s–80s, it was in the context of the rise of abolitionist argument. Representing the colonies entailed representing slavery, and
slavery could be contemplated directly only within the discursive framework of
a call for its elimination.

The representation of the colonial world in eighteenth-century literature
and culture has not, until lately, been widely examined by literary scholars and
theorists. The reasons for this lack of interest are easy to discern. Literary criticism tracks literature, leading to a correlation between the relative paucity of
eighteenth-century representations of colonization and the comparably small
number of critical interpretations. There are, however, a few exceptions. In
these cases the standard procedure is to acknowledge that colonization was not
widely represented in eighteenth-century French culture, and then to respond
to this dearth by cataloging (and indeed, since many of the titles in question
are rather obscure, excavating) the disparate works in which colonization and
slavery are evoked. Since literary scholars are more accustomed to analyzing
representations and discourses than to theorizing their absence, the critical re-
flex in a case where there are few representations to examine is to turn silence
into discourse.

This is a reasonable approach, and it has helped bring to light many obscure
but illuminating texts. Yet it does have the side effect of causing the representation of the colonial world to appear more extensive, less fragmentary, than
it actually was. With this problem in mind, in this book I pursue a different
approach. Rather than taking as my point of departure the scattered works in
which colonies or slavery are evoked, I start from, and indeed insist on, the
premise of a fundamental absence of representation.

Why is it important to dwell on the absence of representation? The main
reason, from my perspective, is that the history of colonial slavery, like that
of several other episodes of atrocity, engages us in a double ethical relation.
It is necessary to contemplate not only the brutality, racism, and indifference
to human life that the Atlantic slave trade entailed but also the attenuated
fashion in which European societies responded to these abuses. Though this
silence was not a direct cause of colonial slavery, it was certainly a condition
of its possibility. It is also one of the aspects of the history of slavery that
holds the greatest contemporary moral relevance. While it is now possible
for us to condemn the inhumanity of colonial slavery from a safe moral vantage point—in France, for example, a law of 2001 established colonial slavery
as a crime against humanity—our ethical relation to silence and avoidance
is both more immediate and more complex.[24] As Myriam Cottias observes,

---

24. Law n° 2001-43, May 21, 2001.

the triangle trade was "the first economy of the global market."[25] As such it brought into existence new, transcontinental networks of production and consumption, linking workers, investors, and consumers in Africa, the Americas, Europe, and Asia. Over the course of the last four centuries, these networks have continued to expand. Today, as in the 1700s, production for the global market often entails exploitation and abuse. Though we may not participate directly in these infractions of workers' and human rights, as consumers in the Western world we often benefit materially from them, and we are sometimes at least peripherally aware of them. As such, like seventeenth- and eighteenth-century observers of the slave trade, we are faced with ethical decisions about whether and how to respond. There are, of course, crucial distinctions to be made between today's sweatshops and *maquiladoras* and the Atlantic slave trade: my purpose here is not to draw a direct analogy between the guilt-by-association produced by contemporary globalization and the historical context of slavery. I do, however, want to point out that our experience as observers of and participants in today's global economy overlaps and resonates with that of people in previous centuries confronted by the transcontinental economy of slavery.

Postcolonial readings of colonial discourse have tended either to emphasize its hegemonic consistency (as in the case of Edward Said's analysis of orientalism) or (following the lead of Homi Bhabha) to expose its constitutive "ambivalence" by exploring patterns of hybridity and mimicry.[26] The silence that shrouded colonial slavery does not fit easily into either of these interpretative frames. It clearly lacks the hypervisibility manifested by orientalist discourse. It also seems to lack the signs of ideological splitting and psychological conflict that are generally associated with ambivalence. In a rich book on seventeenth- and eighteenth-century French colonial or Creole discourses, Doris Garraway suggests that if postcolonial theorists have been slow to consider the representations associated with colonial slavery, it is perhaps because the commodification of human beings that such representations entailed was marked by very little ambivalence.[27] On one level this seems right. But I also want to observe that silence is not necessarily the opposite of speech, and that it is not "univocal" in its meaning. Below I consider the silence surrounding colonial slavery as being symptomatic of a process of displacement. Since displacement entails the bifurcation and disruption of meaning, we can perhaps interpret it as a specific mode of colonial ambivalence.

◦

25. *La Question noire*, 8.
26. Said, *Orientalism;* Bhabha, "Of Mimicry and Man."
27. *Libertine Colony*, xii.

To offer a literary history of the silence enveloping colonial slavery in the most literal sense would mean cataloging all the works in which slavery is *not* represented, or at least those in which slavery really *could* or *should* have been represented but wasn't. This kind of negative literary history is not what I attempt, though in an appendix to this book I do give some indications regarding "absent" or fragmentary representations, particularly in relation to texts regarded as canonical works of the French Enlightenment. Instead, I consider the various ways in which silence spoke: the forms of dislocation and compensation through which silence was translated into representation. In specific terms I argue that in the seventeenth and eighteenth centuries the issue of colonial slavery was regularly projected or "displaced" onto two adjacent cultural terrains. In the first part of this book, titled "East Meets West," I describe a transfer from the colonial arena to the Oriental world, a displacement that was mediated by the widespread perception of the Orient as a culture permeated by slavery. In the second, "Savages and Slaves," I propose that the Americas were predominantly depicted by French observers as a terrain of encounter between Europeans and "noble savages" or "native others." The book's title, *Trading Places,* alludes not only to the commercial activities that were the raison d'être of France's colonies but also to these two major patterns of cultural exchange.

In the course of a reading of Voltaire's Peruvian tragedy, *Alzire* (1736), Christopher Miller observes that whereas Voltaire portrayed enslavement in South America (in *Alzire*) and in the Orient (in his 1764 Oriental tale, *Le blanc et le noir*), he found less to say about slavery as practiced in France's Caribbean colonies. Building on this observation, Miller suggests that Voltaire effectively overwrote the Atlantic triangle connecting France, Africa, and the Antilles with a second triangle of exotic representation anchored in the Orient and South America (74). I agree with this reading, but want to expand it considerably by arguing that the displacements that Miller identifies in the work of Voltaire reflect a much wider correlation between the sparse representation of colonial slavery and the far more extensive depiction of both the Orient and the Amerindian cultures of South America.

That French discomfort with regard to colonial society should be transposed onto representations of Oriental culture is not surprising when we consider that Europeans' fears and desires have very often been projected onto the Muslim East. As Edward Said notes in *Orientalism,* "The Orient has helped to define Europe (or the West) as its contrasting image, idea, personality, experience" (2). In the seventeenth and eighteenth centuries, the Orient served as a mirror for the indirect observation of French society and political culture. The principal medium for this specular exchange was the discourse of "Oriental despotism": the characterization of the Orient as a region subject to authoritarian rule and distinguished by various forms of subordination. Many scholars have observed that Oriental despotism provided a framework for the indirect exploration of the absolutist doctrines of the Bourbon monarchy.[28] I will argue that because the Orient was regarded as a culture permeated by slavery, it also constituted a terrain in which another form of European authoritarianism—the regime of colonial slavery—could be indirectly explored. Locating servitude in the Orient had a number of implications. On the most basic level it shifted attention away from the colonies and projected responsibility elsewhere. Additionally, this displacement also allowed slavery to be surveyed through what might be described as a soft-focus lens. In French representations of the Orient, slavery was often depicted as a domestic, quasi-familial institution that did not involve the physical rigors of plantation slavery, and which had some potentially recuperable social dimensions.

The second pattern of cultural substitution that I discuss in this book relates to the dominant modes of representation of the colonial Americas in eighteenth-century French culture. The New World was imagined across a range of genres and discourses, as a contact zone in which "civilized" though often "barbaric" Europeans encountered "native" and usually "savage" others. By contrast the Americas were much less often portrayed as a creolized society formed from the merger of Amerindian, European, and African cultures. "Native" others were depicted both more extensively and more sympathetically than enslaved Africans, and indeed I would argue that compassion and abundance of representation went hand in hand.

Though both Africans and Amerindians were subject to violence and enslavement in the colonial Americas, their experiences were represented in divergent ways. In eighteenth-century French culture the "black legend" of the Spanish persecution of the Amerindians stood both as an emblem of the moral failings of the conquistadors and as an indictment of the vices associated with civilization.[29] Amerindians, correspondingly, were imagined to embody virtues derived not from exposure to civilized society but rather from proximity to the state of nature. Enslaved people of African descent, by contrast, were not widely portrayed as victims of European imperialism until the end of the eighteenth century, and their suffering was not woven into the fabric of any major philosophical traditions. The Valladolid debates of 1550, in which the Dominican Bartolomé de Las Casas locked horns with the philosopher Juan Ginés de Sepúlveda over the right of Spanish colonists to subjugate and enslave Amerindians, stand to this day as an example of public moral debate. Who now remembers the seventeenth-century Sorbonne inquiry, presided over by

---

28. See, for example, Grosrichard, *Structure du sérail*.

29. Michel de Montaigne's two essays on the New World, "Des Cannibales" (On Cannibals) and "Des Coches" (On Coaches) (1575), were the point of departure for this linkage of proximity to nature and condemnation of civilized barbarism.

Germain Fromageau, in which the legitimacy of the African slave trade was raised as a legal question?[30]

When I speak of the cultural displacement of colonial slavery onto Oriental culture or the discourse of the noble savage, I mean two different though related things. The first is that these thematics occupied a far more central place in eighteenth-century French culture than the Caribbean colonies and their regimen of race-based slavery, an asymmetry that seems disproportionate when we consider the material and strategic importance of the colonial world. This kind of displacement is by no means unfamiliar. In almost every social context, certain issues command attention while others—often the most intractable social questions—remain virtually unexamined. The second is somewhat more context specific, and it mainly concerns the relationship between the colonial world and Oriental discourse. In the first part of this book I discuss a number of texts that initiate discussion of colonization and slavery, but then, by means of discursive or narrative maneuvers such as digression or disjuncture, relocate the question such that the context is transferred to the Oriental world. I also point to similar patterns of displacement in the sphere of material culture, where objects constructed from raw materials derived from colonial sources were often transformed into alluring "Oriental" consumer goods.

To denote the transposition of colonial slavery onto adjacent discursive fields I predominantly use the term "displacement," a concept borrowed from the lexicon of psychoanalysis. Though my analysis of this phenomenon is only loosely based on psychoanalytic theory, I think it is perhaps helpful here to quickly summarize the main tenets of the theory of displacement elaborated by Sigmund Freud. In *The Interpretation of Dreams (1900)*, Freud argues that in the representational economy of dreams, "latent" thoughts of a disturbing nature are often displaced onto neutral representations that appear in the dream's "manifest" content. These manifest representations, Freud further suggests, are usually associated in some manner with the censored ideas. "Displacement" (in German, *Verschiebung*) thus denotes a process of psychic censorship in which challenging ideas are replaced by related but less tendentious concerns.

In this book I draw on the concept of displacement to denote, not processes of repression and substitution occurring within the individual psyche, but rather patterns of representation and nonrepresentation occurring on a broader cultural level. Though it could certainly be argued that individual

---

30. De Lamet and Fromageau, "Règles sur le commerce des esclaves." This case is briefly mentioned by Russell P. Jameson in *Montesquieu et l'esclavage*, 131–34, and by David Brion Davis in *The Problem of Slavery in Western Culture*, 197. The panel of theologians who heard the case determined that it was only legitimate to purchase Africans who were already enslaved. There is no evidence that this rather ambiguous judgment had any impact on the conduct of the slave trade.

writers had their reasons for not wanting to confront the issue of slavery directly (Voltaire, for example, was probably an investor in the *Compagnie des Indes occidentales* (West Indies Company), and Montesquieu's Bordeaux estate did a robust trade in wine with the Antilles), I do not, for the most part, focus on personal disincentives. Rather I examine broad asymmetries and patterns of substitution that transcend individual investments.[31]

Writers, of course, sometimes consciously choose to transpose questions associated with one sociopolitical context onto another, more distant arena. This was the case, for example, with the specular exchange between Bourbon absolutism and Oriental despotism to which I alluded earlier. The displaced representation of colonial slavery, however, was not a form of allegory or conscious self-censorship, but rather the symptom of largely unconscious processes. That is not to say that the topic of slavery was subject to a central mechanism of repression, a claim that would imply an overarching psychoanalytic theory of culture. Rather, I want to suggest, more loosely, that a configuration of different social, cultural, economic, and political forces prevented slavery from becoming a visible issue and diverted representation elsewhere.

Displacement is a form of cultural repression that excludes certain forms of knowledge and forecloses certain questions. But it is also a process that disrupts the production of meaning and serves as a vantage point from which it is possible to observe the workings of power. Does this mean that displacement can be viewed as a site of resistance to the forms of power embodied in colonial regimes?[32] Perhaps, but I think it would be problematic to press this point too far and to emphasize semantic dissonance at the expense of the axis of repression. Displacement speaks to the silencing of the "other," but it is not the other's displaced speech.

Trading Places identifies two different kinds of impediment to representation, obstacles of different natures, but which often worked in tandem and produced a combined effect. One was the pressure to avoid or circumvent discussion of slavery. Slavery was widely felt to be morally problematic yet also believed to be economically beneficial. As a result, at least until the advent of abolitionism, it was either not represented at all or represented as a characteristic of the Eastern world. The second obstacle arose, not from a mechanism of censorship, but rather from the absence of a discursive framework. If a wide array of French observers, including travel writers, missionaries, novelists, and philosophers, all depicted the Americas as a zone of contact between

31. On Montesquieu's business interests and the slave trade, see Lafontant, *Montesquieu et le problème de l'esclavage*, 116, and Chérel, *De Télémaque à Candide*, 281–82.
32. Spivak, "Can the Subaltern Speak?"

Europeans and Amerindians rather than as a site of colonization, slavery, and métissage, it was not simply because these processes were subject to repression but also because writers lacked conceptual models and figurative repertories for representing them. Eighteenth-century Europeans were accustomed to thinking about identity and difference in terms of culture and geography (this was, for example, the model underlying the construct of the Orient). Amerindian culture also fit easily within the established model: the Caribs and other indigenous groups could be understood as "peoples" who belonged to a specific region and who exhibited specific cultural traits. The identity of diasporic Africans, by contrast, did not lend itself to this kind of description. Today we have a rich conceptual vocabulary for speaking about colonial and postcolonial cultures: terms such as "diaspora," "creolization," "hybridity," and "métissage." Eighteenth-century writers, however, lacked these tools and had no precedent for depicting the hybrid and volatile environment of colonial societies. The absence of established discourses also impacted material culture. If artists and craftsmen orientalized furniture and other consumer goods, it was partly because there was a well-developed figurative tradition for representing Oriental culture. By contrast, the Americas constituted an aesthetic tabula rasa to which emblems and symbols had yet to be assigned.

The final section of this book takes a different form from the first two. Rather than addressing silences or displacements, it examines the shift from marginality to discursivity that occurred when, in the late 1760s, France's colonies belatedly became objects of representation and political debate. In emphasizing this transition one of my goals is to bring greater historical differentiation into the analysis of colonial representation.[33] If the pervasive silence of Enlightenment writers on the question of slavery has not been more widely recognized it is partly because scholars have tended to point to the discourses of the 1770s and 1780s as evidence of an energetic critical response. I show that although there was significant engagement with colonial questions in this period, this emphasis represented a decisive rupture with the previous century and a half.

The coalescence of "colonial discourse" that began to take place in the late 1760s was to some extent a function of political events. In 1763, at the end of the Seven Years' War, France lost its North American colonies in Canada (to Britain) and Louisiana (to Spain), a jolting setback that prompted a broad rethinking of the nation's future as a colonial power. Other transcontinental conflicts followed closely on the heels of this defeat: France supported the

---

33. See, on this issue, Frederick Cooper, *Colonialism in Question*, 3.

American colonies in their bid for independence, and then became embroiled in its own colonial conflict in Saint-Domingue. Together these conflicts created a new level of awareness of colonial questions.

But the establishment of the colonies as an object of representation was also the result of cultural forces. Earlier I argued that colonization and slavery only came to be widely represented by French writers when arguments in favor of the abolition of slavery began to gain ground. In the third part of this book I develop this point further to show that French abolitionism was largely predicated on arguments generated within the new field of liberal political economy. I am not the first scholar to point to connections between French liberal economic thought and French abolitionism, but I take this argument further than it has been taken before by suggesting that economic discourse was not just *an* important facet of abolitionism but rather *the* principal conceptual register in which slavery and emancipation were discussed in France between 1763 and the French Revolution. I argue that this economic perspective was present not only where one might expect to find it—in works of political economy—but also in the fictional writing on slavery that appeared in France in the 1770s–90s.

Interest in colonial topics, and particularly in the central question of slavery, rose steadily in the 1770s and 1780s. In 1788, on the eve of the Revolution, slavery was raised to the level of a national political issue by the founding of the Société des amis des noirs (Society of the Friends of Blacks), a pressure group created to inform the public about colonial slavery and to lobby for its abolition.

Slavery was abolished in the French colonies in 1794. It would, however, be hasty to see this event as the culmination of a decade of political activism. Between 1789 and 1793 slavery was discussed relatively little in the Constituent Assembly, debates over colonial affairs revolving rather around the surrogate question of whether political rights should be accorded to colonial planters and to the *gens de couleur libre,* or free black and mixed-race people. What triggered the abolition decree of 1794 was in fact less the emergence of a moral consensus against slavery than the dramatic events unfolding in France's most important colony, Saint-Domingue. The large enslaved population of the island, estimated to stand at around five hundred thousand by 1789, had been in open revolt since 1791.[34] In 1793, in order to discourage its leaders from entering into an alliance with invading British forces, the envoy of the National Assembly, Léger-Félicité Sonthonax, issued a series of proclamations declaring emancipation. The law passed by the convention in 1794 was essentially a ratification of these decrees.

---

34. See Geggus, *Haitian Revolutionary Studies,* 158–70. Geggus estimates the free black and mixed-race population of Saint-Domingue in 1789 to have been around thirty thousand (5).

Emancipation lasted for barely a decade. In 1802 slavery was restored at the behest of Napoleon Bonaparte. Though it is possible to see this reversal as a consequence of the political views and foreign-policy objectives of the soon-to-be emperor, the fact that slavery continued to exist in the French colonies until 1848—a decade and a half after its abolition in the British Empire— certainly suggests a deeper-seated absence of political will.

When we look closely at the abolitionist writing produced by French thinkers in the 1770s–90s, this outcome does not seem all that surprising. The economic framing of calls for emancipation had a decisive impact on the ways in which abolition was envisaged. Most of the principal French advocates of abolition argued that emancipation should occur, not on an immediate basis, as a restitution of fundamental rights, but as a gradual, staggered process, and in such a way that the colonies' social order and economic viability would be preserved. Abolitionism is often approached as a freestanding moral discourse: the belated flowering of a critical response to slavery. But whereas it is certainly accurate to say that French writers formulated moral arguments against slavery, this body of writing also needs to be interpreted within the discursive context in which it was embedded, that is, the framework of emergent economic and political liberalism. This framework both shaped the manner in which emancipation was imagined and, I would argue, contributed to the faltering history of its political implementation.

In *Discours sur le colonialisme* (*Discourse on Colonialism*) (1950), Aimé Césaire observes that beneath the discourses and ideologies in which the colonial web is spun lies the appetite of the merchant.[35] Colonialism is a mosaic made up of many pieces, but its core, Césaire suggests, is economic. Though the annexation of territory and the subordination or enslavement of other peoples have important political, psychological, and sexual dimensions, the first impetus for these predations is usually economic. In its early, Atlantic form in particular, colonialism was a machine of production and manufacture, profit and reinvestment, appetite and consumption. Though colonial ventures were not always profitable, either for individual planters and merchants or for the state (the economic benefits of slavery, challenged by liberal economists at the end of the eighteenth century, are still debated by contemporary historians), colonies nonetheless existed for the purpose of producing commodities and extracting profit.[36] They were hubs in a sprawling system of economic

35. Aimé Césaire, *Discourse on Colonialism*, 32–33.
36. On the economic impact of slavery see Stein, *French Sugar Business*, 37–39, Pétré-Grenouilleau, *L'Argent de la traite*.

connections that linked commerce and manufacture, credit and employment, and that had outlets in the visible cultural domains of luxury and fashion.

Literary critics such as myself are somewhat prone to treating colonization as a discursive phenomenon, anchored in ideology and articulated in texts. But since Old Regime colonialism generated more commodities than texts, in this book I attempt to counteract this propensity by emphasizing the economic and commercial dimensions of colonization and slavery. As noted above, the third section of the book deals at length with the economic discourses that framed discussion of these subjects in the 1770s–90s. In two other chapters I take what might be called a commodity-centered approach to the cultural impact of colonization; that is to say, I explore the transformative impact of colonial expansion on two prominent spheres of material culture. In chapter two I consider how the availability of an array of tropical hardwoods impacted the manufacture of furniture, a domain of material culture that has historically been closely associated with French taste and style. In chapter three I explore the impact of cotton, at first imported from India, but later also grown in the Caribbean and Louisiana, on French textile manufacture and on the realm of fashion. Textiles were the great driver of European economies in the prerevolutionary period, and changes within this industry inevitably had far-reaching social and cultural implications.

In these forays into material culture I approach decorative objects and consumer goods not as a specialist but from the vantage point of a literary scholar. That is to say, I look at textiles and furniture as representational media and make arguments that run parallel to my discussion of texts. Specifically, I suggest that in textiles and furniture we can observe representational displacements that reflect the transfer of colonial interests onto a fascination with Oriental culture. The kind of integrated approach to culture that I take in this book certainly has its pitfalls—those associated with all interdisciplinary research—but I would argue that it also illuminates structures and processes that do not come to light in more narrowly focused research. In the case at hand, for instance, it demonstrates that orientalization was not just a circumscribed tropology or intertextual paradigm but rather the symptom of a far-reaching process of cultural repression and redistribution.

In *The Social Life of Things*, Arjun Appadurai notes that "diversion" or "decontextualization" has long been an important aspect of European aesthetics and a key mechanism in the creation of value.[37] When goods are removed from their original circuits of exchange, their value as commodities is often intensified. They are, so to speak, "decommoditized" and reclassified as aesthetic objects. Eighteenth-century European manufacturers often produced goods that imitated those produced by foreign cultures (chinoiserie prints,

37. *Social Life of Things*, 16–28.

japanning, imitation chinaware, for example) because they understood that the exchange value of this merchandise would be enhanced by the allusion to goods that were seen as cultural artifacts rather than as objects of mass consumption. Building on Appadurai's argument, I would observe that the aesthetics of diversion are historically specific. Today the exchange value of certain commodities—cane sugar, for example—would probably be enhanced by an allusion to Caribbean or tropical provenance. In the eighteenth century this association would have held little meaning or appeal. Raw materials were often "diverted" from their colonial points of origin, but only came to embody value when they were transformed into consumer goods that carried other cultural associations. In the chapters on textiles and furniture I suggest that one fairly widespread process of "re-diversion" involved the transformation of raw materials derived from tropical regions into "exotic" Oriental goods. Imported tropical hardwoods were often sculpted with Oriental motifs or used in combination with Japanese lacquer paneling. And cotton and indigo produced in the Americas were sometimes used to produce delicate chinoiserie prints. An argument of this kind could also be made with regard to coffee, which was long represented as a product of the East even though by the mid-eighteenth century it was predominantly grown in the West.

Approaching the cultural imprint of colonization through the lens of commodities also opens up new possibilities for acknowledging, if not the perspective, then at least the contribution of the colonized and enslaved. A central concern of literary scholarship since the late 1990s has been to get beyond the one-sidedness of colonial discourse and to include the standpoint of the colonized. In the case of colonial slavery, this pluralization of perspectives is particularly difficult to achieve because very few enslaved people had either the means or the opportunity to leave written traces of their experience. There are no known narratives or testimonies written by people enslaved in the French colonies during the eighteenth century: no "francophone Equiano," as Christopher Miller observes (33). The small handful of former slaves in English colonies who wrote autobiographical narratives—for example, Olaudah Equiano and Ottobah Cugoano—were emancipated and became writers after they had traveled from the Caribbean to England.[38] The silence on the French side testifies to the effectiveness of France's policy of keeping slaves out of metropolitan France, where opportunities for emancipation and education might have been more extensive. Though Erick Noël's 2006 study of blacks residing in eighteenth-century France bears the promising title *Being Black in France in the Eighteenth Century,* the documents that Noël explicates are primarily codes of law and cultural representations, and they permit only an oblique reconstruction of the existential experience of enslaved or free black people.

---

38. *Narrative of the Enslavement of Ottobah Cugoano; Interesting Narrative of the Life of Olaudah Equiano.*

But while we encounter little textual residue of the lived experience of slavery, we can point to other legacies and vestiges of enslaved peoples' lives and labor. These traces include oral sources such as folk tales, songs, oral histories, and spiritual traditions.[39] They also include nonlinguistic traces, including buildings, industrial implements, furniture, and clothing: material objects that were made from colonial raw materials or touched by slave labor. Though these artifacts do not directly communicate thoughts or attitudes—they are vestiges of labor rather than indications of agency—they are among the few surviving residues of the daily toil that was the dominant experience of slaves in Europe's plantation colonies.

Steeve O. Buckridge has observed that thinking about objects as components of a material culture "enables us to see objects as a form of visual literacy."[40] Though furniture and textiles do not communicate ideas and mental states in the same manner as texts, they do, nonetheless, exercise what one might call material agency. By providing us with a visual image of "the past" material objects anchor the narratives of social and cultural history. Artifacts that are preserved in colonial settings (i.e., on site in former colonies) are usually integrated into a narrative of colonial history (sometimes to the exclusion of metropolitan vectors). By contrast, decorative objects preserved in the collections of metropolitan museums are generally portrayed as the vestiges of a purely national or domestic history. When we look at a muslin gown or mahogany table in a British or French museum, we are not generally moved to ask whether the timber was felled and loaded aboard a ship by slaves, or whether slaves grew the cotton. As Maxine Berg has observed,[41] museums do not typically encourage this kind of questioning, preferring to direct our attention to what Igor Kopytoff calls the "cultural biography" of things, meaning issues of craftsmanship, sale, and ownership.[42] My discussions of French material culture go against the grain of these curatorial practices in a number of ways. By raising questions about "provenance" that go beyond the conventional criteria of artisanry and ownership, they resituate decorative objects and luxury goods within a trajectory that encompasses colonial as well as metropolitan history. Adjusting the cultural framework within which material objects are studied, I try to release their potential to evoke the submerged experiences of colonized and enslaved workers.

Historiography and Critical Trajectories

Earlier I observed that the marginality of the colonial world within eighteenth-century French culture has carried over into the fields of literary and historical

---

39. A powerful account of these transmissions are given in Joan Dayan, *Haiti, History, and the Gods.*

40. *Language of Dress,* 2.

41. *Luxury and Pleasure in Eighteenth-Century Britain.*

42. "Cultural Biography of Things."

scholarship. I want now to return to this point and to elaborate in more detail on the treatment of the *vieilles colonies* in history and literary history.

It has often been claimed that a time lag besets the representation of contentious periods of history. Henry Rousso has argued, for example, that it took thirty years for the Vichy regime to become a subject of historical study in France, and about the same length of time for historians to turn their attention to the Algerian War.[43] There is, however, a secondary point to be made in this regard, which is that scholars *did* ultimately return to these episodes after a twenty- or thirty-year hiatus. Since the early 1990s, the Algerian War of Independence and France's colonial presence in North Africa have been widely studied and have come to be viewed as formative periods of French history. And in recent sociological and anthropological scholarship, French rule in the Maghreb has been approached as a wellspring of French attitudes toward immigration and cultural diversity. (The militant association Indigènes de la république [Natives of the Republic], for example, speaks strikingly of a "colonial continuum.") By contrast, French colonization in the Caribbean and Indian Ocean was not, at least until the late 1990s, a topic of extensive study or political debate. For example, few questions have been raised about the legacies of France's history of colonial slavery, even though the cultural invisibility of slavery in the eighteenth century undoubtedly has some bearing on the suspicion in which the category of race is held in contemporary French politics and social thought. Given that the disavowal of race is rarely represented as the result of the *overcoming* of a history of racism exemplified by slavery, it seems legitimate to ask whether this disavowal actually reflects a forgetting or denial of this history.

From a historiographical perspective, the first French Empire has for the most part been treated as a colonial prehistory, a preliminary model superseded by the more representative colonial projects of the nineteenth and twentieth centuries. The (in many ways excellent) *Dictionnaire de la colonisation française* (Dictionary of French Colonialism) edited in 2007 by Claude Liauzu, for example, begins its chronology of French colonial history in 1789, a starting point that suggests that the first 150 years of French colonialism can be subsumed under the paradigms associated with the second. As this example illustrates, in French history and public discourse the words *empire* and *colonialism* have often been used as shorthand for the series of colonial ventures initiated in 1830 with the conquest of Algiers.

There are, needless to say, some legitimate reasons for this scholarly emphasis. France and Algeria fought a brutal war of independence that affected an entire generation and which, unlike the French struggle to retain control of Haiti (1791–1803), remains within living memory. The independence of

---

43. *Le Syndrome de Vichy;* "Les raisins verts de la guerre d'Algérie."

France's colonies in the Maghreb was followed by large-scale migration to France, a demographic event that has had a transformative impact on French society, and which now frames the writing of colonial history. But the eclipse of one colonial empire by the next cannot simply be explained away as a function of events. As Françoise Vergès writes, "These islands of sugar, which used to be known as the Vieilles colonies, have been the 'repressed' of French colonialism, territories that had not been conquered militarily, where there had been slavery, and that did not belong to the great narrative of the *mission civilisatrice*."[44] Whereas French colonial rule in Africa and Asia can, at least to an extent, be dressed up in the rhetoric of assimilation and civilizing mission, France's two hundred–year participation in the Atlantic slave trade simply does not lend itself to this kind of recuperation.[45]

There are signs, however, that the history of slavery and the surrogate issues that it raises, most notably the question of race, are now becoming less marginal to the study of French history. Since the mid-1990s more scholarship and more public discussion have focused on the first colonial empire and on France's history of slavery. Several factors have supported this shift, among them the fallout associated with the marking of two important colonial anniversaries: the 150th anniversary of the abolition of slavery in 1998, and the bicentenary of Haiti's independence in 2004.

When the bicentenary of the French Revolution was celebrated in 1989, almost no reference was made either to the first abolition of slavery in 1794, or to the spread of revolutionary fervor to the colonial world. These omissions generated accusations of triumphant nationalism from several quarters, and to rectify the problem the commemoration of a key anniversary in the history of slavery was planned for 1998. These ceremonies, however, in turn became controversial. French officials, led by then president Jacques Chirac, seemed primarily interested in celebrating the humanitarian vision of the Second Republic and Victor Schoelcher, the leading French advocate of abolition in the 1830s–40s. Contesting what they perceived as a metropolitan co-optation of the meaning of abolition, Antilleans (who have been French citizens since 1848) complained that the state was disregarding not only the contribution of slaves to the achievement of emancipation but also the three centuries of colonial slavery that preceded abolition.[46]

The controversy over the memory and commemoration of slavery stirred up in 1998 has continued to reverberate. In 2001 the French Senate approved

44. *Monsters and Revolutionaries*, xiii.
45. When a controversial law was passed in 2005 stipulating that the teaching of colonialism in French schools should acknowledge the positive role played by France, it included the qualification "particularly in North Africa" (Law 2005-158, February 23, 2005, Article 4). It is hard to imagine such a stipulation in the case of the Caribbean, a colonial project that so obviously rested on the foundation of exploitation and servitude.
46. See Reinhardt, *Claims to Memory*, 1–2.

a law, presented by the Guyanese deputy and 2002 presidential candidate, Christiane Taubira, that recognizes colonial slavery as a crime against humanity and imposes penalties for denying its status as such. In 2004, the government appointed a Committee for the Memory of Slavery charged with, among other things, introducing the history of slavery into the curriculum of French schools. In conjunction with these official measures, a number of activist groups or *associations* have been formed to address the history and present-day concerns of the French Antillean community. And, in 2007, life on an eighteenth-century plantation became for the first time a subject of a French television program. Three decades after the iconic U.S. series *Roots,* the French miniseries *Tropiques amers* dramatized the experience of colonial slavery.[47]

Government initiatives and community activism have been accompanied by the publication of several studies of France's history of slavery and racial discrimination. Many of these studies—particularly those authored by French historians—have focused on the history of abolition. Some of these works have a rather official flavor, though others seek to respond to the controversies stirred up in 1998 by emphasizing the role enslaved played in achieving emancipation and by problematizing the teleological narrative that leads from slavery to abolition. They draw attention to the staggered history of abolition in the French context, to the fact that colonial slavery was abolished by France not once but three times: in 1793 (by Sonthonax in Saint-Domingue), in 1794 (by the National Convention), and definitively in 1848.[48]

For most of the past two centuries, the twelve-year struggle against slavery and colonial rule waged in Haiti has registered very little in either French or U.S. historiography. Although C. L. R James's classic study, *The Black Jacobins* (1963), made the case that the Haitian Revolution should be seen as a world-historical event, by most measures it has been—to paraphrase Michel-Rolph Trouillot—a historical nonevent (98). In conjunction with the bicentennial of Haiti in 2004, however, several new studies have undertaken to illuminate the historical significance of the overthrow of colonial rule and have emphasized the interface between the French and Haitian revolutions.[49] This rediscovery has been spearheaded by historians based in North America who have situated Haitian history within the ambit of Atlantic history, a framework that foregrounds transnational connections among Europe, North America, the Caribbean, and Africa. To date, French historians have played a less central role

---

47. The serialzed drama *Tropiques amers,* cowritten by screenwriter Viginie Brac and historian Myriam Cottias, aired on France 3 in 2007.

48. See, for example, Dorigny, *Les abolitions de l'esclavage;* Georgel, Vergès, and Vivien, *L'abolition de l'esclavage;* Vergès, *Abolir l'esclavage;* Jennings, *French Anti-Slavery;* Schmidt, *L'abolition de l'esclavage.*

49. Examples include Geggus, *Haitian Revolutionary Studies;* Dubois, *Avengers of the New World* and *Colony of Citizens.*

in this scholarly renewal, and it is perhaps fair to say that the place of Haiti in Atlantic history still remains to be mapped from the French side.

The expansion in the historical study of the first French colonial empire that has occurred since the early 1990s has been accompanied by a diversification of the kind of questions that are raised. To study colonial history once meant engaging in research on or in the colonies. Colony and metropole were approached as two separate entities, and research was organized around narrowly framed issues such as the demography of colonial society and the social organization of the *habitation*.[50] Though some studies of the slave trade explored transcontinental issues such as the impact of slavery on the rise of entrepreneurial capitalism,[51] most approached the *traite* as an extension of colonial economy.[52] A central concern of recent studies, by contrast, has been to break down divides within and between disciplines by approaching metropole and colony as, in the words of Sue Peabody and Tyler Stovall, a "whole composed of continually interacting parts."[53] As we saw earlier, Peabody's book *"There Are No Slaves in France"* focuses not on colonial legislation on slavery but on laws bearing on the presence of slaves in continental France. Her conclusions are echoed in another work that focuses on slaves and slavery in mainland France, Pierre Boulle's *Race et esclavage dans la France de l'ancien régime* (Race and Slavery during the Old Regime).[54] Eric Saugera's book, *Bordeaux, port négrier* (Bordeaux, Slave Port), to cite another example, combines the tools of French regional and urban history with a focus on the slave trade. Saugera not only shows how the prosperity that derived from the slave trade and *droiture* commerce (commercial voyages between France and the Caribbean without an African leg) contributed to the urban development of Bordeaux but also points to the place of Enlightenment culture within the matrix of social relations formed by the slave trade. In *La Matrice de la race* (The Womb/Matrix of Race), Elsa Dorlin approaches questions of race and colonization from a point of departure in the history of science and sexuality. Through a genealogy of medicine that foregrounds the place of race and sex in the establishment of modern regimes of classification, Dorlin argues that since the mid-seventeenth century these categories have been tightly interwoven,

---

50. The work of Gabriel Debien, long the most influential scholar of France's "old colonies," illustrates this pattern. His principal studies, including *Une indigoterie à Saint-Domingue à la fin du XVIIIe siècle* (1946) and *Esclaves aux Antilles françaises, XVIIe–XVIIIe siècles* (1974), examine the main colonial population groups and the workings of the plantation system.

51. Eric Williams's classic study, *Capitalism and Slavery* (1944), is the most obvious example.

52. See, for example, Pluchon, *La route des esclaves*.

53. *Color of Liberty*, 5.

54. This book comprises essays written between the 1980s and 2000s on a range of subjects including legislation bearing on the residence of slaves and black people in eighteenth-century France, and the construction of the category of race.

and that both women and Africans have regularly embodied the pathological "other" against which norms of health and rationality are defined.

As Dorlin's study illustrates, a key question that has emerged in the wake of 1998 is the place of race in French history. The modern division of humanity into distinct racial subgroups took shape in conjunction with colonial slavery and remains one of the plantation system's most enduring legacies. Going against the grain of France's historical aversion to the discourse of race, in the last five years a number of scholars, as well as a several community associations, have made race and racism the point of departure for sociological analysis and political activism. The category of the "black" and the question of "black identity" form the focal point of Erick Noël's *Being Black in France in the Eighteenth Century* (2006), a broad overview of texts, laws, and images relating to the presence of enslaved and emancipated blacks in Old Regime France, as well as Pap Ndiaye's *La Condition noire: Essai sur une minorité française* (The Black Condition: Essay on a French Minority) (2008), a thoughtful analysis of the historical role of blackness as a mode of cultural identity and as a basis for discrimination and minoration. Whereas French social thought has traditionally emphasized the role of cultural difference in the dynamics of discrimination and marginalization, Ndiaye, in company with a few other current French scholars, focuses on the existence of *minorités visibles:* groups whose exposure to prejudice is more directly linked to skin color than to perceived differences of culture.[55]

Scholars have not been alone in promoting the use of the term "black" in contemporary historical and political debates. A number of community organizations, most notably the CRAN (Conseil représentatif des associations noires de France) (Representative Council of French Black Associations), have positioned themselves as organizations representing, not French Africans or Antilleans, but French blacks.[56] In light of these trends, as Myriam Cottias notes, even mainstream French media have begun to speak for the first time in terms of "la question noire" (the black question) (79).

The methodological concerns to which the historical studies of colonization and slavery published since the early 1990s attest have also been central to recent literary scholarship. As in the field of history, the slave-plantation societies of the old colonies had not, until around 2005, been widely studied by literary

---

55. The place of race in contemporary French politics and social thought is also explored in Fassin and Fassin, *De la question sociale à la question raciale.*

56. The CRAN's attempted linkage of Africans and Antilleans has been rejected by some Antillean organizations, in particular the group Collectif DOM. During a series of heated exchanges in 2006 the association's founder, Patrick Karam, stated that Antilleans, who have been citizens of the French republic since 1848, do not share common ground with Africans.

critics and theorists. They were not, for example, central to the development of the corpus of postcolonial theory and criticism. As Doris Garraway suggests, one reason for this omission may be that "few of the categories and concepts current in postcolonial studies are useful in a discussion of the Old Regime cultures of slavery in which the 'other' was not native and there was so little ambivalence involved in commodifying the human individual" (xii). But if the "other" in postcolonial theory has predominantly been "native," it is not simply because of the emphasis placed on ambivalence and hybridity, or because of the research interests of the pioneer scholars in the field, but also because of the nature of the literary record. Rather, if narratives bearing on relations between "natives" and settlers have been more amply analyzed in postcolonial studies than narratives of colonial slavery, it is in large part because more such narratives exist. This correlation is not limited to studies with a postcolonial orientation. If we perform a survey of all literary criticism bearing on themes such as colonization and cultural encounters, we find that many more critical interpretations have been devoted to Oriental exoticism,[57] and to encounters between natives and colonists,[58] than to literary portraits of colonial slavery. I would contend that the main explanation for this discrepancy is simply that there are many more works in these categories to examine.

Scholars who undertake to explore the literature associated with the first French colonial empire face the preliminary problem of the dearth of relevant texts. Confronted with this lack they generally adopt one or both of two strategies. The first is to catalog all French works in which the colonies, slavery, and people of African descent are portrayed, across genres and historical periods. To give a few examples of this practice, Roger Mercier's *L'Afrique noire dans la littérature française: Les premières images, XVIIe–XVIIIe siècles* (Black Africa in French Literature: The First Images, Seventeenth–Eighteenth Centuries) (1962) catalogs all French representations of contact with Africa and Africans starting from the sixteenth century. Régis Antoine's *Les écrivains français et les Antilles* (French Writers and the Antilles) (1978) undertakes an exhaustive survey of metropolitan French and Caribbean writing on the French Antilles from the establishment of the colonies to the era of negritude. And Léon-François Hoffmann's equally thorough though more historically bounded *Le nègre romantique* (The Romantic Negro) (1973) considers black figures in eighteenth- and nineteenth-century French literature. More recently, Christopher Miller's tour de force study, *The French Atlantic Triangle* (2007), considers the place

57. See, for example, Dufrenoy, *L'orient romanesque en France;* Grosrichard, *Structure du sérail;* Said, *Orientalism;* Lowe, *Critical Terrains;* Dobie, *Foreign Bodies;* Longino, *Orientalism in French Classical Drama.*

58. See, for example, Todorov, *La conquête de l'Amérique (The Conquest of America);* Hulme, *Colonial Encounters;* Berthiaume, *L'Aventure américaine au XVIIIe siècle;* Pratt, *Imperial Eyes;* Van den Abbeele, *Travel as Metaphor;* Boucher, *Cannibal Encounters;* Pagden, *European Encounters with the New World;* Roger, *L'Ennemi américain.*

of the slave trade in French and Francophone culture from the eighteenth century to contemporary times. Emphasizing the triangulated relationships among French, African, and Caribbean writers, Miller brings a new transcontinental momentum to the established critical paradigm.

An overlapping group of studies considers the place of slavery in texts that are considered central to the social and political thought of the French Enlightenment. These include Edward Seeber's *Anti-Slavery Opinion in France during the Second Half of the Eighteenth Century* (1937), and two essays by the distinguished French eighteenth-century scholar Jean Ehrard.[59] Seeber focuses on the latter part of the eighteenth century and on abolitionist writing, the period and genre in which we encounter the greatest number of references to slavery. Ehrard, by contrast, focuses on the overall lack of engagement on the part of the *lumières* with the question of slavery. Michèle Duchet's *Anthropologie et histoire au siècle des lumières* (Anthropology and History in the Century of the *Lumières*) (1971) is not specifically about colonization or slavery, but it touches on both issues frequently in the context of a wide-ranging study of Enlightenment anthropology. Duchet's work has been an important point of departure for the rediscovery, during the past two decades, of the Abbé Raynal's *Histoire politique et philosophique des établissements et du commerce des européens dans les deux Indes* (*History of the Two Indies*), the first attempt to write a history of European colonization.[60]

My own work is indebted to these prior studies, but as indicated earlier, I have significant reservations about the critical practice of gathering together all eighteenth-century, or all "Enlightenment," references to colonial slavery. The studies mentioned above are substantial volumes that explore a wide array of texts in which slavery appears as a topic. Coverage is one of their strengths, but this breadth also tends to confer the false appearance of a strong and continuous tradition of literary representation, while correspondingly camouflaging the marginal and fragmentary nature of these depictions.

Another group of literary studies of Old Regime colonization focus on the last third of the eighteenth century, when representations were, as we have seen, more abundant. This is the strategy of Edward Seeber's *Anti-Slavery Opinion in France during the Second Half of the Eighteenth Century*, and of Hoffmann's *Nègre romantique*, which focuses on revolutionary and Romantic writing, though it includes a chapter on earlier works. *Translating Slavery: Gender and Race in French Women's Writing, 1783–1823* (1994), a volume coedited by Doris Kadish and Françoise Massardier-Kenney, anthologizes and presents critical introductions to late eighteenth- and early nineteenth-century writing on slavery and race by French women. A subsequent anthology edited

---

59. "L'Encyclopédie et l'esclavage colonial," and "L'esclavage devant la conscience des lumières françaises."

60. See also Duchet, *Diderot et l'histoire des deux Indes; ou, L'écriture fragmentaire.*

by Youmna Charara, *Fictions coloniales du dix-huitième siècle* (Colonial Fictions of the Eighteenth Century) (2005), presents and discusses three late eighteenth-century novellas that portray the colonial world. Finally, a number of studies, including eighteenth-century scholar and anticolonial activist Yves Bénot's *Diderot: De l'athéisme à l'anticolonialisme* (Diderot: From Atheism to Anticolonialism), and political theorist Sankar Muthu's *Enlightenment against Empire* (2003), discuss anticolonial perspectives in late eighteenth- and early nineteenth-century literature.

The literary-based studies with which my own work has the greatest affinity are those that identify early French colonization as a site of cultural repression. These include Louis Sala-Molins's *Les misères des Lumières: Sous la raison, l'outrage* (*Dark Side of the Light*), which emphasizes the limited and ambivalent ways in which prominent Enlightenment thinkers responded to colonial slavery,[61] Françoise Vergès's *Monsters and Revolutionaries: Colonial Family Romance and Métissage* (1999), and Catherine Reinhardt's *Claims to Memory: Beyond Slavery and Emancipation in the French Caribbean* (2006). The latter two works explore points of articulation between the colonial past, notably the history of slavery, and present-day debates over citizenship and cultural identity. Bridging the surprisingly deep divide between colonial and postcolonial studies, these studies consider how the problematic memory of a colonial past dominated by slavery and racial hierarchy reverberates—often in the mode of repression—in contemporary society and politics. Vergès considers the imprint of colonial rule, slavery, and métissage in the Indian Ocean "postcolony," La Réunion. She interprets present-day tendencies such as the pursuit of assimilation with metropolitan France as manifestations of a continuing "colonial family romance" that represents France as the *mère patrie* and the colonies as her children, a narrative that obviously obscures the place of slavery in the relationship between colony and metropole (4). Reinhardt's discussion of the memory of slavery in the French Antilles, which also straddles past and present, metropole and colony or Département d'Outre-Mer (DOM; the former French colonies of the Caribbean and Indian Ocean that remain French territories have since 1946 been classified as overseas departments or regions), explores the interweaving of historical and contemporary representations of slavery in the Caribbean and metropolitan France.

We have observed that a number of critical studies of the cultural representation of colonization focus on the relationship between slavery and (the) Enlightenment, understood either as a process of intellectual expansion marked by the development of critical philosophy or as a key period or stage of European history. Discussions of this kind have for the most part drawn the conclusion that Enlightenment philosophy "failed" to respond to the problem of

---

61. The same may be said of Sala-Molins's earlier work, *Le code noir ou le calvaire de Canaan.*

slavery, though at least one study, Sankar Muthu's 2003 book *Enlightenment against Empire,* has identified a late eighteenth and early nineteenth-century tradition of anticolonialism. To this point, scholars who have discussed slavery and Enlightenment have not gone so far as to argue that the philosophers' lack of critical engagement with slavery undermines the very idea of (the) Enlightenment, though building on the critical legacy of Adorno and Horkheimer, one could certainly make an argument of this kind.

For a number of reasons, I do not make the category of "Enlightenment" a central focus of my reflection in this book. This is mostly because the patterns of repression and displacement that I describe in the social and political writings of thinkers such as Montesquieu, Rousseau, and Voltaire are features of a wide range of texts and can also be discerned in material culture. Given this I do not think that it is particularly meaningful to speak in terms of a specific "Enlightenment" response to colonization or slavery prior to the late 1760s. I also find that reading canonical works of political philosophy alongside fictional works, and paraliterary genres such as missionary narratives, allows texts' varied allegiances and political investments to come into focus, offsetting some of the historical abstraction in which the category of "Enlightenment thought" is often enveloped.

At the opposite end of the spectrum, Doris Garraway's compelling book *The Libertine Colony: Creolization in the Early French Caribbean* (2005) focuses not on well-known works of Enlightenment philosophy but on subcanonical and paraliterary genres. Observing that slavery and colonial métissage are among the most disavowed aspects of eighteenth-century social relations, *Libertine Colony* examines not canonical, metropolitan texts in which these encounters are sparsely represented but subcanonical genres grounded in eyewitness observation. Garraway argues that modes of writing such as missionary narratives, and the colonial descriptions and reform proposals authored by Creole magistrates, can be viewed not only as documents of colonial power but also as legacies of creolization: testaments to the participation of indigenous, European, and African populations in a common, albeit highly unequal culture (xi–xii). Taking a new approach to the metropolitan/colonial divide, Garraway considers how colonial/Creole society is represented by writers based in the colonies.

Garraway is certainly right to say that slavery, the racial structure of colonial society, and the range of desires and anxieties inspired by contact between Europeans and Africans are more extensively represented in subcanonical and paraliterary genres than in canonical texts. But I want to make two observations about this argument, one bearing on canonical texts, the other on the subcanonical genres that Garraway explores. The first is that while it is accurate that the colonies and slavery do not figure centrally in eighteenth-century novels and philosophical discourses, we do encounter indirect or displaced representations of these subjects. The disavowal of colonial reality to which

Garraway refers gave rise, not to a simple silence, but rather to a more complex combination of silence and displaced representation. My second point is that although the colonies are represented more extensively in empirical genres such as travel writing and missionary histories, we nonetheless encounter in these works some of the same patterns of emphasis and displacement that are features of more mainstream literature. As I discuss in chapter 4, the missionary authors whom Garraway discusses evince considerably more interest in the "native" dimensions of the Caribbean—the region's indigenous flora, fauna, and human populations—than in slaves, slavery, or the creolized societies that they were engaged in forming.

The final set of remarks that I wish to make with regard to recent scholarship on the literary imprint of colonization concerns the question of eighteenth-century discourses of race. The mid-late eighteenth century was a time of unprecedented reflection on the nature and origins of human physiological diversity. Several major Enlightenment thinkers—for example, Pierre-Louis de Maupertuis, Voltaire, the Comte de Buffon, and Cornelius De Pauw—explored questions such as whether all human beings share a common origin, and to what extent skin color and other physical characteristics are determined by climate and/or physiology and heredity. The period's leading scientific voices contested the theological arguments that had previously been marshaled to explain differences of skin color, notably the claim that the dark skin of Africans is a mark of divine punishment, and instead hypothesized natural causalities relating to climate and physiology.

In a broad sense the linkage between the theorization of race and the colonial order is self-evident. Europe's colonial expansion was obviously an important catalyst for the crystallization of the category of race. Indeed, as Colette Guillaumin has proposed, race can be understood as a signifier that has the effect of naturalizing established relations of domination such as the system of Atlantic slavery.[62] This said, it turns out to be surprisingly difficult to draw direct connections between eighteenth-century writing on human diversity and colonial practice.

For most of the eighteenth century the leading scientific thinkers disagreed about the nature of race. Monogenists such as Buffon squared off against polygenists such as Voltaire, and whereas some writers claimed the causes of physiological variation to be largely environmental, others searched the human body for the physiological causes of blackness. For recent scholars such as Pierre Boulle (24) and Elsa Dorlin (229) these varied explorations constitute

---

62. *L'idéologie raciste.*

the antecedents of "modern racism," which I take to mean the view that humanity is divided into fixed groups identified by different physiological and intellectual characteristics, and the belief that these differences are biological and inherited. Andrew Curran, by contrast, has argued persuasively that eighteenth-century French thinkers predominantly approached human diversity, not as a terrain of fixed and essential differences, but rather as a continuum or spectrum of "varieties."[63] He notes, for example, that midcentury scientists were deeply preoccupied with intermediary or hybrid figures such as the *nègre blanc* (black albino). One of the interesting questions raised by Curran's argument, it seems to me, concerns the relationship between metropolitan racial theory and colonial practice. The theorization of race as an unstable and mutable category seems to have had relatively little impact on what one might call the applied racism of the colonial order. The racial hierarchy of the colonial plantation was put in place at a time when the justification for the enslavement of Africans revolved around theological claims. The shifting debates of eighteenth-century racial science do not appear to have led to a significant modification of this regimen. Correspondingly, I would argue that, beyond the obvious fact that colonization and slavery gave rise to a reflection on race, it is not necessarily possible to correlate the colonial racial order with the currents of metropolitan science.

Over the last decade or so the colonial world has often been described as a "laboratory": a reservoir of samples and a site of offshore experimentation.[64] Scholars including James McClellan and Richard Grove have shown that in the late eighteenth century, fields such as botany and environmental science were given a significant impetus by research conducted in colonial outposts. This should, in theory, also have been the case for racial science. In reality, relatively few Enlightenment theorists of race based their studies directly on colonial evidence. Scientific thinkers such as Buffon and De Pauw were essentially armchair philosophers who pondered the rich spectrum of human diversity from afar.

One exception to this rule can be found in the work of Pierre Barrère, who served as a medical doctor in Guiana, and wrote a treatise on skin color entitled *Dissertation sur la cause physique de la couleur des nègres* (Dissertation on the Physical Cause of the Color of Blacks) (1741) in which he draws evidence from the dissection of the cadaver of an African slave. But Barrère also represents a confirmation of the detachment of racial science from colonial experience to the extent that in a second, better-known work in which he surveys the history, agriculture, and population of French Guiana, he makes very little mention of enslaved Africans and says nothing at all about the causes of skin color.[65] In

---

63. "Rethinking Race History."
64. Grove, *Green Imperialism;* McClellan, *Colonialism and Science.*
65. *Nouvelle relation de la France equinoxale.*

place of these themes, Barrère offers a detailed account of Amerindian culture, a subject that he clearly considered to be of greater interest to his readers.

The most systematic and influential French account of human diversity of the mid-late eighteenth century was the one offered by Buffon in *Histoire naturelle: générale et particulière* (*Natural History: General and Particular*), a pivotal contribution to the natural sciences published in fifteen volumes between 1749 and 1767, with seven volumes of supplements to follow.[66] Given the scope and influence of Buffon's work, I will briefly consider his arguments and his sources of evidence.

Buffon was deeply interested in the issue of what constitutes a species or natural grouping, and he explores this question in the context of human physiological difference in several sections of *Natural History*.[67] Although he was a monogenist—that is, he accepted the theory of a single human origin—he also endorsed the idea that mankind is divided into groups characterized by different physical traits and different levels of intelligence. In designating these groups he uses a number of different terms, including "race," but also "species" and "nation." Buffon argues that variations among human groups are hereditary, but he also claims that they arise from the action of environment over long periods of time ("Varieties," 405). As a result, while he points to the existence of different races, he also recognizes the existence of intermediary and hybrid groups.[68]

One of Buffon's main hypotheses about race is that human beings were all originally white and that dark skin represents a process of "degeneration" from this originary state. The key piece of evidence that he cites in this regard is that while there are *nègres blancs* there are no *blancs nègres* ("Varieties," 389). In the latter part of his career Buffon refined this point by turning to colonial evidence. He argues that "successive intermarriages between whites and blacks lead to lightening of the skin" ("Degeneration," 1017–18). What is fascinating about this claim is that whereas European commentators on race in colonial milieus invariably viewed métissage as a process that *darkens* the skin, Buffon, armed with his belief in originary whiteness, turned colonial taxonomy on its head.

Natural History's arguments about human diversity are grounded in a wide range of scientific and travel literature, as well as in the accumulated lore of orientalism. Buffon's methodology could be characterized as global

66. Georges Louis Leclerc, Comte de Buffon, *Oeuvres*. References in the text are to this edition, my translation.

67. These discussions are concentrated in the long essay titled "Variétés dans l'espèce humaine" (Varieties in the Human Species) (III, 1749), and a later passage titled "De la dégénération des animaux" (On Degeneration in Animals) (XIV, 1766).

68. For example, Buffon describes "Hottentots" as men within the black race "who are beginning to get closer to whites," and "Moors" as whites leaning in the direction of blacks ("Varieties," 371).

and transhistorical, and indeed he is generally dismissive of research that he considers to be too narrow in scope. He makes it clear, for instance, that as far as he is concerned, variations in skin color are due to exposure to the sun over long periods of time, and that dissecting cadavers to locate the anatomical causes of blackness is a sheer waste of time ("Varieties," 402–3). Perhaps for this reason, he is much more interested in the evidence provided by differences among African populations than in the information about race and inheritance that could be gleaned from the colonial world.[69] Perhaps he felt that looking at the colonies as a laboratory of race would correspond to adopting a narrow historical and geographical perspective.

Since the late 1990s, acknowledgments that the category of race has been an important force in French social and political history have led several scholars to undertake genealogies that link contemporary attitudes to race to France's history of colonial slavery. These are important initiatives, and as I have suggested, I view *Trading Places* as a contribution to this project. This said, I think that it is important to avoid conflating the history of racial thought with the history of colonial slavery. To clarify what I mean by this, let us look at the example of a recent work in this area: Elsa Dorlin's 2006 study *Matrice de la race*. In this ambitious work Dorlin proposes that in the seventeenth and eighteenth century, the "othering" of women, Africans, and the enslaved was an integral part of the inner logic of European schemes of rationality, notably in the fields of medicine and natural science. She illustrates the centrality of race and colonization to the economy of modern European thought in various ways. For example, drawing on David Hume's essay *Of National Characters* (1748), Dorlin suggests that the colonies were a "*haut lieu,*" or key site, of the fabrication of French national ideology. What she means by this is that the establishment of settler colonies paved the way for the claim that to be French is to be French anywhere: that national identity is a matter of heredity and not of environment (198). From my perspective this example is problematic for several reasons, one of the most important being that eighteenth-century French writers generally drew a strong distinction between the character of Creoles and that of the metropolitan French. In some versions of this scenario, Creoles were even described as having a distinctive physical appearance. It seems to me significant that Dorlin cites a British source for this idea, and I wonder whether a parallel French source could be located for the same period. In another passage, Dorlin argues that in the late eighteenth century the question of racial mixing emerged as a "problem of the first order" (262). Yet she gives no account of this ostensibly major debate, and as a result it is not clear in

69. Much of what Buffon has to say about the colonies is indeed incorporated into a longer discussion of variations among Africans. See "Varieties," 367–407.

what context (other than perhaps the revolutionary struggle over the political rights of free people of color) this urgent question came to the fore.[70]

In sum, the relationship between discourses of race, métissage, and national identity was less directly pegged to the colonial enterprise than one might anticipate. But I also want here to make a broader point, which is that the relationship between discourses and practices is often circuitous. In the wake of Said's *Orientalism,* we have become accustomed to discerning a close relationship between colonial power and discursive formations. But while this paradigm furnishes a crucial framework for interpreting colonial authority, it needs to be supplemented with other theoretical models. Colonial power has often been exercised or articulated in the mode of discourse, but, as I aim to show, it has also often involved processes of silencing, avoidance, and displacement: mechanisms that psychoanalytic theory helps illuminate.

As stated earlier, this book does not attempt to perform a negative reading of the many eighteenth-century works in which colonial slavery is *not* evoked. I do, however, want to back up my contention that the issue of colonial slavery is only marginally represented in eighteenth-century literature and philosophy, a claim that is not self-evident. To this end I offer, in an appendix, a brief and by no means exhaustive overview of the representation and nonrepresentation of colonization in eighteenth-century French literature. This essay discusses key authors and texts, and situates them in relation to major currents of representation. Many of the authors and works addressed in the appendix (for example, Montesquieu, Voltaire, Rousseau, Diderot, Prévost, Gouges, and Saint-Lambert) also come up for discussion in other places in this book. Others, such as Helvétius, are discussed only in the appendix. I discuss Diderot and d'Alembert's *Encyclopedia* at many points, but the appendix is the only place in which I attempt to survey its contributions to the exploration of colonial questions. Readers interested in an overview of eighteenth-century French approaches to the colonial questions might find it helpful to read this essay before turning to the more specific discussions presented in the chapters that follow.

---

70. Dorlin cites several texts that refer to *métissage* in the context of the seraglio of Constantinople (184–85), and interprets these in light of a work that can be seen as an early instance of eugenics, Charles-Augustin Vandermonde's *Essai sur la manière de perfectionner l'espèce humaine* (Essay on the Manner of Perfecting the Human Race). Two points must be emphasized, however. One is that *métissage* was being associated with oriental rather than colonial slavery, and the other is the isolated nature of the example.

PART I

EAST MEETS WEST

1

Reorienting Slavery

A French epistolary novel of the 1760s tells the story of a feckless European who sells his lover, described as an Amerindian woman born on "the shores of Florida," into slavery. To be more precise, he ships his mistress halfway around the world, from America to Turkey, then sells her to the sultan's palace in Constantinople, where she is installed as a concubine. The obvious question that arises in this context is, why go so far? Since slavery was endemic throughout the Americas in the seventeenth and eighteenth centuries, why bother going all the way to Constantinople to offload an unwanted lover? This far-fetched (and far-flung) plot could perhaps be chalked up to the idiosyncrasies of the writer (Claude Dorat) were it not for the fact that the association of slavery with the Orient, rather than the Americas, was a pervasive tendency of eighteenth-century fiction and philosophy. In this chapter I explore the narrative and discursive modalities of this transfer from West to East, and consider the cultural predispositions, and social and political conditions, that framed this exchange.

To put this East-West axis of exchange into context, it is necessary to take a step back and to consider how the Orient on the one hand, and the colonial world on the other, were positioned in eighteenth-century French culture. As many literary historians and theorists have attested, fascination with the Oriental world was a central feature of Old Regime French culture. Writers and painters obsessively represented the Oriental harem and pored over the characteristics of Oriental despotism. One of the most saturated discursive fields of the period, Oriental exoticism, was manifested across a range of literary genres as well as in many spheres of visual and material culture. By contrast, until a turning point in the late 1760s, cultural representation of the colonial world, particularly France's plantation colonies in the Caribbean and the Indian Ocean, was extremely limited. Despite their considerable economic value, these agricultural outposts were the subject of few literary narratives or visual depictions.

I first began thinking about the relationship between the representation of the colonial world and representations of the Orient while I was working on an earlier book on orientalism. I was struck by the fact that in Edward Said's *Orientalism,* as in a number of the studies published in its wake, eighteenth-century orientalism is not only read as a repository of colonial attitudes and ambitions but also effectively established as *the* site of colonial discourse in this period. The issue that this account raised for me was not so much one of anachronism—it can certainly be argued that eighteenth-century discourses on the Orient paved the way for later colonial ideologies—as one of erasure. That is to say, the critical focus on the political implications of orientalism seemed to overlook the actual sites of French colonialism in the seventeenth and eighteenth centuries.[1] This pattern of emphasis has not been limited to the critical studies inspired by *Orientalism.* Rather, in almost every field of eighteenth-century French studies, more scholarship has been devoted to relations with the East or to Oriental exoticism than to French colonization in the Caribbean and its cultural footprint. Although there are various reasons for this asymmetry, including the continued political resonance of "Western" representations of Muslim societies, the most determining factor is the nature of the "literary record." Whereas representations of the Orient are abundant in eighteenth-century French literature, depictions of the colonial world are scarce.

The relationship between "colonial history" and "orientalist representation" is, however, not simply one of asymmetry. In many literary and paraliterary works it is possible to observe discursive and narrative shifts as a result of which questions relating to colonization are subtly transposed onto an Oriental context. At the fulcrum of this exchange is the question of slavery. The sparse representation of the colonial world in eighteenth-century French culture was largely a function of the difficulty of representing slavery and the social features associated with it, for example, interracial desire and métissage. To represent slavery meant either endorsing its social validity or vigorously condemning it. Intermediate positions generated silence and other forms of avoidance. One mechanism of avoidance that I examine in this and the following two chapters was the displacement of the question of slavery from the disquieting colonial environment onto the less unsettling Oriental context.

This transfer was made possible by the fact that when the regime of slavery was established in the French colonies (roughly speaking, the 1670s), the Orient was already widely regarded by Europeans as a milieu of extreme social and political subordination. Travel narratives and fictions held the power of the

---

1. In addition to *Orientalism,* see Porter, *Haunted Journeys,* and Lowe, *Critical Terrains.*

Ottoman sultan to be absolute, portrayed Oriental women as virtual prisoners of the seraglio, and characterized janissaries and other imperial functionaries as slaves raised to high political office. Because of this representational tradition, the Orient offered a ready-made terrain onto which the question of slavery could be projected. Observing slavery through an Oriental lens allowed commentators to consider its moral and social implications without directly confronting the issue of European responsibility. Orientalization also meant portraying slavery in its mildest, most socially recuperable form, since slavery in the Orient did not usually involve the severe physical and psychological depredations associated with colonial slavery. Finally, the displacement of slavery onto the Orient entailed a process of sexualization. If European writers and artists were preoccupied with slavery in the Orient, it was not simply because they feared that Oriental despotism could potentially spread to France but also because the image of women enclosed in the harem held certain attractions. While slavery in the colonial context produced forms of cultural avoidance, slavery in the Orient aroused desire.

Below I explore the transposition of colonial slavery onto Oriental culture in eighteenth-century literature, considering both the overall economy of representation and patterns of substitution in the narrative structures and discursive systems of texts of various genres. To describe these narrative and tropological patterns I use the term "displacement," a concept used in psychoanalysis to signify the exchange of disturbing latent thoughts for less challenging representations. I borrow the term here, however, to denote not a personal coping mechanism but rather a transindividual pattern of repression and substitution manifested across a range of cultural contexts and media.

Climate, Despotism, and Slavery in Montesquieu

Montesquieu's monumental treatise *On the Spirit of Law* (1748) is the necessary point of departure for any discussion of the representation of colonization and slavery in eighteenth-century French culture. Both Montesquieu's contemporaries and writers of the following generation recognized it as the first significant French meditation on these subjects, and for the quarter century following its publication it shaped the ways in which French writers approached them. *Spirit of Law* is also the eighteenth century's most thorough and influential statement of the tenets of Oriental despotism. Writing at the end of the century, the Orientalist Anquetil-Duperron observed that "the reflections of M. Montesquieu in some sense fixed our ideas about the nature of despotism.... No one has explored this subject in greater depth than he."[2] Much has been written about Montesquieu's account of the Orient and its

2. *Législation orientale*, 9.

implications for his analysis of politics in France. An aspect of this interrelation-ship that has not been widely discussed, however, is the de facto annexation of the question of colonial slavery to the topos of Oriental despotism.

In the second book of *Spirit of Law,* Montesquieu defines despotism as a political system in which "one alone, without law and without rule, draws everything along by his will and his caprices."[3] This form of government is rep-resented from the outset as an Oriental phenomenon and linked with practices that Europeans associated with the Ottoman Empire, such as the abdication of executive power to a vizier and the withdrawal of the sultan to a seraglio staffed by eunuchs (20). A political system with social and cultural dimensions, despotic rule is said to result in the eradication of all personal ambition and courage, and the production of a climate of fear (29–30). Despotism is also said to require the thorough subjugation of women, who rather than being power brokers and consumers of luxury, as they are in other societies, are reduced to being objects of consumption, and are "kept in extreme slavery" (104). In sum, Oriental despotism is characterized as a political regime in which there is neither political nor personal freedom, and under which all men, and in particular all women, are in one sense or another enslaved.

In Montesquieu's account, Oriental despotism is also connected to a num-ber of environmental factors. One tenet of the famous "theory of climates" that he lays out in book 14 is that warm climates produce despotic regimes. In these environments, Montesquieu argues, populations are physically weak and lethargic; people lack courage and as a result they are willing to accept the yoke of absolute rule (232–34). The discussion of slavery that Montesquieu undertakes in the following book (15) takes shape as a continuation of this meditation on the impact of climate on culture.

Montesquieu begins his discussion of slavery by defining it as a relationship in which one man exercises absolute control over the life and property of an-other. As many commentators have noted, he condemns this arrangement un-equivocally, stating that it is good neither for the slave nor for the master. Yet, having taken this firm moral stand, Montesquieu almost immediately begins to qualify what he has said. He suggests, notably, that "civil slavery" is more justified in despotic countries, where people are already subject to "political slavery" (246). Later in the text he returns to and develops these observations about civil and political slavery, and as we shall see, this proves to be one of the most consequential aspects of his discussion of slavery. Initially, however, Montesquieu turns in another direction, embarking on a discussion of the legal arguments about slavery formulated by the great minds of the previous century, most notably the Dutch jurist, Hugo Grotius.

---

3. Montesquieu, *De l'esprit des lois,* 1:131; *Spirit of the Laws,* trans. Cohler, Miller, and Stone, 10. References in the text are to this edition, though I render the title as *On the Spirit of Law.*

Writing against the backdrop of expanding maritime commerce and almost continuous warfare among European states, Grotius sought to formulate principles for the legitimate conduct of warfare and international commerce, drawing on the framework of natural law. It was in this context that in his most influential work, *De iure belli ac pacis* (*The Rights of War and Peace*) (1625), Grotius examined the conditions in which people are enslaved and the legal foundations for this practice.[4] On the whole, Grotius takes an accommodating attitude toward slavery. Though he insists, contra Aristotle, that no one is a slave "by nature," he nonetheless suggests that there are social and political circumstances in which a person may legitimately become a slave. He argues, for instance, that a debtor or destitute person may choose lifelong servitude in return for a guarantee of sustenance, and he puts this kind of arrangement on a par with other social relationships in which one individual enjoys dominion over another: for example, the authority of parents over children (book 2, chapter 5). Elsewhere (book 3, chapters 7–8) Grotius considers slavery as an outcome of warfare, which he identifies as one of the main causes of enslavement. He claims that victorious armies often put their defeated enemies to work rather than putting them to the sword. Since he finds this practice to be humane—or at least morally preferable to wholesale slaughter—he endows this case of enslavement too with a certain degree of legitimacy.

Grotius's position on slavery inevitably appeared problematic to thinkers of the eighteenth-century, who, under the influence of the ideas of John Locke, placed a much higher premium on individual rights. Leading the charge, Montesquieu questioned several aspects of Grotius's account. Above all, as we shall see, he took issue with Grotius's tendency to naturalize slavery by portraying it as a practice that was governed by some kind of social contract and that originated in feelings such as pity and humanity.

In presenting his critique of Grotius's arguments, Montesquieu employs a rhetorical device that is by no means characteristic of *Spirit of Law:* the sustained use of irony expressed via the conditional mood. He writes, for instance, that "one would never believe that pity established slavery" (247), then uses the formula: "I would as soon say that" (*j'aimerais autant dire*) to present a more plausible explanation. In addition to Grotius's claims, Montesquieu presents and dismisses several other contemporary justifications of slavery on religious or legal grounds. For example, Montesquieu writes scathingly in one passage that "I would as soon say that religion gives to those who profess it the right to reduce to servitude those who do not profess it" (249).

In passages such as this he is obviously using the conditional mood to express skepticism toward arguments made in the defense of slavery. But this

---

4. Grotius's discussion of slavery and natural right was developed and debated by Samuel von Pufendorf in *De officio hominis et civis* (*On the Duty of Man and Citizen*) (1673), and Thomas Hobbes in *Leviathan* (1651).

rhetorical device also has the secondary effect of introducing a layer of abstraction into the presentation of what should have been a straightforward rebuttal. Rather than stating in direct terms that he disagrees with the argument that slavery originated in acts of benevolence or pity, or was justified by the spiritual ojective of conversion, Montesquieu says, more ambiguously, that he "would as soon say" that the causes of slavery lay elswhere.

The rhetorical presentation of Montesquieu's argument is, however, not the only question raised by his commentary on slavery. Further issues arise from the fact that the entire discussion is framed as a response to Grotius. This means that forms of slavery that are not addressed by Grotius are also absent from, or at least understated, in Montesquieu's response. The most significant of these omissions is Atlantic slavery, which was in its infancy when Grotius wrote *On the Rights of War* in 1625, but which by 1748 was at its height.

Though modern colonial slavery is largely absent from *Spirit of Law*, Montesquieu does turn to the question of the Atlantic slave trade in one, very short chapter (book 15, chapter 5). In this famous passage, which is widely and justifiably regarded as the first Enlightenment polemic against colonial slavery, Montesquieu, still speaking in the conditional mood, considers the various justifications presented for the enslavement of Africans. He lucidly exposes both the true nature of the Atlantic slave trade and the fundamental causes of its existence. Rejecting arguments based on religion or on perceived racial differences, he implies that the real causes of slavery lie in European prejudice and greed.

> If I had to defend the right we had of making Negroes slaves, here is what I would say: . . . Sugar would be too expensive if the plant producing it were not cultivated by slaves. Those who are concerned are black from head to toe, and they have such flat noses that it is almost impossible to feel sorry for them. One cannot get it into one's mind that god, who is a very wise being, should have put a soul, above all a good soul, in a body that was entirely black. (250)

There would perhaps be no reason to second-guess Montesquieu's use of the conditional mood in this passage were it not for the fact that in the following chapter (book 15, chapter 6) he states that the time has at last come to identify the *real* causes of slavery. He then states, this time in the indicative mood, that these causes are political despotism and warm climates. With this claim he erases not only the spurious explanations that he has previously examined—for example, that slavery arises out of feelings of pity and benevolence—but also his own suggestion that it results from racism and greed (251). Moreover, the formulation of this new argument is accompanied by an abrupt change of scene. As Montesquieu sets about identifying the *real* causes of slavery, readers are transported from the Atlantic triangle to the Oriental world. In the next two books (16–17) Montesquieu mines the topoi of Oriental despotism, offering an intricate account of the subjugation of women in the harem and detailing the subservience of Oriental subjects to the power of their absolute rulers.

In scholarly discussions of the Enlightenment's response to slavery, Montesquieu's chapter on the Atlantic slave trade is frequently quoted, out of context, as an illustration of a gathering polemic. But when this passage is considered in its full textual context, it reads more ambiguously, conveying not unmitigated opposition to colonial slavery but rather a complex combination of opposition and avoidance.

The underlying ambivalence of Montesquieu's critique of slavery was not without consequences for the reception of his arguments. In a fascinating article devoted to the word *nègre* (black/Negro) in seventeenth- and eighteenth-century dictionaries, Lucette Valensi and Simone Delesalle cite a 1762 commercial dictionary, the *Dictionnaire portatif de commerce* (Portable Commercial Dictionary), in which a contributor observes that "it is hard to justify altogether the trade in blacks; but they are indispensable to the cultivation of sugar, tobacco, indigo, etc. Sugar, M. de Montesquieu says, would be too expensive if the plant that produced it were not tended by blacks."[5] The author of this passage, who mistakes the ironic condemnation of unbridled commercialism for a serious justification of slavery, was clearly a deficient reader. But it seems legitimate to ask whether Montesquieu's rhetorical subtlety contributed in some measure to this misreading, and whether his complex mix of irony and conditional phrasing conveyed an underlying reluctance to condemn colonial slavery in more direct terms. His abrupt turn from the triangle trade to the system of Oriental despotism certainly seems to suggest the workings of a process of displacement.

The fact that Montesquieu associates slavery predominantly with the Orient is reflected in the fact that in *Spirit of Law,* colonization and slavery are approached as two distinct issues and examined in two different sections. Slavery, as we have seen, is discussed in book 15, in conjunction with observations on climate, despotism, and Oriental culture. Colonization, on the other hand, is examined in book 21 in the framework of a discussion of commerce.

Montesquieu's account of European colonial expansion focuses almost exclusively on the case of Spain. In a series of arguments that set the tone for much subsequent Enlightenment writing on this issue, he proposes that the conquest of the New World had a disastrous impact on Spain's economy and social fabric. From an economic standpoint, Montesquieu claims, the establishment of colonies led to an influx of gold and silver that produced galloping inflation. From a demographic standpoint it resulted in the rapid depopulation of both metropole and colony (393–97). Drawing the necessary conclusions, Montesquieu expresses the view that establishing far-flung colonies had the destabilizing effect of distending the body politic, making government and administration unwieldy.[6]

---

5. "Le mot 'nègre' dans les dictionnaires français," 103.

6. The arguments presented in book 21 were first sketched in an earlier work, *Considérations sur les richesses de l'Espagne* (Considerations on the Wealth of Spain) (1727). On Montesquieu's

Montesquieu's negative assessment of Spanish colonialism does not, however, appear to extend to all colonial contexts, for at one point he notes summarily that: "Our colonies in the Antilles are admirable; they have objects of commerce that we do not and cannot have; they lack that which is the object of our commerce" (392). There is no further discussion of the specific case of these French colonies. Notably, Montesquieu does not comment on the use of slave labor to produce the valuable colonial commodities to which he alludes.

Earlier we saw that although Montesquieu opens his discussion of slavery with the blanket statement that slavery is by its nature bad, he almost immediately qualifies this assertion by stating that in certain regions, and under certain political regimes, it has a social and political basis. In book 15, chapter 7, having turned to the Oriental context and begun to explore connections between despotism, climate, and slavery, Montesquieu returns to this idea and attempts to resolve the apparent contradiction between claiming that slavery is contrary to nature and finding that it is justified by natural causes. He states, somewhat confusingly, that "slavery is against nature, although in certain countries it may be founded on natural reasons" (252). He follows up this claim with the observation that slavery should be limited to those countries in which such reasons exist, and states that "these countries must be distinguished from those in which even natural reasons reject it, as in the countries of Europe where it has so fortunately been abolished." A little later he concludes in the same spirit that "natural slavery must be limited to certain particular countries of the world" (252). When Montesquieu alludes to "particular countries," it is clear that he has the Orient in mind. Yet when we consider his enthusiastic remarks about the (slave) colonies of the French Antilles and his maneuvering, in book 15, between Atlantic and Oriental contexts, it seems legitimate to wonder whether the countries in which slavery was in some way justified included the "admirable" French colonies of the Antilles. These were, after all, islands with a warm climate that were subject to a form of absolute rule.[7]

The examination of slavery in *Spirit of Law* lays out two interrelated ideas that would have a significant afterlife in eighteenth-century philosophy and economic thought. One is that although slavery is contrary to natural law, it is justified, at least to a limited extent, by natural conditions. This idea resurfaces in arguments made throughout the 1760s and 1770s to the effect that the tropical climate of the colonies mandated African slavery because only Africans possessed the physical strength and endurance required to perform labor in these conditions. In the *Encyclopedia* article "Esclavage" (Slavery) (volume 5, 1765), for example, the Chevalier de Jaucourt argues that

---

discussion of Spanish colonization, see my essay, "Exotic Economies and Colonial History in the *Esprit des lois*."

7. On this point, see also Miller, 66.

environmental conditions in the Antilles meant that slavery was a necessary dimension of tropical agriculture, and opines that, as such, the practice was justified. Though this is of course not what *Spirit of Law* argues, Montesquieu's claims to the effect that, as Laurent Estève has put it, natural rights end where climatic necessity takes over, certainly encouraged this kind of rationalization.[8]

The second influential idea is that slavery is predominantly a feature of Oriental culture, a practice tied to climate, despotic rule, and the subordination of women. This linkage is borne out by the many fictional works of the period, beginning with Montesquieu's own *Persian Letters* (1721), in which women's enclosure in the harem is depicted as a form of sexual slavery.[9]

Slavery and Polygamy in Jean-François Melon

The interconnections of slavery, gender, and Oriental culture were not limited to the work of Montesquieu. Other works of the first half of the eighteenth century similarly associated slavery with the Orient, and with the subordinate status of Oriental women. In this section I consider a pair of works of the 1720s–30s that bring the implications of this triangulated scheme into focus. Their author, Jean-François Melon, had formerly been the secretary of John Law, the economic adviser to the regent and architect of the notorious "Mississippi scheme," a financial speculation that linked public finance to the purchase of shares in the trading company launched to develop France's new colony in Louisiana. After the collapse of Law's "system" in 1720 and the regent's death three years later, Melon retired to private life and turned his hand to the theory of political economy.

Melon, like Montesquieu, used the Oriental world as a sounding board for reflections on French politics and society. In his 1729 novel *Mahmoud le Gasnévide* (Mahmoud the Gaznevid), the life of an Oriental ruler serves as an allegorical framework for the presentation of social and economic ideas about France. Melon's protagonist, Mahmoud, is however not the period's standard Oriental despot. Instead of setting an example to avoid, he is a figure to emulate: an enlightened ruler who takes an active interest in affairs of state, yet who also knows how to step back and listen to discussion and debate. Mahmoud's enlightened policies include, as one might expect given Melon's background in financial administration, a number of economic ideas. As I show in more detail in chapter 6, Melon was concerned with gently moving the prevailing mercantilist orthodoxy in a new direction. He uses Mahmoud as a mouthpiece for ideas such as increasing population, investing in agriculture, and putting

---

8. Estève, *Montesquieu, Rousseau, Diderot*, 59.
9. *Persian Letters*, trans. Mauldon. References in the text are to this translation.

commercial growth and the consolidation of naval power before territorial conquest: principles that would later become mainstays of liberal economic theory. Mahmoud also advocates religious tolerance, supporting the right of the *guèbre* (Zoroastrian, but read Protestant) minority of his empire to freely practice their religion. On a broad range of issues, Mahmoud's policies and political priorities appear diametrically opposed to those associated, at least by its critics, with the reign of Louis XIV.

As Carol Blum has observed, eighteenth-century Oriental fictions provided a convenient cover for the exploration of marital and sexual arrangements that were not permitted in France.[10] *Mahmoud the Gaznevid* is no exception. Melon's Muslim ruler is happily married to a large number of women. He is also a supporter of divorce and a defender of women's rights to initiate or terminate marriage. Symptomatically, it is in the context of his reflection on marriage and gender that Melon raises the issue of slavery.

In one episode Mahmoud receives as a tribute a number of beautiful female slaves from Georgia and Circassia (136–40). He decides to give them as presents to his wives, and the latter, not to be outdone, invite him to "share" the women, presumably as concubines. Most of the women seem content with this arrangement, but one appears downcast, and Mahmoud encourages her to speak up. The slave explains that her mother had always represented marriage as an infringement of women's freedom, and predisposed her against it. Following her mother's advice, she had avoided marrying and lived not only as the mistress of her own fate but also as that of a young male slave whom she had taken as her lover. Though Mahmoud's wives are shocked by the slave's lack of feminine modesty, he defers to the woman and restores her freedom. His wives once again respond in kind by offering to free all of the newly arrived slaves. Most of the women, however, affirm their willingness to remain in the service of Mahmoud and the princesses.

This episode can clearly be read as a case of exploratory Enlightenment thinking about gender and sexuality. But it also illustrates the ways in which orientalization shaped the representation of slavery. As in many other Oriental fictions, slavery is portrayed in *Mahmoud the Gaznevid* as as a mild and flexible institution, a domestic arrangement akin to the extended family, rather than as a form of oppression or the ultimate violation of personal freedom.

The subject of slavery is raised in a different context in Melon's best-known work, an economic treatise titled *Essai politique sur le commerce* (*Political Essay upon Commerce*) (1734).[11] In the course of a wide-ranging treatment of economic questions, Melon refers on several occasions to the subject of the colonies. In statements that parallel those of Montesquieu, he decries the Spanish presence in the Americas but speaks favorably of the agricultural

10. *Strength in Numbers.*
11. *Essai politique sur le commerce* (1734).

colonies established by England and France (52–56). Turning to the question of whether the use of slave labor in these territories was morally legitimate, he argues, in what one would have to describe as an extreme gesture of naturalization, that since slavery was practiced in the colonies its use must be justified (61). Yet Melon does not seem to be altogether at ease with the moral questions raised by colonial slavery, a practice with which he must have been somewhat familiar from his days as Law's secretary. He notes that the black codes of 1685 and 1724 had moderated the behavior of masters in salutary ways, and calls for further reforms in the same spirit.[12] The regime of slavery that Melon imagines, however, is far removed from the order enforced by the *Black Code*. It is a world in which masters provide for their slaves' education, in which marriage and familial ties are encouraged, and in which slaves are emancipated and given a modest pension at the end of their active lives. We do not have to look far for the source of this domesticated model of slavery. It is a vision that Melon himself had previously explored in his Oriental novel.

Given that Melon imagines slavery's transformation into a mild institution modeled on the family, we should perhaps not be surprised to find him asking, in one passage, whether slavery should be domesticated in the other sense of the word, that is, brought home to metropolitan France (61). In *The Problem of Slavery in Western Culture*, David Brion Davis suggests that Melon answered this question in the affirmative, on the grounds that slavery provided to the slaves themselves a degree of material security that was not enjoyed by laborers in Europe. "Even in Europe," Davis interprets Melon as saying, "slavery would be preferable to a system that deprived the worker of economic and social security" (152). This reading is not entirely accurate. Though Melon finds himself unable to argue against the proposal on the basis of individual liberties (espousing a kind of proto-utilitarianism, he argues that any social practice may be deemed acceptable if it benefits the greatest number of people), in the end he concludes that this step would create fear and disorder and would therefore be destabilizing to the state (62). Nonetheless, Davis is right to say that Melon's exploration of slavery demonstrates "how the principles of the early Enlightenment could be applied to a defense of human bondage" (152).

The question of whether it would be salutory to bring slavery home to France was revived again at other points in the century. Erick Noël notes that in 1752 Trudaine de Montigny, the future *intendant,* or comptroller, of France, argued in a treatise on the improvement of the French textile industry that the East India Company should import free and enslaved Indians to work

---

12. Melon was one of several mid-eighteenth-century writers who viewed the *Black Code* as a reform document introduced to limit the power of masters in positive ways. There has been some discussion among historians as to whether this was in fact one of the intentions of the document, and as to whether the code in fact exercised a moderating influence. See, for example, Sala-Molins, *Le code noir,* and Goveia, *West Indian Slave Laws.*

in the cotton and silk industries (53–54). The same idea was mooted by President Dugas in a 1755 speech before the Academy of Lyon. Toward the end of the century, a number of political economists picked up where Melon had left off by unfavorably comparing the predicament of the French day laborer with that of the colonial slave. Myriam Cottias and Arlette Farge have recently unearthed an anonymous 1797 pamphlet titled *De la nécessité d'adopter l'esclavage en France* (On the Need to Adopt Slavery in France), in which a domestic regime of slavery in France is considered as a plausible solution to the acute destitution of the poor in the age of the French Revolution.[13] For Cottias and Farge this call for the expansion of slavery is a symptom of the contradiction between Enlightenment values and colonial ideology. But while the pamphlet can certainly be read in this way, I think it is important to note that the possibility of introducing slavery in continental France had been raised on previous occasions, and that as *Political Essay* illustrates, it was predominantly explored within the framework of proposals for enlightened economic reform. As such, as David Brion Davis suggests with respect to Melon, the idea of expanding slavery was not so much in contradiction with Enlightenment perspectives as in harmony with them. Smoothing over any potential tensions was the representation of slavery, not as an extreme and violent form of domination in which the slave was removed from his or her family of origin, but as a quasi-domestic arrangement on the Oriental model.

When we read Melon alongside Montesquieu, several representational patterns come into focus. In the work of both writers, slavery is at once orientalized and naturalized—its naturalization being to some extent a function of its Oriental translation. It is portrayed as a natural corollary of Oriental climate and of the political and social arrangements that Europeans associated with these environmental conditions: despotism, polygamy, and the enclosure of women in the harem. The recurrent representation of these Oriental domestic arrangements by European writers has been widely and correctly interpreted as a mode of indirect commentary on French government and society. But these stock representations can also be read as indirect or displaced representations of French *colonial* society. Their main effect, from this point of view, was to attenuate the harsh image of slavery by portraying the relationship between master and slave as a kind of hierarchical family structure rather than as an instance of naked coercion.

Montesquieu, Slavery, and the *Encyclopedia*

"Everything is in the Encyclopedia," writes Jean Ehrard, referring not to the comprehensive scope of this great compendium of Emlightenment thought,

---

13. Cottias and Farge, *De la nécessité d'adopter l'esclavage en France.*

but rather, more narrowly, to its presentation of the topic of slavery.[14] "Everything," however, should be taken to mean not the entire range of possible representations but the more circumscribed set of ideas about slavery that circulated in France in the first half of the eighteenth century. There are two main points to be made about how this tradition of representation played out in Diderot and d'Alembert's *Encyclopedia*. The first is that despite the emphasis that the work's editors placed on commerce and manufacture, colonial commerce and the slave trade occupy as marginal a place in the *Encyclopedia* as in other contemporary texts. Having combed the *Encyclopedia* for references to the Atlantic slave trade, Ehrard found only thirty-three, most of which are cursory, and many of which portray slavery in a neutral or positive light.[15] Colonial slavery is not evoked in the celebrated articles devoted to rights, justice, and political equality, pieces such as Diderot's "Droit naturel" (Natural Law) (volume 5, 1755), or Rousseau's "Économie" (Economy) (volume 5, 1755). Even more surprisingly, it is virtually absent from Louis de Jaucourt's article "Slavery," which vehemently condemns enslavement as an infringement of personal and political rights, yet represents the practice as a phenomenon of the ancient world and of medieval society rather than as a contemporary problem.[16] The second point to be emphasized is that the representations of slavery in general that are gathered in the *Encyclopedia* are strongly influenced by Montesquieu's discussion of the subject in *Spirit of Law*. This means that slavery is treated in many articles as an Oriental practice, and by extension that it is often naturalized, that is, partially justified as a function of climate and/or culture.

As Ehrard points out, Montesquieu's reflections on slavery are referenced directly in two passages of the *Encyclopedia*, the "Eulogy of Montesquieu" by d'Alembert that appears as a prefatory text to volume 5, and the article "Slavery" by the Chevalier de Jaucourt.[17] D'Alembert's "Eulogy of Montesquieu" was written following Montesquieu's death in 1754. It is both a survey of Montesquieu's contributions to contemporary philosophy and an attempt to defend his ideas against the objections of reactionary critics. Since *Spirit of Law* had been placed on the papal *Index Librorum Prohibitorum* in 1751 on the grounds that Montesquieu's theory of climates legitimized practices such as polygamy that were prohibited by Catholic doctrine, it was this aspect of Montesquieu's thought that d'Alembert primarily sought to elucidate. The

14. "L'Esclavage devant la conscience des lumières françaises," 146.
15. "L'Encyclopédie et l'esclavage colonial."
16. In one paragraph, Jaucourt observes in passing that one cannot serve religion by reducing those whom one hopes to convert to servitude, and that the conquerors of the Americas were wrong to follow this maxim. In another he alludes, again fleetingly, to the contrast between the metaphorical use of slavery as code for political subjugation in Europe and real enslavement in the colonies.
17. "L'Esclavage devant la conscience des lumières françaises," 146.

main point that d'Alembert attempts to make is indeed that Montesquieu viewed law as a corrective to natural and cultural conditions. He cites as an example Montesquieu's argument that in warm countries governments should counteract the population's natural propensity for indolence by making work mandatory. Considering that this is d'Alembert's approach, one might expect him to say on the issue of slavery—or at least to claim that Montesquieu had said—that even if warm climates promote slavery, enslavement is nonetheless contrary to natural law, and laws should be instituted to prohibit it. This is, of course, not exactly how Montesquieu's argument unfolds, and it is not what d'Alembert says either. After breaking slavery down into three categories—civil, domestic, and political—d'Alembert instead offers a qualified justification of the institution on a range of cultural and environmental grounds. He argues, for example, that loss of liberty can be "tolerated" in countries where men are relatively powerless in relation to the state, particularly if by becoming slaves of the regime, individuals find ways to advance their own interests. He was presumably thinking of high-placed functionaries of the Ottoman Empire who, though in a formal sense enslaved, were also powerful and wealthy. With regard to the domestic servitude of women, d'Alembert emphasizes that Montesquieu's position is not, in a straightforward sense, that polygamy or enclosure in the harem is justified, but rather that environmental conditions such as the precocious age at which women reach sexual maturity in warm climates constituted mitigating factors. Significantly, d'Alembert says nothing at all about Montesquieu's discussion of the Atlantic slave trade. Rather, adhering to the main thrust of Montesquieu's presentation of slavery, his discussion remains firmly anchored in the discourse of Oriental despotism.

The article on "Slavery" written by Jaucourt (volume 5, 1755) opens with the acknowledgment that the author had borrowed many of his ideas on the subject from *Spirit of Law*. Jaucourt was not misrepresenting this debt. The article, for example, reprises Montesquieu's claim that slavery is contrary to natural law and seconds his rejection of Grotius's characterization of slavery as an outgrowth of pity or benevolence. To support these arguments, Jaucourt holds up examples drawn from the Bible, the Roman Empire, and feudal serfdom. He says nothing, however, about slavery in the modern period, and indeed the first part of the article concludes with the observation that slavery had been eradicated from most parts of Europe at the end of the fifteenth century. In the closing section, Jaucourt considers the practice of slavery in the Oriental world. Closely following Montesquieu, he overlays orientalization with naturalization, arguing that "though based on a natural reason, it is nonetheless true that slavery is against nature." (Montesquieu, we recall, formulates the relationship the other way around, stating that although slavery is contrary to natural law, it has natural causes.) Jaucourt adds, again paraphrasing *Spirit of Law*, that for some people in Muslim countries slavery constitutes a form of *jouissance,* both because of the voluptuous conditions of life in the harem and because Oriental peoples are naturally averse to work:

> In all Mahometan states servitude is rewarded by the idleness allowed to slaves who serve for pleasure. It is this laziness that makes the harems of the orient places of delight for those against whom they are made. People who fear only work can find happiness in these tranquil places; but this perturbs the very foundation of the establishment of slavery.

If we turn from "Slavery" to "Despotism" (volume 4, 1754), another article by Jaucourt, we encounter parallel statements linking the political culture of despotism to the generalization of servitude. Jaucourt writes, for instance, that "as all men there [the Orient] are equal, no one can set himself above others; as all men there are slaves, one cannot set oneself above anything." In the same vein he states (not without circularity) that "women there are all slaves; and since it is permitted to have several wives, a thousand considerations make it necessary to keep them enclosed."

For Jean Ehrard, d'Alembert's and Jaucourt's readings of Montesquieu represent two fundamentally different interpretations of the representation of slavery in *Spirit of Law,* and by extension two fundamentally different perspectives on slavery itself. He argues that whereas d'Alembert largely accepts slavery as a climatic fatality, Jaucourt condemns the institution in even stronger terms than Montesquieu. This reading seems to me to be only partially justified. Jaucourt does place more emphasis than Montesquieu, and certainly more than d'Alembert, on the idea that slavery is contrary to the inherent natural freedom of human beings, as well as on the idea that the right to own property does not extend to a right to own people. It is nonetheless important to note that Jaucourt makes almost no reference to slavery in his own time, preferring to base his arguments on the practices of the ancient world, on feudal serfdom, and on Oriental despotism.[18] As such he offers a partial reading of *On the Spirit of Law,* one that develops Montesquieu's arguments against Grotius and embraces his thinking on climate and the Orient, yet fails to reprise his condemnation of the Atlantic slave trade. This omission is perhaps not all that surprising. Montesquieu, after all, places considerably more emphasis on refuting seventeenth-century juridical arguments and weighing the social effects of climate and political culture than on addressing the specific historical and cultural foundations of colonial slavery. From my perspective Jaucourt's analysis, much like d'Alembert's, manifests a pattern of attenuated condemnation/qualified justification, in which climate and Oriental culture constitute the mitigating factors.

18. This difference of interpretation arises in part from Ehrard's perception that Jaucourt addresses the Atlantic slave trade in the article "Slavery." As noted above, however, the subject is mentioned only indirectly in two brief passages (see n. 16). Jaucourt does, on the other hand, discuss and condemn the slave trade in the article "Black Slave Trade."

I note above that relatively few *Encyclopedia* articles address the Atlantic slave trade as a specific form of enslavement, and suggest that this omission was interwoven with the period's tendency to orientalize slavery. There are, however, some exceptions to this rule: articles that speak in direct terms about slavery in a colonial setting. The *Encyclopedia* article that is most forthright in its condemnation of the practice is Jaucourt's "Traite des noirs" (Black Slave Trade), which characterizes the Atlantic slave trade as a violation of natural law. It perhaps is not incidental that the article appeared in 1765, a time when awareness of colonial issues and opposition to the slave trade were on the rise, or that it concludes with remarks to the effect that the abolition of slavery would not be detrimental to the colonial economy. As I show in the final section of this book, the idea that emancipation would be beneficial rather than harmful to colonial economies was a key tenet of French abolitionism in the 1760s–90s.

Most other references to colonial slavery in the *Encyclopedia* adopt a more neutral approach. Conforming to the pattern of naturalization that I describe above, they depict slavery as an integral facet of the colonies' physical environment or economic system. In articles devoted to tropical agriculture, for example, slaves are portrayed as necessary components of the machine of colonial production. In a similar vein, the article "Esclave" (Slave) by Boucher d'Argis, recites the articles of the *Black Code* yet passes no comment whatsoever on the practices that they regulated. The message that the article conveys is that being a slave meant being subject to the legal code that regulated slavery. In a similar fashion, the article "Nègres" (Blacks) collapses the difference between "black" and "enslaved African," a fusion of meanings that causes enslavement to appear as a natural attribute of blackness, rather than as a contingent socio-political condition imposed by Europeans.[19]

Narrative Displacements

Up to this point I have considered discursive mappings of slavery onto Oriental culture in the context of philosophical literature. Turning to other modes of displacement, I will now consider the workings of this mechanism in fictional narratives. In fiction as in philosophy, colonization, and by extension the Atlantic slave trade, were not widely represented before the 1770s. By contrast, the Orient and its various forms of slavery—polygamy, despotism, capture by Barbary pirates—were widely represented across a range of genres. Below I consider several works of fiction in which the "reorientation" of slavery occurs not in the form of conceptual exchanges but through various narrative devices.

19. On this conflation, see also Delesalle and Valensi, 87–89.

For a preliminary example of how displacement may be read in the narrative structure of fiction let us go back to a work that we have already considered briefly: Montesquieu's *Persian Letters*. Although in this novel slavery is more or less synonymous with Oriental polygamy, there are a few passing allusions to the practice of slavery in other geopolitical contexts. In one letter, for example, the "Chief black eunuch" who oversees Usbek's harem confides to his master that he had been "abducted at the age of fifteen from my homeland in the heart of Africa" (84). Though he proceeds to describe how he became a eunuch in a harem, this enslaved black man's allusion to his abduction from Africa certainly brings the protocols of the Atlantic slave trade to mind.

The plot of Montesquieu's novel unfolds on two fronts, Paris and Isfahan, distant locations connected by an allegorical thread. The harem plot set in Isfahan reaches its climax when Usbek's wives rise up in revolt against their absent husband and master, demanding, at least through their actions, the freedom to leave the harem and select their own sexual partners. On the Paris end, the plot culminates with the financial collapse of John Law's Mississippi scheme (185–86). As several critics have noted, it is possible to draw a correlation between, on the one hand, the "unveiling" of the women of the harem and the unmasking of male authoritarianism that it betokens, and, on the other, the manner in which Law's financial speculations turned the class structure of French society inside out (Usbek's friend and fellow-traveler Rica observes that "the foreigner has turned the state inside out the way an old-clothes dealer turns a coat" [186]).[20] I want to note that there is also a colonial dimension to this story, an unstated parallel between the slave revolt that occurs in the harem and the failed investment scheme by means of which Law, in cahoots with the Mississippi Company, sought to accelerate the growth of the brand new French (slave) colony in Louisiana. Beneath the Oriental slave revolt—an uprising that betokens enlightened self-liberation—the shadow of colonial slavery obtrudes.

Moving East: Claude Dorat's *Letter from Zéila*

At the start of this chapter I presented a summary of a fictional narrative to which I now want to return. The text in question is a suite of heroic epistles by Claude Dorat published under the titles *Lettre de Zéila, jeune sauvage, esclave à Constantinople; Réponse de Valcour;* and *Lettre de Valcour à son père* (Letter from Zéila, a Young Savage Enslaved in Constantinople; Valcour's Reply; Letter from Valcour to His Father) (1764–67). In this fictional correspondence Dorat draws on the narrative core of a well-known group of stories, the transnational "Inkle and Yarico" saga.[21] This corpus, which I discuss at greater

---

20. See, for example, Pucci, "Letters from the Harem."
21. Dorat, *Lettres en vers et oeuvres mêlées.*

length in chapter 4, centers on the romance of a mixed-race couple: Inkle, a European man, and Yarico, a woman variously portrayed as an Amerindian and as an African. The pair meet somewhere in the Americas, usually in the aftermath of a shipwreck. The woman saves the man's life, and the two fall in love. Later, however, the European ungratefully abandons the woman, and in some versions of the story sells her into slavery.

Dorat's version of the story begins, typically enough, in the "bois de la Floride" (forests of Florida). But as we have seen, the narrative takes a curious twist when the male protagonist, a Frenchman named Valcour, rather than simply abandoning Zéila in "Florida" or selling her to a nearby plantation, decides to take her and their young son to Constantinople, where he sells them to a merchant. This merchant, in turn, sells Zéila, whose orientalized name seems to prefigure her fate, to the sultan's harem, where she is installed as a concubine. Valcour sets sail for Europe, and Zéila, in despair, writes him a letter in which she complains of the way he has mistreated her, and pleads for the restoration of her freedom and honor. Moved by the eloquence of her pleas, Valcour repents and sails back to Constantinople. In an early performance of what Ella Shohat calls the "orientalist rescue trope," Valcour earns his credentials as a civilized European man by saving a helpless woman from enslavement by an Oriental despot.[22]

When Zéila describes the sultan's palace in her letter to Valcour, she represents it as an environment deformed by slavery of every kind: "I see only objects that wound my eyes. Here, under an iron yoke, man crawls, downcast, and dismal slavery banishes virtue. Here all rights are void; and, to compound this crime, under the common oppressor, each subject in turn oppresses" (1:98). Her description sums up the basic tenets of Oriental despotism as articulated by Montesquieu. The absence of civil and political rights leads to the annihilation of virtue and courage. And though every man is subject to the absolute power of the sultan, each also manages to carve out a sphere of absolute dominion within the confines of his household. Zéila's reference to the "iron yoke" beneath which men crawl may perhaps be viewed as an image more consonant with the rigors of plantation slavery than with conditions in the Oriental harem, but as yokes and chains are common metaphors of French classical literature, and this is a conspicuously classical text, I will not push this reading too far.[23]

Zéila's letter draws a stark contrast between the Oriental world, an environment permeated by slavery, and Florida, which is portrayed as a land of unfettered freedom. In one passage, for example, she imagines returning to her homeland to raise her son as a free human being, a kind of "noble savage"

---

22. Shohat, "Rupture and Return."

23. By the 1760s the heroic epistle was such an outmoded genre that Dorat felt compelled to devote several pages to defending it.

in the mold of Rousseau: "There my dear son, rejoicing in his own being, will learn by my care how one lives without masters. And I will leave him, as his sole inheritance, strength and virtue, the treasures of the savage" (1:101). Her idealized description gives no inkling of the existence of any form of developed society in the Americas, let alone of the presence of the most extreme forms of human servitude.

Letter to Zéila was written in the mid-1760s, at a time when France was still smarting over the loss of her North American colonies and the architects of French foreign policy were beginning to consider new colonial prospects in Egypt and other parts of Africa. Given this historical backdrop, it is tempting to read Dorat's tale of a French man rescuing a woman from the clutches of the Ottoman sultan as a veiled allusion to the "reorientation" of France's colonial ambitions. Yet as we have begun to see, Dorat's transposition of the Inkle and Yarico story from the Americas to the Orient also reflects a long-standing pattern of cultural displacement. It seems almost as if, in order for Zéila to be represented as a slave, she must first be relocated to the Orient, the quintessential location of slavery. This perception is reinforced by Zéila's depiction of "Florida" as a land of uncompromised freedom, and by the absence of any reference to the practice of slavery in the Americas. Situated in this longer historical context, Zéila's enforced migration from West to East seems to protect the fiction that slavery was an Oriental phenomenon—a condition from which Europeans might one day be able to rescue subject peoples—rather than a condition routinely imposed on Africans who were transplanted to the West.

Barbary Captivity and Atlantic Slavery

The fear of capture and enslavement at the hands of Barbary pirates was a common theme of European literature from the seventeenth century to (at least) the nineteenth. Though "Barbary captivity" narratives are not always studied in the same frame as the discourse of Oriental despotism, they overlap with this body of representations in many respects, including the representation of pirates as Oriental agents of enslavement and the preoccupation with women imprisoned in the harem. Emphasizing these continuities, in the next two sections I consider Barbary captivity as a discourse in which slavery is represented as an Oriental phenomenon.

Linda Colley's popular historical study, *Captives,* portrays seizure and servitude as endemic realities of the Mediterranean world between the start of the sixteenth century and the end of the eighteenth.[24] According to Colley, North African Muslims were regularly captured by European vessels and in

---

24. There is a fairly extensive recent literature on slavery in the Mediterranean. Works devoted to piracy and captivity include Davis, *Christian Slaves, Muslim Masters,* and Matar, *Piracy, Slavery and Redemption.*

some instances put to work on the galleys, while in turn European Christians were often captured by "Barbary corsairs" and held as hostages or slaves in the North African client states of the Ottoman Empire. Colley calculates that "in all, over the course of the seventeenth and eighteenth centuries, there were probably twenty thousand or more British captives of Barbary" (44). Though Colley focuses on the British captives who were held in North Africa, she notes that these twenty thousand "represented only a fraction of the total number of men and women confined in North Africa over this period. There were also French, Neopolitans, Dutch, German, Scandinavian, Portuguese, American, and above all Spanish captives and slaves" (44). The specific case of French captives has been examined in an essay by Gillian Weiss, who notes that despite the long-standing diplomatic alliance between France and Turkey, and despite France's adherence to the "freedom principle"—the axiom that slavery had been banished from French soil with the abolition of feudal serfdom in 1315—"French privateers and the Knights of Malta persisted in trawling for Muslims, and Barbary corsairs continued to prey on France's merchant vessels and its maritime provinces."[25]

The Atlantic slave trade, both because of its sheer magnitude and because of its deep moral and social implications, has largely come to overshadow the history of slavery in the Mediterranean world. Yet as Colley and Weiss both note, for many Europeans living in the seventeenth and eighteenth centuries, capture by Barbary pirates loomed larger on the horizon than enslavement in a remote colonial context. Barbary captivity certainly had a major cultural resonance in this period. Weiss notes that religious processions of redeemed slaves periodically passed through French villages, and that printed narratives "depicted abduction, torment, and emancipation for the reading public" (10–11). Stories of abduction and enslavement also spilled over into fictional genres. Many seventeenth- and eighteenth-century French tales and novels—for example, Alain-René Lesage's *Histoire de Gil Blas de Santillane* (*Adventures of Gil Blas*) (1715–35) and Voltaire's *Candide*—contain episodes describing the experience of capture at the hands of Barbary corsairs.

For Colley, the enslavement of British subjects by extra-European peoples represented "the underbelly of empire," a zone of vulnerability which, try as it might, Britain could never fully bring under control. She argues that as the British Empire grew in size and prestige, the enslavement of Britons became increasingly difficult to tolerate, and she gestures to the patriotic anthem, "Rule, Britannia," which was first performed in 1740, and which proclaims with suspect overconfidence that "Britons never, never, never shall be slaves," as one sign of this growing discomfort (47). Building on this claim, Colley suggests that the associations that the words *slave* and *slavery* triggered for

---

25. Weiss, "Barbary Captivity and the French Idea of Freedom," 233.

British people probably changed significantly in the 1720s–30s. She suggests that before 1730 the experience of enslavement was predominantly associated with captivity in the Mediterranean, whereas afterward, slavery became virtually synonymous with the Atlantic slave trade, a context in which it was Britons who exercised dominion (64).

Gillian Weiss makes a parallel argument about the cultural geography of slavery in the French context, though she locates the shift in meaning to an earlier historical moment: the late seventeenth century. Weiss observes that treaties signed between France and rulers in Algiers, Tunis, and Tripoli in the 1680s and 1690s included clauses that prohibited the enslavement of French subjects and outlined procedures for their liberation in the event that they were captured. As a result of these measures, Weiss finds, the number of French subjects in captivity in North Africa declined rapidly (248). Weiss suggests that one reason that French ministers began to treat piracy and captivity with a greater degree of concern in the 1680s was that they had begun to perceive the enslavement of French subjects as an affront to national prestige. She notes that in the 1630s France had begun to expand its frontiers by establishing far-flung colonies in the Caribbean and Indian Ocean, and suggests that this empire building was accompanied by a growing sense of national identity and pride. Along the same lines as Colley, Weiss argues that at the same time that enslavement of French subjects in North Africa became increasingly difficult to tolerate, slavery became more strongly associated with the Atlantic world. As evidence of this trend, she notes (citing Delesalle and Valensi's useful article) that the term *nègre* was first used in a French dictionary to designate an enslaved African in 1704.[26]

This sequence of arguments has a persuasive internal logic, but as I stress throughout this book, the relationship between cultural representation and the social, economic, and political processes involved in colonization was rarely straightforward or transparent. Though Weiss is correct to say that France's colonial empire began to register in empirical genres such as commercial treatises and dictionaries at the end of the seventeenth century, it was not until significantly later that it began to register in other cultural productions. Conversely, though the number of French captives held in the Maghreb may have begun to decline in the late seventeenth century as a result of state intervention, Barbary captivity did not by any means disappear as a topic of literary representation. To the contrary, the experiences of French protagonists enslaved in the Ottoman Empire were the subject of memoirs and novels well into the nineteenth century.[27]

---

26. The dictionary to which Weiss refers is *Dictionnaire universel français et latin* (Universal French and Latin Dictionary) of 1704. Delesalle and Valensi actually cite Furetière's *Universal Dictionary* of 1684 as the first work in which the meanings of the words *black* and *slave* converge.

27. One nineteenth-century example is P. J. Dumont's personal captivity narrative, *Histoire de l'esclavage en Afrique* (1819).

Let us consider, by way of an example, Nicolas Fromaget's 1742 narrative, *Le cousin de Mahomet et la folie salutaire* (The Prophet's Cousin), a work that is part Oriental tale, part picaresque novel. The narrative is represented as the memoir of a naive young man who runs away from school, has a series of adventures, and finally ends up as a slave in an Ottoman harem.[28] Needless to say, this course of events provides a pretext for the observation, at close quarters, of a number of cloistered Oriental beauties. During his years of servitude, the narrator manages to have affairs with several of these inaccessible women; he is at one point almost made into a eunuch, and he loses several masters to the autocratic violence of various sultans and viziers. In short, the narrator experiences at first hand the aspects of Oriental despotism most often underscored by French writers.

The hero's existence as a slave in the Ottoman Empire is at times a dangerous one, but it is not for the most part portrayed as an adverse condition from either a physical or a psychological point of view. Fromaget's depiction of Oriental servitude indeed resonates with Jaucourt's claim in the *Encyclopedia* that slavery in the Orient is in some cases more of a pleasure than a punishment. Fromaget also does not seem to find the idea of a Frenchman serving for several years as a domestic slave to be either anomalous or disturbing. In Constantinople the hero comes into contact with many Europeans who are in the same position as himself: French, Italian, and Spanish men and women who have served as slaves in Ottoman households over a period of several years. Far from repressing the idea that Frenchmen could be made into slaves, *The Prophet's Cousin* seems almost to embrace it. As the narrator's first encounter with slavery occurs while he is en route from Paris to Marseille, one implication of the novel would indeed seem to be that French people were perpetually exposed to the dangers of seizure and enslavement.[29]

The lasting vitality of the captivity narrative as a genre suggests a need to view the relationship between imperial power and literary representation as a more complex process than the rather straightforward translation that Colley and Weiss describe. When we consider that the "underbelly of empire" (i.e., the enslavement of Europeans) is evoked in many literary texts, including such canonical works as *Robinson Crusoe, Gulliver's Travels,* and *Candide,* it seems necessary, in particular, to entertain the idea that in literary narratives power is not always rendered as power.

A helpful model for thinking about this kind of disjuncture is the idea of "anticonquest" laid out by Mary-Louise Pratt in her influential book, *Imperial*

---

28. Fromaget, *Prophet's Cousin,* translated by Eric Sutton.

29. On the road to Marseille the narrator falls in with a company of convicts condemned to serve on the galleys. After a disagreement with the party's guards, he finds himself summarily accused of theft and thrown in among the prisoners. He is released only when the captain of the archers decides, on what seem to be purely subjective grounds, that he is in reality an honest young man.

Eyes. Pratt notes that many colonial-era narratives depict European travelers and explorers, not as strong and commanding figures, but as isolated and vulnerable wanderers who are threatened by aggressive and dangerous natives (38–86). She proposes that this kind of narrative had the dual effect of softening the realities of conquest while tacitly justifying the use of violence by Europeans. The prevalent use of the rhetoric of anticonquest in our own imperialistic times certainly lends support to Pratt's contention that the acknowledgment of vulnerability often supports, rather than contradicts, the exercise of power. In the context of the eighteenth century, it seems to me plausible to suggest that by representing European servitude in the Orient, rather than African slavery in the New World, writers participated in a strategic form of displacement whereby attention was directed away from a context in which Europeans were the primary perpetrators toward a situation in which they figured as victims.

Belated Orientalization: Bernardin de Saint-Pierre's *Empsaël and Zoraïde*

Unlike the other works examined in this chapter, the play that I turn to now, Jacques-Henri Bernardin de Saint-Pierre's *Empsaël et Zoraïde* (1792), was written at a time when colonization and slavery had ceased to be marginal or neglected topics. Completed during the French Revolution, the play is indeed a vehicle for the abolitionist arguments that coalesced in the 1770s and 1780s, arguments of which Bernardin de Saint-Pierre was a noted proponent.[30] Yet although *Empsaël and Zoraïde* confronts the issue of slavery directly, and from an abolitionist perspective, the pattern of West-East displacement that I identify as a feature of earlier literary representation continues to reverberate in its structure. Below I consider it as a hybrid text: a work in which colonial slavery and its Oriental shadow come together in a tangled dramatic configuration.

Bernardin de Saint-Pierre had the opportunity to experience slavery at close range, having served as a colonial engineer in Île de France from 1768 to 1771. His observations of the colony later furnished the inspiration for several texts, notably *Voyage à l'île de France, à l'île de Bourbon, au Cap de Bonne-Espérance* (Voyage to the Island of Mauritius) (1773) and *Études de la Nature* (Studies of Nature) (1784). Bernardin's best-known work, the novel *Paul and Virginia,* which is set in the Île de France, was published in a supplement to *Studies of Nature* in 1788. The practice of slavery is addressed in several of these works. In *Voyage to the Island of Mauritius,* for example, Bernardin gives a somber account of the harsh treatment meted out to the colony's Malagasy slaves. He

---

30. Bernardin was not a member of the Society of the Friends of Blacks, but he corresponded regularly with its founder, Jacques-Pierre Brissot, and praised its work in several texts, notably *Voeux d'un solitaire* (Wishes of a Solitary Man) (1789), and *Suite des voeux* (Sequel to the Wishes) (1792).

dwells on the cruel punishments inflicted on them, and on the frequent separation of families. In a postface he asks whether the luxuries produced by slave
labor were worth the suffering that they occasioned, and criticizes thinkers of
the previous generation for not condemning slavery strenuously enough.

Bernardin began to write a play about colonial slavery in 1775, but he didn't
finish the work until many years later. By the time the final version was completed (probably 1792), France's most important colony, Saint-Domingue,
was in the throes of a massive slave insurrection, and a heated debate over the
future of the colonies and slavery was unfolding in the Constituent Assembly.
Curiously, however, the action of *Empsaël and Zoraïde* is set, not in the Antilles or the Indian Ocean, but on the Barbary Coast, and its enslaved characters
are not Africans but white Europeans who are held captive by a Tunisian ruler
named Moulay Ismael.

It must be emphasized at this point that Bernardin's intentions in depicting
slavery in the guise of Barbary captivity were not to avoid the subject of the
Atlantic slave trade. On the contrary, in depicting slavery through the lens of a
situation in which whites are enslaved by blacks, he was deliberately trying to
cast the iniquity of the colonial order in a fresh light. To this end, Bernardin
portrays the play's Tunisian Muslim characters, Moulay Ismael and his chief
minister Empsael, as black men of sub-Saharan descent, and designates them
with the words *nègre* and *mulâtre:* terms borrowed from the lexicon of New
World slavery. The substitution of black for white masters is in many respects
an effective political strategy. As Roger Little writes in the introduction to a recent critical edition, "A delicious and biting irony undergirds this drama, a reversal of the traditional roles on which the master is always white and his slaves
just as invariably black" (ix–x). The play's black characters express convictions
such as that "black is the natural color of man and of woman" (49). As Léon-
François Hoffmann explains, when racial utterances such as these were placed
in the mouth of a black character, they challenged the deep-seated prejudices
that underpinned colonial slavery (94).

In other ways, however, the play's Oriental setting could be said to de-
tract from its polemic against colonial slavery. Captivity and enslavement in the
Maghreb were somewhat different from slavery in a colonial setting. Though
the living conditions of Barbary captives were not always good, European slaves
or prisoners were not usually forced to perform hard physical labor. Some were
allowed to come and go with relative freedom, and many received visits from
compatriots charged with securing their freedom. All of these conditions are
reflected in Bernardin's drama, where the European captives enjoy a similar
amount of freedom of movement and scarcely seem to perform any work. The
Oriental setting particularly shapes the manner in which the enslavement of
women is depicted. The play's enslaved female characters, including the eponymous Zoraïde, occupy domestic positions and are valued for their beauty and
sexual appeal. None of them is forced to work in the cane fields, or to endure
a twelve-hour shift in a sugar mill.

When we begin to consider Bernardin's staging of slavery from the perspective of what it doesn't represent, other omissions, or perhaps displacements, come into focus. Though Bernardin obviously knew that several European nations, including France, participated in the Atlantic slave trade, his play lays the blame for colonial slavery squarely at the feet of Spain. Tapping into the "black legend" of Spanish brutality, Bernardin holds Spain responsible, not only for the conquest of the Americas, but also for the practice of slavery in the Caribbean in the eighteenth century. The main figure among the enslaved male characters is Don Ozorio, a Spanish nobleman who, before he was taken captive during a transatlantic voyage, had been the owner of a Caribbean plantation. As the plot slowly unravels, it is revealed that Empsael had for years toiled as a slave in the fields of this very plantation. Before he gets around to forgiving his former master for the years he spent in servitude, he devotes several passionate speeches to the cruel treatment of slaves on Spanish plantations. He decries, in particular, the hypocritical emphasis that Spanish colonists placed on converting slaves to Christianity, a critique that feeds into the play's important subtheme of religious intolerance.[31]

Don Ozorio's plantation is said to be located in "Saint-Domingue," a name used in the eighteenth century to designate both the French colony on the island of Hispaniola (today Haiti) and (as presumably in this instance) the neighboring Spanish colony (now the Dominican Republic). By 1792 the French colony had outstripped its Spanish neighbor by every economic measure and had a far larger enslaved population. It was also very much in the news, since for several years its various population groups had been engaged in major uprisings. In light of this historical context, Bernardin's decision to depict his colonial protagonist as a plantation owner from Spanish Saint-Domingue, rather than from the neighboring French colony, seems somewhat curious. In *Voyage to the Island of Mauritus,* Bernardin complains that when philosophers condemned the massacre of Mexicans by the conquistadors, they tended to write as if genocide in the Americas were a thing of the past rather than an ongoing reality of the colonial world. I submit that he perhaps falls, in *Empsaël and Zoraïde,* into a similar trap.

The combination of orientalization and "hispanicization" deployed in the play can be said to have a number of consequences. One is to allow Bernardin to portray the slave trade in a critical light without directly denouncing France. This approach can in turn be related to the tenor of French antislavery writing in the 1780s–90s. Most writers who denounced slavery in this period

---

31. One weakness of *Empsaël and Zoraïde,* both politically and aesthetically, is that it tries to do too much, notably to deal with both slavery and religious intolerance. Bernardin's decision to broach this second issue may have been influenced by the example of Voltaire's highly successful tragedy *Zaïre* (1732), which also explores the issue of intolerance through the story of a powerful Muslim ruler who loves an enslaved Christian woman. In *Empsaël and Zoraïde,* however, the pairing of the well-worn critique of religious persecution with the relatively new political topic of slavery is rather distracting.

defended, and in some cases even celebrated, the existence of French colonies. Abolition was indeed sometimes advocated on the grounds that it would save the colonies and position France to launch new colonial ventures in Africa. In *Voeux d'un solitaire* (*The Wishes of a Solitary Man*), a sequel to *Studies of Nature,* Bernardin himself argues that it would be beneficial for France to establish new agricultural colonies on the African coast. Traces of this political perspective can be read in *Empsaël and Zoraïde.* One of play's characters is named Anthony Bénézet after the French-born Pennsylvania Quaker who was one of the first vocal opponents of slavery. In the play he serves as a mouthpiece for the argument that if Africans were to begin cultivating crops such as sugar and cotton, they would be able to bring the slave trade to an end (117).[32]

Bernardin's choice of the Barbary Coast as a setting for his attack on colonial slavery is thus not only a revival of earlier displacements onto the Orient or the Maghreb but also a reflection of the formulation of new proposals to replace the plantations of the Caribbean with "free" agricultural settlements in coastal Africa. In the shifting terrains of Oriental and abolitionist discourses, the ongoing practice of slavery in the colonies of the Antilles and Indian Ocean fades from view. Caught in the divide between the old current of orientalization and the rise of a new colonial vision, colonial slavery is never fully actualized as an object of representation in its own right.

When we consider literary representations of colonial slavery in relation to depictions of Oriental servitude, we notice first the glaring asymmetry. The Oriental world is depicted extensively, the colonial milieu scarcely at all. What this pattern of representation initially seems to betoken is indifference to colonization and slavery and to the social and ethical questions that these practices raised. While people were captivated by the Orient, they were simply not that interested in the colonial world. But I believe that the nature of the relationship between colonialism and Oriental exoticism was in reality more complex. In a number of eighteenth-century texts, including several highly influential works, Orient and colonies converge in ways that suggest, not outright indifference, but rather an underlying reluctance to examine slavery directly, or, to make this point in another way, a need to examine slavery indirectly, via the trope of orientalization. The next two chapters offer further evidence of a broad-based process of displacement. Turning from texts to material culture, I explore the relationship between the Oriental and the colonial in cultural media other than literature.

---

32. When Bénézet tries this argument out on Empsaël, the black leader lucidly retorts that Europeans would respond by seizing African land, an interpretation that seems more than justified when we consider Bernardin's own proposals for new French settlements!

2

Oriental Veneers

In 2004 the Metropolitan Museum of Art in New York City mounted a small exhibition of exquisite ceramics, silverware, and furniture created for the consumption of the new hot beverages popularized in Europe in the seventeenth and eighteenth centuries.[1] The presentational materials for the exhibit drew attention to the Eastern origins of coffee and tea, as well as to the Oriental motifs that adorn many of the elegant pieces created for their enjoyment. Coffee and tea came to Europe from the East, the exhibit's curators explained, and to capture these origins, European craftsmen created silver coffee and chocolate pots and porcelain demitasses in Oriental styles. A point that was not made, however, was that by the mid-eighteenth century most of the coffee and chocolate consumed in Europe, along with the sugar with which these drinks were usually prepared, were imported from Europe's plantation colonies in the Americas, particularly that "pearl of the Antilles," the French colony of Saint-Domingue. And though the informational panels explained that the English predilection for tea never really took off in coffee-addicted France, they did not clarify the geopolitical reasons for these national preferences, for instance, the fact that by the mid-eighteenth century the most significant French colonial and commercial networks lay to the west, while Britain was consolidating and expanding its hold on India.

These omissions can be attributed to several different factors. On one level, the museum's team of curators was simply following the lead of eighteenth-century craftsmen, who also underscored Oriental associations while making

---

1. Chocolate, Coffee, Tea, Metropolitan Museum of Art, February–July, 2004.

little of the colonial provenance of many raw materials. As in the field of literary studies, scholarship and interpretation in art history are aligned with the dominant historical modes of representation. Yet in the case of material culture, there is a further dimension to this story. Museum curators typically concentrate on matters such as artistry, craftsmanship, and the history of ownership—the aspects that Igor Kopytoff has called the "cultural biography" of things.[2] The social and economic processes that support these cultural dimensions command their attention to a lesser degree. There is perhaps even some degree of resistance to the idea of approaching delicate porcelain coffee cups or elegant mahogany tea chests as by-products of colonial agribusiness. At first glance, the history of luxury furniture seems to have little to do with this kind of material reality, or indeed with the social and economic concerns of people beyond the (literally) gilded elite world of which such furniture is seen as a vestige. Yet practices of consumption and aesthetic appreciation are stages in the cycle of production, and in the eighteenth century this cycle began with the cultivation and harvesting of raw materials and marshaled a workforce that included, in some instances, the enslaved population of Europe's plantation colonies.

In the seventeenth and eighteenth centuries, French material culture was enriched by the growth of maritime commerce and the development of commercial networks that linked Europe to Asia, Africa, and the Americas. From the colonies established in the Atlantic and Indian oceans in the mid-1600s came aliments such as coffee, sugar, and cocoa; raw materials employed in the textile industry, including cotton, indigo, and cochineal; and tropical woods and resins used in pharmacology, shipbuilding, and furniture making. The influx of these various materials stimulated an array of changes in both production and consumption.

Commercial relations with the East were widely referenced in French art, literature, and material culture. Given this, one would perhaps expect to encounter a parallel set of references to colonial environments and their principal exports. In fact, the impact of colonial commerce on France's economic and material life did not register strongly, and it was not until much later that tropical or colonial origins came to be promoted as a marker of quality and luxury. Wood imported from colonial sources, known as *bois des îles*, was a costly commodity that was used primarily as a veneer and retailed as a luxury. In Flaubert's *Madame Bovary* (1857), for example, the *palissandre* (rosewood) desk in which Emma Bovary keeps her love letters, and which her husband, Charles, opens to his chagrin in the aftermath of her death, serves as a general symbol for the heroine's destructive taste for elegant and expensive goods.[3] But rosewood desks such as Emma's were not represented or marketed as *colonial* goods. Instead, tropical woods were absorbed into consumer goods that

2. Kopytoff, "Cultural Biography of Things."
3. Flaubert, *Madame Bovary*, 320–21.

conjured other cultural associations, including, in many instances, the exotic world of the Orient.

In this chapter I consider how imported tropical hardwoods and related materials such as tortoiseshell and mother-of-pearl transformed French furnishing styles in the seventeenth and eighteenth centuries. I also revisit the well-known story of how commerce and contact with the Orient shaped French material culture, and consider the various ways in which Oriental exoticism was manifested in the domain of furniture. Juxtaposing these two historical threads, I highlight the contrast between the prevalent, not to say obsessive, referencing of the Oriental world and the overall invisibility of colonial origins. We have seen that the relationship between the "Oriental" exoticism and the "colonial" in this period was defined not only by asymmetry but also by displacement. Below I give further examples of this process. I show that in the case of furniture, raw materials derived from colonial sources, particularly tropical hardwoods, were often turned into chairs, tables, or armoires adorned with Oriental motifs or styled in a recognizably Oriental fashion. As in other parts of this book, I attribute this pattern of effacement and projection to two primary factors. On one level the obstacle was simply that there was no readily available thematic repertory or figurative tradition for the representation of the rapidly changing human and ecological realities of Europe's island colonies. Whereas Turkey, Persia, Japan, and China could be evoked with a parasol or pagoda, a sofa or a turban, there was no parallel set of themes or images through which colonial society could be portrayed. A second issue was that because of their culture of slavery, the colonies presented a significant representational challenge. There was little superficial exoticism to be derived from the depiction of plantation agriculture or from the contemplation of colonial servitude. In view of these issues I suggest that furniture makers and *marchands de modes* participated in a process of aestheticization whereby attractive associations were accentuated, and potentially negative or compromising ones minimized. This is not to say that craftsmen and merchants engaged in deliberate efforts of misrepresentation or concealment. Rather, I suggest that an array of subjacent cultural and economic forces led them to make little of colonial origins, while emphasizing Oriental connections.

Before going further, a few qualifications are necessary. First I want to emphasize that orientalization was only one of several processes by means of which colonial commodities were integrated into the French decorative tradition. Tropical woods were perhaps just as often associated with pastoral or neoclassical imagery as with Oriental motifs. But if the volume of pieces of furniture in which West was translated into East was in real terms small, these exchanges nonetheless appear significant when furniture is examined alongside other cultural productions, for example, literature and textiles. This is a case where an integrated cultural perspective clarifies patterns that do not come to light in more narrowly focused work.

Cross-disciplinary perspectives of course have their limitations, and indeed the second qualification that I need to offer here is that I approach eighteenth-century material culture as a literary scholar, rather than as a specialist in the history of furniture (or, in the next chapter, textiles). What this means in broad terms is that I consider furniture as a representational medium that shares certain themes and motifs with literature and the visual arts. Furniture obviously signifies in other ways, through formal and material properties about which I will have relatively little to say.

Colonial Commerce and the Furniture Revolution

During the seventeenth and eighteenth centuries French furniture underwent a series of significant transformations, many of which were connected to the impact of transcontinental commerce. Cultural historians have rightly emphasized the impact of contact and commerce with the Orient, especially China and Japan, on French furnishing styles. Below I consider the impact of colonial commercial networks. The main story in this regard concerns the impact of tropical hardwoods imported from the Indian Ocean, the Caribbean, and Central America. As I will show, the arrival on the European market of colorful and resistant materials such as ebony, mahogany, and tulip- and sandalwood vastly expanded the options of craftsmen and consumers, contributing to an upheaval in techniques and forms.

The quest for wood was an important feature of the early history of colonial expansion. By 1600 many European nations had run short of timber and were beginning to look elsewhere for supplies. As European explorers moved west, they named several territories, including Madeira and Brazil, for their plentiful reserves of timber. They also referred to the Africans whom they imported to labor in their colonies as "bois d'ébène" (ebony wood), a label that identifies slaves with one of the most prized colonial trade goods. No European nation ever succeeded in meeting the needs of its domestic building and shipbuilding industries from colonial sources. But in the forests of the Caribbean and Central America, European settlers and explorers discovered woods with other desirable properties: combinations of color, resistance, and fragrance that made them valuable to manufacturers in the drug, perfume, and dye industries, and in particular to furniture makers.

Evidence of the significance of this trade in woods can be found in several travel narratives. For example, in his account of a voyage undertaken in 1607, the French naturalist Jean Mocquet recalls that during a stopover in Guiana, he collected *citrin* (sandalwood) to sell to an apothecary in La Rochelle, while his ship's crew loaded a cargo comprising seventy thousand pounds of aloe, red and yellow *citrin*, and *bois de rose* (tulipwood).[4] In a later work on colonial

---

4. Mocquet, *Voyages en Afrique, Asie, Indes occidentales et orientales*, 86–94.

Guiana, the physician and naturalist Pierre Barrère recalls that it was the quest for *bois de Brésil* and other prized hardwoods that first brought French sailors to the shores of Guiana. He also notes that hardwoods such as "guaiac, crabwood (*bois de crabe*), ironwood (*bois de fer*), kingwood (*bois violet*), ebony, [and] tulipwood (*bois de rose*)" had since continued to figure among Guiana's principal exports.[5]

The colonial trade in tropical hardwoods served as a catalyst for a number of major furnishing trends. Until the end of the seventeenth century, ebony was only imported in small quantities and used in the form of a veneer. Starting in around the 1630s, however, Portuguese, Dutch, and later French merchants began shipping large quantities of ebony from their colonial outposts in Madagascar and Mauritius.[6] As a result of this increased supply, solid ebony became a fashionable choice for chairs, tables, and interior paneling. Inspired by the beauty of the wood, craftsmen experimented with form and design, giving rise, by the end of the century, to a vogue for ornately sculpted ebony furniture.

As this example illustrates, access to new materials had a direct impact on the craft of furniture making. The very distinction drawn in French between a *menuisier*—a craftsman who builds furniture—and an *ébéniste*—a specialist who executes sculpture, marquetry, and veneers—dates to the late seventeenth century, as does the existence of a specialized trade guild of *maîtres ébénistes-menuisiers* (established in 1638). Indeed, I think it would not be an exaggeration to say that the arrival of tropical hardwoods on the European market led to an overhaul of the furniture-making industry that paved the way for the transformation of the luxury furniture market into a branch of the decorative arts.

One of the most important aspects of this metamorphosis was the refinement of veneering techniques, including inlaying and marquetry. Before the seventeenth century, the color of a piece of wood was sometimes altered by the use of heat, or vegetable stains and varnishes. In the age of colonial imports the need for these treatments was greatly reduced, as woods ranging in color from pale yellow to deep purple became available. By juxtaposing these various colors, artisans were able to create eye-catching designs that turned furniture into a canvas for art.

The first real star of French *ébénisterie* was the Dutch-born *ébéniste* André Boulle, who made many pieces for Louis XIV's château at Versailles. Boulle was particularly known for marquetry compositions (known as "Boulle marquetry")

---

5. *Nouvelle relation de la France équinoxale*, 3–4, 116. Barrère's narrative was published in the 1740s but concerned the author's posting to Guiana in the 1720s.

6. In his study of the colonial roots of environmentalism, Richard Grove notes of Mauritius (Île de France) that "during the Dutch period the rate of deforestation on the island became closely correlated with the state of the European market for luxury goods" (132). By the time of the French takeover of Mauritius in 1721, the island's ebony reserves had already been greatly depleted, especially in coastal areas. On the Portuguese and Dutch ebony trade in the Indian Ocean, see Evers and Hookoomsing, *Globalization and the South-West Indian Ocean*.

that combined ebony from the Indian Ocean with Caribbean tortoiseshell and red or gold-hued copper.[7] In later years leading craftsmen abandoned these dramatic contrasts for a more subdued decorative style in which color contrasts were created by juxtaposing different kinds of wood—a technique known as "painting in wood."[8] When in 1685 Alexandre-Jean Oppenordt was engaged to create a parquetry floor for the state apartments at Versailles, his contract stipulated that rather than resorting to stains or fire in order to alter the color of the woods employed in his design, he would rely on the natural color of oak, coral wood, *bois de lis des Indes*,[9] and green and black ebony. Figure 1 shows a parquet floor of a slightly later period (ca. 1715-20). Though the black-and-white reproduction does not do justice to its intricate combination of satinwood, tulipwood, and olivewood, it does at least suggest the contrasts and nuances of color that could be obtained from tropical hardwoods.

In an account of the marquetry techniques that he and other contemporary *ébénistes* practiced, André Roubo mentions the use of "rare colored woods that come to us from abroad and are known by the names of bois des Indes, brazilwood, mahogany of all kinds, satinwood, cedar, olive, and aromatic laurel."[10] As Roubo notes, craftsmen did not always distinguish clearly among the different varieties of wood that were imported from the Antilles, Central America, and the Indian Ocean, often referring to them collectively as "bois des îles" or "bois des Indes." But despite the vagueness of these expressions we can, nonetheless, identify some of the most popular tropical hardwoods employed by eighteenth-century craftsmen.[11]

Woods that were frequently used in marquetry included *palissandre* (rosewood), a veined grey or purplish wood found mostly in the Antilles, and *amarante* (purple wood) from Central America, which was made fashionable by Charles Crescent, furniture maker to the regent, Philippe d'Orléans. *Bois de citron* (lemonwood) from the Antilles, which had a pale lemon color and a pleasant aroma, and *bois de rose* (tulipwood), primarily imported from Brazil, were also prized materials. All of these woods were used almost exclusively as veneers, imported in small quantities, and sold by the pound. Woods from the Caribbean and Central America that were imported in larger quantities and used to build furniture included *campêche* (campeachy/logwood), *gaïac* (lignum vitae/guaiac), and mahogany.

7. In terms of the total value of imports, over the course of the eighteenth century, tortoiseshell was a more important commodity than any tropical wood, including ebony and mahogany. See Chaussat and Chaussat, *Les meubles de Port Rochelais,* 30.

8. See Ramond, *Marquetry,* 79.

9. Janneau, *Le meuble de l'ébénisterie,* 39. It is hard to know which variety of wood was designated by the term *bois de lis des Indes,* which literally means "lily of the Indies wood."

10. Roubo, *L'art du menuisier,* 1:22–23.

11. On exotic woods and their botanical names and provenance, see *Mobilier créole,* 14–29, Chaussat and Chaussat, 141–42.

Figure 1. German parquet, circa 1715–20. Veneered in satinwood, tulipwood, and olive-wood. J. Paul Getty Museum, Los Angeles.

Mahogany, or *acajou,* was the queen of the exotic hardwoods, the wood that had the most profound and lasting impact on European furniture design. It was also a material whose history was closely intertwined with that of colonial expansion, since it was purportedly discovered by Columbus when he first landed in Hispaniola. The term *acajou*/mahogany actually covers several related species, the two principal varieties being *Swietana mahogani,* known in French as *acajou de Saint-Domingue* or *de Cuba,* a tree that is indigenous to the greater Antilles; and *swietana macrophylla,* known in French as *acajou du Honduras.*[12] *Acajou de Cuba* was introduced into the French colonies of Martinique and Guadeloupe around 1740, with *acajou de Honduras* following much later, around 1900. Interestingly—I would even say symptomatically—in spite of

12. The French word is derived from the Portuguese *acajoba,* the English from a Spanish term, both words originating in pre-Columbian Central American languages.

mahogany's New World provenance, several eighteenth-century French writers borrowed the exotic resonance of the word *acajou* to name their Oriental characters. Charles Simon Favart, for example, composed a popular comic opera entitled *Acajou* (1744), while Charles Duclos wrote an Oriental tale titled *Acajou and Zirphile* (1744).

Historians of British art have dubbed the eighteenth century the "age of mahogany" in recognition of the material's enormous impact on material culture. In France the taste for gilded, painted, and upholstered furniture lasted longer, with solid mahogany furniture not really becoming a widespread trend until the end of the century.[13] Mahogany furniture was, however, prevalent at an earlier moment in the colonies, as well as in west coast ports such as Bordeaux, Nantes, La Rochelle, and Rouen: wealthy and cultured centers in which the circulation of colonial imports gave rise to distinctive furnishing fashions.

Circum-Atlantic Furniture

The furnishing styles specific to France's west coast ports in the eighteenth and nineteenth centuries have historically been grouped under the label "port furniture."[14] I will take a slightly different approach to these regional trends by thinking of them as instances of a "circum-Atlantic" culture and situating them in relation to the circuits of colonial commerce. The idea of "Atlantic history" or the "Atlantic world" has not enjoyed much currency in French historiography, where the status of the nation as the central organizing category has on the whole been subject to less revision than in the North American or British contexts. I will suggest, though, that in many cultural domains, including that of furniture, it is necessary to adopt the regional and transcontinental framework of Atlantic history.[15] In the case of furniture, for example, we find that styles popular in Bordeaux and La Rochelle shared many characteristics with those that were prevalent in England and in the colonies of the Caribbean, locations connected not only through commercial ties but also by cultural affinities.

French regional styles typically evolved at a slower pace than fashionable Parisian furniture. On the west coast, for example, elements of the French

13. In 1753 Mme de Pompadour ordered six mahogany commodes for her residence at Crécy from a prominent Parisian *marchand de modes* (a retailer of fashionable objects and linens). The taste for mahogany did not, however, become prevalent in France until the 1780s–90s.

14. On the category of port furniture, see Chaussat and Chaussat, 15–16, and Du Pasquier, *Bordeaux Musée des arts décoratifs*, 113–15.

15. Major discussions of "Atlantic," "Atlantic-rim," and "circum-Atlantic" history and culture include Gilroy, *The Black Atlantic;* Roach, *Cities of the Dead;* and Bailyn, *Atlantic History.* French historiography has been more receptive to the category of the "Mediterranean world," a concept explored by Fernand Braudel in *La Méditerranée et le monde méditerranéen a l'époque de Philippe II,* and reactivated as a strategy of international relations under the presidency of Nicolas Sarkozy.

regency style (roughly 1700–30) remained popular well into the nineteenth century.[16] In at least one respect, however, the port cities of the Atlantic were in the decorative vanguard. Though in England the natural beauty of wood, rather than gilding or sculpting, became the focal point of furniture in the early 1750s, in France this shift did not take place until the end of the eighteenth century. The one exception to this rule was the west coast. As archival sources such as probate inventories show, the elegant townhouses of districts such as Les Chartrons in Bordeaux and the Île Feydeau in Nantes were often decorated with furniture that reflected the colonial origins of their owners' fortunes. These furnishings included pieces crafted in solid mahogany, which became popular on the Atlantic coast well before they started to appear in Paris and other regions of France.

In the next few paragraphs I explore some of the styles of furniture that were (and remain) associated with the west coast region, and that attest to the impact of colonial commerce and the coalescence of a circum-Atlantic style. The main focus is on mahogany, though other materials, notably cane, are also discussed.

Among the most striking examples of circum-Atlantic furniture were the solid (and often massive) mahogany armoires used in cities such as Bordeaux and Nantes to store linens and display fine china. Figure 2 shows an armoire of this kind: a regency-style *armoire bordelaise* in sculpted *acajou moucheté* (dappled mahogany). In a fascinating study of the lifestyle of the nobility of the Bordeaux region in the eighteenth century, Michel Figeac explains that armoires such as this one were much more prevalent in the homes of well-off *bordelais* than in the *hôtels* or *châteaux* of surrounding regions. He calculates that between 1680 and 1730, over 39 percent of the probate inventories executed for aristocratic residences in and around Bordeaux recorded the presence of an armoire, with the figure rising to over 92 percent, and an average of over six armoires per inventory, between 1760 and 1794.[17]

In an equally interesting and in many ways complementary study of Bordeaux's history as slave port, Eric Saugera makes reference to an unusual armoire housed in a stately residence in Agen, a town located to the southeast of Bordeaux. He explains that the interior surfaces of the doors of the armoire are painted with scenes representing two black domestics, a woman on the left side, a man on the right (288–89, 305). Though the provenance of this piece is unknown, Saugera speculates that it may once have belonged to a merchant by the name of Nègre who is known to have lived on the same street. Whatever its history, this curious armoire might be said to testify in an unusually direct way to the region's involvement in colonial commerce, as well as to underlying connections between mahogany and "bois d'ébène."

16. Chaussat and Chaussat, 45.
17. Figeac, *La douceur des lumières*, 289, 296.

Figure 2. Regency-style *armoire bordelaise,* first half of the eighteenth century. Sculpted *acajou moucheté.* Musée des arts décoratifs, Bordeaux.

A second piece of furniture commonly found in noble and bourgeois residences in eighteenth-century Bordeaux and La Rochelle was the solid mahogany *commode,* or chest of drawers.[18] These came in a range of different styles, each one characteristic of one of the region's main ports. Figure 3 shows a midcentury *commode en tombeau* with three rows of drawers arranged in an inverted pyramid, a style associated with Bordeaux. In La Rochelle *commodes* were more box-like and had no tapering at the bottom. The chests of drawers that were prevalent on the Atlantic coast of France in the mid-eighteenth century are very similar to those manufactured in England in the same period.[19] They can in fact be seen as crossover pieces that illustrate the close ties between the west coast and England.

The commercial and cultural currents linking the French Atlantic to Britain, the Netherlands, and the colonial world are also illustrated by the chair or daybed made from rattan or cane. In the seventeenth century, Dutch merchants encountered rattan latticework in Indonesia and began importing it to Europe. Strong, mobile, and relatively inexpensive, rattan chairs and daybeds became fashionable in the Netherlands and Britain in the late seventeenth century. They arrived in Bordeaux soon afterwards, though it was only much later that cane furniture became popular in Paris.[20] Light, aerated, and easy to clean, chairs made from local cane were also widely used in the Caribbean and Indian Ocean colonies.

One of the most distinctive pieces of circum-Atlantic furniture was the table crafted from lignum vitae or guaiac (figure 4). Guaiac tables usually have turned legs, and feet joined by a stretcher, often in the form of a cross-link. Tables of this design were prevalent in France during the reign of Louis XIV, but they passed out of fashion, at least in Paris, at the end of the seventeenth century. In the region around Rochefort and La Rochelle, however, the cross-link style remained current for a much longer period. This was in part because lignum vitae—a veined wood of contrasting colors that was one of the most commonly imported tropical hardwoods—was difficult to work other than by turning, and in part because it was used in the shipbuilding industry, and Rochefort was home to a naval shipyard.

The landscapist Claude-Joseph Vernet's *Vue du port de La Rochelle prise de la petite rive* (View of the Port of Rochelle taken from the Little Bank) (1763), one of a series of fifteen paintings of French ports that Vernet completed under the aegis of a royal commission, depicts an activity that must have been a

18. The *commode,* or chest of drawers, was a relatively late addition to standard European furniture, first making its appearance around 1690. Its invention was probably tied to the gradual expansion of consumers' wardrobes and to the resulting need to create more storage space.

19. The connection between England and the Bordeaux area was in some measure a legacy of the English presence in region in the Middle Ages. In the seventeenth and eighteenth centuries, this old connection was renewed through commercial relationships.

20. See Du Pasquier, 40, 51.

Figure 3. Mahogany *commode bordelaise,* or *en tombeau,* mid-eighteenth century. Musée des arts décoratifs, Bordeaux.

common sight in the port of La Rochelle: a cargo of timber is being trans-ferred from a ship onto the busy docks (figure 5).[21] Was the wood that was being unloaded mahogany, or perhaps guaiac?[22] Had it been shipped from one of France's Caribbean colonies or from the Île de France? And had it perhaps been loaded aboard the vessel at the point of origin by a corps of enslaved laborers? These are purely speculative questions, of course, but they are ones that invite us to consider this well-known painting in a new light, such that we see it not only as a patriotic image of France's thriving ports and naval bases but also as a document of the interconnected global trajectory linking colonial raw materials to domestic crafts and industries.

How did the furniture of France's west coast compare with furniture preva-lent in the French colonies? Unfortunately very little early French 'Creole' furniture has survived. The few antique pieces that can be seen on public

21. In 1753 Vernet received a commission to paint views of all of France's major ports. In-tended to showcase France's prosperous ports and naval power, these landscapes were, ironically, completed during the Seven Years' War, a conflict that dealt a severe blow to the navy and mari-time commerce.

22. The summaries of ships' cargoes printed in the *Journal de Guyenne* (a periodical published in Bordeaux, 1785–91) indicate that logwood, guaiac, and mahogany were the most commonly imported tropical woods.

Figure 4. Table with turned legs and stretcher, late seventeenth or early eighteenth century. Guaiac with an oak top. Musée du nouveau monde, La Rochelle.

display in museums and plantation houses in Martinique and Guadeloupe are for the most part nineteenth-century creations imported from former English colonies such as Barbados or Dominica, or from the United States. From the small handful of surviving eighteenth-century pieces we can, however, discern a number of trends. These include the widespread use of solid mahogany, a wood valued in the Caribbean not only for its beauty but also for its resistance to humidity. The standard furniture of the *case du maître* on a French *habitation* generally included mahogany armoires, chests, and four-poster beds. Cane was a popular choice for seat furniture because upholstery was vulnerable to humidity and insects. Figure 6 shows late eighteenth-/early nineteenth-century Creole dining furniture displayed in the Museum of History and Ethnography in Fort de France, Martinique.

Written sources reinforce the evidence of the surviving antique pieces. For example, in his exhaustive description of Saint-Domingue at the end of the eighteenth century, the Creole writer Moreau de Saint-Méry observes that white colonists and free people of color typically furnished their homes with armoires and chairs crafted from locally available materials such as mahogany

Figure 5. Claude-Joseph Vernet, *Vue du port de La Rochelle prise de la petite rive* (1762). Oil on canvas. Musée national de la marine, Paris.

Figure 6. Reconstruction of an early nineteenth-century Creole dining room with mahogany table, armoire, and cane chairs. Musée ethnographique et historique, Fort de France, Martinique.

and cane.[23] A sale inventory conducted for a plantation in Les Abricots, Saint-Domingue, at around the same time gives the following account of the contents of the master's house: "Mahogany bergère with its cushion, in bad condition...mahogany bed with a straw mattress, pillow, cotton mosquito net and printed cotton coverlet, all in bad condition...a bad cedar armoire, used as a cupboard. Another armoire in mahogany, with copper bolts and locks...mahogany table."[24] Though the assessor clearly didn't think much of Les Abricots's furniture, his rapid denomination of the pieces included in the sale suggests that they were standard items for a Caribbean plantation house.

Depending on how narrowly furniture is defined, certain items that European settlers adapted from the material culture of indigenous people could

23. Moreau de Saint-Méry, 1:90.
24. *Inventaire et mise en possession de l'habitation Valette,* September, 27, 1792. Archive, Musée du nouveau monde, La Rochelle (87–4–2).

also be included in the category of Creole furnishings. Early colonial narratives include admiring descriptions of the pirogues, hammmocks, woven storage baskets, and wooden stools crafted by "Carib" and "Galibi" Indians. In his discussion of colonial Guiana, for example, Pierre Barrère describes hammocks as "useful pieces of furniture," and accurately predicts that these mobile "American beds" would one day prove popular in France (137).

One of the most important questions raised by the production of furniture both in the colonies and metropolitan France concerns the role of enslaved and free black craftsmen and laborers. When the colonial population expanded during the sugar boom of the late 1600s, skilled workers, including carpenters, were in short supply. The French authorities tried to encourage carpenters to move to the colonies with the promise that after ten years' service, they would automatically obtain the rank of master and enjoy the right to open their own boutique in Paris.[25] These inducements were, however, not particularly successful, and in order to avoid paying the high wages commanded by the few French artisans resident in the colonies, colonists often elected to train their slaves as woodworkers.

From the evidence of estate inventories, advertisements for slave auctions, and published descriptions of the colonies, it is clear that slaves with special skills, including carpenters, were highly valued.[26] "Nègres à talent" were often hired out to perform specific jobs, and in some cases they were allowed to earn money for their own account. They were considerably more likely than field slaves to be able to win or buy their freedom. In a study of free people of color in Fort Royal (now Fort de France) from the late seventeenth to the early nineteenth century, Émile Hayot finds that many artisans were free black men, and that after masonry, carpentry was one of the most common professions of this group.[27] For 1710 alone, Hayot identifies fifty-four free black or mixed-race *menuisiers* (carpenters) in the parish records of Fort Royal.

Colonists also sometimes brought their slaves to France to learn carpentry skills. Erick Noël has shown that of the thousand or so cases in which enslaved or free blacks who registered with the Black Police stated their profession, about a third declared themselves to be artisans, most of the others being domestic servants. Among the artisans (just under three hundred people) forty-two are listed as woodworkers of some kind (116). Censuses of people of color conducted in 1777 and 1807 in the Bordeaux region testify to the presence of a small number of men, designated as "mulattoes," whose profession is given as *menuisier* or *ébéniste*.[28] According to Noël there was also a contingent of

---

25. These promises offered a shortcut for artisans wishing to reduce the lengthy period of apprenticeship and practice required to become a master under the French guild system. See *Mobilier créole*, 60–61.

26. See, for example, Labat, *Nouveau voyage aux isles de l'Amérique* 4:186–88. References hereafter in the text are to this edition.

27. Hayot, *Les gens de couleur libres du Fort-Royal*, 30–34.

28. Document in the Archives régionales de la Gironde: ARG 1M 332.

black woodworkers in Nantes (117). He speculates that in a city in which many residents owned or had an interest in a colonial plantation, slaves were being trained to perform skilled labor on return to the colonies (117). Unfortunately, archival documents offer only a limited picture of the number of enslaved and free blacks who learned or practiced woodwork in France in the eighteenth century. Over the course of the century, a series of laws restricted the presence of slaves in metropolitan France, and since both slave owners and former slaves had an interest in evading these controls, the numbers recorded in police censuses and port records undoubtedly underrepresent the size of this group.

To date relatively little research has been undertaken on the skilled labor performed by enslaved people or free people of color in either the colonies or metropolitan France. This is no doubt in part because it is very difficult to document these activities, but it is perhaps also a sign that we predominantly associate slavery with agricultural work and other forms of hard physical labor, and fail to raise questions about slaves' contributions to the erection of buildings or the creation of luxury furniture. In cities such as Bordeaux and Nantes, historians and museum curators generally take it as a given that eighteenth-century furniture was often built from materials sourced in the colonies. Outside this region, however, questions about sources and offshore production are rarely raised. As I noted earlier, the elegant artifacts of Old Regime culture on display in our leading museums do not signal their colonial origins in the same way that they sometimes highlight Asian provenance or design. As a result we have to make the connection between furniture and wood for ourselves, applying an interdisciplinary historiography that interweaves the national history of material culture with the transcontinental history of colonial commerce.

Furniture and the Oriental Exotic

The eighteenth century is generally hailed as the golden age of French furniture. The panoply of forms, styles, and techniques that came into existence between the waning years of Louis XIV and the downfall of Napoleon's empire took root and has been reproduced and recycled ever since. But while these styles are closely associated with ideas about French taste and indeed French culture, they cannot be described without reference to the foreign influences with which they were deeply imbued. Arjun Appadurai has written of the tendency of consumer cultures to produce what he calls "aesthetics of diversion," that is, strategies for attenuating the commodity status of consumer objects by portraying them as the rare and authentic artifacts of a distant culture.[29] These aesthetics played an important role in the cultural system of eighteenth-century Europe, the birthplace of the world's first mass consumer culture. In this context of rapid economic and social change, manufacturers used references to

29. *Social Life of Things*, xv–xvi.

alien cultures to lend their products the allure of authentic value. The foreign cultures that were most widely borrowed from, referenced, and imitated in this process of diversion were without question those of the Orient.

Though references to the Orient in seventeenth- and eighteenth-century culture are often grouped together, in the case of material culture I think it is helpful to separate them into two different types. After discovering the so-phisticated material culture of China and Japan in the mid-1600s, Europeans spent the next century busily importing and imitating decorative objects such as porcelain ware and lacquer paneling and screens. In the European appetite for these goods we can read an implicit homage to China and Japan and their rich cultural traditions. The case of the Near and Middle East was strikingly different. Allusions to the material culture of regions such as Turkey and Persia were predominantly linguistic (they in fact perfectly illustrate the circular rela-tion of fashion and vocabulary that contemporary commentators viewed as a scourge of the age).[30] They also tapped into the long-standing association of the Muslim Orient with cultural traits such as sensuality and indolence. The objects most often dignified with Turkish or Arabic-sounding names were, for example, comfortable chairs and beds.

Below I consider the Oriental exoticism of French furniture from two differ-ent angles. First I consider what the orientalized beds and chairs that flooded the French market in the late seventeenth century tell us about the scope of eighteenth-century orientalism. Following that, I turn to Chinese and Japa-nese references and explore a number of instances in which materials of colo-nial origin were fashioned in a manifestly Oriental style.

Furniture and Oriental Discourse

In the mid-seventeenth century a new range of comfortable chairs entered the repertory of French furniture. *Lits de repos, canapés, sofas, ottomanes, turquoises, paphoses,* and *duchesses* reflected the period's predilection for informality, as well as its heightened concern with sociability (see, for example, figure 7). Many of these new models accommodated more than one person, and if we exclude benches and church pews, they were the first European chairs that seated sev-eral occupants side by side. The Oriental, feminine names that were often conferred on these chairs signaled a distant allusion to the Turkish *divan:* the row of cushions arranged against a wall that European travelers encountered in their voyages to the East. More immediately operative, however, was a chain of

---

30. Louis-Sébastien Mercier wrote of the lexicon of furniture, "I believe that the inventory of our furniture would very much surprise an ancient were he to return to this world. The language of the bailiffs and auctioneers who know the names of this immense mass of superfluities is an idiom that is very detailed, very rich, and utterly unknown to the poor." "Légères observations" (Frivolous Observations), *Tableau de Paris* 2 vols. (Paris: Mercure de France, 1994), 1: 852–60.

Figure 7. Ottomane ceintrée. Drawing by Jean-Charles Delafosse, circa 1770. Bibliothèque nationale de France.

associations linking widespread ideas about the Orient to ideas about femininity, sociability, and sexuality. In her entertaining and erudite book on the history of luxury in France, Joan DeJean comments on a late seventeenth-century fashion plate in which a stylish young woman shows off her impeccable but, for the period, informal attire, by lounging seductively on a sofa, the period's stylish but informal new chair.[31] As DeJean notes, the chair mirrors the clothes, and both apparel and furniture tap into the multiple cross-referencing of fashion, relaxed decorum, femininity, sexuality, and the Orient.

This system of cross-referencing is reflected in the scattered representations of furniture that appear in eighteenth-century French literature.[32] Though it is a critical commonplace that, unlike the realist novels of the nineteenth century, eighteenth-century French novels pay little attention to decor, a number of works from this period allude to furnishings, and in particular to the newly fashionable "Oriental" daybeds and chairs. For example, in La Morlière's *Angola* (1746), an erotic fairy tale with philosophical overtones, the Fairy Lumineuse bans *tabourets* (the stools that courtiers occupied at Versailles) from her court because they reinforce social distinctions. Instead she chooses for

31. Joan DeJean, *The Essence of Style*, 69, fig. 3.4.
32. On these interwoven associations, see also my discussion of Oriental chairs and their literary avatars in *Foreign Bodies*, 147–216.

her palace comfortable "Oriental" furniture that promotes conversation and a sense of equality, while at the same time creating an atmosphere tinged with sensuality. In some other novels of the period the presence of an Oriental chair signals the potential for erotic commerce in more explicit ways. In libertine novels such as Marivaux's *Paysan parvenu* (The Fortunate Peasant) (1735) and Laclos's *Liaisons dangereuses* (*Dangerous Liaisons*) (1787), references to a sofa, *ottomane,* or *chaise longue* serve as preludes to scenes of seduction.[33] In these narratives, the close resemblance between the reclining chair and the bed appear to serve as an emblematic reminder of the permeable boundary between social and sexual exchange that is the genre's central preoccupation.

In two midcentury Oriental tales with libertine overtones, *Le canapé couleur de feu* (The Flame-Colored Sofa), attributed to Fougeret de Monbrun (1741), and *Le sopha* (1742) by Crébillon fils, protagonists unexpectedly find themselves transformed into chairs. In Crébillon's novel the protagonist, having been turned into a sofa, discovers that he is in a position to learn the truth about women's conduct in matters of intimacy. The testimony he offers is, however, less a titillating description of clandestine encounters than a moralizing commentary on the degeneration of true passion into the social performance of sexual conquest. A related point of view, articulated in a very different register, can be read in Jean-Jacques Rousseau's *Lettre à d'Alembert sur les spectacles* (Letter to d'Alembert on the Theater) (1758). Rousseau wrote this long public letter as a response to d'Alembert, who in the *Encyclopedia* article "Geneva" (volume 7, 1757) had called for the establishment of a public theater in the Calvinist city-state. In his rejection of d'Alembert's arguments, Rousseau advocates that the serious business of philosophical reflection be divorced from frivolous modes of social interaction, which he associates with aristocratic circles and female influence. In a much-cited passage, Rousseau complains that "every woman in Paris gathers in her apartments a harem of men more womanish than she," inviting his readers to imagine these guests pacing up and down in frustration, "while the idol lays stretched out motionless on her chaise-longue, with only her tongue and her eyes active."[34] Mining the contemporary trope of the harem as a confining prison in which men were emasculated by their contact with women, Rousseau imagines the salon hostess as an Oriental despot, stretched out languidly on a sofa, exercising her undemocratic power over a coterie of literary eunuchs.

These literary references to Oriental chairs and beds convey the depth and complexity of eighteenth-century French orientalist discourse. As the different representations discussed above illustrate, words, images and styles that evoked the Orient triggered a complex chain of associations relating to gender and sexuality, fashion and style, and political dispositions ranging from despotism

---

33. Choderlos de Laclos, *Dangerous Liaisons,* trans. Douglas Parmée, 146, 278. Marivaux, *Le paysan parvenu,* 221.

34. Rousseau, *Letter to d'Alembert on the Theatre,* trans. Allan Bloom, 100–01.

to egalitarianism. In this broad, cross-platform system of signification, an Oriental reference in the domain of furniture could be translated into a fictional narrative, or into the argument of a philosophical treatise. There was, by contrast, no equivalent system of references to the colonial world, a milieu that still remained largely outside the frame of cultural discourse.

East Meets West

Many Oriental crazes hit France in the last decades of the seventeenth century. There was the fashion for delicate blue-and-white porcelain from China, and the vogue for hand-painted silk. There was also the infatuation with lacquerware: Chinese and Japanese screens, chests, and boxes coated in a lustrous resin dyed black or red, and decorated with intricate gold-leaf relief painting. Initially, European merchants imported lacquer objects and furnishings from the Far East. Chinese and Japanese furniture, however, consisted of a relatively limited range of pieces, and as a result importers soon began transferring lacquer panels from imported screens and two-door cabinets to domestically made chests and commodes.[35] Joan DeJean explains that one new piece of furniture—the *cabinet*—came into existence in this context. With its broad rectangular lines, the *cabinet* provided an ample surface on which these reassigned panels could be mounted (244). A number of prominent eighteenth-century *ébénistes*—for example, Bernard Van Risenburgh (known as BVRB) and, later in the century, Martin Carlin—made the tasteful incorporation of lacquer panels into elegant French furniture a signature feature of their style.

By the end of the seventeenth century European craftsmen had also begun trying to manufacture their own lacquer. DeJean notes that by the 1690s the term *lachinage* was used to designate both authentic Asian lacquerware and the cheaper domestic imitations that had started to come onto the market (243). But lacquer techniques proved hard to replicate, and for several decades European craftsmen succeeded only in producing very inferior imitations. This situation changed in 1714, when a craftsman called Gaston Martin obtained a royal patent for a new method of applying *vernis façon de la Chine* (Chinese-style varnish). *Vernis Martin* quickly became a brand name, and in 1748 the workshop in which Martin's four sons produced their trademark product was awarded the prestigious title of *manufacture royale*.[36]

Artisans used *vernis Martin* in two different ways. In some instances it was used as an inexpensive substitute for imported Asian lacquer. In others it was applied to mask the splintered borders of reassigned lacquer panels. Transferring panels was a delicate matter that required skilled craftsmanship. In addition to smoothing over splintered edges with *vernis Martin*, *ébénistes* had to consider

35. See Jarry, *Chinoiseries*, 133.
36. On the development and use of *vernis Martin*, see Wolvesperges, *Le meuble français en laque*, 23–129.

the wood that would be positioned around the lacquer. Sometimes their goal was to give the illusion of a unified lacquer surface. At other times they tried to harmonize the wooden border with the strong palette of the lacquer. To find appropriate matches they turned to the wide range of color choices offered by tropical hardwoods. Red lacquer from China was sometimes edged with bronze moldings and coordinated with marquetry executed in warm-toned purple wood and tulipwood (see, for example, figure 8). Black lacquer was often paired with ebony or ebony veneer, since the wood's deep color and natural sheen made it possible to conceal the border joining the lacquer to the wood (see figure 9).

Even when lacquer furniture was manufactured or refashioned in France it invariably gestured to the Oriental origins of the technique. French imitation lacquer was decorated with recognizably Chinese or Japanese figures such as parasols and pagodas. Oriental origins were also referenced in the trade vocabulary. In English the practice of coating wood with varnish to obtain a hard, lustrous surface was known as "japanning," or applying "China polish," while in French lacquer was widely known as "bois de la Chine," a conflation of veneer with wood in which the wood, which was often of colonial origin, effectively disappeared beneath the lustrous Oriental surface.[37]

Earlier we saw that one of the most significant growth areas in French furniture in the seventeenth and eighteenth centuries was the perfection of veneers, inlaying, and marquetry: the techniques by which a plain wood surface is overlaid with a layer of a more precious material, or a decorative or figurative pattern is composed from tiny pieces of wood. Marquetry was one of the most emblematic styles of eighteenth-century French furniture. The product of an encounter between costly materials and highly skilled craftsman, it projected luxury and refined taste.

Several of the period's leading *ébénistes,* such as Roger Van der Cruse Lacroix and Christophe Wolff, made *chinoiserie* motifs a central feature of their marquetry designs.[38] In their eyes there was no better way to valorize the elegance and beauty of their compositions than to harness the appeal of Oriental culture. Figure 10 shows a late eighteenth-century rolltop desk in which marquetry is used to compose a detailed miniature painting. This was the signature style of David Roentgen, a prominent *ébéniste* who produced many pieces like this one, in which tonal designs are used to portray Chinese hunting or fishing scenes.[39]

A different type of merger between colonial wood and Oriental imagery was the clean-lined mahogany side chair or armchair. In the 1750s the English cabinetmaker Thomas Chippendale earned an international reputation for his elegant mahogany chairs. One of his most popular models had a cutout back featuring geometrical designs of Chinese inspiration. In 1751 an engraver

---

37. Ibid., 71.
38. Jarry, 196–97.
39. See Salverte, *Les ébénistes du dix-huitième siècle,* 277.

Figure 8. Armoire with red Chinese lacquer, purple wood and tulipwood marquetry, and gilt bronze moldings. Bernard Van Risenburgh, circa 1750–55. Musée du Louvre, Paris. Réunion des musées nationaux/Art Resource, NY.

named Matthew Darly published his *New Book of Chinese, Gothic and Modern Chairs,* a technical treatise devoted to the craft of cutting out seat backs in the Gothic or Chinese style.[40] Darly subsequently entered into a partnership with Chippendale, and together they manufactured an entire collection

40. See Jarry, 148.

Figure 9. Three-panel commode with Japanese lacquer, ebony veneer, bronze ornaments, and white marble top. By Martin Carlin. Musée du Louvre, Paris. Réunion des musées nationaux/Art Resource, NY.

of mahogany chairs with sculptured chinoiserie backs. These chairs made their way to France as a result of the tastes of Anglophile clients, and by the 1780s French manufacturers were producing their own variations on the Chippendale model. The immense popularity of this style is illustrated by the fact that chinoiserie dining chairs can be seen today in museums throughout Europe and North America.

In the 1780s a new kind of Oriental design was introduced alongside the established chinoiserie style. In this new variation the backs of mahogany chairs were often decorated with Egyptian motifs such as sphinxes or lotus flowers. This style is generally known as *retour d'Égypte* in reference to the enthusiasm for all things Egyptian that overtook France in the aftermath of Napoleon's Egyptian expedition of 1797–99. In reality, the vogue for Egypt began about a decade before the expedition, Napoleon's campaign in Upper Egypt being as much as symptom as a cause of French Egyptptomania. Figure 11 shows a French faux-mahogany chair with a *retour d'Égypte* lotus-motif back in the collection of the Musée des arts décoratifs in Bordeaux.

We have seen that the national style of the golden age of French furniture was permeated with references to the exotic cultures of Turkey, China, and Japan. Oriental inspiration was registered in the imitation of techniques and

Figure 10. Cylinder-fall desk by David Roentgen, circa 1776. Oak, cedar, and mahogany, with marquetry of maple, tulipwood, ebony, mother-of-pearl, and brass. Metropolitan Museum of Art/Art Resource, NY.

styles, and conveyed through vocabulary and decorative motifs. There was, as I have argued, every incentive to make this connection, since the high market value of decorative objects was directly tied to their exotic cachet. We have also seen that the appeal of the Orient traversed media as diverse as furniture and literature, such that the allure of an elegant sofa could be translated with remarkable fluidity into a plot of a philosophical tale.

The high visibility and discursive presence of the Orient contrasted sharply with the cultural position of the colonial world. The geographic origins of the

Figure 11. Retour d'Égypte chair, circa 1800. One of a set of six by the Jacob brothers. Beech stained to resemble mahogany. Collection du Musée des arts décoratifs, Bordeaux.

hardwoods that played a key role in the evolution of French furniture making registered little, either in styles or designs, or in literary representations. A few references to the colonial sources of wood appear in empirical literatures, as, for example, in the treatises of craftsmen such as André Roubo, and in the narratives of travelers such as Jean Mocquet and Jean-Baptiste Labat, but it was not until the 1770s that colonial materials began to register significantly in other literary genres.[41]

41. The Dominican missionary Jean-Baptiste Labat describes the different varieties of wood that he encountered in Guadeloupe and Martinique, and mentions making furniture and other objects from them. *Nouveau voyage aux isles de l'Amérique,* 1:378–79, 2:109–10, 3:207–19.

In this decade tropical woods and the natural environment from which they were derived abruptly became an object of literary representation. A small group of naturalists with experience of colonial environments began to research the structure of the tropical ecosystem and to publicize the environmental hazards of colonial agriculture. Two noted botanists, Pierre Poivre and Philibert Commerson, studied the environmental impact of deforestation in the Indian Ocean colony of Île de France.[42] The literary voice of their school was Bernardin de Saint-Pierre, a writer who, having served as an engineer in the Île de France in the late 1760s, translated his environmentalist concerns into a series of widely read works. His best-selling novel, *Paul and Virginia* (1788), is a narrative which, read closely, has as much to do with trees as with human beings.

Other aspects of the colonial milieu also began to be exoticized in the 1770s–90s. Notably, this period produced the first significant literary representations of colonial slavery. This wave of tropical exoticism carried over to a limited extent into the field of the decorative arts. Perhaps the most obvious example was the turn-of-the-nineteenth-century fashion for *pendules au nègre:* gold clocks decorated with the sculptured figure of a black man or woman. In material culture as in literature, representations of this kind must be interpreted against the backdrop of the rise of abolitionism in the 1780s, and the abolition of slavery in 1794. That is to say, the representation of slavery and by extension the colonial world was made possible by the rise of a discourse that condemned colonial servitude. Given this correlation, it is not surprising that tropical exoticism waned quickly after the reinstantiation of slavery in 1802. It was not until the second half of the nineteenth century that images relating to colonial life began to reappear. A true colonial imagery—a stock of images employed to advertise tropical commodities and magnify imperial power—came into being only in the late nineteenth century, after the definitive abolition of slavery in 1848.[43] During the era of slavery it would have been much more difficult to exoticize life on a Caribbean plantation by the depiction of a leafy palm tree or a stately plantation house.

The plantation colonies of the Caribbean and Indian Ocean resembled in many respects the offshore production sites of our contemporary world. In both cases crops/commodities that were originally produced elsewhere were/ are pushed into mass production by the use of low-cost labor. And in both cases goods produced in these sites, or produced using raw materials grown there, were/are identified with the place of cultural origin or design rather

---

42. On the environmentalism of Bernardin de St. Pierre, Philibert Commerson, and Pierre Poivre, see Grove, *Green Imperialism.*

43. See Dana Hale, "French Images of Race on Product Trademarks during the Third Republic," *The Color of Liberty: Histories of Race in France,* ed. Sue Peabody and Tyler Stovall (Durham, N.C.: Duke University Press, 2003), 137.

than with the place of production. Nike sneakers are associated with the energy and ingenuity of the United States, not with the "developing world" locations in which they are chiefly manufactured. In the eighteenth century the incentive to underrepresent the conditions of "offshore production" was even greater than it is today, since these conditions of production included the regime of slavery, colonial violence, and ecological devastation.

3

The "Fabric of Two Worlds"

In a poem of 1666, a somewhat obscure writer named Pierre Le Jolle poked fun at the exotically named goods purveyed by the Company of the Indies:

> How many pieces of cotton
> Do these many bales contain?
> Those two hundred are Percales,
> And those over there are Mauris.
> These others are Salampouris
> ....
> Hamans, Adathaïs, Dungris....[1]

Rehearsing the names conferred on the various types of exotic fabric traded by the company, the poem registers a lexical explosion in the domain of textiles and gestures toward changes in commerce and consumption. Specifically, Le Jolle draws attention to a recent development in the French textile market: the import, from India, of a dazzling array of cotton fabrics. In the span of a few decades these Indian imports not only expanded the vocabulary of textiles but also exercised a transformative impact on the textile industry and French fashion.

To our post-Saidian eyes, the aspect of this historical episode that perhaps stands out most is the reverse influence of Indian enterprise on European material culture. This cultural transfer, however, had several other subtexts. The influx of Indian cotton had a galvanizing effect on France's domestic textile

---

The title of this chapter is borrowed from M. D. C. Crawford's *Heritage of Cotton: The Fabric of Two Worlds.*

1. Cited in d'Allemagne, *La toile imprimée et les indiennes de traite*, 38–39.

industry, stimulating rapid change in almost every branch of production and consumption. One facet of this expansion was increased production of raw materials such as cotton and indigo in France's Caribbean colonies, and the identification of these settlements as important markets for cotton textiles. In this chapter I explore the colonial dimensions of industrial modernization in the sphere of textiles. Focusing on the history of cotton I explore a cultural geography in which textiles and fashions remained closely associated with Eastern cultures, although both production and consumption were progressively being relocated to the West.

Mapping the Textile Revolution

Prior to the cotton revolution of the late seventeenth century, textiles were manufactured in small workshops on hand machinery operated by skilled workers and predominantly retailed on a regional level. By the mid-nineteenth century they were frequently mass-produced in factories on heavy machinery operated by unskilled workers, and national and international markets had emerged alongside the established regional circuits of production and distribution. A crucial catalyst for these changes, as Maxine Berg has shown in the case of England, was the introduction of printed Indian cotton into European markets in the mid-seventeenth century.[2] Raw and woven cotton had been imported into western Europe from the Levant since the Middle Ages, but these small-scale imports had never had a major impact on European textiles. Matters changed when the Dutch and British East India Companies, followed after 1664 by their French counterpart, took over Portuguese trading positions in India and began to import hand-painted and block-printed textiles. These brightly colored textiles were known in Portuguese as *palampores*, in England as chintz or calicos, and in France as *toiles peintes* (painted cloth) or *indiennes*. They were immensely popular, and almost immediately French and British manufacturers began to produce their own domestic "knockoffs" of these exotic Eastern goods.

The popularity of *indiennes* spearheaded a dramatic rise in the consumption of cotton textiles. Drawing on the evidence of probate inventories, the cultural historian Daniel Roche has charted a rise in the percentage of cotton clothing in French wardrobes from only 3–8 percent in 1700 to 25–40 percent, depending on social class, in 1789.[3] One reason for this dramatic increase was that the demand for cotton cut across the social spectrum. Clair Hughes explains that before cotton's mass penetration of the European textile market "formal clothing for both men and women with any claims to prosperity and fashion

---

2. Berg, *Luxury and Pleasure in Eighteenth-Century Britain.* The histories of French and British textiles in the seventeenth to nineteenth centuries run broadly parallel, though in the mid-eighteenth century England overtook France both in technical innovation and scale of production.

3. Roche, *La culture des apparences,* 127, 137.

was of silk, satin or velvet. Wool or fustian (a coarse linen and cotton mixture) was worn further down the social scale, or for informal, country wear." But as cotton fabric from India came to be widely available, people of all social classes made cotton clothing an important part of their wardrobes.[4] Cotton textiles met the basic needs of the lower classes, brought fashionable variety to the wardrobes of bourgeois consumers, and in their most luxurious forms, appealed to elite consumers who were attracted by exotic new fashions.

The vogue for *toiles peintes,* which had the multiple advantages of being relatively inexpensive, colorful, light, and easy to clean and maintain, helped stimulate a broad array of changes in production and manufacture.[5] Berg writes of Britain that the pressure to imitate imported prints "sparked the growth of the cotton industry and the rapidly mechanizing processes which accompanied it" (85). In turn, the expansion and mechanization of the cotton industry led to changes in patterns of consumption. As Beverly Lemire has shown, again with regard to Britain, the arrival of Indian printed cotton helped to launch a new, consumer-based chapter in the history of textiles and fashion.[6] Calicos and *toiles peintes* were the first commodities of the mass consumer culture that we associate with nineteenth- and twentieth-century textiles. Hughes indeed makes an apt comparison when she writes that "muslins were to the late eighteenth and early nineteenth centuries what synthetic fibers were to the mid twentieth century—they transformed life" (36).

As the poem cited above illustrates, the Indian influence on European textiles and clothing was registered in the adoption of a rich new vocabulary. Many of the terms used today to denote types of fabric or styles of clothing reference seventeenth- and eighteenth-century trading relationships between Europe, India, and the Levant. In the eighteenth century this vocabulary was even more extensive.[7] English words such as cotton, indigo, calico, damask, dungaree, chintz, muslin, shawl, gingham, seersucker, cashmere, and twill gestured to the Eastern origins of certain textiles, as did French terms such as *indiennes, bayadères* (a kind of woven silk with bands running parallel to the weave), *damasc, cashmere, percale, contouche* (a gown or *sacque* loosely based on a Turkish caftan called a *gontos*),[8] *foulard, persienne* (a printed silk fabric that was popular in the 1720s), *circassienne* (an orientalized version of the coat-dress or mantua that was the foundation of women's dress in the 1780s), *robe à la turque* (a variant of the *robe à la polonaise* that was a popular dress style in the 1770s–90s), *châle* (shawl; from the Persian *shal*), and *mousselines.* Another set of terms, including *siamoises* (striped silk and linen cloth), *pékins* (printed

4. Hughes, *Dressed in Fiction,* 36.
5. On the reorganization of the textile industry, see Reddy, *Rise of Market Culture.*
6. See Lemire, *Fashion's Favourite,* esp. 18–19, 198.
7. On this vocabulary, see Burnard, *Chintz and Cotton,* and Vrignaud, *Vêture et parure en France au dix-huitième siècle.*
8. See Ribeiro, *Dress in Eighteenth-Century Europe,* 35.

taffeta), *nankins* (in England, nankeens),[9] and *manches à pagode* (tight-fitting sleeves with a funnel opening),[10] testified to a parallel influence of Chinese silk on the French textile market, as well as to cross-fertilizations between Indian and Chinese exoticisms. Though Marcel Mauss claims in *The Gift* that a distinguishing feature of modern Western societies is that they strive to separate words and things, this grid of exotic terms suggests, to the contrary, the embedding of consumer goods in an intricate web of words and associations.[11]

Vocabulary was not the only medium through which the Asian origins of cotton textile manufacture were registered in European culture. Eastern provenance was also captured in Indian- or chinoiserie-inspired prints, motifs, and designs, in literary representations of fabric and clothing, and in the intense, long-running economic and political debates waged in both England and France over the changes occurring in the textile industry. Though these changes were in reality multifaceted, for almost a century a single issue—the impact of Indian imports on domestic industry—became the focal point of debates over textiles, labor, manufacturing standards, and economic growth.

But if cotton and the clothing manufactured from it were strongly associated with the Orient, other cultural and commercial vectors also contributed to the transformation of textile production and consumption. Starting in the late seventeenth century, European entrepreneurs began to manufacture their own *toiles peintes*. At first they printed on undyed woven cotton imported from India and the Near East. Beginning in around 1700, however, there was a gradual transition to domestically woven cloth. The cotton fiber required to supply French weavers was also at first supplied from the East (Turkey, Syria, Egypt, and India). Gradually, however, Europe's Caribbean and North American colonies, and after 1776 the southern United States, became significant exporters of raw cotton and several widely used dyestuffs. M. D. C. Crawford, from whose sweeping study of the history of cotton I borrow the title of this chapter, estimates that by 1770, 70 percent of the needs of the Lancashire mills were supplied by cotton grown in the British West Indies and Louisiana.[12] France, too, increasingly imported raw cotton from the Americas. By the 1780s cotton was the second-largest export, after sugar, of France's most productive colony, Saint-Domingue.[13] By 1787, according to Léo Elisabeth, 20 percent of Martinique's *habitations* were devoted to the cultivation of cotton.[14]

9. A term that in different periods denoted hand-painted Chinese silk, unbleached silk, and a fine yellowish cotton cloth.

10. See Émile Quicherat, *Histoire du costume en France*, 554.

11. Marcel Mauss, *The Gift*.

12. Crawford, 129. In the 1790s, following the introduction of Eli Whitney's cotton gin, the southern states overtook the Caribbean as Britain's major supplier of raw cotton.

13. Banks, 33. See also May, *Histoire économique de la Martinique*, 96–97.

14. Elisabeth, *La Société martiniquaise aux XVIIè et XVIIIè siècles*, 42.

Europe's American and Caribbean colonies were not only major producers of raw cotton, they were also important consumers of cotton textiles. Low-quality cotton cloth, known in French as *guinées* and in English as Osnaburg, was in great demand in the colonies as a material in which to outfit slaves. And more-refined cotton fabrics were popular among the white population and free people of color because they were better suited to the region's warm, humid climate than traditional woolens and silks. Cotton was also one of the most important exchange goods used in the purchase of slaves. From the beginnings of the *traite,* European merchants traded blue or striped cotton for African slaves. M. Chambon, the author of a work titled *Commerce de l'Amérique par Marseille* (1764) (Commerce with the Americas via Marseilles), notes that "of all the fabrics used in Guinea, none is more sought after than *toiles peintes.* A beautiful *indienne* will always fetch more than another more costly cloth, either because the variety of colors is more to the taste of Negroes, or because the lightness of the cloth is more suited to these hot climates."[15] Though this dyed or printed cotton was initially purchased in India, by the end of the seventeenth century a significant share of this lucrative market had been captured by manufacturers in French ports such as Nantes and Marseilles.

But if the geography of production and consumption shifted over the course of the eighteenth century, these changes registered very little in the modes of cultural representation associated with textiles. Cotton and silk fabrics continued to go by Oriental or pseudo-Oriental names and retained their exotic Eastern aura. The reasons for this cultural image were complex. One factor was that whereas the contributions of India, China, and the Levant to the history of material culture were widely known and relatively easy to capture in words and images, the Caribbean colonies had not yet become established as an exotic location. Another was that for a variety of reasons, not least their dependency on slave labor, these island outposts posed a particular representational challenge. In the absence of discourse and other forms of representation, the colonial contribution to the transformation of the European textile industry was masked by the continued association of cotton and silk, and the raw materials required to produce them, with the opulent East. As I observe in the previous chapter with regard to furniture, this pattern of representation in some respects prefigured the dynamics of today's globalized textile and clothing industries. Just as the unpaid labor of slaves was overshadowed by the emphasis placed on Oriental provenance, so today the labor of low-paid textile and garment workers in "offshore" sweatshops and maquiladoras is similarly effaced by the appendage of prestigious metropolitan labels.

---

15. Chambon, *Le Commerce de l'Amérique,* 2:389. Chambon was a former receiver-general of taxes, and his book is a richly detailed account of the history and contemporary state of French commerce, focusing on the port of Marseilles.

Below I offer a series of mappings of the cultural geography of the eighteenth century's emergent global market in textiles. The main story that I tell concerns the rise of cotton and its impact on modes of production and consumption. But there are several backstories—for example, with respect to the transcontinental trade in dyes. As in the two previous chapters, I highlight the contrast between the valorization of Eastern origins and the relative invisibility of the colonial mode of production.

Before proceeding, however, I need to qualify the distinction that I make in this book between the "Oriental" and the "colonial" in light of the specific geography of the history of textiles. France, like England, had a colonial as well as a commercial presence in India. From the mid-seventeenth century it operated five trading bases on the Indian subcontinent. These trading positions, known as *comptoirs,* were basically fortified French enclaves with a few civil institutions. Commodities, including textiles, were traded through them, and they were also the site of manufacturing activities: in several of the French settlements there were factories staffed by Indian weavers. As we have seen, France also had two colonies in the Indian Ocean: the Île Bourbon and the Île de France, both plantation colonies similar to those of the Antilles. For the purposes of what follows I primarily situate the French commercial and colonial presence in the Indian subcontinent in relation to the currents of orientalist discourse, while connecting its ventures in the Indian Ocean to the colonial enterprise in the Caribbean. There are, however, points of intersection and zones of hybridity that need to be acknowledged. Notably, while slavery was not the main system of labor in the *comptoirs,* it was not altogether absent from them either. There was significant transcontinental commerce between French India and the Indian Ocean colonies and, particularly in the formative years of the latter, slaves were imported from India as well as from Africa.[16] The records of the Black Police also show that Indians, listed as *nègres du Bengal* or *nègres de Pondichéry,* were among the slaves brought to metropolitan France in the latter part of the eighteenth century.[17]

The Oriental Paradox

In the seventeenth and eighteenth centuries, as we have begun to observe, textiles and clothing were widely associated with Oriental materials, styles, and manufacturing techniques. This is not to say, however, that the Orient was predominantly represented as a place of creativity and entrepreneurial

16. On Indian slaves in the Mascareignes, see Weber, *Compagnies et comptoirs,* 30–34.

17. Erick Noël explains that following the institution of the Black Police, Indians were classified as "people of color" and required to register with the authorities. In the 1777 census they are variously represented as *nègres indiens, du Bengal,* and *de Pondichéry,* a scheme of classification that suggests, on the one hand, that the experience of enslavement entailed assimilation with people of African descent, and on the other that Indian origins were perceived as a differentiating factor.

dynamism. To the contrary, the Orient was typically imagined as a static, unchanging environment, subject to despotic governance and unfavorable to business. In the eyes of many European observers the Orient appeared, in particular, as a world without fashion where clothing remained the same for generations on end. When the liberal philosopher Jean-Baptiste Say commented, at the beginning of the nineteenth century, that French villagers "are a bit Turkish when it comes to clothes," he was voicing a widespread view that in the monotonous East nothing, particularly not styles of clothing, ever changed.

Why was it that at a time when Asian imports were galvanizing European markets, the Orient was so often represented as a world mired in tradition? The foundations of this paradox, I suggest, lay in the oppositional processes of European identity formation. Although Europe's economic and cultural dominance was largely achieved as a result of commercial relationships with other parts of the world, in the sphere of cultural representation, Europe's dynamism was typically contrasted with the stagnation perceived to reign elsewhere, most notably in the societies of its principal "other," the Orient. To develop this point further I will consider some textual examples: passages in French literary works in which Oriental identity is approached through the lens of dress. To start, I return to Montesquieu's epistolary novel, *Persian Letters,* in which a group of Oriental travelers observe French mores and fashions, and find their own clothing and comportment scrutinized in turn.

After his arrival in Paris, Rica, the most outgoing of the novel's Persian travelers, is dismayed to find that when he trades his Oriental garments for European clothes he ceases to be an object of interest, and instead falls into a kind of existential void. "Divested of everything foreign in my garb, I found myself estimated at my proper rate. I had reason to complain of my tailor, who had made me lose so suddenly the attention and good opinion of the public; for I sank immediately into the merest nonentity" (60), he complains to a friend back home. Rica's account of his vestimentary demise obviously satirizes the superficial exoticism of a French public captivated by the spectacle of foreign visitors. But it also coheres to a widespread perception of Oriental dress as costume rather than clothing.

I would argue that if, when he takes off his Persian garments, Rica sinks into an existential void, it is because in European orientalism clothing was understood to be a kind of uniform: dictated by nation and social station, and constitutive of identity. This perspective is widely reflected in the period's travel narratives as well as in the collections of prints depicting typical Turkish, Greek, and Levantine costumes that frequently accompanied them. For example, in the most widely circulating of these collections, the Dutch artist Jean-Baptiste Vanmour's *Recueil de cent estampes représentant différentes nations du Levant* (Collection of a Hundred Prints Representing Different Nations of the Levant), the peoples of the Ottoman Empire are classified according to their function within the state, with each engraving representing the costume of a different social order.[18] In this representational tradition, Oriental dress was perceived not as a product of individual choice or as a passing fashion but as the outward signifier of region, religion, profession, and marital status. In an age when France and Britain had abandoned the sumptuary laws that prescribed different fabrics and colors for different social classes, the Orient was imagined, somewhat nostalgically, as a place where dress could still confidently be taken as a gauge of social identity. Going by the evidence of Louis-Sébastien Mercier's *Tableau de Paris* (1781–88), this perception still held currency at the end of the eighteenth century. Using the Orient as a foil against which to contrast the transience of French fashion, Mercier asks: "Why don't we laugh at oriental apparel, which never changes?" He answers his own question with the observation that, unlike contrived French fashions, Oriental dress conforms to the natural shape of the body.[19] In another passage Mercier claims that the skill of cutting and sewing cloth is quite unknown in the Orient, where people still dress "à la primitive" (in the primitive style), that is, by draping cloth around their bodies.[20] In both instances Oriental clothing, and implicitly the Orient itself, are represented as unchanging and determined by culture.

Oriental clothing was not only widely perceived as costume, it was also often worn as such, both in theatrical performances and at courtly entertainments. As the *fêtes galantes* of the painter Antoine Watteau document, masquerade became popular in France during the hedonistic years of the regency (1715–23). Revelers at masques and carnivals often wore exotic Oriental attire. The carnival season of 1700, for example, opened with festivities based on the theme of the "King of China," with the ruler of China serving as a surrogate for the magnificence of Louis XIV. In 1748 the pupils of the French Academy in Rome devised an elaborate Turkish procession in which students dressed up as members of the Ottoman court. One of the participants, Joseph-Marie Vien, made drawings for the procession that were later turned into an ethnographic guide to Oriental costume.[21] Louis XV's Mistress, Madame de Pompadour, a leader of fashion and important patron of the arts, also enjoyed posing in Oriental attire. She was portrayed as a Turkish sultana by Carle Van Loo in two over-door paintings of the early 1750s.

As these various examples suggest, one reason for the appeal of Oriental costume was that it allowed social and political gestures to be made obliquely, without direct reference to French politics and society. The vogue for costumes, including Oriental disguises, also correlated with the period's intense concern

18. Vanmour, *Recueil de cent estampes représentant différentes nations du Levant.*
19. "Habillements," *Tableau de Paris,* 1:125.
20. "Tailleurs," *Tableau de Paris,* 1:958–59.
21. See Ribeiro, *Dress in Eighteenth-Century Europe,* 249–50.

with social mobility. Donning a costume meant changing identities, at least for a while, invoking the possibility that the clothes might make the man.

The socially transformative potential of clothing is a central theme of one of the most famous representations of Oriental clothing in French literature: Molière's comedy, *Le bourgeois gentilhomme* (*The Bourgeois Gentleman*) (1670).[22] Aspiring to appear as a gentleman rather than as a merchant, the play's social climbing protagonist, M. Jourdain, undergoes what would today be called a makeover. He hires a team of professionals, including a dancing master, a music tutor, and a philosopher, and charges them with turning him into a paragon of gentility and elegance. To complete their work a tailor decks Jourdain out in a flowing floral robe, said to be worn by people of quality in the morning (13–15). Though the tailor is a scoundrel who is intent on fleecing his gullible client, he is not misrepresenting this sartorial trend. Morning gowns, or *Wentke*, first imported from India by the Dutch East India Company in the early seventeenth century, were fashionable items in England and France in the 1670s–80s. As Jourdain is far from being a man of style, he inevitably cuts a ridiculous figure in this exotic garment and succeeds only in provoking the laughter of his family and servants.

Oriental costume returns in the final act of the play, in which Cléonte, a worthy young man whom Jourdain rejects as a son-in-law because he is a bourgeois rather than a gentleman, schemes to win approval by disguising himself as the son of the "Grand Turc" (the Turkish sultan). Appearing before Jourdain in full Turkish mufti, Cléonte claims that having learned of his reputation as a prominent French gentleman, and having become enamored of his daughter, he has come to claim her hand (73–85). The plot unfolds in the mode of farce as Jourdain is put through his paces in an elaborate, and at times menacing, Oriental ceremony. In this closing *divertissement* the protagonist's utmost desire is fulfilled: he is raised to the ranks of the (Turkish) nobility as a "Mamamouchi."

In both episodes of the play, Oriental costume figures the potential for a change in social standing. In act 2, social promotion is connected to the dynamism of the fashion system. In act 4, by contrast, the Orient serves as a screen for a parody of bourgeois ennoblement, and provides a safe framework for the examination of controversial topics such as *arrivisme* and social mobility. These different takes on Oriental costume reflect the workings of a deeply rooted paradox. In act 2, the morning gown, an exotic import fresh off the boat, as it were, from India, captures the mobility of fashion associated with the Orient.

---

22. *Le bourgeois gentilhomme; Bourgeois Gentleman*, trans. Bernard Sahlins. References in the text are to this edition. A parallel work in English letters is Daniel Defoe's *Roxana; or, The Fortunate Mistress* (1724), in which a Turkish dress emblematizes the heroine's rise from modest bourgeois wife to opulent royal mistress. As Defoe was a staunch critic of luxury and of the Eastern trade, the dress also figures the contaminating effects of imported finery.

Bourgeois Gentleman can in fact be viewed as an early case of "product placement," an interpretation corroborated by the fact that it purportedly inspired Louis XIV to purchase morning gowns for himself and several members of his entourage.[23] In act 4, by contrast, costume becomes synonymous with Turkish custom and social rigidity. In this dispensation, Jourdain can rise socially only by moving laterally, from one culture to another.

The Age of *Indiennes*

In the introduction to *Orientalism* Edward Said notes that "the Orient is an integral part of European *material* civilization and culture." In the end, however, Said comments very little on commerce with (or commodification of) the Orient, focusing rather on the merger between textuality and political expansionism. The critical literature that has built on the foundations of *Orientalism* has for the most part followed suit. Over the last two decades a number of studies have been devoted to orientalism in literature, painting, and photography, but to date relatively little has been written about the sphere of material culture. This lacuna is problematic, because in order to contextualize a work such as *Bourgeois Gentleman* it is not enough to inventory literary and political factors such as the growing importance of travel writing, the pervasive discourse of Oriental despotism, or the gradual decline of the Ottoman Empire. It is also necessary to factor in aspects of material history such as the social and economic upheavals to which the import of Indian cotton textiles gave rise. Commerce with India, and in particular the import of *indiennes*, had a profound impact on early modern European societies. Manufacturers and consumers alike were enticed by the artistry and commercial dynamism of the East, but these popular imports also gave rise to processes of retrenchment and cultural resistance: forces that are reflected in many of the textual representations described by Said.

Indian cotton textiles such as the morning gowns featured in *Bourgeois Gentleman* were first imported in bulk into northern Europe in around the 1650s. These exotic fabrics initially featured traditional Indian motifs such as large, lush flowers. Their designs were, however, rapidly adjusted to reflect European tastes. Textile historian Beverly Lemire explains that by the end of the seventeenth century the British East India Company required that "goods made in India conform to the fashions in Europe, while still retaining that aura of oriental exoticism" (13).

Fairly quickly, French and English manufacturers also began to produce their own imitation *indiennes*. Raynal's *History of the Two Indies* (book 3) notes that French cotton printers, or *indienneurs*, initially imitated the patterns favored

---

23. In light of the satirical context in which morning gowns are presented, this decision may seem surprising. Presumably the king felt confident that, unlike M. Jourdain, he could successfully carry off this high-fashion look.

by craftsmen on the Coromandel Coast, but later started to turn out their own less ornate designs (1:337). Less costly than imported fabrics, these domestic imitations brought *indiennes* within the reach of even the most humble consumers. The wide availability of "knockoffs" indeed gave rise to some anxieties about quality and the preservation of social distinctions. Joan DeJean cites a 1673 issue of the *Mercure galant,* in which discerning consumers are warned to be on the lookout for cheap, printed imitations of the hand-painted *manteaux chinois* (Chinese coatdresses, or mantuas) that were the height of fashion that year.[24]

As the case of Chinese mantuas attests, *indiennes* had an impact on the shape and cut of French clothing. With fabric becoming more significant than form, drapey styles such as the mantua replaced the tightly fitted jacket-and-skirt ensembles that had previously dominated women's fashion. As Clare Haru Crowston observes, "In the eighteenth century fashion lay not in cut or design, but primarily in textile patterns and decorations."[25]

The *indiennes* revolution was, however, slowed down in both England and France at the end of the seventeenth century. Anxious about competition from abroad, and fearing the collapse of France's highly regulated system of standards and protocols, manufacturers and workers in the traditional wool, linen, and silk industries began to demand controls, both on the import of *indiennes* and on the production of domestic imitations. In both nations these protests were successful, and far-reaching prohibitions were established. In France it was illegal to either import or manufacture printed or painted cotton from 1686 to 1759. In England imports of "chintz" were banned in 1701, and, under the provisions of the Calico Act of 1720, domestic printing on cotton was also banned for three decades.

Commercial protectionism in France must be understood in light of the policies on manufacture established in the 1660s–70s during the ascendancy of Jean-Baptiste Colbert. Louis XIV's powerful first minister was the scion of a prominent family of Rheims drapers, and as such he took an active interest in France's textile industries. Determined to bring about improvements in the quality of French manufacture, Colbert reorganized and in some respects strengthened the medieval guild system. Producers of high-quality goods were rewarded with recognition as "manufactures royales" (royal manufacturers), an honor accompanied by lucrative contracts to supply fabrics to the court.[26] Colbert also reorganized the French dye industry, which had grown and diversified as a result of the introduction of colorants from Asia and the Americas.[27]

---

24. DeJean, *Essence of Style,* 64–65.
25. Crowston, *Fabricating Women,* 134.
26. DeJean, 2.
27. Colbert organized the French dye industry into several hierarchical categories. From 1671 makers of "grand et bon teint" were permitted to dye wool and broadcloth, and enjoyed a monopoly over prestigious colors such as scarlet. The hues that they produced were standardized, and

It was because of the legacy of *colbertisme* that in the debate over *indiennes,* quality as well as the preservation of jobs emerged as a key issue. If, in 1686, domestic imitations were banned along with foreign imports, it was because advocates of the traditional industries were able to claim that the quality of the French prints was poor. *Indiennage* did not meet the high standards of other domestic textile manufacture, they argued, and as such it threatened to undermine the spirit of Colbert's reforms. Advocates of a ban could also claim that allowing domestic production effectively meant opening the door to contraband, since customers would inevitably prefer authentic Indian goods to substandard French imitations.[28]

This argument was effectively invalidated in the 1740s, when the French print and dye industry reaped the benefits of two acts of international industrial espionage. Two French travelers, a naval officer and a Jesuit priest, secretly observed Indian colorfast dye techniques and published detailed accounts of the procedure.[29] After the exposure of these trade secrets, opponents of the ban could legitimately claim that French manufacturers had become able to produce printed fabrics of the same high quality as their Indian counterparts.

Though the 1686 ban was draconian, it did not bring domestic cotton printing to a complete standstill. For one thing, the law banning *toiles peintes* contained a number of loopholes, which meant that certain categories of imports and certain forms of domestic production remained legal. A significant exception, for example, involved the city of Marseilles, which had been established as a free port in 1669. As a result of its special status, Marseilles enjoyed the right to conduct free direct commerce with the Levant. Marseilles entrepreneurs were also allowed to print on cotton, a privilege that was conferred in order to promote exports to the Levant, but which also reflected concern with meeting the demands of the slave trade. The fundamental problem with loopholes such

---

they were expected to generate them with little variation. "Petit teint" dyers, on the other hand, were licensed to dye other fabrics, and also to redye clothing. The colors that they produced were more variable, and they were not required to meet the same uniform standards as "grand et bon teint" craftsmen.

28. The technological superiority of Indian craftsmen stemmed from their mastery of colorfast dye techniques. In the process of resist dyeing, hot wax was applied to undyed cloth, which was then submerged in a bath of color. The waxed areas did not absorb the dye, and as a result a contrast pattern was produced. Both wax and dye could be applied with wood blocks to create a simple pattern, or painted on by hand to achieve a more complex design. The French term *toiles peintes* refers to the technique of hand painting, though it was also used more loosely to refer to both block-printed and painted fabrics. A second dimension of Indian print and dye techniques was the use of mordants: solutions containing alum or iron acetate that fixed the dye to prevent it from running or fading. As European dyed and printed fabric was prone to discoloration, these Indian techniques represented a real advance.

29. In 1734 M. de Beaulieu, a naval officer stationed at the French trading post in Pondichéry, dispatched an account of resist and mordant dye techniques and a set of fabric samples to a chemist in France (the samples are now in the Musée de l'histoire naturelle). In 1742 Father Coeurdoux, a Jesuit missionary, published a second detailed account of Indian techniques in the *Lettres édifiantes et curieuses.*

as this was that it was all but impossible to differentiate between legitimate Levantine imports and illicit Indian goods, or between cotton printed legally in Marseilles and cloth printed illegally elsewhere in France.

A second significant loophole involved what could be called the reorientalization of a domestic knockoff. In the 1690s the city of Rouen began producing a blended cotton fabric that would become one of the most successful and adaptable textiles of the following century. A textile manufacturer named Delarue, finding himself overstocked with cotton, decided to weave his surplus inventory with silk. The result was a subtly striped, cream-colored material that Delarue sold to make underskirts. Subsequently silk was replaced by a less-expensive linen warp, and the fabric became a staple of France's petticoat industry. Both striped cotton petticoats and the fabric from which they were made became known as *siamoises,* since the material reminded people of the striped garments worn by the Siamese ambassadors who had toured France to much fanfare in 1686. Whatever their exotic associations, *siamoises* were big business. According to Édgard Depitre, Rouen alone counted fifteen thousand *siamoises* workers by 1727.[30] This profitable industry quickly spread to other cities, where striped underskirts were manufactured under local names such as "rouenneries de Marseille."[31]

The prohibition on *toiles peintes* was favored by manufacturers and workers in the wool and silk industries, as well as by those who clung to the tenets of *colbertisme,* but opposed by a number of other groups. These groups included representatives of the port cities, including merchants involved in colonial commerce, and members of the new school of liberal economics that was taking form in the 1750–60s. Over time this second coalition gained ground. Between 1749 and 1759 printing on wool, blended fabrics, and silk was reauthorized, and in 1749 printing on cotton imported by the Company of the Indies or woven in France was also allowed. At the close of the 1750s, the last remaining provisions of the ban became the subject of a full-blown public controversy, with prominent authors weighing in on either side. Perhaps the most noteworthy contribution to this debate was a 1758 opuscule titled *Réflexions sur les avantages de la libre fabrication et de l'usage des toiles peintes en France* (Reflections on the Advantages of the Free Manufacture and Use of Calicos in France) by Abbé Morellet, a liberal economic thinker who went on to write a memoir criticizing the monopoly exercised by the Company of the Indies.[32] For Morellet, the debate over *toiles peintes* provided a public platform from which to offer opinions about a broader set of social and economic problems. In addition to advocating free trade and the deregulation of manufacture, the philosopher decried the self-interested position of the guilds and upheld

---

30. Depitre, *La toile peinte en France,* x.
31. Biehn, *En jupon piqué et robe d'indienne,* 28.
32. *Réflexions sur les avantages de la libre fabrication et de l'usage des toiles peintes en France.*

freedom of consumption as an inalienable right. Morellet's arguments against the ban were also, at least to a certain extent, inspired by egalitarian principles and the period's trenchant critique of harsh forms of punishment. He observes that if the ban was to remain in place, then the rich and powerful ought to be policed and punished to the same degree as the poor and vulnerable (39). He opines that "citizens will never get used to seeing an unfortunate man sent to the galleys, or a family ruined over a piece of calico" (41). In the end, Morellet goes so far as to observe that if the quality of French printed cotton was low, this was of no great consequence, because the textile industry was in any event bound to furnish clothing to the poor.

In 1759 the prohibition on *toiles peintes* was lifted in a climate of growing support for free trade and against the backdrop of war with England and looming economic crisis. In the aftermath of this repeal, cotton manufacture and *indiennage* rapidly gained momentum, with new workshops opening in key textile centers such as Rouen, Nantes, Lyons, Marseilles, Paris, and Mulhouse. William Reddy describes the burgeoning French cotton industry as "the most progressive and most rapidly expanding sector of the whole French textile industry in the eighteenth century, having grown from nothing in 1700 to providing work for perhaps three hundred thousand cottagers by 1780."[33] In Nantes alone there were nine cotton manufactures employing twelve hundred people and producing one hundred twelve thousand bolts of cloth a year by 1783.[34]

This rapid expansion both stimulated and was made possible by the introduction of new technologies that streamlined and refined production. One of many areas of technological innovation was the introduction, in the early 1750s, of copperplate printing. First used in the field of paper printing, copper plates allowed printers to execute intricate designs and therefore expand the range of fabrics that they were able to produce.[35] For the first time fabrics adorned with figurative motifs—scenes representing people, animals, and buildings rather than simple flowers—became widely available.

Among the earliest and most popular of these figurative designs were chinoiserie scenes. Chinese and Japanese-style images of birds, pagodas, and hunting parties had long been popular subjects of engravings and had also been featured on wallpaper. In the 1760s they began to appear on bedcovers, wall hangings, curtains, and clothing. The most illustrious French manufacturer of *toiles peintes* in the latter part of the eighteenth century was Jean-Christophe Oberkampf, a German Protestant who in 1760 established a print works at

33. Reddy, *Rise of Market Culture*, 24.
34. Depitre, *La toile peinte en France*, 15.
35. From around 1785 copperplate printing gave way to cylinder printing, which accelerated the pace of production, though rollers were less flexible than copper plates and more geared to production for the mass market.

Jouy-en-Josas, near Versailles. *Toiles de Jouy,* which are still reproduced today by upscale home-furnishing retailers, became a brand name tied to a specific image: a red or deep blue print on crisp, high-quality white cotton. Among Jouy's signature prints were chinoiserie designs featuring emblematic Oriental motifs such as parasols, pagodas, luxuriant foliage, exotic birds, hunting or fishing parties, and tea ceremonies. The very first fabric manufactured at Jouy, "The Chinese Man with a Wheelbarrow," was in fact a red chinoiserie print on a white background (figure 12).

Oberkampf recruited a number of prominent artists to create chinoiserie designs for his workshop. Among these were Jean-Antoine Fraisse, author of a *Livre de dessins chinois* (Book of Chinese Drawings);[36] the celebrated painter François Boucher, whose *Scènes chinoises* (Chinese scenes) were reproduced in various branches of the decorative arts; and Jean Pillement, whose collections of chinoiserie designs were consulted by many different *indienneurs.*[37] Since global commerce involves circles as well as circuits of exchange, it is perhaps not surprising that by the middle of the eighteenth century Indian manufacturers were also copying these designs. Craftsmen on India's Coromandel Coast imitated the recycled Oriental imagery of their French counterparts, wooing European customers with a new line of custom-made polychrome textiles.[38]

The Oriental imagery of the prints popularized in the second half of the eighteenth century played on the Oriental origins of printed cotton cloth. Consumers were in effect reminded of the Eastern roots of *toiles peintes* by the overlay of exotic Chinese or Japanese imagery. Since Oriental provenance had from the outset been a factor in the success of these versatile textiles, it stood to reason that manufacturers, whether Indian or European, would continue to mine this profitable vein.

Indiennage and the West Indies

But if *indiennage* was connected to the East on a number of different levels, it was also tied into the circuits of colonial commerce and directly associated with both slavery and the slave trade. From the very beginnings of the Atlantic slave trade, woven cotton was one of the most common basic units of exchange. The value of slaves and the goods exchanged to purchase them was often measured in terms of *pieces* of cloth. Slaves were frequently designated by the term *pièces d'Inde,* a euphemism that registered the perceived equivalence between human beings and other transnational commodities. Long before *indiennes*

36. Fraisse, *Livre de dessins chinois.*

37. Jean Pillement's collections of chinoiserie designs included *Oeuvres de fleurs, ornements, cartouches, figures et sujets chinois* (Paris: Leviers, 1776); *Recueil de différents panneaux chinois;* and *Cahier de parasols chinois.* On chinoiserie designs, see Jarry, *Chinoiseries,* 13–14.

38. See Berg, *Luxury and Pleasure in Eighteenth-Century Britain,* 54.

Figure 12. The Chinese Man with a Wheelbarrow, 1760. Woodblock print on cotton. Musée de la Toile de Jouy. Photograph Marc Walter.

became popular in Europe, Indian dyed and printed cotton was traded for slaves on the coast of west Africa. Raynal's *History of the Two Indies* notes that among the diverse cotton textiles manufactured on the Coromandel Coast of India, "there are a large number that are dyed blue or with red and blue stripes that are good for the slave trade" (3:328). The blue cloth preferred by African slave traders, along with other basic cotton textiles used to clothe slaves, came to be known as *guinées* as a result of their association with the "Guinea trade."

The memoirs of Jean-François Landolphe, a slave trader who kept a detailed journal of his voyages of the 1760s–80s, offer a window onto this exchange of textiles for slaves. In an account of a voyage to Benin in 1769, Landolphe records purchases of a locally produced fine straw-colored cloth, as well as sales of a variety of French textiles.[39] The fabrics enumerated in his accounts include one Cholet kerchief, one Nîmes silk kerchief, a half piece of printed calico, one piece of Breton cotton, one piece of Rouen cotton, one piece of white baft, one piece of dress Cholet, one piece of Nîmes silk-satin, and a piece of Indian chintz. The list communicates the complex regional specialization of Old Regime French textile manufacture, but also testifies to the impact of new developments, notably the rising importance of domestically woven cotton and various cotton blends.[40]

The clothing worn by slaves in France's Caribbean colonies was, at least in principle, regulated by the *Black Code,* article 25 of which stipulated that masters should each year provide either two suits made of "toile" (cotton or linen cloth) or an equivalent measure of cloth from which the slaves could make their own clothing. In his *History of Jamaica* (1774), the English planter Edward Long notes that "checked linen, striped hollands [a coarse-woven cotton fabric], fustain blanketing, long ells and baize, Kendal cotton, Ozna-burgs [another coarse cotton], canvas, coarse hats, woolen caps, cotton and silk handkerchiefs" were all imported in large quantities as clothing for slaves.[41] He also mentions that slaves sometimes dyed their own clothes with indigo and other colorants. Perhaps unsurprisingly, Long gives no indications as to agency. Did slaves choose to dye their clothes, or was this work that they were required to do? In another passage Long wishes that Jamaica's white popula-tion would adopt the light cotton clothes favored by their neighbors in the Spanish colonies, which he describes as better suited to the tropical climate than heavy English woolens.

Many of the loopholes to the 1686 ban on printed cotton concerned either the slave trade or the business of supplying cotton to the colonies. One of

39. Landolphe, *Mémoires du Capitaine Landolphe.*
40. On the regional specialization of Old Regime textile manufacture, see Reddy, "Structure of a Cultural Crisis," 267.
41. Long, *History of Jamaica,* 2:493.

the reasons given for the exemption of Marseilles, for example, was the city's central role in supplying the triangle trade. In 1722, when Rouen's nascent cotton-weaving industry came under attack by local officials concerned that the region's agricultural workforce was being siphoned off to work in *toileries* (cotton/linen workshops), the argument that won the day was that cotton woven in Rouen was sorely needed in the colonies.[42] The ban on printed cotton had been extended to the colonies in 1733, but the strong demand for light, washable clothing in these tropical environments meant that the interdiction was never enforceable (even advocates of prohibition agreed that wool was too heavy and that silk didn't wear well in a tropical climate). As a result, supplying the colonial market remained a strong incentive for domestic *indiennage*.[43]

France's domestic cotton industry grew most rapidly in west coast ports such as Rouen and Nantes that had strong connections to the Antilles. The first major French cotton manufacture was established in Nantes. The second, the prestigious *manufacture royale* of Darnétal, was established in 1746 in the vicinity of Rouen.[44] The reasons for this west coast dominance are fairly evident. Cities such as Nantes and Rouen were links in a commercial chain that connected Paris, the Seine, and the towns of the Loire valley to the circuits of Atlantic trade.[45] Rouen, a traditional textile center, had established a lucrative niche as a supplier of linen and fustian "slave shirts" to the Spanish colonies as early as the sixteenth century. Indeed, in his work on Marseilles's commerce with the Americas, M. Chambon represents the manufacture of *anabases*—a striped white and blue cloth used in the slave trade—as a specialty of Rouen (2:381). Later on (seventeenth–eighteenth century) Rouen led the way in the production of textiles for the French colonial market.

In *Reflections on the Advantages of the Free Manufacture and Use of Calicos*, Abbé Morellet devotes an entire chapter to the importance of supplying the colonial market with light and inexpensive cotton clothing. He writes that "besides our exports for the slave trade, we have a considerable market in our French islands of America; the people and the blacks there are dressed in cotton cloth that we import from India" (43). Later he observes that weaving this cloth domestically would be more cost effective. Morellet also underscores the growing importance of the colonies as producers of cotton. In the same work he notes that "we have raw materials as cheaply as any nation in Europe: the cotton we get from the Levant in return for our woolens; cotton from our colonies; and cotton from India" (68), and after a quick cost analysis he concludes that "if we encourage the cultivation of cotton in our colonies and especially in Louisiana," then French manufacturers could undercut India (72).

---

42. Chassagne, *Le coton et ses patrons,* 26–30.
43. Depitre, *La toile peinte en France,* 97.
44. Chassagne, *Le coton et ses patrons,* 38.
45. Both also had large Protestant communities of skilled artisans and good water supplies.

Morellet's views echo those of Diderot, whose *Encyclopedia* article "Cotton" (volume 4, 1754) cites experiments conducted by a M. Jore of Rouen as evidence that France could produce muslins as fine as those made in India. After giving an account of the various American varieties and methods of cultivation based on the writings of the missionaries Jean-Baptiste Du Tertre and Jean-Baptiste Labat, Diderot claims, enthusiastically, that Antillean cotton is the finest in the world.[46] What is striking about this discussion, however, is that while Diderot describes the cultivation of cotton in painstaking detail, he makes no reference to the generalized use of slave labor in the colonial system of production. Slavery does not enter into Morellet's discussion of cotton manufacture either. Although in his discussion of the ramifications of the ban on *toiles peintes* Morellet hammers home the social dimensions of the issue, condemning harsh punishments and advocating the manufacture of clothing for the poor, he says nothing about the moral questions raised by the cultivation of cotton on colonial plantations.

In summary, we have seen that cotton was popularized in western Europe in the wake of the introduction of Indian printed fabrics. These Eastern origins were reflected in the vocabulary of textiles, in public debates that pitted French manufacturers against perceived Indian competitors, in the ambivalent testimony of fictional narratives, and in decorative traditions such as *chinoiserie*. But although cotton arrived in Europe from the East, over the course of the eighteenth century the geography of both production and consumption shifted. Cotton was increasingly spun and woven in France, often for export to the Americas or Africa, while the raw cotton required to supply European manufacturers was increasingly imported from colonial sources, particularly Louisiana and the Antilles. These developments did not, however, give rise to a change of terminology or to the popularization of a "tropical" imagery to parallel the Oriental "exotic." Though by the mid-eighteenth century cotton had become what M. D. C. Crawford has called "the fabric of two worlds," it remained associated with only one.

Global Color

Prior to the expansion of maritime commerce in the early sixteenth century, the dyes used by French textile manufacturers were made almost exclusively from local botanicals such as *garance* (madder) and *guède* (woad). Though indigo was introduced to Europe by Marco Polo, it was imported in significant quantities only after the opening of the sea route to India in 1497. Saffron, another Eastern dyestuff, also began to penetrate the European market at this

46. Labat, *Nouveau voyage aux îles de l'Amérique;* Du Tertre, *Histoire générale des Antilles habitées par les Français* (General History of the Antilles Inhabited by the French). References in the text are to this edition.

time. Following the discovery of the Americas, a second wave of new dyes entered the global market. By the mid-seventeenth century colorants such as *rouge de Brésil* (a dye derived from the bark of brazilwood), roucou, and cochineal had come to be widely used in textiles and painting.[47] Indigo was also native to the Americas, though settlers preferred to cultivate more familiar varieties imported from Asia. This transplantation was highly successful, and indigo quickly became the Americas' most important dye export.

In this section I consider these various colorants both as trade goods that traveled along global circuits of exchange and as objects of cultural representation that participated in narrative and discursive economies. I look first at two dyestuffs specific to the Americas, then turn to indigo, by far the most important coloring agent produced in the French colonies.

The rust-colored dye known as roucou is derived from the seeds of the urucú tree. When ground into a paste and mixed with oil, these seeds yield a rich, reddish pigment. The indigenous people of the Caribbean basin applied roucou paste to their bodies for decorative and symbolic purposes, though also because it had the properties of a sunscreen and insect repellent. Many European observers of the early colonial Caribbean allude to the indigenous population's use of roucou. Almost uniformly they characterize it as a body paint, highlighting decorative purposes over practical applications.

In Voltaire's *Essay on Universal History,* the use of roucou and other pigments as body paints serves as the point of departure for a philosophical meditation. Undertaking to refute a claim made by the Jesuit missionary Joseph-François Lafitau in his influential *Customs of the American Savages,* Voltaire offers a contrasting perspective on the relationship between nature and culture. In response to Lafitau's claim that the blackness of Africans and the bronze skin tone of Amerindians was the residue of a centuries-old practice of body painting, Voltaire asserted that skin color is determined biologically, and not by cultural practices. "Let him suppose that Caribs are only born red and negresses black because their first fathers painted themselves black or red," he writes dismissively (1:29).[48] If Voltaire took the trouble to counter Lafitau's claim, it is of course not simply because he wanted to refute what he saw as an absurd metalepsis. Rather, he was staking out a position that supported his own polygenist view of human origins, a theory strongly opposed by the Catholic Church, which held that all human beings belong to a single family descended from Adam.

Voltaire's observations about dyestuffs and diversity later attracted the attention of Chambon, the author of *Commerce with the Americas.* A devout Catholic as well as a strong advocate of trade, Chambon seems to have been

---

47. In *Dictionnaire universel de commerce,* Jacques Savary des Brûlons explains that roucou and *rouge de Brésil* were often mixed with European dyes to obtain precise shades, 1:374; 2:1407.

48. See also *Essai sur les mœurs,* 2:330–44 for Voltaire's polygenist theory of human diversity, and on cochineal as a colonial export.

happy to seize an opportunity to take a few digs at the philosophical constituency, represented by Voltaire. In his discussion of roucou, Chambon notes that "savages and Caribs" love the substance with a passion, and on the basis of this observation mocks Voltaire for viewing "red men" as members of a different human group: "The Caribs are red, the Orenokos black, and we would be too if we continually smeared ourselves with rocou, or black substances. Our garbellers [i.e., dye mixers], others will say grabellers, of vermillion, cochineal, and indigo are red and blue, and our smithies are black" (1:376–77). Whereas for Voltaire skin color is a fact of nature, for Chambon it also has cultural dimensions. Chambon indeed seems to suggest that whatever their biological differences, human beings are alike to the extent that they are all cultural agents.[49]

What is striking about Chambon's refutation of Voltaire is, however, not only the mix of humanism and Catholic orthodoxy that he brings to bear on the question, but also the fact that he takes what might be called a commodity-centered approach to the question of human diversity. That is to say, Chambon's argument that the differences between people are less significant than one might imagine is framed by his focus on the exchange of commercial goods and techniques. Trade, Chambon seems tacitly to suggest, not only demystifies difference but also gradually attenuates it. Chambon's point is brought home when we take into account that the use of roucou was not limited to Amerindian culture. By the mid-eighteenth century roucou was also a significant colonial export crop, particularly in French Guiana, where an extended rainy season and perennial shortage of slave labor prevented the development of a sugar monoculture. (In his account of Guiana in the 1720s Pierre Barrère identifies roucou as the colony's main export crop and observes that "it is very useful in dyeworks since it is used to make yellow, red, and other colors."[50])

Cochineal, a brilliant scarlet pigment, was discovered by the Spanish at the time of the conquest of the Americas in the late sixteenth century. Having learned how to produce cochineal from Inca and Aztec craftsmen, Spanish missionaries protected this knowledge as a valuable trade secret. Though a related dye called *lac* had been used for centuries in Asia, the method of making cochineal long remained a mystery, and Spain enjoyed a valuable monopoly over the global supply (cochineal was known in English as "Spanish red"). Until the mid-eighteenth century French authors debated whether the dye was derived from the cochineal fly or from the nopal cactus, of which the fly is a parasite.

With Spain controlling the market, cochineal long remained a rare and expensive product. Provincial weavers generally had to send fabric to Paris to be dyed with cochineal at the prestigious *manufacture royale* des Gobelins. The

---

49. In Book 15 of the 1780 edition of Raynal's *History of the Two Indies,* it is held that the skin color of native North Americans resulted both from exposure to the sun and from the use of natural dyes that helped repel insects (4:11–12). The author opines that this color is unattractive, but only to European eyes.

50. Barrère, *Nouvelle relation de la France,* 96.

Spanish monopoly was finally broken in 1776 when a French naturalist named Thiéry de Menonville traveled to Mexico, secretly obtained samples of both flies and nopal plants, and carried them to Saint-Domingue. Though his samples did not thrive in this new environment, an indigenous strain of the cochineal fly was identified in the colony, and by the late 1780s Saint-Domingue boasted several functioning *nopaleries*.[51] In the wake of this breakthrough a number of French authors wrote about cochineal production in Saint-Domingue from a nationalistic perspective, portraying it as a sign of France's rising commercial strength. This note is sounded, for example, in Raynal's *History of the Two Indies*, where cochineal is celebrated as an example of the economic and social benefits to be reaped from international commerce (3:475).

Indigo, which is derived from the foliage of a leguminous tropical plant, has been used as a dye in Asia, Africa, and the Mediterranean since ancient times. After the collapse of the Roman Empire, indigo disappeared from Europe and was reintroduced only in the sixteenth century after the opening of the sea route to Asia. It was an Asian variety of the indigo plant, known as *Indigofera tinctoria*, that European settlers planted in the Caribbean and continental Americas.

Indigo has a number of characteristics that made it a prized colonial cash crop. In tropical climates it grows easily and matures rapidly (two and a half months from seed to harvest), and the dye that it yields has excellent properties of absorption and colorfastness, generating a deep, purplish hue. In the seventeenth and eighteenth centuries its chief rival in France was woad, another plant-based dye. Woad, however, produces a lighter color than indigo and is less resistant to fading.

In ways that parallel the story of cotton, the introduction of indigo into the European market initially generated considerable resistance. Indigo imports were subject to extensive controls in France until 1664.[52] As indigo became a key export of the French colonies in the Antilles, however, attitudes began to shift.[53] By the 1750s France had come to dominate the global indigo market, generating six hundred thousand *livres* a year to meet not only 80 percent of its own demand but also the needs of its European neighbors, and even those of the Levant, which had formerly been the world's leading exporter of the dye. In the span of a century, colonial agriculture effected a reversal that turned the merchants of Marseilles into the principal suppliers of Levantine dyers, rather than their leading customers.[54]

---

51. Vrignaud, *Vêture et parure*, 65.

52. Chambon, *Le Commerce de l'Amérique*, 373–74.

53. On the production of indigo in the French colonies, see Debien, *Une indigoterie à Saint-Domingue*, 8–12.

54. Rambert, *Histoire du commerce de Marseille*, 6:404. According to this study, indigo was the third-most-important colonial import, following sugar and coffee, slightly ahead of cotton.

Indigo, like cotton, encapsulates the globalization of agribusiness in the seventeenth and eighteenth centuries. Native to Asia, or at least first widely cultivated there, it was transplanted to the Americas in the mid-seventeenth century. By the end of the century, Western imports had come to far outstrip imports from Asia. By the time the great Swedish naturalist Carl Linnaeus coined the botanical name *Indigofera tinctoria* (loosely, "dyestuff made in India") in 1753, indigo was predominantly grown and made in places other than India, notably French colonies such as Saint-Domingue and Louisiana. The name conferred by Linnaeus was in a sense stuck in a time warp. It registered the influence of Eastern craft but not the labor (and skill) of the Western-hemisphere producers who had captured the global market. Condensing place of production and place of origin, the botanical name overlooks the impact of globalized commerce on the production and consumption of commodities.

Much the same can be said of the discussion of indigo that appears in Pierre Pomet's comprehensive *Histoire générale des drogues* (General History of Drugs) (1694; revised 1712).[55] Though Pomet locates indigo production in Bengal and Surat he refers throughout the text to the labor of "nègres," as though he were referring to the Americas, or as though slave labor were a necessary feature of indigo production. Above I noted that Indian slaves who made their way to France in later years were sometimes classified as "nègres du Bengal." In a text of the 1690s, however, I think that the association of black slavery with the Indian subcontinent probably bespeaks a kind of unconscious transfer: the displacement of the colonial mode of production from West to East.

Encyclopedic Spaces

In Diderot and d'Alembert's *Encyclopedia* the specialized world of manufacture and commerce was brought to the attention of the general reading public. The work's editors and many of its contributing writers were deeply interested in the state of craft and industry in France; indeed, as its full title suggests, one of its principal objectives was to give *métiers* (artisanal professions) the same dignity accorded to the abstract sciences and arts. In his "Prospectus" (published in 1750 as an advertisement to potential *Encyclopedia* subscribers) Diderot writes that "too much has been written on the sciences, not enough on most of the liberal arts, and almost nothing has been written on the mechanical arts." To remedy this omission the *Encyclopedia* included not only articles on craft and manufacture but also detailed diagrams of workshops and machinery. This celebration of the mechanical arts was, of course, not without social and political implications. It announced a vision of society in which the

---

55. Pomet's *History* was corrected and updated by two leading French botanists, Nicolas Lemery and Joseph Pitton de Tournefort, and republished in English under the title *A Compleat History of Druggs*. See 16–17.

traditional aristocratic disdain for trade and manufacture was superseded by admiration for artisanry and entrepreneurship, and the social transformations that they supported.

In the *Encyclopedia*'s survey of French craft and industry, the large and rapidly changing textiles, clothing, and fashion industries inevitably occupied a central place. Daniel Roche has identified as many as 3,036 articles in which this set of topics is addressed (414). The fact that a number of these articles, including the entry for "Cotton," were written by Diderot illustrates the importance accorded to this crucial sector of French manufacture. In his discussion of this corpus of articles, Roche points to a number of broad themes and tendencies. Many of the articles on textiles formulate a Rousseauist critique of cumbersome formal clothing and express a general preference for apparel that accommodates rather than constrains the movement of the body. The *Encyclopedia* also upholds the broadly positive view of material refinement that had been handed down by Bernard Mandeville. The article "Luxe" (Luxury) (volume 9, 1765) by Saint-Lambert, for example, acknowledges the positive social effects of consumption while marking certain limits and suggesting that overindulgence can be a cause of social degeneration. Finally, many articles express an enthusiastic view of the expansion of commerce and the introduction of new technologies.

I want to think about the *Encyclopedia*'s presentation of textiles from the perspective of cultural geography. Although the *Encyclopedia* is not often analyzed in terms of a geographic compass, a comparison of the ways in which the Orient and the Americas are represented in its volumes yields revealing results. Roche's inventory of articles dealing with clothing and textiles provides a helpful starting point, since it classifies articles by the regions that they evoke as well as by other criteria. By Roche's count, 131 articles deal directly and/or principally with textiles and clothing in Asia, as compared with sixty-three for Europe, and two each for Africa and the Americas (424). What these figures convey is the strong association of textiles and fashion with Eastern materials, crafts, and styles. One reason for this linkage lay in the cultural imprint of vocabulary. Whereas a vast array of terms—words such as *indiennes, siamoises,* and indigo—alluded to Eastern origins, there was no equivalent vocabulary to denote that a product was "made in America." In a text ordered as a dictionary, this asymmetry had obvious consequences. But invisibility was not, as we shall see, simply a function of an article's title, for even in entries in which colonial production is very much at issue, the colonial environment is often accorded less importance than other world regions.

A case in point is the article "Indigo" (volume 8, 1765) by Le Romain. After a brief description of the indigo plant, which is said to be "very common in the Antilles, in Saint-Domingue, in almost all of the warm countries of America, and in several parts of the East Indies, from which it seems to have taken its name," the article explains how indigo is produced, starting with an account of the various tools and utensils that are required. The production method described in the article is said to be that of the "islands of the Americas." Presumably this method was more familiar to the author than, for example, Indian techniques, having already been described by missionaries such as Du Tertre and Labat, as well as by Pomet.

In his account of indigo production in the Antilles, Le Romain relies heavily on the impersonal subject "one," and on the passive voice. He describes, for example, one phase of the process as follows: "One opens the taps through which this colored water flows into the stirring drum; one immediately cleans the soaking vat in order to make room for new plants, and by this means the work is continued without interruption." The effect of this phrasing is to make the labor involved in making indigo tablets appear to happen virtually without human effort. The active voice and conjugated verbs are used only in one short paragraph, in which Le Romain explains the role of the master *indigotier* (indigo maker). "To prevent...mishaps," he writes, "the indigo maker carefully watches the different processes occurring in the stirring drum." Reaching the end of his account, Le Romain acknowledges that "the bad odor that is exhaled from the baths when they are in operation causes the death of many workers; it is one of the main causes of the decrease in the number of indigo plantations in the French islands." He does not explain that the workers killed in this manner were predominantly enslaved, nor does he note that slaves as well as indigo makers had to be careful and skilled.

In the second part of the article, Le Romain turns his attention to the use of indigo in the manufacture of *indiennes*. "Here is how indigo is prepared in the dyeing of cloth in the East Indies," he states, marking a change in subject that also involves a transfer from West to East Indies. This change of geographic context is accompanied by a change in tone and syntax: "The worker having reduced a certain amount of indigo to powder puts it into a big earthenware vase that he fills with cold water; he adds a proportionate quantity of lime that has been partially pulverized; then he sniffs the indigo to make sure it doesn't smell sour, and if it does, he adds more lime to take away the smell." As this sentence illustrates, in the second half of the article workers are individuated, and their labor is portrayed as a skill and described in a series of active verbs.

The volume of plates devoted to "Agriculture and Rustic Economy" includes an illustration of an *indigoterie* (figure 13). Divided vertically into three segments, the illustration presents the standard view of an indigo plantation in this period (it is very similar, for example, to the illustration that appears in Labat's *New Voyage* [see figure 16]). It depicts the succession of vats and drums in which the indigo mixture was beaten and stirred. Underneath these images is a legend that lists, alphabetically, the various buildings and utensils involved in the production process. Included among these utensils are the "negroes," who are listed alongside, and on the same basis as, tools and implements. As in the article "Indigo," in which slave labor is evoked in a depersonalized, passive

Figure 13. "Indigoterie et Manioc," *Recueil de planches sur les sciences, les arts libéraux et les arts mécaniques.* Livorno: 1771–78. Vol. 1. Courtesy of the Rare Book and Manuscript Library, Columbia University.

voice, enslaved workers are rendered here as machinery: moving parts to be set in motion by a skilled overseer.

Diderot's article "Cotton" represents a somewhat different case. Writing against the backdrop of the prohibition of *toiles peintes,* Diderot advocates the lifting of the ban on the grounds that French manufacturers were perfectly equipped to compete with their Indian counterparts. As seen earlier, he cites the experiments of a certain Jore of Rouen as evidence that French craftsmen had the capacity to produce muslins of the same high quality as those made in India. He also notes that France had access to an abundant supply of cheap, high-quality raw cotton from the Antilles. Drawing on Jore and missionaries such as Du Tertre and Labat, he claims, in what was probably an exaggeration, that the Caribbean colonies had become France's principal suppliers of raw cotton, and that "the French islands of the Americas supply the best cottons used in the workshops of Rouen and Troyes. Even our neighbors in other countries purchase their cotton from Guadeloupe, Saint-Domingue, and adjacent countries." In a polemical context in which the point was to show that France could out-manufacture India, the Caribbean colonies are fleetingly celebrated as the world leader in raw cotton production. We can draw a parallel here with the enthusiasm for French cochineal production in Saint-Domingue that followed in the wake of Menonville's act of industrial espionage. In both instances the colonial production of raw materials became visible in light of a nationalistic celebration of commerce.

The Triumph of Cotton

In mid-eighteenth-century France dress and fashion were matters of considerable moral and political significance. Long-running arguments about the corrupting effects of luxury took on a new life as they converged with new discourses advocating the abandonment of artifice and the embrace of nature. In the 1740s, medical writers began to issue warnings about the physiological dangers posed by tight, restrictive clothing such as corsets and stays. Their arguments gained ground after the publication in 1762 of Jean-Jacques Rousseau's pedagogical novel *Émile; ou, De l'éducation* (*Emile; or, On Education*), in which the clothing that is appropriate for children is reviewed alongside other aspects of their education and upbringing.

In the second book of *Émile,* Rousseau argues that children's clothing should allow for the abundant physical exercise that he advocates throughout the novel: "The limbs of a growing body ought to have room in their garments. Nothing ought to hinder either their movements or their growth; nothing too tight; nothing that clings to the body; no belts. French dress, constraining and unhealthy for men, is particularly pernicious for children."[56]

56. *Emile; or, On Education,* translated by Allan Bloom, 126. Subsequent references in the text are to this edition.

Rousseau suggests that children be dressed in light fabrics, even in winter, and preferably in the bright colors that they instinctively prefer (366–67). He also advocates avoiding costly fabrics since these create in children's minds a pernicious connection between luxury and merit.

In book 5, which deals specifically with the education of girls, Rousseau broaches the thorny question of female dress. In a widely discussed passage, he claims that little girls' love of dressing up is innate, and proposes that coquetry in moderation is a positive attribute. He goes on to say that simple, form-fitting gowns are far more seductive than ornate dresses that alter the shape of the body and conceal women's natural charms. In place of the dominant fashions of his age, he proposes a return to the simple, flowing robes of ancient Greece, both because of the freedom of movement that these styles allowed, and because they revealed the contours of the body. I will quote this passage at length because it reads, on one level, as a visionary piece of fashion journalism, an argument for a return to the past that anticipates the major trends of the following three decades:

> It is known that comfortable clothing which did not hinder the body contributed a great deal to leaving both sexes among the Greeks with those beautiful proportions seen in their statues—statues which still serve as models for art today, when disfigured nature has ceased furnishing art with models among us. They had not a single one of these gothic shackles, these multitudes of ligatures which squeeze our bodies on all sides. Their women were ignorant of the use of these whalebone corsets with which our women counterfeit their waists rather than display them. I cannot believe that this abuse, pushed to an inconceivable extent in England, will not finally cause the species to degenerate, and I even maintain that the attraction that it offers is in bad taste. It is not attractive to see a woman cut in half like a wasp. That is shocking to the sight and it makes the imagination suffer. (372–73)

Advocating taste rather than fashion, Rousseau continues: "Give some ribbons, gauze, muslin and flowers to a tasteful young girl who despises fashion. Without diamonds, tassels, or lace she is going to produce for herself an outfit that will make her a hundred times more charming than all the brilliant rags of La Duchapt would."[57] As on other matters, Rousseau was ahead of his time when it came to questions of dress. In subsequent decades his antifashion ideal would become nothing short of the height of fashion. In the 1780s, plain white muslin gowns set off by simple trimmings such as ribbons, gauze, and flowers became a high-fashion look, while in the 1790s, toga-like dresses inspired by ancient Greece and Rome were all the rage. In the Directory period, modish women adopted straight, unadorned shifts of transparent white muslin that hugged the contours of the body, often leaving very little to the imagination. What I

57. La Duchapt was a well-known milliner of the period.

want to highlight in the present context is that the "back to nature" philosophy that underpinned these various trends provided an ideological foundation for the manufacturing and consumer revolution that elevated humble cotton over traditional luxury fabrics such as velvet, taffeta, and silk.

The transformation that Daniel Roche has called the "triumph of cotton" resulted from several factors.[58] We have seen that France's cotton weaving and printing industries grew rapidly after the reauthorization of *indiennage* in 1759. This expansion was accelerated by several factors, including the spread of mechanization. Serge Chassagne notes that whereas in 1780 there was only one mechanized spinning workshop in the whole of France, by 1814 there were 272.[59] New technologies and the use of materials grown cheaply in the colonies also contributed to a change in the ratio of clothing price to consumer income.[60] Clothes of all kinds became, at least in relative terms, more affordable, and this was particularly true of cotton garments. Giving an example that pertains to women's dress in the 1770s, Clare Crowston writes that "a cotton dress was half the price of a taffeta one, permitting women to buy more dresses or to begin buying custom-made garments for the first time" (162). Historians of dress generally concur that the 1770s–80s were a time of diversification in which people of all classes, and in particular women, owned not only more clothing than ever before, but also a greater range of pieces. The rise of flexible and affordable cotton was one of the key factors that enabled people of all classes to expand and diversify their wardrobes.

In 1783 cotton received a powerful new marketing image when Marie-Antoinette was portrayed by her favorite painter, Elisabeth Vigée-Lebrun, wearing a simple white muslin gown with a loosely gathered "peasant" neckline, cinched at the waist by a ribbon (figure 14). When this painting was exhibited in the biannual Salon it proved so controversial that it had to be withdrawn. Apparently not all segments of the public were ready to accept a portrait of the queen wearing a dress that, to the uncultivated eye, closely resembled an undergarment. By 1783, the muslin shift dress, first called a "gaulle," and later known as a "chemise à la reine," had been in fashion for several years among elite French and English women.[61] But to the uninitiated, as Caroline Weber

---

58. Roche, 143–44.

59. Chassagne, *Le coton et ses patrons*, 258–59. Mechanized production and the rise of a historically unregulated sector also contributed to the collapse of the guild system. The corporations were reformed by controller-general and free-trade advocate Anne-Robert-Jacques Turgot in 1776 and, after a short period of reinstatement following Turgot's dismissal, definitively abolished by the Constituent Assembly in 1791.

60. See Ribeiro, *Dress in Eighteenth-Century Europe*, 85.

61. Caroline Weber shows that the formality of Marie-Antoinette's wardrobe was relaxed over a period of several years, as the stiff "robe à la française" (dress in the French style) was replaced by the looser "robe à la polonaise" (dress in the Polish style) and finally by the frothy "gaulle." *Queen of Fashion*, 145–52.

Figure 14. Elisabeth Vigée-Lebrun, *Marie-Antoinette,* 1783. Oil on canvas. Private collection. Bildarchiv Preussischer Kulturbesitz/Art Resource, NY.

explains, this informal dress style signaled that the queen was not meeting expectations and did not deserve queenly respect (161).

    Marie-Antoinette is of course notorious for the pleasure that she took in "slumming": playing the part of a milkmaid or shepherdess at the *hameau,* her miniature farm in the park of Versailles. The queen's predilection for simple cotton dresses cut in a "peasant" style can perhaps be seen as another instance of this predilection for fashionably crossing social boundaries, a return to "nature" inspired by a selective appropriation of Rousseau's ideas. Much has been written about the queen's comportment and clothes, and about broad socio-cultural processes such as the "democratization" of fashion. My contribution here will be to highlight the role of cotton in this multilayered history.

Despite, or perhaps because of, the controversy over Vigée-Lebrun's intimate portrait, the white muslin shift dress rapidly became a staple of fashionable women's wardrobes. The vogue for transparent white muslin gowns remained a constant through the first decade of the nineteenth century, though dress styles evolved in various ways. In the 1790s the peasant-influenced look of the "chemise à la reine" gave way to fashions inspired by the neoclassical aesthetic that dominated the decade. Silhouettes became straighter, the waistline was no longer defined, and as a result the bust became the focal point of a woman's figure. The silhouettes of directory and empire can be seen as a reflection of the emphasis placed on motherhood and breastfeeding in the social discourses of the period. At the end of the decade the traumatic impact of the Terror reverberated in many ways, one outlet for social anxiety being fashion. As young Parisians embraced lifestyles of reckless self-abandonment, fashions became topical and extreme. Ultrafashionable young men were known as "incroyables" (literally, incredibles), their female counterparts as "merveilleuses" (marvels). The latter wore diaphanous cotton dresses that molded the bust and clung to the contours of the body, leaving nothing to the imagination.

In these decades, cotton continued to be associated in various ways with the Oriental world. The fine diaphanous fabric prized by fashionable women, for example, was known as *mousseline,* a term derived from the name Mosul, a city in present-day Iraq. This was also the age of the Oriental accessory. Simple white muslin gowns were accented with bold printed pieces such as Indian cashmere stoles, and turban-style head coverings of wrapped, Oriental fabric. Portraits of the period show prominent women such as Rose de Beauharnais—the future Empress Josephine—and the young Germaine de Staël wearing this orientalized style.

The colonial sources of these fabrics and fashions remained less visible but they were nonetheless significant. Above I note that the cultivation of cotton and indigo in France's plantation colonies contributed to the rising popularity of cotton in the second half of the eighteenth century. Here I suggest something further, which is that cultural traditions as well as raw materials may have made their way from colonies to metropole. As Sara Melzer observes in an article devoted to seventeenth-century writing on New France, we tend to assume that discourses and ideas radiated outward from the metropole to the colonial margin, but in some instances it is possible to map reverse trajectories: patterns of transmission in which concepts and trends that crystallized in the colonial milieu were exported back to continental France.[62] I would like to point to a few possible reverse trajectories in the domain of taste and fashion.

---

62. Melzer, "The Magic of French Culture," 137, "Une 'seconde France,'" 81–83.

Aileen Ribeiro proposes that the white shift dresses popularized by Marie-Antoinette may have been inspired, not only by neoclassical and pastoral currents, but also by styles worn in the colonies. She notes that in the Antilles, where the warm, humid climate made light cotton clothing a desirable choice, "simple tubes of white muslin had for some time been worn by ladies on the plantations." She also observes that the indigo used to blue-rinse muslin to a startling whiteness also came from the colonies.[63] Even the "Oriental" turbans with which fashionable directory women accessorized their dresses may have had a colonial origin. Though these turbans are usually viewed as examples of Eastern influence in a period of rampant Egyptomania (Ribeiro writes, for example, that "the Egyptian Expedition...produced a fashion for turbans"[64]), it is possible that this fashion made its way to France, not from Egypt, but from the Caribbean, where, as Helen B. Foster has noted, head wraps had been worn by women of color since early colonial times.[65]

In the 1770s the Italian painter Agostino Brunias toured the islands of the Caribbean, producing detailed visual accounts of the lifestyles of its populations. His vivid paintings portray white Creoles, free people of color, and the enslaved engaging in daily routines such as visiting markets, shopping in town, and participating in dances and festivities. Brunias is very attentive to styles of dress. His socially conscious images capture the fashionable looks of the period, documenting crossovers from whites to free people of color and vice versa. In the painting of a linen market reproduced in figure 15, for example, women of various classes and races are shown wearing head wraps strikingly similar to those soon after popularized in Paris.[66]

Though the trajectories of fashion are often hard to document, it is perhaps not incidental that several of the most fashionable wearers of cotton shifts and head wraps in the Directory period had colonial backgrounds. In an age in which the colonies had emerged from obscurity to become a focus of interest and debate, a number of Creole women, including Rose de Beauharnais and her friend Fortunée Hamelin, established themselves on the Paris scene as celebrated beauties and leaders of fashion.

The Colonial Triumph of Cotton

In his exhaustive description of Saint-Domingue in the late 1780s and early 1790s, the Creole magistrate Moreau de Saint-Méry represents dress as an important signifier of social identities. As several readers have observed, Moreau's account of the colony is characterized by an obsessive classification of the

---

63. Ribeiro, *Dress in Eighteenth-Century Europe*, 227–28.
64. Ribeiro, *Fashion in the French Revolution*, 131.
65. Foster, *New Raiments of Self*, 276–81.
66. Brunias, *A Linen Market*, Dominica, ca. 1780.

Figure 15. Agostino Brunias, *Linen Market, Dominica,* ca. 1780. Oil on canvas. Yale Center for British Art, Paul Mellon Collection.

population into different racial groups. At one juncture, for example, he lays out a complex taxonomy identifying 128 possible forms of mixed-race descent: a veritable "calculus of color," in the words of Werner Sollors.[67] As Sollors and other critics have shown, Moreau's preoccupation with métissage and its demographic repercussions reflects on the one hand a concern with policing racial boundaries, and on the other what Robert J.C. Young has termed a "covert theory of desire."[68] In this highly charged context, dress operated both as a marker of racial boundaries and as a mechanism of social mobility. Clothing signaled barriers, but it was also a site of seduction and erotic commerce.

Moreau's description of Saint-Domingue includes numerous observations on the dress of the white elite. He alludes to, for example, their preference for

67. Sollors, *Neither White nor Black Yet Both,* 115.
68. Young, *Colonial Desire,* 9.

white muslin, which he describes as a "livrée coloniale," or colonial livery.[69] Moreau also examines the clothing and sense of style of free people of color and slaves. In many cases these commentaries unfold into reflections on sexual relations between blacks and whites. In one passage, for example, Moreau observes that if a white man wanted to win the affections of a mixed-race slave, he had only to take her to a *marchand de modes* and deck her out in *mousselines* and *indiennes,* and his desires would soon be fulfilled.[70]

Free women of color, particularly the category of *mulâtresses,* occupy a central position in Moreau's account of social relationships in Saint-Domingue. He underscores their sensuality, repeatedly emphasizing their appetite for carnal pleasure, and laying the blame for the libertine morals of the colony at their feet. As Doris Garraway has observed, Moreau effectively projects his own desire, and that of men of his social class, onto mixed-race women (159). He blames the prevalence of social "disorders" on their "seductions," saying little about white men's desire or their power to command sexual favors. One of the sensual passions of women of color on which Moreau dwells is their taste for material consumption. He observes, for instance, that "all the finest productions of India" were imported to adorn their charms, drawing—as in the case of enslaved women—an implicit link between the purchase of clothing and the procurement of sexual favors.[71] In this formulation desire is located in women of color rather than in the white men who, it is implied, used clothes to pay for sex. As the aberrant social structure of the colony was thoroughly naturalized for Moreau, he offers no reflection on the social and economic forces that may have led women in subordinate positions to exchange sex for clothing, or on the sense of security and elevated social status that elegant apparel can confer.

Moreau's allusions to the seductive attractions of Indian fabrics resonate across colonial waters with a cry uttered by Bernardin de Saint-Pierre in the 1803 preface to his celebrated novel, *Paul and Virginia.* In an apostrophe to his female compatriots, Bernardin writes: "Oh Frenchwomen, it is for you today that the Indian woman weaves the lightest cottons and the brightest silks."[72] But while Bernardin rightly draws attention to the relationship between consumption and production, his focus on fine Oriental muslins and their hardworking Indian producers somewhat overshadows the labor of cotton textile workers closer to home: the enslaved labor force of France's plantation colonies and the emergent French industrial working class. Bernardin was in fact by no means insensible to the labor of the enslaved. In an earlier work, *Voyage à l'Île de France* (Voyage to the Île de France) (1773), he had indeed

69. Médéric-Louis-Elie Moreau de Saint-Méry, *Description topographique, physique, civile, politique et historique de la partie française de l'isle Saint-Domingue,* 2 vols. (Philadelphia: Dupont, 1797), 1:20. References below in the text are to this edition.

70. Ibid., 1:60.

71. Ibid., 1:93.

72. Bernardin, *Paul et Virginie,* 77.

addressed Frenchwomen in a way that emphasized the colonial provenance of the fashionable goods they consumed and the relationship between luxury and slavery: "The beautiful pink and red hues that women wear; the cotton wool with which they line their skirts; the sugar, the coffee, the chocolate for their breakfasts, the rouge with which they show off their pallor; the hands of unfortunate blacks have prepared all of these for them. Women of feeling, you weep over tragedies, yet the things that give you pleasure are soaked in the tears and tainted with the blood of men" (Letter 12).[73] Much could be said about the gendered attack on luxury staged in this passage, and about the metaphors of natural and artificial color deployed in the service of this critique. I will highlight only the small but suggestive difference of emphasis between Bernardin's best-selling work of fiction, in which backbreaking labor is attributed to Oriental workers, and the assault on slavery that appears in more narrowly focused empirical writing on the colonial world.

In the 1780s–90s opponents of colonial slavery formulated the argument that free men are more productive than an enslaved workforce, and that European nations would increase their profits and expand their markets by abolishing the slave trade and establishing new colonies in Africa. One of the main claims made by these activists was that Europe's new colonial subjects, along with its emancipated slaves, would prove to be major consumers of European manufactured goods, and in particular of European textiles. In an open letter published in the report of a British commission investigating the slave trade (1788), the former slave Olaudah Equiano observes along these lines that indigo and cotton could be grown more profitably by free workers in Africa:

> Cotton and indigo grow spontaneously in some parts of Africa: a consideration of this is of no small consequence to the manufacturing towns of Great Britain.... It opens a most immense, glorious and happy prospect. The clothing, etc. of a continent ten thousand miles in circumference, and immensely rich in productions of every denomination, would make an interesting return indeed for our manufactories, a free Trade being established.[74]

Framing his argument in terms of contemporary economic discourses, Equianao opines that if slavery were abolished, Africa would quickly be established as a major market for British goods. Equating not only commerce but also clothing with civilization, Equiano, like other antislavery writers of his generation, imagines a benevolent form of colonialism in which commerce and humanity would be reconciled, with Africa emerging as both a major producer of raw materials for the British textiles industry and as a leading consumer of British-made clothing.

73. Bernardin, *Voyage à l'Île de France*, 1:58.
74. *Life of Olaudah Equiano*, 178.

Giving voice to what I think is probably the dominant critical perspective on the relationship between fashion and social history, Clair Hughes writes that "dress is a visible aspect of history, a material index of social and historical change" (2). In this chapter I have argued that this is true, but only to a point. The textile and clothing fashions of seventeenth and eighteenth century France reflected historical processes such as the rise of consumer culture and the gradual breakdown of the social hierarchy. Yet not all aspects of social and material history were directly translated into cultural representations. I would therefore qualify Hughes's statement with the observation that like other cultural productions, textiles and fashion can be sites of repression and displacement. In eighteenth-century France the Oriental world was referenced and represented as a point of origin for new textiles, techniques, and styles. In sharp contrast, the important role of Europe's colonies as producers of raw materials and consumers of cotton textiles long remained largely invisible. It was only at the end of the eighteenth century, in an era of turmoil and upheaval, that the colonial axis of another revolution, the revolution in textiles and apparel, came slowly into focus.

PART II

SAVAGES AND SLAVES

4

The Trope of
Colonial Encounter

In his deliciously acerbic short story "The Dread Redeemer Lazarus Morell," Jorge Luis Borges presents the following cautionary tale of well-intentioned injustice: "In 1517, the Spanish missionary Bartolomé de Las Casas, taking great pity on the Indians who were languishing in the hellish workpits of Antillean gold mines, suggested to Charles V, king of Spain, a scheme for importing blacks, so that they might languish in the hellish workpits of Antillean gold mines."[1] Having pointed to the absurdity of this substitution, Borges's narrator goes on to observe that had the exchange of African for Amerindian labor not taken place, the history of the New World would have been very different. There would have been no American Civil War, no jazz or voodoo, neither the heroic biography of Toussaint Louverture nor the scurrilous career of Lazarus Morell, a scoundrel who lured slaves from southern plantations with the promise of freedom, only to resell them later for his own profit.

In this short but telling tale, two different but related themes come together. The famed Spanish missionary Las Casas is implied to have felt more sympathy for indigenous people than for the transplanted Africans whom he designated to take their place. Whether or not this characterization is historically accurate, what can be said is that until the twentieth century the persecution and suffering of the indigenous peoples of the Americas garnered more notice and elicited more sympathy from European observers than the plight of enslaved Africans. Encounters between Amerindians and Europeans are far more widely represented in seventeenth- and eighteenth-century European

---

1. Borges, "Dread Redeemer Lazarus Morell."

literature than exchanges with diasporic Africans, even though, by the late seventeenth century, contact between Europeans and Africans or Creoles of African descent was more extensive in most regions than encounters between natives and settlers. To this asymmetrical history of compassion and representation Borges juxtaposes the vast historical scope of the African diaspora in the Americas: the plethora of events and cultural forms that would not have come into being but for the Atlantic slave trade. Whatever the motivations of Las Casas's proposal, the story implies, it unleashed powerful forces that changed the face of the world.

This chapter and the next explore the implications of the paradox articulated in Borges's story. That is to say, they consider the bifurcated, though relational, representation of indigenous Americans and diasporic Africans in seventeenth- and eighteenth-century French culture. In chapter 5 I consider how these representations inform Enlightenment meditations on the state of nature and the development of human society. First, however, I consider how Amerindians and enslaved blacks are depicted in narrative works that recount the formative years of the French Caribbean, and in fictional representations of the French presence in the Americas. I argue that whereas inaugural encounters between "natives" and "settlers" were central to the imagining of colonial contact, slavery and the creolized societies that formed around it captured relatively little attention. I attribute this asymmetry to two principal factors. One is the difficulty of representing the problematic subject of slavery. The other stems from the discursive challenges involved in portraying the diasporic identities created in the vortex of the Americas. Whereas encounters between different cultural groups could be mapped within the framework of literary narrative, the processual character of colonial history proved to be a more elusive subject of representation.

These patterns of representation have carried over into the scholarship devoted to European writing on the Americas. Until the mid-2000s, relatively little scholarship was devoted to textual representations of the New World's slave-plantation societies. By contrast, there is a well-developed critical literature bearing on "encounters" between Europeans and Amerindians in North and South America and the Caribbean. This corpus includes influential studies such as D. W. Meinig's *The Shaping of America: A Geographical Perspective on Five Hundred Years of History* (1986–2004), Peter Hulme's *Colonial Encounters: Europe and the Native Caribbean, 1492–1797* (1986), Philip Boucher's *Cannibal Encounters: Europeans and Island Caribs, 1492–1763*, Tzvetan Todorov's *La conquête de l'Amérique: La question de l'autre* (*The Conquest of America: The Question of the Other*), Mary Louise Pratt's *Imperial Eyes: Travel Writing and Transculturation* (1992), and Anthony Pagden's *European Encounters with the New World* (1993). Though these works are diverse in scope and methodology, they nonetheless display a certain number of commonalities. They share, in particular, a collective focus on the moment or experience of "first encounter": what Todorov calls the "extreme and exemplary encounter" between Europeans and Amerindians in the wake of 1492, and what Meinig describes as the "sudden and harsh encounter between two old worlds that transformed both and integrated them into a single new world."[2]

While there can be no question that the first disorienting meetings of Amerindians and Europeans and the political and epistemological fallout of this contact is a subject of immense historical and philosophical significance, the emphasis placed on colonial first encounters perhaps calls for some level of analysis. In this collective focus we can perhaps discern what Michael Taussig has called the quest for "a decent fix of straightforward Othering," an epistemological and aesthetic preference for alterity in its purest forms.[3] With its symmetry and metaphorical closure, the trope of the colonial first encounter leaves little room for the acknowledgment of hybridity and creolization. Gyan Prakash has argued that colonial ethnography produced the category of the "native" to embody the prehistorical other of civilized man.[4] The first major instantiation of this model occurred in the Enlightenment's inexorable narrative of mankind's journey from the primitive to the civilized or modern. This chapter and the next explore the remarkable power of the narrative to overshadow all other chronologies and modes of colonial interaction.

Africans and Amerindians in Early Colonial Narrative

In the first few decades of the French presence in the Caribbean, interaction with 'indigenous' peoples was a daily reality and a matter of life and death. Settlers relied on the people whom, following Spanish practice, they called *Caraïbes* (Caribs) for information about the local environment.[5] Their very survival indeed depended on the establishment of trading relationships in which manufactured goods such as glass and ironware were exchanged for food. When relations were hostile, colonies grew slowly, if they were not destroyed outright.[6]

The life-or-death importance of "native-settler" relations to the development of the fledgling colonies is reflected in the central position that these

---

2. Todorov, *Conquest of America;* Meinig, *Shaping of America,* 1:64–65.
3. Taussig, *Mimesis and Alterity,* 143.
4. Prakash, "After Colonialism," 5–7.
5. The term *Carib,* with its overtones of "cannibal," appears to have originated with the first European encounters with indigenous Antilleans. As Peter Hulme explains, it is unclear whether, and in what sense, the group identity that it denotes had meaning before Columbus's first voyage. See *Colonial Encounters,* 50–87. French missionaries writing in the seventeenth and eighteenth century clearly presume the term to denote an authentic category of identity. Whether the "Caribs" viewed themselves as "Caribs" is impossible to know, as their perspective can only be reconstructed through the accounts of external observers.
6. Jean-Baptiste Du Tertre notes that after the five-year war between French and Caribs ended in 1640, Martinique and Guadeloupe grew rapidly. *Histoire générale des Antilles,* 1:208.

exchanges occupy in the first group of narratives devoted to France's colonial outposts. The fact that many of these works were composed by missionaries who had been sent to the Antilles to convert the Caribs further explains the emphasis placed on Amerindian culture and on relations between the Caribs and the French.

But while interactions with Caribs were unquestionably a central feature of settler experience in the 1620s–50s, by as early as 1660 matters had changed substantially. French settlers first arrived in Guadeloupe and Martinique in 1635. They established a number of small settlements, as well as satellite footholds in Grenada, St. Lucia, and coastal Guiana. Confronted with French expansionism, the Caribs mobilized to defend their territory and way of life. They launched aggressive guerilla attacks on isolated settlements, and the French in turn retaliated, usually on a bigger scale. After two decades of escalating violence, the Caribs were forced out of Martinique and Guadeloupe. By the terms of a 1658 treaty the Amerindian population of the Caribbean was given—that is to say, confined to—the islands of Dominica and St. Vincent. In later decades France and Britain (also a signatory to the treaty) violated the terms of this agreement by establishing settlements in these Carib sanctuaries. In 1795 the last surviving Carib population in the Antilles was deported from St. Vincent to a small island off the coast of Venezuela. In French Guiana the fate of the "indigenous" population was roughly similar. Although the colony for a long time remained fragile, its Amerindian population shrank precipitously from an estimated twenty to thirty thousand at the start of the seventeenth century to a mere two thousand by 1750.[7]

The removal of the Caribs was an important preliminary for the transformation of Martinique and Guadeloupe into full-blown plantation colonies. Beginning in the 1650s these islands underwent a process of social and ecological transformation that turned them from remote outposts in which *pétun* (tobacco) and other local plants were grown on a small scale into centers of agribusiness geared to the production of sugarcane. Before 1650 agricultural labor in the colonies was performed by the settlers and a small cohort of *engagés* (indentured servants), though manpower was also provided by a small number of enslaved Amerindians and by a few African slaves captured from British or Spanish vessels or purchased from Dutch traders.[8] As tobacco gave way to sugar, the demand for labor escalated rapidly, and following the lead of other European nations, France entered the Atlantic slave trade. Monopoly slave-trading companies were established in the 1670s and 1680s, and by 1720 the number of African slaves in Saint-Domingue alone had reached forty-seven thousand.[9]

---

7. See Labat, *Voyage aux îles d'Amérique* (1992 edition), 97–101.

8. Kenneth Banks estimates that by 1642 there were already about twelve hundred African or Afro-Brazilian slaves in the French Antilles, alongside some three thousand French settlers. *Chasing Empire across the Sea*, 31.

9. Ibid., 81.

One might expect that as the Caribs were relegated to the margins of colonial society, they also became less central to colonial narrative, and, correspondingly, that as enslaved Africans became more numerous, they also became more significant subjects of representation. But this is not the pattern that we encounter in early colonial histories and travel narratives. Rather, Amerindians continued to occupy a central place in colonial narrative long after they had been removed from colonized territories, while enslaved Africans occupied a marginal position despite their growing numbers. Régis Antoine has hypothesized that missionaries (the principal authors of colonial narratives) continued to dwell on hostilities with the Caribs even after these clashes had declined in importance because these dramatic stories appealed to donors.[10] I believe that the issue runs deeper than this interpretation suggests. In the following two sections of this chapter, through readings of the two most widely circulated early histories of the French Caribbean, I propose that missionaries were not simply concerned with promoting an enticing image of the Caribbean to outsiders, but rather, for a variety of reasons, continued to regard the colonies as terrains of encounter between European and indigenous peoples.

Absence and Ambivalence in Du Tertre's *General History of the Antilles*

Unlike colonial competitors such as Britain and the Netherlands, France saw the Christianization of indigenous and enslaved populations as a fundamental aspect of its colonial expansion. Beginning in the 1630s the Dominican and Jesuit orders sent a cohort of priests to the Antilles to implement this mission. Among the most literate members of colonial society, several of these missionaries went on to publish descriptions of the French colonies in their formative decades.

In her study of early writing on the French Caribbean, Doris Garraway signals the importance of paraliterary works such as the narratives of missionaries, given the virtual absence of colonial experience from more literary canonical genres.[11] She reads these texts both as narratives of colonial history and as historical documents that testify to the formation of a Creole society (17–21). Correspondingly, she argues that to read them is to perform something other than the now-familiar work of colonial-discourse analysis, a mode of reading that has the side effect of reaffirming the centrality of European power.

I find Garraway's interpretation of missionary narratives as colonial/Creole texts to be compelling, but I also think that when we classify these works it is important to take certain aspects of their representational economy into account. Specifically, it seems to me necessary to think about the fact that the French missionaries wrote far more about Carib culture and native-settler

10. Antoine, *Les écrivains français,* 49.
11. Garraway, *Libertine Colony,* 4–10.

relations than about slaves and slavery. In light of this selectiveness, I want to propose that while these texts unquestionably entertain a different relation to colonial experience than more-mainstream metropolitan writings, they nonetheless manifest similar patterns of emphasis and avoidance, and gravitate toward the same figures and themes.

As Peter Hulme has noted, French missionary writings constitute one of the primary sources of information about the now-vanished Carib culture.[12] The main figure in this ethnographic tradition was Raymond Breton, a Dominican priest who lived alone with the Caribs of Dominica for four and a half years and who authored a Carib grammar and a Carib-French dictionary,[13] but other missionaries took a keen interest in Carib customs and culture, too. Below I consider the two most widely read missionary narratives bearing on the early French Caribbean: Jean-Baptiste Du Tertre's *General History of the Antilles* and Jean-Baptiste Labat's *New Voyage to the Islands of the Americas*. Following the lead of Hulme and Garraway, I discuss these texts' complex representation of the Caribs. But I also bring a new dimension to this discussion by exploring the relationship between this ethnographic project and the representation of slavery.

Du Tertre's *General History of the Antilles* was the first French account of the Caribbean to penetrate beyond the narrow circle of readers who had a direct interest in colonial ventures. Its account of Amerindian culture influenced many canonical French writers, including Rousseau and Chateaubriand. A naval officer turned priest, Du Tertre arrived in Guadeloupe in 1640 and remained for seven years, ultimately becoming the superior of the colony's Dominican mission. A decade later (1656–57) he returned for a shorter, second visit. His first account of his experience and of the French settlements in the Antilles was published in 1654 under the title *Histoire générale des isles de Saint Christophe, de la Guadeloupe, de la Martinique* (General History of the Islands of St. Christophe, Guadeloupe, and Martinique). A revised and expanded version of this work, titled *General History of the Antilles,* was published in 1667–71.[14] As Doris Garraway has noted, there are substantial differences between the two versions. Whereas the earlier text is a narrative history

---

12. See note 5, above.

13. Breton, *Petit catéchisme,* and *Dictionnaire caraïbe-français.* Breton's "dictionary" is actually more akin to an encyclopedia that explicates Carib concepts and practices.

14. Du Tertre, *Histoire générale des îles.* Du Tertre notes in the preface to the later *Histoire générale* that in 1658 a volume entitled *Histoire naturelle et morale des îles Antilles de l'Amérique* was published in Rotterdam by Charles (sometimes known as "César") de Rochefort. He claims that Rochefort had obtained and reproduced various manuscripts devoted to the colonies, including a preliminary version his own 1654 text and Father Breton's *Carib Dictionary.* The 1667–71 *General History* seems to have been in part a response to this act of plagiarism. At several points in his narrative, Du Tertre refutes claims made by Rochefort, a Protestant, regarding the poor record of achievement of the Dominican mission. The addition of extensive new material also had the effect of rendering Rochefort's account obsolete.

of the colonies with a strong personal inflection, the revised edition not only provides readers with a history of the colonies' founding and development but also offers a comprehensive description of their ecology, agriculture, and social organization. Garraway's reading focuses on the earlier text, which, as she explains, is more direct in its treatment of issues such as sexuality and métissage that are her core concerns (52). I consider rather the revised and expanded text of 1667–71. This is because it was this version that was read by Enlightenment thinkers such as Rousseau and Voltaire, and because the later work was published after the expulsion of the Caribs, at a time when the colonies' population of enslaved Africans was on the rise.

The opening volume of *General History* offers what could literally be called a blow-by-blow account of the French Antilles from the arrival of the first settlers on the island of Saint-Christophe (today St. Kitts) in 1626 to the sale of Martinique and Guadeloupe to the Company of the West Indies in 1664. It recounts the struggle for domination waged between French and English settlers on St. Kitts and revisits the endless petty squabbles that divided the French leaders. The main focus of the narrative, however, is the changing relationship between colonists and Caribs. Du Tertre could scarcely be accused of sugarcoating these dealings; to the contrary, he offers an explicit account of the brutal violence perpetrated by the French (1:81–92). But while Du Tertre criticizes what he sees as the excesses of the French settlers, he does not fundamentally question their right to establish and defend settlements in the Antilles. As a result, his account of Carib-French relations unfolds as a double-handed narrative of condemnation and legitimation. He laments the excessive violence committed by the French while at the same time blaming the Caribs for their irrationally aggressive behavior.

General History's second volume turns from history to "natural history." Du Tertre describes the islands' geography, plants, and animal life, and in the final two sections (treatises 7–8), considers their human inhabitants. In treatise 7 the colonies' population of "savages" is examined at length, while Europeans are considered in somewhat less detail. In treatise 8, Du Tertre turns his attention to the colonies' enslaved population.

In a passage titled "Of the Savages in General," Du Tertre paints an idealized portrait of the Caribs as a people living close to nature in a state of uncorrupted innocence. Echoing Montaigne's famous essay "On Cannibals," he argues that the Caribs should be thought of as "savage" only in the sense that they are "wild," that is, without culture or clothing. He also suggests that although the Caribs have little knowledge of the world, they are fundamentally good. Again echoing Montaigne, he contrasts them with Europeans, who have amassed a great deal of knowledge yet are in many respects corrupt. In an illustration accompanying this passage, male and female Caribs are shown standing naked beside a fruit-bearing tree, an image that calls to mind the Garden of Eden (2:356). Since, as Garraway notes, the fruit is still on the tree and not in the hands of the female Carib, the reader seems to be invited to view the Carib couple as a kind of prelapsarian Adam and Eve. This iconography, however, raises the thorny question of how contact with corrupt Europeans could possibly be of benefit to the Caribs. Apparently recognizing this issue, Du Tertre observes that it pains him to see creatures who are good and innocent barred from salvation because they do not know God.

In other sections of *General History,* however, unembellished nature and uncivilized humans are represented in much less favorable terms. In a passage in the first volume, for example, Du Tertre states that before the arrival of the French "everything in the islands was repellent"; there was nothing there of any interest, just a "barbarous people" and "uncultivated land." He goes on to say that since the arrival of the French, the savages had happily been "brought to reason."

Du Tertre also casts acts of violence perpetrated by the Caribs in a strongly negative light, attributing them to the machinations of their shamans, or *boyé,* rather than to a genuine need for self-defense. In a number of passages he complains of the "artifice" with which the *boyé* tried to convince their fellows that the French were plotting to confiscate their land (1:4; 1:201–2). In order to grasp the utter incongruity of these remarks we have to recall the historical context: *General History* was published in 1667, almost a full decade after most of the Caribbean was annexed by Britain and France.

In Du Tertre's narrative the Caribs manifest the kind of good savage/bad savage dichotomy that Michael Taussig has identified as an organizing subtext of European writing on the Americas.[15] On the one hand, the Caribs embody the philosophical figure of the "good savage" as constructed by Montaigne. On the other, however, the concrete realities of interaction pulled Du Tertre in a different direction, causing him to view the Caribs in a less favorable light. Straddling these two perspectives, Du Tertre writes admiringly about the absence of inequality and authority among the Caribs in one moment, while in the next chastising them for failing to teach their children proper manners (2:376).

A second polarizing issue was the question of Christianity. The primary rationale for the missionaries' presence in the colonies was the conversion of the Carib population. This population, however, turned out to be exceptionally resistant to the Christian message. Du Tertre notes that in twelve years of unflinching service, Raymond Breton had managed to achieve only four conversions, all cases in which the convert was on the brink of death (2:414). Forced to explain why a people whom he and other missionaries had portrayed as so ideally suited for evangelization had resisted the Christian message, he falls back on claims such as that the Caribs saw the French as a violent and dissolute people (ibid.), an explanation that allows him to rebuke the colonists for their

15. Taussig, *Mimesis and Alterity,* 142.

transgressive behavior, while at the same time avoiding the controversial subject of Carib spiritual beliefs.

If in Du Tertre's narrative the Caribs constitute a subject of "ideological splitting" along the lines discussed by Homi Bhabha, enslaved Africans stand almost entirely outside the frame of discourse.[16] Whereas the islands' "native" population is immediately established as an object of interest, the presence of African slaves is paradoxically so naturalized that it is effectively taken for granted. Du Tertre indeed refers so little to slaves and slavery (with the exception of treatise 8) that one might be led to think that there were hardly any enslaved Africans in the French Caribbean in the 1650s–60s. In fact, though Africans were not transported on French vessels until around 1670, they were present in the French colonies almost from their foundation. According to Adrien Dessalles, black inhabitants marginally outnumbered whites in Martinique by as early as 1664, both populations standing at a little over two thousand.[17]

Du Tertre first alludes to Africans when he is giving an account of fighting between French and English settlers on St. Kitts in the late 1620s.[18] He notes in passing that the French contingent was reinforced by a group of "twenty blacks." In subsequent passages he refers to a promise of freedom made to a group of five hundred blacks if they helped the French to defeat the English "heretics" (1:61), and explains that a quarrel that had erupted between the two French leaders, M. de Poincy and M. de la Grange, had to do with the ownership of a cargo of African slaves (1:131). At a later point in the narrative, Du Tertre alludes to a slave revolt and describes the pursuit and execution of rebels and Maroons that followed this rebellion (1:153, 1:500). He observes with satisfaction that the culprits had been tracked down and publicly hanged and quartered, noting in an aside that the children who were involved in this episode had "merely" had their ears cut off. What is striking about this passage, beyond the apparent absence of moral qualms, is that Du Tertre provides the details of a slave revolt without having previously established the existence of slavery. At no point in the *General History* does he state when or how enslaved Africans first arrived in the colonies, nor does he say how many were present at any given time. The only section of *General History* in which enslaved Africans are represented at length is the closing treatise of the second volume, a section devoted exclusively to the islands' enslaved population, and to which I now turn.

---

16. Bhabha, "Of Mimicry and Man."

17. Dessalles, *Histoire générale des Antilles* 5 vols. (Paris: Libraire-éditeur, 1847–48), 1:559–661.

18. Enslaved Africans are mentioned in one of the royal letters patent that Du Tertre reproduces in his history as a documentary source. This letter—written in the name of Louis XIV—recalls that the capture of a Spanish vessel carrying a cargo of slaves had a transformative impact on the French settlement in St. Kitts (1:59). Interestingly, however, this transformative episode is not mentioned directly in Du Tertre's narrative.

As a preliminary to his discussion of enslaved Africans Du Tertre makes a series of exculpatory statements to the effect that, since he is not a jurist, he cannot pretend to assess the legitimacy of slavery. In spite of this caveat he does, nonetheless, undertake to refute the accusation, levied by people whom he characterizes as "more pious than learned," that Christians were being bought and sold in a land governed by the laws of France. With a nod to the "freedom law"—the principle that slavery had been eradicated from France at the time of the abolition of feudal serfdom—he characterizes France as the nation that led the world in its abhorrence of servitude (2:483).[19] But having made this claim, Du Tertre proceeds over the next fifty pages to show the opposite: that is, that slaves, including Christians, were regularly bought and sold in territories under French rule. This pattern of denial immediately followed by unacknowledged affirmation signals both the strength of the French doxa that, to quote the title of Sue Peabody's book on this subject, "there are no slaves in France," and the mythifying power of this doctrine to obscure French involvement in slavery.[20] Du Tertre can in fact be seen as the first in a long line of French writers whose characterization of France as the land of freedom (or, in another variant, of human rights) served to mask the nation's history of colonial slavery.

If Du Tertre's unconvincing attempts to dissociate slavery from French national culture suggest at least a degree of discomfort with the practice, the passage that immediately follows illustrates the main reason why he, like other French observers, found it possible to overcome these qualms. In a pragmatic aside Du Tertre notes that the colonies' "poor slaves" were their most valuable economic assets. "All the wealth of the country comes from their work" (2:483–84), he explains. Economics, it seems, trumped Du Tertre's legal and moral scruples regarding the sale and exploitation of Christians and potential converts.

In two articles on the writing of early colonial missionaries, Sue Peabody argues that representations of enslaved Africans evolved significantly between the very first narratives of this kind—the handful of works published between 1640 and 1659, including Du Tertre's first colonial history—and texts of the 1660s–80s, a period defined by the transition from tobacco to sugar and by a rapid rise in the use of slave labor.[21] She contends that missionaries wrote more,

---

19. Sue Peabody suggests that one difference between the 1654 and 1667 versions of *Histoire générale* is that whereas a passage in the first version appears to question the legitimacy of slavery, in the later work Du Tertre simply states that he is not qualified to raise the question, and instead contents himself with defending the settlers against accusations of mistreatment. This reading stems from a mistranslation in the English translation that Peabody consults. As noted above, the legitimacy of colonial slavery remains at least nominally at issue in the second edition. I would add that the passage of the first edition in which Peabody finds evidence for a genuine interrogation of the legitimacy of slavery (*Histoire générale des îles de St. Christophe*, 473) is just as ambivalent as the passage of the later edition. See Peabody, "'Nation Born to Slavery,'" 115, 118.

20. Peabody, *"There Are No Slaves in France."* I am grateful to Toby Wikström for helping clarify this point.

21. Peabody, "'Nation Born to Slavery,'" and "'Dangerous Zeal.'" The group of "earlier" texts discussed in these articles are, in addition to Du Tertre's first history: Jacques Bouton,

and wrote in more positive terms, about enslaved Africans as the latter became more numerous and better established in the French colonies. Whereas the works of the earlier group of writers (including writings by Jacques Bouton, Pierre Pelleprat, and André Chevillard, and the 1654 *General History*) painted enslaved Africans in a few broad brushstrokes, describing in derogatory terms their low intelligence and unpleasant odor, subsequent works, including a letter to a patron written by a Jesuit named Jean Mongin and the later version of *General History*, offered more-nuanced portraits, evoking positive traits such as fidelity, love of children, and a capacity for religious fervor that was sorely lacking among the Caribs. Peabody sees the main reasons for this change of attitude as being the birth of Creole children able to communicate in French and the fact that missionaries could no longer focus their evangelizing mission on the Caribs.

Peabody's arguments about early colonial writing grow out of an attempt to offer an alternative to the long-running debate over whether racial prejudices provided the foundation for Atlantic slavery or slavery gave rise to the conditions in which race became an all-determining category, a debate that has been a fixture of the historiography of slavery.[22] She argues, I think convincingly, that ideas of racial difference are best understood to be embedded in the social and economic relations within which they occur, and not as transhistorical categories with fixed meanings and uniform social implications. But while I agree with Peabody's general arguments with regard to the historical inscription of race, I am less persuaded by her more specific claims about the portrayal of Africans in early colonial narrative. It is, first of all, rather difficult to establish patterns when the number of texts under consideration is so small. I wonder, in fact, whether the reason that Peabody examines only two post-1660 works—*General History* and the letter sent by Mongin—is that missionary writing about the Antilles dropped off sharply after 1720, a decline that in itself seems to belie the claim that as missionaries became more familiar with enslaved Africans they represented them more often.[23] But there

---

Relation de l'establissement de françois depuis l'an 1635 en l'isle de Martinique, l'une des Antilles de l'Amérique (1640); Pierre Pelleprat, *Relations des missions des pères de la compagnie de Jésus dans les isles et dans la terre ferme de l'Amérique méridionale* (1655); and André Chevillard, *Les desseins de son eminence de Richelieu pour l'Amérique ce qui s'est passé de plus remarquable depuis l'établissement des colonies* (1659). The "later" works are Jean Mongin, "Lettre à une personne de condition du Languedoc écrite de l'Île de Saint-Christophe au mois de mai, 1682," reprinted in *Bulletin de la société d'histoire de la Guadeloupe*, nos. 60–62 (1984), 73–125, and *General History*.

22. As Peabody notes, helpful summaries of these debates are offered in Fredrickson, *Racism*, and Davis, "Constructing Race."

23. Whereas Jesuits based in New France continued to publish accounts of their missions through outlets such as the *Journal de Trévoux* and the *Lettres édifiantes et curieuses,* the only significant missionary narratives relating to the Antilles produced after 1700 were the two editions of Labat's *New Voyage* (1722, 1742), both of which appeared several decades after the author's mission to the Antilles in 1693–1706, and *Histoire de l'Isle espagnole ou de Saint-Domingue* (History of Hispaniola or Saint-Domingue) (1730–31) by the Jesuit Pierre-Francois-Xavier de Charlevoix.

are other interpretative issues to be considered here as well. Peabody notes that whereas the 1654 *General History* devotes only eight pages to the condition and characteristics of enslaved Africans, this reflection is expanded into a fifty-page "treatise" in the 1667 text.[24] While this is accurate, it should be noted that the work as a whole grew from a single volume to four volumes, and that the closing treatise of volume 2 remains the only section of the text in which slaves and slavery are discussed. As we have seen, slaves are scarcely mentioned in the narrative of the colonies' founding and development. It is also necessary to consider the different terms in which slaves and Caribs are described. Peabody observes that the treatise devoted to slaves includes "detailed chapters on marriage, childrearing, food, housing, dress, work, entertainment, and death among black slaves that very much parallel earlier ethnographies of Amerindians or Africans in their native lands."[25] While this is again true, there are important differences to be made between Du Tertre's discussion of slaves and his description of Caribs. Specifically, I want to suggest that whereas he approaches Carib beliefs, customs, and behavior as being determined by culture and natural environment (and, at the risk of rehearsing a well-worn critique of anthropological representation, as being unaffected by historical change), his writing on slaves grapples with the challenge of describing practices and modes of behavior that are strongly determined by historical contingencies.

This distinction is an important factor in helping us understand the marginal position of transplanted Africans in early colonial histories. Like other European observers, missionaries were accustomed to describing cultural differences that were relatively stable and strongly linked to geography. By contrast, they had little experience in accounting for the processes of hybridization and social adaptation that we have come to associate with diasporic formations. Du Tertre and his contemporaries faced the relatively new task of describing the character traits and behavior, not of a homogeneous "people," but rather of a diverse group of individuals who had been removed from their birth lands, and whose daily lives were organized around rules imposed by Europeans. Section headings such as "On the Way in which Slaves are Married" and "On the Way in which Slaves are Dressed" testify to the fact that major areas of slaves' social experience were governed, not by the norms of a "native" culture, but rather by the structure and routines of colonial society.

Perhaps inevitably, Du Tertre at times lost sight of this historicity and falls back on sweeping generalizations about slaves' character and behavior. In one passage, for example, he writes that "the moods of most of these slaves are

---

Charlevoix, who is better known for his *Histoire de la Nouvelle France* (History of New France) (1744), spent little time in Saint-Domingue. His history of the colony is actually a revised and corrected edition of a manuscript by an earlier Jesuit missionary, Jean-Baptiste Le Pers, who spent over two decades in Saint-Domingue in the early eighteenth century.

24. Peabody, "'Nation Born to Slavery,'" 116.

25. Ibid., 118.

like those strange colors that sometimes appear green, sometimes gold." He goes on to qualify this assertion with the observation that these mood swings seemed to have something to do with the treatment meted out by masters (2:496), yet having made this obvious point, he quickly falls back into anthropological generalizations about slaves' arrogance, gaiety, love of music and song, and propensity for larceny. On this last point he pauses again, wondering whether slaves stole because of the deprivations they suffered or because stealing was a quintessential trait of African culture. Citing his own discussions with slaves as evidence, he opts, self-reassuringly, for the second interpretation (2:297). In these various back-and-forths we see Du Tertre wavering between ethnographic and historical representation, struggling to find an adequate conceptual framework within which to anchor thinking about identity and difference in the context of a rapidly creolizing colonial society.

Memorializing Natives/Naturalizing Slaves: Labat's *New Voyage*

The tension between ethnographic and historical or sociological interpretation is also a central feature of the most widely read missionary account of the early French Antilles: Jean-Baptiste Labat's *Nouveau voyage aux isles d'Amérique* (New Voyage to the Islands of America), published in 1722 and reissued posthumously in an expanded edition in 1742 (the edition that I consider here).[26] Labat, who like Du Tertre was a Dominican, arrived in the Caribbean in 1693 at the height of the sugar boom. He spent over a decade in Martinique and Guadeloupe, rising to the rank of *vice-préfet apostolique*. An amateur engineer and tireless entrepreneur, Labat's name is still associated in the Antilles with the history of sugar and rum. As Lafcadio Hearn and, more recently, Doris Garraway have noted, Labat is also remembered by black Antilleans as a cruel and malevolent spirit.[27] In the preface to his narrative Labat remarks that although colleagues and acquaintances had urged him to publish an informational treatise on colonial affairs, he had preferred to lay before his readers a memoir based on personal experience (1:xxxi). In reality, *New Voyage* is a hybrid text in which personal reminiscences offered in a garrulous and engaging style are juxtaposed with long descriptive passages, some of a highly technical nature. Given his entrepreneurial experience, Labat unsurprisingly devotes many pages to the production of the leading tropical commodities. Below I consider Labat's references to the enslaved workers who manned this agro-industrial complex in conjunction with his discussion of the Caribs. I point to patterns of emphasis and omission that are in many ways similar to those

26. Labat, *Nouveau voyage aux isles de l'Amérique* (1722, 1742).
27. Misbehaving children are still sometimes cautioned that Père Labat will get them. See Hearn, *Two Years in the French West Indies*, 142–83; Garraway, *Libertine Colony*, 92.

encountered in Du Tertre, though they also reflect the changing demographic circumstances of the period.

Scholarly discussions of *New Voyage* have generally focused on Labat's ethnographic writing on the Caribs. What these commentaries often seem to miss, however, is the fact that Labat arrived in Martinique almost forty years after the Caribs were expelled. Given this chronology Labat's writing on the island's precolonial population necessarily takes a retrospective form. This commemorative approach to Carib culture is announced early in the narrative. In his account of his first journey across Martinique from the port of St. Pierre to the Dominican mission at Fonds St. Jacques (situated on the island's Atlantic coast), Labat recalls that he and his guides—two black slaves employed by the mission—had come upon a cross erected by Father Raymond Breton in 1658. Labat explains that the monument commemorated a skirmish between settlers and Caribs in the aftermath of which the northern end of the island, known as Capesterre, had been ceded to the Dominicans. The cross, in other words, commemorated a landgrab in which the Caribs had been forced out and the Dominicans had moved in. This story of dispossession may seem somewhat incongruous given Raymond Breton's reputation as the man who spent over a decade trying to bring the Caribs to God. But perhaps the cross can be seen to do double duty in Labat's narrative, standing both as a monument and as a symbol. In the first guise it marks the separation between the island's past, embodied by the Caribs, and its present, represented by Labat and his two black guides. As a symbol, on the other hand, it marks the abiding association of the island with the Caribs, as well as the iconic pairing of missionary and Carib. In the wider representational economy of *New Voyage,* this bifurcation plays out in the fact that although the pragmatic Labat makes it clear that he views the conversion of the Caribs as an idea belonging to the past (in one passage he states bluntly that the Jesuit mission on St. Vincent was a complete waste of money [2:287], while in another he claims that the Caribs were simply not the kind of people inclined to embrace a new faith [2:89]), he nonetheless remains deeply curious about the Caribs and loses no opportunity to write about them.

Labat observes that he had been in the Antilles for about ten months before he had the opportunity to see any "savages" (2:74). His account of this first encounter runs for several pages, with Labat offering a detailed description of the Caribs' physical appearance, clothing, and ornaments, as well as an overview of their beliefs and customs. It rehashes, and was no doubt informed by, the earlier commentaries of Du Tertre and Breton, whom Labat acknowledges in his preface as his chief precursors (1:v). Labat, however, departs from his predecessors' approach to the subject in at least one important respect. Whereas Du Tertre represents objects such as hammocks, pirogues, and reed baskets as essential implements of the Carib way of life, Labat views them as cultural artifacts: emblematic objects that he was eager to acquire for his personal use, and that he planned to carry back to France to show off to his friends. Labat approaches Carib material culture, in other words, as a source of potential souvenirs. The word "souvenir," of course, literally means a memory. Here I use it to connote not only Labat's desire to preserve the memory of his travels through the possession of a material token but also, in a stronger sense, his perception of Carib culture as an object for memorialization.

This commemorative perspective on Carib culture surfaces at several points in the narrative. Perhaps the most striking case is a passage in which Labat recounts a visit that he made to Dominica, one of the two islands designated as a Carib sanctuary by the treaty of 1658 (6:95–154). This visit gave Labat an opportunity to take a longer look at Amerindian mores and customs and to lay before his readers a more detailed account. What stands out about this discussion, however, is that although the Caribs remained the dominant cultural group on Dominica, Labat speaks of them as though they were relics of the past, infusing his account of their way of life with a kind of proleptic nostalgia.

The most memorable moment of Labat's stay on Dominica seems to have been a visit to the *carbet*, or meeting house, presided over by Mme Ouvernard, a formidable Carib matriarch whom Labat estimates to be over a hundred years old (6:95–97). He relates that she had once been the mistress of the English governor of St. Kitts, and that she had borne this Englishman many children, including a famous Carib chief named Ouvernard who is mentioned by Du Tertre. In his reconstruction of their conversation, Labat recalls that Mme Ouvernard asked him when Father Breton, who had died some thirty years earlier, was likely to return. He remembers answering that his venerable colleague would undoubtedly return soon, noting in an aside that it would have been futile to tell her the truth since Caribs only believe what they see with their own eyes. This comment obviously reflects Labat's low opinion of the Caribs' conceptual abilities. But I think that it also conveys something further, that is to say, his impression that the Caribs of Dominica were living in the past, having been overtaken by the forces of history. The same perspective resurfaces when Labat recounts his leave-taking from Mme Ouvernard. Noting once again that trying to convert the Caribs was a fool's errand, he remarks that "to turn them into resolute Christians one would have to remove them from their country for ever" (6:168–69). Here it is Labat who seems to lose sight of history, forgetting that the Caribs, having been deemed inassimilable, had already been expelled from the greater portion of their birth lands.

Slavery and the enslaved inevitably figure more prominently in Labat's description of the Antilles at the height of the sugar boom than they do in Du Tertre's account of the colonies in their formative years. But the way in which Labat writes about slavery is in many ways consistent with the manner in which his predecessor broached the subject. That is to say, although Labat refers to slaves at many points in *New Voyage,* they are almost always mentioned in an oblique and extemporary fashion, as fixtures of the colonial economy rather than as objects of interest in their own right. This objectification can be observed throughout the text, but it is most acute in sections that describe the production of tropical commodities: passages in which Labat is keen to describe the workings of colonial agriculture, yet apparently reluctant to make slavery the focal point of his discussion.

The narrative portion of *New Voyage* is punctuated by several detailed accounts of the production of tropical commodities, including indigo, cotton, and sugar. These long and rather technical descriptions tend to position the reader as a potential colonial entrepreneur, explaining how "one" or "you" might go about producing the commodity in question. Like the author of a how-to book, Labat offers detailed advice on how to select a loyal foreman (4:173–74), how to prevent slaves employed in positions of responsibility from cheating you (3:406), and how to care for and manage other slaves (4:198–205). In these passages the role of the planter or estate manager is almost always explained in the active voice, and the pronoun "one" is used to foster identification between Labat, his readers, and colonial entrepreneurs. The labor of enslaved workers, by contrast, is generally described in the passive voice, and slaves are almost always designated in the plural as "they" or "them." In this social grammar, agency and dynamism are ascribed to colonists, while slaves are depicted as moving parts in the colonial machine.

This reification of slave labor is reinforced by the illustrations that accompany the text. In these drawings slaves are depicted alongside buildings, tools, and machinery as sketchy, undifferentiated figures, while in the legends that accompanying the illustrations, slaves are listed among the components of industrial matériel (1:269) (see figure 16). These textual and graphical representations, which were important sources for the articles and plates devoted to tropical agriculture in Diderot and d'Alembert's *Encyclopedia,* reflect not only the dehumanization of the enslaved worker but also a corresponding tendency to naturalize slavery as a facet of colonial existence. In this economy of representation slaves certainly figure, yet they rarely become an object of interpretation.

There are, however, a few exceptions to this rule: passages in which Labat surveys the colonies' enslaved workforce through an anthropological rather than an entrepreneurial lens. The most significant of these is a chapter titled "On the black slaves whom we employ in the islands; on trade with their countries," (volume 4, chapter 9) in which Labat discusses the different African nations represented among the colony's enslaved population, the various languages spoken by slaves, and a few other cultural characteristics (4:444). It is certainly not incidental that in this chapter, one of the few places in *New Voyage* where slaves are envisaged as people rather than as machinery, they are also approached as Africans. When considered in light of their African origins, slaves, like Caribs, are perceived as members of cultural groups that have their own languages and customs. By contrast, when they are considered

Figure 16. Indigoterie. Jean-Baptiste Labat, *Nouveau voyage aux isles de l'Amérique,* 1742. Reproduced with permission of The Huntington Library, San Marino, California.

within a purely colonial framework, they are reduced to the functionality of the instrument of production.

The grounds of this distinction are clarified in a passage in which Labat comments on a claim made by another missionary, Father Braguez, to the effect that Africans are resistant to conversion (4:443). Qualifying his colleague's claim, Labat contends that Africans convert readily when removed from their native lands but betray the promises of their baptism as soon as they are given the opportunity to return to Africa, a claim that broadly parallels his argument that the Caribs could be converted if they were first removed from their ancestral lands (6:168–69). What I want to draw from this passage is that when Labat approaches slaves as Africans, he recognizes their agency and capacity to resist the overtures of colonial ideology. When he considers them as slaves he does not.

The chapter touching on the slave trade with Africa is one of only two moments in the text in which the legitimacy of slavery is called into question. In the course of his discussion of the slave trade, Labat raises the question whether this commerce in human beings had ever been legally sanctioned. By way of an answer he alludes to the purported decision by Louis XIII to permit slavery in the French colonies in the interests of bringing Africans to God (4:420).[28] He also invokes the arguments of jurists such as Hugo Grotius, who had categorized individuals sold into slavery as criminals and prisoners of war. Like later commentators, including Montesquieu and Rousseau, Labat treats Grotius's representation of the reasons for which people were enslaved with skepticism. He contends that many slaves had simply been kidnapped by unscrupulous traders (4:425). But instead of drawing the conclusion that the Atlantic slave trade could *not* be justified, Labat contents himself with citing legal precedent. He notes that the Sorbonne had previously examined as a "question of conscience" whether it was permissible to abduct people from their homes if such abductions were an established custom of the country in question (4:427–29).[29] Though he reports that the court decided that abduction was *not* legally justified, he adds that this decision was not "received" in the islands, where people felt that if judges owned plantations they would think differently. Since Labat does not challenge this perspective, it seems fair to assume that he was in agreement that practical considerations outweighed the niceties of legal theory. In the end, what his reference to an official "debate" effectively achieves is the rapid foreclosure of the legal and moral questions that he had previously affected to raise.

Earlier we saw Du Tertre struggling with the question of whether slaves' behavior was determined by the particularities of their social condition or by factors linked to culture and race. Unsurprisingly, these kinds of questions also

---

28. As Christopher Miller notes, Labat's reference to Louis XIII's decision to allow slavery in the French Antillean colonies (which appears in both 1722 and 1742 texts) was cited by many subsequent writers, including Montesquieu, though there does not seem to be a historical basis for the claim beyond Labat's assertion. If this anecdote was repeated by later commentators, it was presumably, as Miller suggests, because it conveyed the impression that slavery had a precise, legally sanctioned starting point. *French Atlantic Triangle*, 18–19.

29. The Sorbonne case presented by Adrien Auguste De Lamet de Bussy and Germain Fromageau is presented in "Règles sur le commerce des esclaves en général, et des nègres en particulier," *Dictionnaire des cas de conscience* (Paris: J. B. Coignard, 1733). It is mentioned briefly in Jameson, *Montesquieu et l'esclavage*, 131–34; Davis, *Problem of Slavery*, 197; and Noël, *Être noir en France*, 38–9, but has not otherwise been the object of much discussion. There is in fact a striking contrast to be drawn between this low-profile debate on the enslavement of Africans and the much better known "Valladolid Controversies," in which the Dominican Bartolomé de las Casas squared off against the philosopher Juan Ginés de Sepúlveda over the enslavement of Amerindians.

surface in the more anthropologically slanted passages of Labat's narrative. This is true, for example, of an uncharacteristically poignant passage in which (Labat discusses the fate of a young African boy who had been presented to him as a "gift,")but who had fallen into a deep depression and begun eating dirt (2:11–12). Labat notes first that the Mina people (from the "Slave Coast" or today's Togo) were particularly subject to melancholy and would often cut their own throats over a mere trifle. Having stated this purported anthropological "fact," however, he goes on to say that slaves often killed themselves to spite their masters, or because their "foolish imagination" led them to believe that after their death they would be able to travel back to their birth land (a belief also mentioned by Du Tertre [*General History,* 2:516]). Labat explains that although the young boy had been baptized and had told him that he loved him, he nonetheless wanted to die so that he could return home to his father. In the end Labat admits sadly that the boy did die, then abruptly launches into a discussion of the various nasty means used to prevent slave suicide in the British colonies (2:15–16). Though this shift from sympathy to rationalization is certainly not to Labat's credit, I am nonetheless inclined to read it, not as a sign of utter moral indifference, but rather as an indication that Labat was unable fully to confront the emotional and ethical implications of viewing a black slave as a fellow human being. I would argue, in other words, that sensing the underlying contradiction, Labat reverts to a perspective on which human individuality is subordinated to the logic of colonial production.

In a study of medical discourses relating to sexuality and colonization, Elsa Dorlin observes that in medical treatises of the mid-eighteenth century, slaves, like women, were often portrayed as physiologically deficient or abnormal. Both slaves and women were claimed to be subject to specific diseases, including most notably pica, a disorder characterized by depression and a propensity for eating dirt, coal, and other nonnutritive substances.[30] Dorlin suggests that in the case of slaves pathologization provided a counterpoint to the claim that only Africans possessed the physical strength and endurance necessary to labor in the tropics. Since Africans were being ascribed unusual strength, they also had to be shown to be vulnerable, in other words. I want to suggest an additional interpretation, which is that pathologization drew attention away from the conditions in which slaves lived and worked and directed it toward supposed biological or cultural traits, a pattern illustrated in Labat's vacillating attempt to portray slave suicide as a cultural phenomenon.

Like many aspects of Labat's writing on colonial society, his observations about the Mina and melancholy later came to be recycled elsewhere. His conclusions are echoed, for example, in the *Encyclopedia* article "Negroes Considered as Slaves in the Colonies of America." At the end of the eighteenth century, when

---

30. Dorlin, *La matrice de la race,* 246–50.

an abolitionist movement was beginning to take shape, the rehashing of Labat began to take a new turn. In Raynal's *History of the Two Indies,* Labat's remarks about the Mina are reprised, but suicide by slaves is portrayed not as a cultural phenomenon but as a response to the harsh conditions of the colonial regime.[31]

The representation of enslaved Africans comes together with Labat's commemorative approach to Carib culture in the frontispiece engraving to *New Voyage* (see figure 17). A tondo portrait of Labat appears against the backdrop of a landscape in which signs of civilization are juxtaposed with emblems of tropical nature. The portrait is held aloft by a kneeling figure who appears, at first glance, to be a young man of African origin. He closely resembles the anonymous workers portrayed in the text's illustrations of tropical agriculture, except that he is arrayed in a feathered skirt and headdress. As Doris Garraway observes, "The identity of this personage is rendered ambiguous due to his feathered garment and black skin" (132). For Garraway, the juxtaposition of an indigenous/black figure and an orderly colonial landscape stands as a visual representation of the "indigenization" that Labat undergoes: the entrepreneur-priest's self-adaptation to local conditions in the interests of controlling them (132–34). This interpretation is convincing insofar as Labat is concerned, but I think that there is more to be said about the ambiguous black figure that holds his portrait aloft. I want to suggest that this figure, like Labat, is subtly indigenized. Though he at first appears to be of African descent, he is rendered ambiguously African/Amerindian by virtue of his attire. Perhaps it could be said that this racial ambiguity inscribes the nostalgic tendency of colonial narratives, including *New Voyage,* to highlight the encounter with the Caribs even after the Caribs had been expelled from the colonies, while underrepresenting the role of enslaved Africans. Viewed in this light, the Amerindian accoutrements worn by the kneeling figure can be interpreted as symptoms of a wider tendency to cloak the realities of slavery in a veneer of residual exoticism.

Colonial Representation in Eighteenth-Century Fiction

In the remainder of this chapter I turn from the empirical genre of travel writing to the representation of colonial environments in fictional genres. Works of fiction, of course, entertain a different relation to history than travel writing and missionary narratives. Whereas in these empirical genres the "setting" of a narrative is largely determined by the experiences of the writer, in fiction it is the result of a process of selection. By extension, whereas in the case of empirical genres it is legitimate to point to significant elements of an author's experience that have been glossed over or repressed, in fiction the question of

---

31. Raynal, *History of the Two Indies* (1780 edition), 7:164.

Figure 17. Portrait of Jean-Baptiste Labat. *Nouveau voyage aux isles de l'Amérique,* 1742. Frontispiece, volume 1. Reproduced with permission of The Huntington Library, San Marino, California.

"omission" or displacement is complicated by the ubiquity of figures such as metaphor and allegory. Nonetheless, without overlooking these representational specificities, I think it can be argued that eighteenth-century fictions that depict the colonial Americas manifest patterns of omission and substitution similar to those seen in travel writing, a genre from which they frequently drew inspiration. Below I discuss the economy of colonial representation in two eighteenth-century fictions. The first, which is not one text but many, is the "Inkle and Yarico" saga: a transnational corpus of stories that portray the love affair between a European sailor and a woman variously portrayed as an Amerindian and/or an African. The second is *Cleveland,* a multivolume novel by Abbé Prévost. This selection of texts may perhaps appear somewhat arbitrary. It is in fact strongly determined by the "literary record," that is, by the fact that before the 1770s only a handful of French fictions adopted the colonial Americas as their geographic setting.

Racial Indeterminacy in *Inkle and Yarico*

The Inkle and Yarico corpus is composed of roughly forty-five texts written between 1604 and 1830 by authors from Britain, France, Switzerland, and Germany in genres including travelogues, philosophical commentaries, plays, ballets, and verse elegies.[32] Some were written by well-known or soon-to-be well-known writers, such as Richard Steele, Sébastien Chamfort, and Abbé Raynal. Others were the work of more-obscure figures, including several anonymous contributors to popular reviews. David Brion Davis has characterized Inkle and Yarico as a "great folk epic," and indeed the corpus appears more like a branched medieval legend than the product of an age defined by stricter notions of literary property.[33] Because of its long historical span and broad, indeed transnational author- and readership, Inkle and Yarico constitutes an important point of reference in thinking about the cultural representation of the colonization of the New World.

The outline of the Inkle and Yarico story is prefigured in a passage that appears in the French explorer Jean Mocquet's *Voyages to Africa, Asia, and the West and East Indies* (1617). Written before the topoi of contact between Europeans and Amerindians had fully crystallized, the *Voyages* depict the latter with a fluctuating mix of curiosity, admiration, and fear. One episode of Mocquet's narrative, however, stands out for its self-conscious literariness, and for the overlay of references to classical literature. Perhaps not incidentally, this story is related by a secondary narrator, a figure described as an "English

---

32. On the Inkle and Yarico corpus, see Price, *Inkle and Yarico Album.* On English versions, see Felsenstein, *English Trader.* There has been at least one postcolonial reworking of the story, the Guyanese-British novelist Beryl Gilroy's *Inkle and Yarico.*

33. Davis, *Problem of Slavery,* 10–11.

pilot." In his episode the pilot recounts how, having been shipwrecked during an earlier voyage, he was saved by an Amerindian woman. He lived with this woman for several years in the forest, and she gave birth to a child. One day, however, he flagged down an English vessel, and after going aboard he began to feel ashamed of his naked Indian lover and decided to abandon her. Realizing that she had been betrayed, the woman stood weeping on the shore until, in a final fit of despair, she tore their child in two, casting one half into the sea, and taking the other with her. The ship's crew, who had watched this scene in bewilderment, asked the pilot why he had abandoned the woman. He retorted in his own defense that she was "only a savage."[34]

A story in many ways similar to Mocquet's appeared a half century later in Richard Ligon's *A True and Exact History of the Island of Barbados* (1657).[35] It is unclear whether Ligon, who had for a short while been a planter in Barbados, was acquainted with the passage in Mocquet's *Voyage*. As Peter Hulme has observed, the issue of transmission is in any case less significant than the formation of narrative topoi signaled by the similarities between these two texts.[36] In his telling of the story, Ligon explains that although during his career as a planter he did not own many "Indian" slaves, he, like other settlers, occasionally bought women captured from the mainland or from neighboring islands because they were "better used than the negroes in certain things" (54). This observation leads him to recall an incident in which an Amerindian slave who was pregnant by a "Christian" took herself into the woods, delivered her child, and returned shortly afterwards with a bouncing baby boy. In recounting this story Ligon emphasizes not only the woman's self-reliance but also her agreeable physical appearance. He emphasizes in particular her "bright bay" color, perhaps in order to differentiate her from his African slaves, whom he seems to have found not only less able but also less attractive. Later in the narrative, Ligon clarifies the circumstances behind the birthing episode. It appears that the woman and her lover had escaped together to Barbados, but having arrived in the colony the European had changed his mind and sold the woman at auction, presumably to Ligon himself. Ligon concludes, philosophically, "So poor Yarico for her love, lost her liberty." He does not, however, seem to be inspired to pass any kind of broader judgment, either on slavery as an institution or on his own position as the owner of the unfortunate "Yarico" (54–55).

Another half century later the story of Yarico entered the literary mainstream. It was reprised in a periodical widely read in both Britain and France: Joseph Addison and Richard Steele's *Spectator*. In one issue of this influential journal of social and political commentary, Steele describes a visit to a literary salon

---

34. Mocquet, *Voyages*, 148–50. The episode appears in a section dated 1604 in which Mocquet recounts his travels to the lands of the "Amazones, Caripous et Caribes."

35. Ligon, *True and Exact History*.

36. Hulme, *Colonial Encounters*, 256–58.

where the guests were discussing the different degrees of fidelity demonstrated by men and women.[37] Defending the honor of the female sex, the hostess, a lady named Arietta, retells Ligon's tale. Though it is not clear how Steele knew Ligon's story, or why he chose to rework it in this context, the fact that he too owned property in Barbados may have had some bearing. In Steele's retelling, Ligon's cursory narrative is transformed from a brief sentimental episode into a full-blown literary allegory for relations between the sexes, and between people of different cultures. In this embellished version, the English protagonist, named for the first time as Thomas "Inkle," is escaping from a party of warlike Amerindians when he comes upon an Indian maid. The two instantly fall in love and for a time live together in the wilderness. After a few years, however, they are rescued by a passing ship and taken to Barbados. Regretting the time and profit lost in this romantic idyll, Inkle pragmatically decides to sell his lover into slavery. When she informs him that she is expecting their child, he churlishly responds by raising the asking price (1:37).

Critical commentaries on the Inkle and Yarico story have generally emphasized the fact that, unlike other well-known European/Amerindian pairings—Prospero and Caliban, Crusoe and Friday—the pairing of Inkle and Yarico represents the relationship between colonizer and colonized as a sentimental bond, and as a result subtly naturalizes it. Though the European is always shown to betray the love of the woman who has saved his life, the representation of his bad faith is counterbalanced by the suggestion that the woman—who symbolizes the land and its natural resources—bestows herself freely. In a study of colonial narratives by German writers, Susanne Zantop develops this argument, proposing that Inkle's abandonment of Yarico, which is followed in some versions of the story by the Englishman's return to Europe, bespeaks criticism, not of Inkle's exploitation of his lover, but rather of his failure to turn their short-lived romance into a durable bond.[38] The dereliction to which the corpus gestures, in other words, is not the act of conquest but the failure of European nations to implement a sustained colonial project.

What Zantop's reading brings into focus is that critical commentaries have generally approached Inkle and Yarico as an allegory of colonization, while making little of the fact that it also concerns the practice of slavery. In most versions of the story, though, Inkle doesn't merely leave Yarico, he also sells her into slavery, usually in a well-established plantation colony such as Barbados. Given this largely neglected aspect of the narrative, I suggest that while the Inkle and Yarico stories invite us to approach colonial experience as an encounter between Europe and America, colonizer and colonized, their subtext of colonial slavery gestures to patterns of domination and exploitation that are less subject to recuperation in the mode of romantic naturalization.

37. Addison and Steele, *Spectator* 1:34–37.
38. Zantop, *Colonial Fantasies*, 122–26.

In the discussion that follows I shift the emphasis away from the figure of colonial encounter toward the stories' subtext of slavery. Specifically, I consider how the Inkle and Yarico texts represent Amerindian and African populations. What I principally argue is that the shadow of slavery comes to the fore in the stories' negotiation of the question of race: that is, in their engagement with the interpretative grid that tied enslavement to the matrix of phenotype and geographic/cultural origin.

To begin to develop this reading I would like to return to Steele's version of the story. Looking more closely at this narrative we find that the relationship between the Amerindian woman and the European man is portrayed as the attraction of two contrasting physical types. "If the *European* was highly charmed with the limbs, features and wild graces of the naked *American*," Steele writes, "the *American* was no less taken with the dress, complexion and shape of an European, covered from head to foot." He adds later that Yarico "would sometimes play with his [Inkle's] hair, and delight in the opposition of its color to that of her fingers" (1:36). The words *European* and *American* are italicized throughout the story, underscoring the representative status of the two young lovers.

In later versions of the story the contrasting physical and cultural features of the two protagonists are similarly emphasized. A 1726 verse version, for instance, recounts that Inkle "viewed her [Yarico's] naked beauties with surprise/Her well-proportioned limbs and sprightly eyes,"[39] while in an accompanying verse epistle, Yarico reports to Inkle that she had been "Charmed with thy face, like polished ivory fair/Thy beauteous features and enticing hair."[40] It is obviously not incidental that in these references to physical features, Inkle is attracted to Yarico's body, while Yarico admires the European's face, a distribution of desire that aligns with a wider set of divisions between mind and body, intellect and labor. But what is perhaps even more interesting about the stories' references to physical differences is that, despite the details that are supplied, the geographic and cultural origins of the heroine become increasingly difficult to decipher. In the 1726 verse version that I have just cited, for example, the heroine is introduced as a "negro virgin" but later represented as a "faithful Indian maid."

Circling back to the question of the relationship between literary representation and colonial history that I touched on earlier, what one would perhaps expect to observe in this context is a pattern whereby the depiction of European-Amerindian encounters that is central to early colonial literature transitioned, over time, to a focus on relations between Europeans and Africans. Inkle and Yarico stories are of course works of fiction, and as such not

---

39. Seymour, "Story of Inkle and Yarico, Taken out of the Eleventh *Spectator*," in *New Miscellany*. See also Felsenstein, *English Trader*, 89–94.

40. Seymour, "An Epistle from Yarico to Inkle, after he had sold her for a slave," in *New Miscellany*, 38–41. See Felsenstein, *English Trader*, 95–98.

directly governed by the imperatives of historical referentiality. Nonetheless, given their strong intertextuality with travel literature and the fact that they undertake to comment on colonial experience, I think it is legitimate to consider how they reflect the demographic shifts occurring in the Americas between the sixteenth and eighteenth centuries. Earlier we saw that African or Africanized figures began to appear in Inkle and Yarico stories in the 1720s. What happened after this point, however, is somewhat surprising. When we consider Inkle and Yarico stories of the mid- and late eighteenth century, we find that in most cases the heroine either remained Amerindian or else became indeterminately or interchangeably African and Amerindian. Over the long term, other colonial vectors, notably the Orient, emerged, taking the story in new directions.

I tend to think that it is symptomatic that among the French versions of the story there are no overtly African Yaricos, and that geographic and cultural displacements are particularly thick on the ground. The brief retelling of the story that appears in Abbé Raynal's *History of the Two Indies,* for example, essentially returns to Ligon's original version and renders Yarico as an Amerindian maid (7:229). The frontispiece illustration that accompanies this narrative could be seen to tell a different story. It shows a dark-skinned woman in a half-skirt or loincloth and shackles. In the absence of explicit markers of Amerindian origins, perhaps the most obvious reading of this figure would be that she is an enslaved woman of African origin (figure 18).[41] Another case in point is Sébastien Chamfort's comedy *La jeune Indienne* (The Young Indian) (1764), in which an Amerindian heroine called Betti is transported from the coastal island of her birth to the southern city of Charleston, where, after various plot twists, she is happily married to her English lover, Belton.[42] Though the second half of the story is set in the Carolinas, a colony where slavery was prevalent, and although the protagonists are married as a result of the good offices of a Quaker, a member of a religious sect that by the 1760s had become known for its advocacy of abolition, Chamfort makes no reference whatsoever to the practice of slavery. In another French retelling that I discuss in chapter 1—Claude Dorat's suite of heroic poems, *Letter to Zeila, Valcour's Reply,* and *Letters from Valcour to His Father*—a heroine born to the primitive forests of Florida is transported to the Orient, where she becomes a harem slave. Orientalization is also a feature of a late-eighteenth-century version, Lucien Bonaparte's novel *The Indian Tribe,* in which the virtuous heroine, now called "Stellina," is sold to Portuguese merchants in Ceylon.[43]

When critics have commented on the uncertainty surrounding Yarico's "race" or cultural origins, they have for the most part attributed it either to

---

41. Different versions of this illustration appear in the various editions, but in each case the female figure is ambiguously African/Amerindian.

42. Chamfort, *Oeuvres,* 2:124–72.

43. Bonaparte, *La tribu indienne.*

Figure 18. "An Englishman Sells His Mistress in Barbados." Raynal, *Histoire politique et philosophique des établissements et du commerce des Européens dans les deux Indes,* 1780. Frontispiece, volume 3. Courtesy of the Rare Book and Manuscript Library, Columbia University.

confusion on the part of metropolitan authors or to the progressive blurring of racial boundaries between different population groups as a result of métissage. In his study of English versions of the story, for example, Frank Felsenstein suggests that the problem was confusion. He writes that while "Ligon's stated preference for the American Indian over the African slave... reveals an eyewitness's ability to discriminate between the two... later... renditions of the Inkle and Yarico tale... reveal a repeated ineptitude or inability in distinguishing one group from the other" (15). Peter Hulme, on the other hand, interprets Yarico's successively Amerindian/African appearance as a reflection of the gradual formation of mixed-race populations such as the "Black Caribs" of St. Vincent, a group that arose from (or at least was perceived to have been created by) intermarriage between Amerindians and African Maroons.

While I find both of these interpretations plausible, I want to lay out a somewhat different approach, proposing a reading that situates the Inkle and Yarico corpus within the wider representational asymmetry that I describe in this book. What I suggest, then, is that the vagueness of Yarico's identity reflects writers' propensity to emphasize "native-settler" encounters rather than contact arising from slavery. Whereas Hulme's interpretation of the alternately indigenous/African appearance of Yarico suggests a correlation between literature and historical events, I propose that the indeterminacy of Yarico's origins reflects rather a displacement of the history of Atlantic slavery onto a commemoration of the encounter between Amerindians and Europeans. Hulme himself points to this kind of displacement in readings of two other major English narratives of colonial relations, Behn's *Oroonoko* and Defoe's *Robinson Crusoe*. He aptly characterizes Aphra Behn's eponymous hero, for example, as "a deafricanized African with an American name" (241),[44] and notes that when Defoe provides a physical description of Friday he goes out of his way to indicate that his character was *not* an African: "His hair was long and black, not curled like wool.... The color of his skin was not quite black... his nose small, not flat like the negroes," and so on (Hulme, 205). I view Yarico as yet another example of the trope of indigenization: a symptom of the broad-based cultural displacement by which first encounters between Europeans and Amerindians overshadowed later encounters between Europeans and enslaved Africans and, by extension, the phenomenon of Atlantic slavery.

Colonial (Dis)locations in *Cleveland*

Racial indeterminacy is also a feature of Abbé Prévost's multivolume novel, *Le philosophe anglais; ou, Histoire de Monsieur Cleveland, fils naturel de Cromwell, écrite par lui-même, et traduite de l'anglais* (*The English Philosopher; or, History*

44. Behn, *Oroonoko*.

of M. Cleveland, Illegitimate Son of Cromwell, Written by Himself and Translated from the English) (1731–39). *Cleveland*, as the text is more generally known, followed closely on the heels of another lengthy work, *Mémoires et avantures d'un homme de qualité qui s'est retiré du monde* (*Memoirs and Adventures of a Man of Quality*) (1728–31), the last volume of which is Prévost's masterpiece, *History of the Chevalier des Grieux and Manon Lescaut* (1731).[45] The famous closing episode of *Manon Lescaut* transports Manon and her doggedly faithful lover, the Chevalier des Grieux, to the fledgling colony of Louisiana. Though the two lovers initially hope to make a fresh start in the New World, they soon fall prey to the corrupt colonial regime and are forced to flee into the wilderness where Manon tragically dies. In *Cleveland* this brief episode is paralleled by a much longer, but less well-known sequence in which the eponymous hero follows his lover, Fanny, to the Americas. In both works, as Marie-Christine Pioffet writes, the vast physical expanse of the New World provides a backdrop commensurate with the heroes' unbounded passion.[46]

If Prévost produced two of the small handful of mid-eighteenth-century French fictions that represent Europe's colonies, it was not by pure chance. Several factors disposed him to be more attuned to the colonial world than other French writers of the period. Prévost spent a number of years in England, where colonial affairs were discussed more widely and more openly than in France. It was in an English periodical, for example, that he first read the speech of a purported Jamaican Maroon, Moses Bom Saam, a discourse that he later republished in his own journal, *Le pour et contre* (For and Against).[47] Prévost was also the editor of a fifteen-volume collection of travel narratives published under the title *General History of Voyages* (1746–59). Inevitably, some of these narratives included descriptions of the colonial Americas.[48]

In *Cleveland*, set in the 1650s, the hero's journey to the New World in pursuit of his beloved Fanny unfolds as a veritable colonial odyssey. Cleveland and various secondary characters shuttle back and forth between Spanish Cuba, portrayed as a highly developed colonial milieu, and various small French and English outposts in the Caribbean, Florida, and Virginia. They finally end up as the guests or hostages of a Native American nation called the Abaquis. Because Cleveland spends much of his American odyssey in North America, critical studies of the novel have tended (quite legitimately) to focus on Prévost's debt to travel writing devoted to this continent, for example, Baron de Lahontan's *Nouveaux voyages dans l'Amérique septentrionale* (*New Voyages to North America*) (1703), and Louis Hennepin's *Description de la Louisiane* (Description

---

45. Prévost, *Cleveland; Mémoires et avantures.*
46. Pioffet, "L'espace américain," 77.
47. *Le Pour et contre*, nos. 223–24 (1735), 201–13, in Prévost, *Le Pour et contre*, vol. 6.
48. Prévost, *Histoire générale.* Other editors continued the collection after Prévost gave up the editorship.

of Louisiana) (1683).[49] What is less often noted is that Cleveland's American travels begin and end in the Caribbean. During his first attempt to catch up with Fanny, the hero finds himself imprisoned on the small island of Nevis, where he is forced to work as an indentured servant. He escapes to the Atlantic island of St. Helena, from which, after various adventures, he hurries back to the Caribbean. After a brief stop in Martinique, which is portrayed as a remote outpost populated by Caribs and a single French missionary (2:130), he finally makes his way to the bustling city of Havana (2:138).[50]

To zero in on Cleveland's Caribbean itinerary like this is, as I have suggested, to read against the grain of the novel, which presents a longer and discursively richer account of the hero's travels in North America. What I want to achieve through this emphasis, however, is a dialogue between the novel's two colonial milieus. As a point of departure for this reading I consider the mediating role played by a racially ambiguous character named Iglou.

We first encounter Iglou in Havana, where the colonial governor, Don Francisco, presents him to Cleveland as a gift. In this initial meeting he is designated simply as an "esclave nègre" (black slave). It is only later that we learn that his name is Iglou, and that other details of his background start to emerge. Don Francisco characterizes Iglou as a man who is well qualified to serve Cleveland as a guide because he has traveled throughout the Americas and is familiar with the continents' major languages. When the two men reach the English settlement at Jamestown and head inland, this experience becomes apparent. Iglou reassures Cleveland that he knows the country well, having been born, not in Cuba or Africa, but among the savages of North America. In a short account of his life, he relates that as a youth he had been captured by the Spanish and taken as a slave to Havana. Far from feeling embittered by this experience, however, Iglou explains that he had always been treated well by his masters and as a result had formed a favorable opinion of Europeans (2:196).

Besides the problematic softening of colonial slavery that Iglou's narrative betokens, two questions seem to arise from this narrative twist. First, why does Iglou initially appear in the guise of a "black slave"? That is, why doesn't Don Francisco say from the outset that if Iglou is an ideal companion/guide for Cleveland, it is because he is a Native American? And second, what narrative or discursive maneuvers does this change of identity enable?[51]

---

49. See, for example, Stewart, "L'Amérique," 879.

50. Stewart proposes Labat as a possible model for the French missionary. Given the period in which the novel is set and the apparent seclusion of the French priest, this personage seems more likely to have been based on Raymond Breton. Ibid., 870.

51. In *Le nègre romantique* Léon-François Hoffmann mentions a novel titled *Mourat et Iglou; ou, Indamena, anecdote tirée des mémoires sur l'Île Saint-Christophe* (1782) in which the eponymous Iglou is an enslaved character of indeterminate origin (82).

The second question is relatively easy to answer. With Iglou recast as a "native informant," Prévost can bring Cleveland and his party, including Fanny, with whom he has been reunited, into the orbit of the Abaqui nation, a sympathetic and physically attractive Native American people (2:196). The hero's stay among the Abaquis allows Prévost to open a long parenthesis in which he ponders issues such as the impact of the transfer of European knowledge and values to other cultural groups. The Abaquis recognize Cleveland as a man of superior wisdom and ultimately invite him to govern them. He immediately sets about "civilizing" them (Prévost's term), by instilling principles of discipline and European morality (2:251). As Pierre Berthiaume has noted, however, the goals of Cleveland's program of reform are at best vague, and his methods of implementing them are self-defeating.[52] One of the main problems seems to be that Cleveland has very ambivalent feelings about the Abaquis' proximity to the "state of nature." On the one hand, he is afraid of setting them on a path that will lead to "luxe" and "mollesse" (luxury and idleness) (2:260), the vices of civilized society. On the other, he is dismayed by the Abaquis' indolence, even in the face of grave dangers, as well as by their propensity for superstition. Several Abaqui cultural practices—for example, the exposure of newborns who appear weak or who bear unusual birthmarks—strike him as barbaric and in need of reasoned reform.

Cleveland and Fanny work through some of these questions in a long dialogue in which they debate the relative merits of nature and civilization and discuss the goals of acculturation. Fanny argues that both Europeans and Native Americans fail to live up to the highest standards of humanity, the former because of their lapses into luxury and vice, the latter due to their vulgarity and barbarism. The goal of acculturation, she suggests, should be to steer the Abaquis to a point that is neither beneath nor beyond "reason," which is for her the core of all moral values (2:312). Fanny's preference for a stage of human development located somewhere between pure nature and highly developed society anticipates Rousseau's *Second Discourse,* in which the second or intermediate stage of human development is characterized as the longest and happiest phase of human history. There are differences to be observed here, however, since Rousseau's theory of human "perfectibility"—the idea that human beings possess an innate capacity to evolve in new directions—made it impossible for him to represent this stage as a goal in its own right. As a result, in *Social Contract* Rousseau asked which codes of law and which forms of government would be most likely to curtail the negative effects of social and economic development. Cleveland, on the other hand—I won't say Prévost, since the author clearly tries to distance himself from the immature political thinking of his protagonist—does not make the connection between

---

52. Berthiaume, "Abaquis et Nopandes."

political structures and social outcomes. One of the main deficiencies of his "civilizing mission" is indeed that he tries to achieve his political ends by resorting to problematic means. During the ceremony in which he is installed as governor of the Abaquis, to give one example, he informs the members of the tribe that if they fail to show him obedience, they will be punished by the sun, which is the object of their worship. Through political manipulations of this kind, as Berthiaume writes, Cleveland attempts to inculcate reason by exploiting the very credulity and superstition that he is striving to eradicate (97, 99). In the end the Abaquis, who have been decimated by an epidemic, are torn apart by internal dissent, with some members of the tribe remaining loyal to Cleveland, and others breaking away.

The Abaqui episode of *Cleveland* can clearly be read as an allegory for the repercussions of colonial contact. Viewed in this way, it must be said to cast cultural transfer in a conspicuously negative light. Prolonged contact between Europeans and Native Americans is shown to generate confusion over the ideal state of humanity and the best ways to achieve it. It is also portrayed as a source of dissension and perhaps also as a vector of disease. But while Prévost casts doubt on the possibility of exerting a positive transformative impact on another people, what he never really questions is the underlying benevolence of the colonial venture. Though the process of acculturation may not succeed, the intentions behind it are shown to be pure. This representation would have been less plausible, of course, had Prévost undertaken to allegorize colonial contact in the Caribbean, where relationships between European and non-European peoples were defined by the regime of slavery. But although Cleveland's Caribbean tour—Nevis–St. Helena–Martinique–Cuba—offers ample opportunity for a reflection on colonial slavery, Prévost, in a quite literal sense, steers away from this topic, exploring instead a colonial setting which, while flawed, had some potentially redeeming features.

Returning, in light of this point, to Iglou, the black-slave-turned-good-savage, I want to propose that the racial ambiguity of this character may be read as a narrative trace of the displacement of moral and political discourse away from colonization as practiced in the Caribbean toward the North American context, and by extension toward a more abstract philosophical meditation on colonization as a medium of cultural transfer.

Aztecs, Incas, and Slaves

Native North Americans were not the only "noble savages" who interested French authors. The idealization of indigenous culture and countervailing critique of European colonial intervention was also a feature of literary discourse on the Aztec and Inca peoples of Central and South America. Next to the Hurons and Iroquois of New France, these were the Amerindian groups most widely represented in eighteenth-century French culture.

As critics including Edward Seeber and more recently Christopher Miller have observed, French interest in the Aztecs and Incas paralleled, and was in some respects interwoven with, the fascination exerted by Oriental culture.[53] Representations of Amerindian protagonists with names such as Zilia, Zamore, and Alzire are interwoven on many levels with the stories told about Oriental characters such as Zadig, Zaki, or Zaïde.[54] Both modes of exoticism involved the exploration of another "advanced" culture: a civilization with well-defined social and cultural systems. The vogue for Incas and Aztecs, however, also built on other foundations, namely those laid by Montaigne in his seminal essay "On Coaches" (1575). Writing in the wake of Montaigne, eighteenth-century writers lamented the destruction of the once flourishing Aztec and Inca civilizations at the hands of the conquistadors. The "black legend" of Spanish barbarism in the Americas served as a powerful vehicle for reflection on the modalities of conquest and the ethics of cultural difference. But as we shall see, it was also a discourse that allowed for the displacement of moral questions from the French context to the Spanish, and from the eighteenth century onto an earlier historical period.

In this section I consider two well-known midcentury works that depict the transformative encounter between the civilized peoples of South America and Spanish invaders: Voltaire's tragedy *Alzire; ou, Les Américains* (Alzire; or, The Americans) (1736), and Françoise de Graffigny's epistolary novel *Lettres d'une Péruvienne* (*Letters of a Peruvian Woman*) (1747), a work partly inspired by the popularity of *Alzire*. In my readings of these two texts I ask how the condemnation of atrocities perpetrated by the Spanish in sixteenth-century America intersected with questions raised by the still-unfolding history of French colonial expansion. One aspect of this reflection concerns the way in which these two texts frame the experience of colonization. As we shall see, both Voltaire and Graffigny emphasize the adaptation of colonized subjects to the codes of the dominant Spanish or French culture. Building on my reading of *Cleveland,* I suggest that these explorations of processes that have since come to be known as "acculturation" and "assimilation" occurred at the expense of a reflection on colonial regimes that were grounded in the thoroughgoing moral and physical subjugation of the colonized.

53. Seeber provides a long list of flexibly Oriental/East Indian/South American names (*Anti-Slavery Opinion,* 137), and Miller similarly notes the exchangeability of American and Oriental names and registers (*French Atlantic Triangle,* 146).

54. Examples of Aztec/Inca exoticism in this period include Thomas-Simon Gueullette's Inca pastiche of the *Thousand and One Nights, Mille et une heure [sic], contes péruviens* (The Thousand and One Hours, Peruvian Tales); Jean-François Marmontel's *Les Incas; ou, La destruction de l'empire du Pérou* (The Incas or the Destruction of the Peruvian Empire); and the works by Graffigny and Voltaire discussed below.

From Enslavement to Acculturation: Voltaire's *Alzire*

Voltaire's American tragedy *Alzire* was one of the writer's most successful and influential plays.[55] It had a good run at the Comédie française in 1736, and, as Christopher Miller has shown, a significant circum-Atlantic afterlife, with performances staged on Gorée Island (1766) and in the Caribbean colony of Saint-Domingue (1765–82) (71–78). The play, however, is set not in Africa or the French Caribbean, but in the South American city of Lima in the aftermath of the Spanish conquest. Its ostensible theme is religious intolerance, but as Miller rightly observes, *Alzire* has other important dimensions, for it is "directly concerned with conquest, colonialism, and slavery" (71).

At the opening of the play the defeated Aztec ruler, Montèze, has converted to Christianity and is urging his daughter Alzire to do the same. Montèze also wants Alzire to marry the new Spanish governor, Gusman, in order to cement the relationship between the conquered "Americans" and their new Spanish overlords. Alzire hesitates, however, feeling torn between her duty to her father and people, and her fidelity to the memory of her fiancé, Zamore, whom she believes to have been killed by Gusman. She finally decides to wed Gusman only to learn, shortly afterward, that Zamore is still alive. Zamore attempts to assassinate Gusman, whom he views as a bloodthirsty tyrant, and in response the Spanish colonists demand revenge. The cycle of violence is brought to an end when Gusman's father, the devout but tolerant Alvarez, promises clemency if Zamore agrees to become a Christian. In the play's denouement, Gusman, on his deathbed, forgives Zamore and repents his violent treatment of the Aztecs. He encourages Zamore to convert, but does not make Christianization a condition of his future freedom.

As this summary suggests, *Alzire* does not stage a full-frontal attack on religious intolerance but rather deploys a more subtle combination of attack and rearguard defense. In his preface to the play, Voltaire actually identifies its primary subject as the superiority of the true spirit of religion over the dictates of natural virtue: "I have tried to show how much the true spirit of religion triumphs over the virtues of nature," he writes (i). Instead of championing natural law over religion, Voltaire places religious fanatics and men who obey the dictates of nature on the same level, while setting tolerant Christians such as Alvarez, or Gusman at the hour of his death, on a higher moral plane. This perspective may reflect Voltaire's deistic leanings, or perhaps anxiety about possible censorship: it was one thing to criticize a few Spanish fanatics, another to question the moral supremacy of Catholicism in a publicly performed play. But there is clearly also a current of what might be called colonial paternalism in Voltaire's embrace of tolerant Christianity. This note

---

55. Voltaire, *Alzire; ou, Les Américains.* References in the text are to this edition, my translation.

is particularly evident in the final speech of the play, in which a reformed Gusman pleads: "Know that my clemency has surpassed my crimes. Instruct America: teach its kings that Christians were born to give them laws" (77). Since the play ends on these words, Voltaire appears to be saying that there *is* such a thing as legitimate colonial rule, that is, governance that undertakes to educate and enlighten rather than to persecute and destroy, and to be suggesting that Christian universalism constitutes a legitimate medium for this cultural transfer.

Beneath this civilizing discourse, however, runs a more skeptical subtext. Prior to the final scene in which the problems of Alzire and Zamore are serendipitously resolved, the two Amerindian protagonists devote themselves to mourning their lost freedom and the destruction of their hereditary culture, while characterizing their Spanish overlords as bloodthirsty tyrants. The lexicon in which they voice these anticolonial protests is, for the most part, that of slavery. Alzire and Zamore state repeatedly that in depriving the Aztecs of their political and cultural autonomy, the Spanish have effectively turned them into "slaves." Their speeches are filled with references, both literal and figural, to slaves, shackles, masters, and yokes. In one impassioned speech Alzire characterizes herself as the "slave of a barbarian, wife of a Christian" (61). In another she claims that the unfamiliar trappings of European civilization, particularly its cavalry and firearms, had enabled the Spanish to reduce the entire world to slavery (27). Though the vocabulary of slavery is pervasive throughout French classical tragedy, where it serves as a metaphor for the self-surrender that accompanies passion, in *Alzire*, a play in which military conquest and religious conversion are accorded more attention than personal feelings, it takes on a more literal meaning, signifying the loss of political self-determination and the dismantling of cultural identity.

It seems to me that the brisk resolution of political tensions that occurs at the end of the play—Gusman's belated embrace of a kinder, gentler form of Christianity; his decision to pardon Zamore; and the suggestion that the Aztecs would henceforth be able, with clear conscience, to convert and acculturate— does not convincingly sweep away the impassioned rhetoric of political liberty and cultural autonomy that dominates the rest of the play. At the end of the day, Gusman's personal transformation and Zamore's potential conversion constitute a rather fragile basis for this kind of political accommodation. Uncontained by this too-rapid resolution, the play's recurrent allusions to slaves, masters, and chains gesture toward forms of colonial rule that were not recuperable as vehicles for the civilizing mission, colonial orders that included the slave system practiced in many European colonies in Voltaire's own time. This colonial order is of course not represented directly in *Alzire*, or indeed in any French representation of the "black legend" of Spanish barbarism, yet it simmers beneath the surface of these pious condemnations.

Colonial Chronologies in Graffigny

Françoise de Graffigny's epistolary novel, *Letters of a Peruvian Woman*, was published in 1747, some ten years after *Alzire's* staging at the Comédie française. Though a best seller in its day, like many other works by eighteenth-century women the book fell out of view in the early nineteenth century.[56] In the late 1980s feminist scholarship on the forgotten writing of eighteenth-century women led to its rediscovery as an important contribution to Enlightenment philosophy. New editions were published in 1993 and 2001, and the novel has since become a fixture of eighteenth-century survey courses, as well as the object of numerous critical studies.[57]

Like *Alzire,* by which it is clearly influenced, *Letters of a Peruvian Woman* explores relations between Europeans and Amerindians in the wake of the Spanish conquest. Graffigny, however, takes the representation of the colonial encounter in a somewhat different direction than Voltaire. Whereas *Alzire* deals with the repercussions of conquest in the newly colonized continent, in *Letters of a Peruvian Woman* the heroine, who has sometimes been compared to a postcolonial immigrant, is displaced from her homeland and transported to Europe.

The novel is comprised of letters addressed by a young Peruvian princess named Zilia to her fiancé, Aza, the heir to the Incan throne. In these letters Zilia remembers how, on the eve of her marriage, conquistadors ransacked the Temple of the Sun where she lived with the other royal virgins, took her captive, and set her aboard a vessel bound for Spain. Once at sea, the Spanish ship was engaged by a French vessel, and Zilia, along with a cargo of Peruvian gold, was transferred to the French ship and set on a new course to France. In her letters Zilia confides to Aza that although she spoke no French, she instinctively preferred the French to her haughty Spanish captors. She is particularly impressed by their gallant captain, Déterville, who, after their arrival in France, invites her to take up residence in his mother's château.

Many of Zilia's letters concern her adaptation to French culture. They convey her first impressions of institutions, behaviors, and technologies with which she was previously unfamiliar, and which are defamiliarized and as a result denaturalized under her ingenuous gaze. Graffigny's "Peruvian Letters" has often been compared with another text in which French culture is viewed through the eyes of a group of cultural outsiders: Montesquieu's *Persian Letters*. As scholars have observed, however, *Letters of a Peruvian Woman* brings a new dimension to Montesquieu's use of the trope of critical alterity

---

56. No new editions were published between 1835 and 1966.

57. Graffigny, *Lettres d'une péruvienne*. Recent critical commentaries include Altman, "Woman's Place in the Enlightenment Sun"; "Making Room for 'Peru'"; Douthwaite, "Relocating the Exotic Other"; Dobie, "Graffigny's Writing Subject"; and Piroux, "Encyclopedist."

by inventing a protagonist who is at once foreign and female. A point often made in this connection is that whereas Montesquieu sets (at least part of) his novel in the Oriental seraglio, Graffigny eschewed the popular harem plot with its cloistered female figures and instead elected the Inca temple of Peru as her *locus tragicus*.[58] This geographical transfer from East to West is, however, not only significant in terms of the novel's prioritization of questions of gender. It also introduces a colonial dimension into the dynamics of cultural critique. Whereas Montesquieu's Persians travel to Europe more or less of their own accord, Zilia, as a colonized subject, is transported to Europe by force in the wake of the conquest and occupation of her homeland.[59] As several readers have observed, *Letters of a Peruvian Woman* offers both a critical examination of French mores on the domestic front and a critical commentary on European colonial rule.

A point that has been virtually absent from this discussion, however, is that the colonial setting depicted in the novel is the Spanish Americas in the sixteenth century rather than the French colonies in a more contemporary historical moment. Considering the text in light of this point I want to explore the relationship between Graffigny's participation in the "black legend" of Spanish barbarism and the unrepresented context of French colonial rule. As in the case of *Alzire,* I propose that Graffigny's return to the scene of the Spanish conquest two centuries after the fact produced a focus on processes of acculturation and assimilation rather than a sustained examination of disappropriation and enslavement.

After she has been living in France for some time, Zilia learns that Aza, who had been captured and brought to Spain, had abandoned the idea of returning to Peru to lead some form of resistance movement, and instead decided to assimilate into Spanish society by marrying a wealthy Spanish lady. With Zilia released from her engagement, Déterville promptly declares his love and proposes marriage. In a plot twist that has been extensively analyzed, Zilia turns down his offer, preferring to live independently in a house bought with the gold captured from the Spanish vessel. The novel thus concludes, not with a fairy-tale marriage, but with Zilia living comfortably in her country house, spending her days happily at work in her library. This unconventional ending clearly has a strong feminist resonance, and it is primarily from this perspective that it has been discussed by recent scholars. There is, however, a further dimension to Zilia's refusal of marriage, to the extent that what she is rejecting is not only subordination to a husband but also assimilation to French culture. Whereas Aza marries and assimilates, Zilia positions herself as an exile and, though she continues to reside in France, she also affirms the cultural identity of her country of origin.

58. See, for example, Douthwaite, "Relocating the Exotic Other," 461.
59. On the colonial thread of the novel, see Altman, "Graffigny's Epistemology."

As Jack Undank has noted, one of the most important features of the country house purchased with Zilia's Peruvian gold is its quiet, well-stocked library. Zilia is fortunate enough to have access to a "room of her own," a quiet place of reflection and study in which she can embark on the process that Hélène Cixous has called "coming to writing."[60] It is presumably in her library that Zilia translates her letters, originally composed in Peruvian *quipu*—a form of notation composed of a system of knotted colored cords—into French prose. The letters offer a detailed description of the library, and in particular of a small inner chamber of which Zilia is particularly fond. She describes a room decorated with Peruvian artifacts and adorned with frescoes depicting scenes of Peruvian life. For Janet Altman, one of the leading feminist scholars of Graffigny, this room is a site of ideal accommodation in which both women's literacy and the cultural difference of Peru are acknowledged and given space. There is, however, perhaps some element of what might be called "museumification" at work in the reconstruction of Peruvian decor within a French country château.[61] That is to say, the novel seems to relegate Peruvian culture to the past, situating it as a precolonial tradition that, having been dismantled by the conquistadors, is available to be reassembled in a faraway "metropolitan" setting.

Focusing on this commemorative approach to Peru leads us to ponder the country's ongoing history under Spanish rule, a reality from which Zilia, like Aza, has obviously become detached. It also draws our attention to a curious feature of the novel's colonial subtext: the seeming temporal anomaly by which Zilia leaves Peru in the mid-sixteenth century, at the time of the Spanish conquest, but arrives in France some two centuries later, in the mid-eighteenth century.

To the extent that critics have commented on this two-hundred-year time warp, they have generally explained it in terms of the interplay between realist and subjectivist modes of writing. Though this reading is certainly plausible, it seems to me that there is a somewhat more concrete point to be made about the hiatus between departure and arrival. What is significant about this interval in my view is that it allows Graffigny to represent colonial violence as an atrocity perpetrated by the Spanish in the distant past rather than as an ongoing offense in which members of her own nation were implicated. Considered from this perspective, the temporal sequence of the novel seems akin to the syntax of a dream narrative in which a painful or disturbing moment is elided by a seamless transition.

Letters of a Peruvian Woman is clearly attuned to the ethical questions raised by human diversity. Peruvians are portrayed, not as savages or idolaters, but as the cultural equals of Europeans. Yet despite these modes of openness, the text is surprisingly chauvinistic when it comes to evaluating France's role in

60. Undank, "Graffigny's Room"; Cixous, *Coming to Writing*.
61. See Altman, "Making Room for 'Peru.'"

world affairs. From the outset, as we have noted, the French are favorably compared with the Spanish, who absorb all responsibility for crimes committed in the New World. Déterville's victory over the ship carrying Zilia to Spain is recorded as a propitious event that enables him to gallantly "rescue" Zilia. There is no discussion of what his ship was doing off the American coast, and correspondingly no acknowledgment of French commercial and colonial activity in Atlantic waters. This is not to say that the realities of French colonial expansion do not intrude into the economy of the novel. They do. Yet as in many other texts of the French Enlightenment, colonial history is legible, not in the positive presence of images and discourses, but rather in the traces left by the absence or erasure of representation. In *Letters of a Peruvian Woman* this pattern of repression and displacement is primarily marked in the fracturing of the representational framework that Gérard Genette calls the "time of history": the narrative presentation of the period of time within which a story unfolds.[62] In its awkward narrative suspension between two historical moments, the novel points obliquely toward its own representational silence, gesturing by means of elision to what it does not say.

I have suggested that although by as early as 1670, contact between "natives" and settlers in the French Caribbean had sharply diminished, travelogues and fictional narratives continued to portray colonization in the guise of an encounter between Europeans and Amerindians, while according a relatively marginal place to the Atlantic slave trade and to the creolized slave societies that formed in its orbit. We have observed that many French writers who took up the pen to write about the colonial Americas did so in order to pass judgment on the injustices and vicissitudes of colonial rule. Some condemned the brutality and intolerance of the conquistadors, adding their voices to the "black legend" of Spanish imperial barbarism. Others began to ask whether it was possible or desirable to transmit European knowledge and values to extra-European peoples. As the examples that I have considered suggest, eighteenth-century French writers took a range of perspectives on this issue, with some—for example, the Voltaire of *Alzire*—endorsing the basic principle of what would later be formalized as the civilizing mission, while others—for example, Prévost—worried about cultural incompatibility and the dilution of customs and values. Yet though these are clearly important questions, they are questions that address themselves more to certain colonial contexts than to others.

It was undoubtedly meaningful to consider the risks and benefits of acculturation and assimilation with regard to eighteenth-century North and South

---

62. Genette, *Figures III*.

America, but such questioning could have had little relevancy to the milieu of the slave-plantation colonies of the Caribbean, where there was little if any attempt to enlighten or instruct. In this regard, the critical examination of colonization undertaken by Enlightenment writers was a partial one. While certain injustices and dilemmas were highlighted, other features of colonial rule were virtually ignored. It might even be fair to say that the critique of one form of colonial abuse masked, and thus indirectly supported, the neglect of others.

As a coda to this observation I would add that selective critical analysis of colonial practice has by no means been limited to eighteenth-century culture. Contemporary French historians and political commentators have written extensively about the ideology of the civilizing mission, and about the implications of assimilationism and its contemporary legacies in the context of postcolonial immigration. By comparison, the fundamentally coercive order of plantation slavery has been the object of much less discussion, either in the field of French history or in the wider context of public commemoration and debate.

5

Slaves and the Noble Savage

In a well-known reflection on the categories employed to describe human diversity in contemporary France, the philosopher Étienne Balibar observes that although French social thought and political discourse have largely abjured the concept of race, ideas relating to cultural difference have been marshaled in ways that closely parallel the deployment of race in other national contexts.[1] The colonial doctrine of assimilation allowed colonized subjects to become French citizens, regardless of parentage or phenotype, if they were willing to renounce practices considered antithetical to French mores (particularly those associated with Islam) and if they could demonstrate mastery of key French skills. In the era of postcolonial immigration, by the same token, the validity of race has consistently been questioned, while differences associated with culture have been strongly emphasized. In Balibar's eyes, the postcolonial French preoccupation with cultural difference effectively amounts to racial thinking, constituting in its most extreme forms a kind of "neo-racism" or a "racism without races."

The emphasis that French social thought places on differences of culture reflects an underlying epistemological and political framework in which cultures are understood to be self-contained and relatively homogeneous, and in which difference is located in the intervals between them. It is possible to draw a structural connection between this understanding of culture and the historical disavowal of race. That is to say, if phenotype and claims about biology or

---

1. Balibar, "Is There a Neo-Racism?"

genetics are not considered determining, it is in large part because they do not correspond to cultural boundaries.

How do these tendencies of contemporary French social thought bear on cultural representations of colonization in the eighteenth century? Balibar, like several other commentators on contemporary French attitudes to diversity, views the perspectives that prevail today as continuations of doctrines forged during the colonial era. When genealogies of this kind are posited, the colonial regimes that are referenced are usually those of the nineteenth and twentieth century, particularly French rule in North and West Africa.[2] There are certainly many valid reasons for this emphasis, not least the significant migration to France from these regions that has occurred over the last half century. Yet it is also true that colonial historiography has tended to treat France's "first" and "second" colonial empires as two distinct formations, separated by the abolition of slavery in 1848. In lieu of this tendency, I propose that colonial history should be considered as a kind of palimpsest, with early ideas and practices resurfacing in later dispositions. For example, I suggest that the color-blind/culture-conscious orientation of contemporary French social thought can be retraced not only to the policy of assimilation essayed in Algeria, but also to ideological and discursive features of the first colonial empire. By this I mean not only that a preliminary form of assimilation, known as *francisation* (Frenchification), was attempted in Canada in the seventeenth century but also in a broader sense that from the earliest stages of empire, French writers devoted considerable attention to differences between cultural groups, particularly Europeans and Amerindians, while saying little about forms of diversity that ensued from colonial contact and the Atlantic slave trade: the forms of diversity that are elsewhere most often considered under the rubric of race.

In this chapter, as in the previous one, I propose that in eighteenth-century French representations of the Americas, Amerindians were more widely depicted than diasporic Africans and, correspondingly, that human diversity was predominantly thought of in terms of cultural difference. In the previous chapter I examined contrasting representations of Africans and Amerindians in missionary narratives and colonial fictions. Below I consider how this economy of thought was manifested in Enlightenment social and political philosophy. The "theme of the noble savage" is perhaps more a retrospective construction of literary history than a genuine category of eighteenth-century literature. Nonetheless, we will see that representations of the "savage" peoples of the Americas and Africa performed an important corroborative function in a range of discourses in which the advantages of civilization were weighed against the munificence of nature. Though eighteenth-century political thinkers also made

---

2. The sociologist Nacira Guénif-Souilamas, for example, argues in a 2006 essay that assimilation is the very principle of colonization, and indeed that colonization should be viewed as a form of assimilation. See "La république aristocratique," 7–8.

abundant reference to the institution of slavery, which they adopted as a metaphor for social inequality and political coercion, these references were almost always figurative appropriations divorced from empirical referents.

In this chapter I read questions of race, slavery, and cultural diversity in the Enlightenment against the grain of their philosophical abstraction, highlighting the colonial subtexts of seminal philosophical discourses. This means, for example, resituating the noble "savage" within the historical context of the colonial Americas, and interrogating the relationship between metaphors of political servitude and the colonial regime of slavery. This kind of reading opens up what the literary scholar Sara Melzer has called "reverse trajectories": conceptual genealogies in which colonies figure, not as remote outposts subject to metropolitan discourses, but rather as sites in which key discourses coalesced.[3] Taking this kind of approach, I explore the reverse trajectories of a group of key Enlightenment concepts: discourses relating to the "state of nature," natural law, and man's originary freedom, and, conversely, to the various forms of political and social subjection manifested in European society.

Between Savages and Slaves: Rousseau's *Second Discourse*

It is a striking fact that despite the enormous body of writing devoted to Rousseau's *Second Discourse*, the *Discours sur l'origine et les fondements de l'inégalité parmi les hommes* (*Discourse on the Origin and Foundations of Inequality among Men*) (1755), and despite this text's unquestioned influence on twentieth-century anthropology, relatively little has been said about Rousseau's use of ethnography to illustrate his description of the "state of pure nature."[4] Although, as Timothy O'Hagan observes, Rousseau's account of this primitive condition differs from the earlier meditations of Locke and Hobbes in its rigorous reconstruction of the experience of originary man, the references to the mores of actual "savage" populations with which Rousseau supports his account have rarely been subject to examination.[5]

Second Discourse was written in response to the question posed by the Academy of Dijon in its 1754 essay competition. The Academy asked: What is the origin of inequality among men, and is it authorized by natural law? Rousseau responded that in order to be able to reflect on inequality as it is embodied in contemporary laws and social structures it is first necessary to understand

---

3. Melzer, "The Magic of French Culture" and "Une 'seconde France'?"

4. Rousseau, *Discours sur l'origine de l'inégalité*. References in the text are to *Discourses*, translated by Victor Gourevitch.

5. O'Hagan, "Rousseau," 19–20. An exception to this rule is Muthu's *Enlightenment against Empire* (discussed below), which does consider the implications of the anthropological methodology of *Second Discourse* for colonial ideology.

mankind's "original constitution," and to retrace its journey from this originary state to the social and political condition of modern Europeans.

But Rousseau also famously problematized his account of the "state of nature" by characterizing it, in his preface, not as a historical description of early
man, but rather as a hypothesis based on the nature of things. He states to this
effect that

> it is no light undertaking to disentangle what is original from what is artificial
> in man's present nature, and to know accurately a state which no longer exists,
> which perhaps never did exist, which probably never will exist, and about which it
> is nonetheless necessary to have exact notions in order accurately to judge of our
> present state. (125)

The account of the state of nature in the *Discourse* proper opens in a similar
vein with a bold injunction to set aside "the facts":

> Let us therefore begin by setting aside all the facts, for they do not affect the ques-
> tion. The inquiries that may be pursued regarding this subject ought not to be
> taken for historical truths, but only for hypothetical reasonings; better suited to
> evaluate the nature of things than to show their genuine origin. (132)

A great deal of commentary has been devoted to these enigmatic lines.
Two leading figures of French anthropology, Émile Durkheim and Claude
Lévi-Strauss, took them to mean that Rousseau was advocating a synchronic
or structural approach to anthropology rather than a diachronic or historical
method.[6] Literary theorist Paul de Man, by contrast, argued that Rousseau had
effectively suspended the distinction between empirical reference (including
historical referentiality) and the figurative structure of language.[7] What from
my point of view complicates this question further is the fact that, having problematized reference and historical exposition, Rousseau proceeds to illustrate
his "hypothetical" account of the state of nature with ethnographic references
to the way of life of real "savage" peoples. He seems in other words to be
saying that although originary humans may not have lived in the manner he
describes—and, indeed, may not have existed at all—indications as to their way
of life are furnished by the character and behavior of contemporary savages as
described in the accounts of travelers and missionaries.

I will not attempt to unravel this epistemological knot, an endeavor that
would require not only a close reading of *Second Discourse* but also consideration of the many brilliant interpretations devoted to its rhetoric and arguments.

---

6. See, for example, Durkheim, *Montesquieu and Rousseau*, 67; Lévi-Strauss, *Anthropologie
structurale*, 319; *Tristes tropiques*, 467–70.

7. De Man, "Metaphor (Second Discourse)," 135–59.

I do, however, want to make two more-limited points about Rousseau's methodology and the critical readings that it has generated. The first is that, despite the many commentaries devoted to the epistemological implications of the text's opening paragraph, readers have largely failed to comment on the added layer of complexity introduced by Rousseau's ethnographic references to real "savages." The second point, which is related to the first, is that Rousseau's enigmatic problematization of his own account of the state of nature seems to have led readers to overlook his subsequent use of ethnographic references and, by extension, to ignore the historical context of exploration and colonization that framed and informed the text.

Because the ethnographic allusions of *Second Discourse* have been subject to little scrutiny, it often seems to be assumed that the "savages" to whom Rousseau refers are those who figure most prominently in eighteenth-century philosophy, that is, native North Americans. One of Rousseau's first influential readers, Voltaire, certainly made the assumption that the models for his originary humans were "the savages of Canada."[8] In fact, the main ethnographic referents of *Second Discourse* are not the Hurons or Iroquois of New France but rather the Amerindians of the Caribbean basin. Rousseau learned about these peoples, at least insofar as we can tell from his footnotes, by reading François (Francisco) Coréal's descriptions of the indigenous peoples of the Spanish Americas, and Jean-Baptiste Du Tertre's account of the Caribs.[9] The influence of Du Tertre, as we shall see, is clearly evidenced in the text's allusions to the mores of the Caribs.

Rousseau describes the first humans as beings whose capacity for sensation greatly exceeded their ability to reason and form ideas. Living in an eternal present they had little sense of the future, and no idea of changing the conditions of their existence. Such, he adds, "is still nowadays the extent of the Carib's foresight: he sells his cotton bed in the morning and comes weeping to buy it back in the evening, for not having foreseen that he would need it the following night" (143). (The missionary Jean-Baptiste Labat makes more or less the same claim in a passage in which he recounts his purchase of a hammock from a group of improvident Caribs.)[10] Rousseau also conjectures that early men had few passions. Their desire for the opposite sex was purely physical and did not involve feelings such as jealousy, which arise out of love for a specific individual. Once again, he turns to the Caribs to make his point: "The Caribs, which of all existing peoples has so far deviated least from the state of

8. Letter to Jean-Jacques Rousseau, August 30, 1755, in *Correspondence,* 259–60.
9. Coréal, *Voyages de François Coréal;* Du Tertre, *Histoire générale des Antilles.* A third important reference, as the footnotes to the text attest, was "Kolben," i.e., Kolb, *Description du Cap de Bonne-Espérance.*
10. Labat, *Nouveau voyage,* 2:115.

nature, are in fact also the most peaceful in their loves and the least given to jealousy, even though they live in a scorching climate which always seems to rouse these passions to greater activity" (156).

The mores of modern-day "savages" come up again when Rousseau turns from man's originary state to the second stage of human development: the age that followed the formation of families and other social relations but preceded the institution of laws and private property. Whereas in the first part of the text Caribs are said to illustrate the rude good health and limited emotional palette of man in his earliest state, in this later section "primitive" peoples are held to embody the intermediary stage of human development. Rousseau indeed points to the fact that almost all the savages encountered by Europeans lived in huts clustered in small communities to prove that this was/is the longest, most sustainable phase of human history:

> Occupying a just mean between the indolence of the primitive state and the petulant activity of our amour propre, [it] must have been the happiest and the longest lasting epoch. The more one reflects on it, the more one finds that this state was the least subject to revolutions, the best for man, and that he must have left it only by some fatal accident, which, for the sake of the common utility should never have occurred. The example of the savages, almost all of whom have been found at this point, seems to confirm that mankind was made always to remain in it, that this state is the genuine youth of the world, and that all subsequent progress has been so many steps in appearance toward the perfection of the individual, and in effect toward the decrepitude of the species. (167)

Voltaire makes a similar claim in *Essay on Universal History,* where he writes that "all people were for centuries what the inhabitants of several of the southern shores of Africa, those of several islands, and half of the Americans are today" (1:13).

The second part of *Second Discourse* sketches man's trajectory from the long, happy middle phase of human history to modern society. In this account Rousseau explains how moral and political inequality came to exist alongside naturally occurring physical differences, and how the institution of laws, hierarchies, and governments legitimized these forms of inequality. He famously identifies the root cause of these pernicious developments as the institution of private property: "The first man who, having enclosed a piece of land, to whom it occurred to say *this is mine,* and find people sufficiently simple to believe him, was the true father of civil society" (164). In the pages that follow, Rousseau argues that the consequences of the establishment of property had been resoundingly negative: "How many crimes, wars, murders, how many miseries and horrors mankind would have been spared by him who, pulling up the stakes or filling in the ditch, had cried out: beware of listening to this impostor. You are lost if you forget that the fruits are everyone's and the earth no one's" (164). The development of society is represented as the progressive polarization of rich and poor, and the refinement of art and science is said to have led to the proliferation of commodities on which people had grown dependent. This dependency is in turn blamed for a loss of physical vigor and, since people also became dependent on each other, personal autonomy. At several points in *Second Discourse* Rousseau observes that when present-day "savages" such as the Caribs are presented with a choice between their accustomed freedom and the material advantages of advanced civilization, they invariably pick the former (128, 177, 187). When we consider the downward spiral of political authoritarianism and social control that Rousseau describes, this decision to "run for the woods" seems more than justified.

Rousseau depicts the transition to life in society as a difficult process of adaptation. In order to underscore the degree of sacrifice and self-discipline required to participate in the social order, he draws on the vocabulary of the most extreme form of subjugation to the will of another, that is to say, the lexicon of slavery. It is said, for example, that

> the moment one man needed the help of another; as soon as it was found to be useful for one to have provisions for two, equality disappeared, property appeared, work became necessary, and vast forests changed into smiling fields that had to be watered with the sweat of men, and where slavery and misery were soon seen to sprout and grow together with the harvests. (167)

But for Rousseau the evils of socialization do not end with economic inequality and the uneven distribution of power. The complex demands imposed by social relationships also entail a form of subjection: "Man, who had previously been free and independent, is now so to speak subjugated by... the whole of nature, and especially to those of his kind, whose slave he in a sense becomes even by becoming their master; rich, he needs their services, poor he needs their help" (170). This passage, in which even masters are characterized as slaves of the social system, harkens back to Rousseau's *First Discourse, the Discours sur les sciences et les arts* (*Discourse on the Sciences and the Arts*), in which the rebirth of art and science is held responsible for fostering a culture of luxury and dependency: "This is how luxury, dissoluteness and slavery have at all times been the punishment visited upon our prideful efforts to leave the happy ignorance in which eternal wisdom has placed us," Rousseau laments in the earlier text.[11]

Rousseau breaks down the process of the institution of law and government into three distinct phases: the establishment of private property, which, as we have seen, is represented both as the foundation of organized society and as the origin of inequality; the institution of positive laws and of a magistrature empowered to interpret and enforce them; and the gradual replacement of

---

11. Rousseau, *Discours sur les sciences et les arts; Discourses,* 14.

legitimate political power with arbitrary and abusive rule. Each of these stages is held to correspond to a specific mode and degree of inequality: "The state of rich and poor was authorized by the first epoch, that of powerful and weak by the second, and by the third that of master and slave, which is the last degree of inequality, and the state to which the others finally lead, until new revolutions either dissolve the government entirely or bring it closer to legitimate institution" (182). To qualify the final degree of political and social inequality, Rousseau, like other French thinkers of the early- and mid-eighteenth century, uses the term "despotism." Deploying a complex historical model, he characterizes despotic rule both as an end point and as a return to the conditions of the "state of nature," a condition in which force, rather than law, reigned supreme.

Rousseau's discussion of despotism owes much to Montesquieu's *Spirit of Laws*, which also portrays despotic government as the most extreme form of exercise of royal power.[12] Rousseau also follows Montesquieu in drawing a connection between despotic government and civil slavery. He writes that "wherever despotism rules...it suffers no other master; as soon as it speaks, there is no consulting probity or duty, and the blindest obedience is the only virtue left to slaves" (185). Reprising Montesquieu's cautionary tale of monarchy's potential, and indeed perhaps inevitable, slide into despotism, Rousseau gestures to a cyclical pattern in which governments become arbitrary and repressive, are overthrown and for a time redeemed, and then descend again into tyranny and subjugation. Montesquieu—to the extent that he does propose a political solution to this pattern—emphasizes the importance of respecting the principles of monarchic rule, and champions moderating forces such as the checks-and-balances system of the English constitution. Rousseau, by contrast, lays out in *Du contrat social* (*On the Social Contract*), the work that builds on the theoretical groundwork of *Second Discourse*, what he perceives as the most legitimate and stable foundations for government and the social order.

The contemporary point of reference that Rousseau, like Montesquieu, provides for arbitrary, despotic governance under which all men are effectively enslaved is the repressive, inherently unstable reign of the Oriental sultan. Mobilizing the trope of Oriental despotism, Rousseau writes that "the despot is master only so long as he is the stronger, and...as soon as he can be expelled he cannot object to violence. The uprising that finally strangles or dethrones a sultan is as lawful an action as those by which, the day before, he disposed of his subjects' lives and goods. Force alone maintains him" (186). In an adjacent passage he contrasts the many constraints imposed on contemporary Europeans with the untrammeled freedom of the Amerindian: "What a sight the difficult and envied labors of a European statesman would be for a Carib! How many cruel deaths would not this indolent savage prefer to the honor of such a life"

---

12. On Montesquieu, despotism, and slavery, see above, 37–43.

(187). In this sequence of passages we can discern a trajectory leading from the untrammeled freedom of "primitive" peoples to the absolute servitude of subjects of despotism, or, to reference the empirical referents cited by Rousseau, from the Caribbean "savage" to the Oriental subaltern. Between these two extremes—between the polarities of nature and hypercivilization, freedom and subjugation, West and East—stands the contemporary European, who looks with nostalgia on the vanishing world of the savage, while striving to avoid the condition of social and political servitude embodied by the Oriental other.

One group is, however, strikingly absent from this philosophical and geopolitical schema, and that is the population of human beings subject to literal regimes of slavery, namely the millions of Africans transported across the Atlantic to labor, often in real chains, in European colonies. In *Second Discourse,* as in many other Enlightenment texts, the condition of these diasporic Africans is overshadowed by the prevailing cultural currents of orientalism and primitivism. It should perhaps be added that what Rousseau has to say about Amerindians scarcely qualifies as an engagement with the historical process of colonization either. We saw in the previous chapter that the Caribs, whom Rousseau, following Du Tertre, represents as contemporary exponents of the condition of originary man, had by 1755 been decimated as a population, and forced to retreat to the two outlying islands of Dominica and St. Vincent. Rousseau makes no reference to these upheavals, offering instead an account of Amerindian culture that is frozen in a precolonial past.

The opening lines of *On the Social Contract* pick up where Rousseau left off at the end of *Second Discourse.* That is to say, they characterize the political subordination experienced by members of developed societies as tantamount to enslavement. In perhaps his most famous passage, Rousseau writes that "man is born free, and everywhere he is in chains. One man thinks himself the master of others, but he is more of a slave than they." This bold statement proclaims, however, not that all men are in a formal sense enslaved, but rather that people everywhere are subject to regimes of social discipline and political oppression.[13] Under the influence of these lines subsequent French political thinkers would similarly contest political authoritarianism by characterizing it as a form of slavery. The revolutionary journalist Jean-Paul Marat, for example, provocatively titled his first work, a diatribe against princes, *The Chains of Slavery* (1774).[14]

Social Contract does not, however, consider slavery only in metaphorical terms. An entire chapter (book 1, chapter 4) is devoted to slavery of a more literal kind. In this section Rousseau asks whether slavery can in any circumstances be reconciled with right—whether, that is, it ever has a legitimate legal and political basis (221–25, 8–13). In raising this question he is entering into

---

13. Rousseau, *On the Social Contract,* translated by Frederick Watkins, 3.
14. Marat, *Chains of Slavery.* Marat wrote this work in English.

a debate with Grotius, who had argued that the enslavement of a people may be considered a legitimate outcome of war if it prevents the annihilation of the defeated group.[15] Dissenting from this conclusion, Rousseau argues that from the standpoint of reason it is impossible for an individual to alienate or sell his own liberty, and correspondingly that an entire people cannot elect or be forced to surrender its freedom. Slavery and right, Rousseau concludes, are simply contradictory terms (225, 13).

In this passage, as in the chapters of *On the Spirit of Law* in which Montesquieu attacks Grotius's position on slavery, an Enlightenment thinker challenges the arguments of the previous age from a perspective framed by a new emphasis on individual liberty. In both Rousseau and Montesquieu, however, this challenge is circumscribed by the fact that the question is explored in the terms established by Grotius and other theorists of the previous century: thinkers who drew their examples from the Bible and classical antiquity rather than the contemporary colonial context, and who focused on the enslavement of entire peoples rather than on individual bondage. Guided by Grotius's example, Rousseau, as we have seen, moves swiftly away from the subject of individual bondage to the servitude of entire peoples, a form of enslavement that in the mid-eighteenth century was much less prevalent than individual chattel slavery.

In summary, then, we have seen that key elements of Rousseau's political thought, notably in *Second Discourse*, are supported by ethnographic references to modern-day "savages," most often in the guise of the Caribs of the Antilles. Rousseau refers to Amerindians on an empirical basis, yet he describes them as though they lived in a static environment unmarked by historical change. Most glaring is his failure to mention the far-reaching social and cultural changes that had ensued from the European colonization of the Americas. Turning from savages to slaves, we find that enslaved Africans figure less prominently than Amerindians in Rousseau's anthropological discourse because they do not embody the forms of extreme alterity that he is at pains to describe. When Rousseau does refer to slavery, it is generally in metaphorical terms, to register the oppressive effects of political disenfranchisement in his own society. In this trope slaves become surrogates for contemporary Europeans, with the result that differences between political subservience and colonial slavery are thoroughly effaced.

The Savage Critique of Civilized Slavery

While Caribs occupy a central place in Rousseau's *Second Discourse*, they do not figure prominently in other eighteenth-century political discourses. If we

---

15. See above, 39–40.

survey the canonical texts of the French Enlightenment, we find that the Amerindians who appear most often are not the indigenous populations of the Caribbean but rather the Huron and Iroquois nations of France's colonies in Canada. This focus can be attributed to several interrelated factors. One was that Jesuit missionaries based in New France published accounts of their interaction with Native Americans well into the 1770s, whereas the Dominicans based in the Caribbean stopped producing narrative histories around the 1720s, when their mission transitioned from the Christianization of "savages" to the salvation of colonists and slaves. As previously observed, the colonial environments that were represented most extensively were those that involved encounters between "natives" and settlers. Colonies that presented problematic moral and social features such as slavery and miscegenation were rarely put under a spotlight. A related aspect of this pattern of representation was that the Caribs, when they were depicted at all, were portrayed as primitive people with limited conceptual powers. By contrast, the Hurons and Iroquois of New France were portrayed in several influential texts as rustic philosophers endowed with a superior capacity for reason. In these works "savages" are claimed to be more civilized than civilized Europeans, their superior capacity to reason and form moral judgments being attributed to their greater proximity to nature. Below I consider a cluster of eighteenth-century texts in which European cultural, religious, and political practices are critiqued from the perspective of native North American protagonists who serve as ciphers for the injunctions of natural law.

The first major work of this kind was *Nouveaux voyages dans l'Amérique Septentrionale* (*New Voyages to North America*) (1703), a popular travelogue published at the turn of the eighteenth century that went through twenty-five editions by 1758 and had a major influence both on later writing about New France and on philosophical discussions of nature and freedom.[16] Its author, Louis Armand, Baron de Lahontan (1666–1715?) was an army officer and cartographer who served in New France for over a decade (1683–94), and who traveled widely in Quebec and the Great Lakes region. As a participant in several French campaigns against the Iroquois (who were allied with the British), Lahontan sometimes lived for months at a time in Huron and Algonquin villages. He became proficient in several Amerindian languages and developed a detailed knowledge of Huron cultural practices. He was, in short, as Sankar Muthu suggests, a seventeenth-century precursor of the modern-day participant-observer (24). Lahontan was also a turbulent individual who had a somewhat checkered military career. He distinguished himself in skirmishes against British troops but afterward fell afoul of the governor of Newfoundland and was forced to flee to Europe, where he was branded a deserter and deprived of his rights of inheritance. Living in exile

---

16. Lahontan, *Nouveaux voyages; New Voyages to North America*. In the English translation several passages are rearranged, and the (unnamed) translator adopts a more moralistic attitude toward the Hurons' resistance to Christianity.

in the Netherlands, he recounted his Canadian travels in Canada in *New Voyages,* and also translated his experiences into a philosophical dialogue, *Dialogues d'un sauvage avec M. le Baron de Lahontan* (*Dialogues of a Savage with M. le Baron de Lahontan*) (1704).[17]

To understand Lahontan's affinity for native North Americans, and in a broader sense the literary appeal of these nations, it is necessary to evoke the specific form of colonial rule practiced in New France. Shortly after the founding of the French colonies in Canada at the beginning of the seventeenth century, it became obvious that the state would prove unable to send enough settlers to ensure the survival of the colony. To compensate for this deficit, colonial administrators formed alliances with local Amerindian populations, hoping ultimately to integrate them into colonial society. This policy involved a two-pronged strategy of evangelization and cultural assimilation.[18] Jesuit and Recollet priests undertook a mission of conversion, while secular officials launched a program of *francisation* (Frenchification) geared to replace practices such as nomadism and collective ownership with French modes of social organization. Schools were opened for the instruction of Amerindian children, and officials encouraged intermarriage between indigenous women and French men. The 1627 charter of the Compagnie de la Nouvelle France (New France Company) declared that any savage who was brought to the Christian faith would be considered fully French and would enjoy the right to live and own property in France. Along the same lines, in an oft-cited letter of 1667, Jean-Baptiste Colbert urged the *intendant* (civil administrator) of New France to make greater efforts to promote intermarriage, so as to create in the colony "un même peuple et un même sang" (one people and one blood).

Assimilation has often served as a watchword for French colonial policy, though it was only ever one of the protocols followed in France's colonies at any given historical moment. If it has garnered more attention than other policies, it is no doubt in part because it conveys a somewhat positive image of France as a colonial power. By attempting to assimilate at least some of its subject peoples, France showed that it saw them not as irremediably inferior others, but rather as potential citizens.

The doctrine of assimilation rests on a view of colonized peoples as "others" who, if given adequate cultural training, could learn to be French. In this respect it is aligned with the self-representation of France as a nation in which race enjoys little currency: a society in which culture is a more important criterion of citizenship than skin color or descent. But though French writers

17. Lahontan, *Dialogues de Monsieur le Baron de Lahontan*. A translation of the *Dialogues* as *A Conference or Dialogue between the Author and Adario...* is included in *New Voyages* (2:90–121). References are given to this edition in text.

18. On the policy of *francisation*, see Jaenen, "Problems of Assimilation," and Aubert, "'The Blood of France.'"

and subsequently French historians have emphasized assimilation, the historical scope of this doctrine was in reality very limited. New France was the only Old Regime *colonie* in which assimilation was attempted on a large scale, and it was not implemented there with any great degree of success. By the turn of the eighteenth century the policy of Frenchification had come under severe strain, and officials had begun to explore other models, notably those in place in the Caribbean. Historian Guillaume Aubert notes that in 1709 it became legal for colonists in New France to own Amerindian war captives, a right long enjoyed by colonists in the Caribbean. According to Aubert, this step was just one symptom of a wider political shift by which, as the strategy of Frenchification faltered, policy was remodeled on practices in the Antilles, an environment in which slavery was endemic and race was a defining factor.[19]

The writings of Lahontan were both a product of and a reaction to the policy and ideology of assimilation. It was because of this policy that Lahontan lived in proximity to indigenous people and became familiar with their languages and way of life. But this proximity also made him skeptical as to the plausibility of converting and "Frenchifiying" the Hurons, and about the desirability of this transformation.[20] In both *New Voyages* and *Dialogues of a Savage*, Lahontan emphasizes Amerindians' deep resistance to Christianity. In passages that echo comments made by Du Tertre and Labat, he notes that while they would play along with the missionaries for a while, the Hurons rarely made any firm commitments. Lahontan, however, was far from being perturbed by this reluctance to embrace Catholicism. Instead of interpreting the Hurons' resistance as a sign of their libertine nature, he sees it as a manifestation of their instinct for social and political freedom. In passages that foreshadow and likely influenced Rousseau, Lahontan comments favorably on Native Americans' distaste for private property and the technological advances of European society. He also claims that the Hurons looked down on the hierarchical and obedient French, considering them to be little better than "slaves" (2:8). Without thoroughly idealizing the Hurons, Lahontan portrays them as rational beings who resisted Christianity and French cultural norms for perfectly valid reasons. In a few passages he even goes so far as to brand them as "philosophes rustiques" (rustic/natural philosophers) (2:104; 2:12).[21]

The translation of the savage into the rustic philosopher is developed further in a philosophical companion piece to *New Voyages*, the *Dialogues of a Savage with M. le Baron de Lahontan*. In this fictional dialogue, Lahontan converses with an Amerindian named Adario, a character based, at least according to the text's preface, on "The Rat," a Huron chief mentioned frequently in *New*

---

19. Aubert, "'The Blood of France,'" 20.

20. See, for example, 2:92–98.

21. In other passages Lahontan comments favorably on the Hurons' skills and knowledge, e.g., their use of hieroglyphs to communicate and their ability to make maps (2:104–10).

Voyages. Refashioned into Adario, The Rat is portrayed as a Native American who has visited France and observed French customs at close range. Like the Persian, Siamese, and Peruvian travelers imagined by other eighteenth-century French writers, Adario participates in a strategy of critical alterity: the examination of French religious, cultural, and political life from the uninformed, and by implication innocent, standpoint of a cultural outsider. But whereas Montesquieu's Persians respond to French society in ways determined by their own highly developed culture, Adario's responses are shaped by his ignorance of civilized society and his immersion in nature.

The conversation between Lahontan and Adario revolves primarily around the subject of religion. Mimicking the discourse of colonial missionaries, Lahontan urges Adario to secure his salvation by converting to Christianity. The arguments he presents are more dogmatic than rational, however, and Adario meets them with a stalwart display of skepticism and common sense. He declares himself ready to accept that the universe is governed by a great spirit or divine being, but rejects as foundationless key Catholic doctrines such as papal infallibility (2:117–180) and the existence of heaven and hell (2:103). In passages that find their echo in Rousseau, Adario suggests that "primitive" societies are in many respects superior to advanced European ones. He observes that by living packed into congested cities where vice is rampant, Europeans have lost the robust health and long life span enjoyed by savages (2:160). He is also critical of Europeans' obsession with money, which he characterizes as "the father of luxury, lasciviousness, intrigues, tricks, lying" (2:140), and he identifies private property as the root cause of pernicious social inequalities (2:154–55). On the political front, Adario complains that Europeans are wont to set positive laws above natural goodness (2:123) and to sacrifice freedom to obedience (2:124). In a number of passages he goes so far as to characterize the subservience of Europeans as a de facto form of enslavement. I will come back later to these metaphorical allusions to slavery—another instance in which Lahontan's thought anticipates Rousseau's.

The strategy of critical alterity deployed in *Dialogues of a Savage* was reprised in several mid-eighteenth-century works. There is, indeed, a veritable subgenre of fictional texts in which Native North American travelers serve as mouthpieces for the critical examination of European mores from a primitivist perspective. One example is Jean-Henri Maubert de Gouvest's *Lettres iroquoises* (Iroquois Letters) (1752), in which an Iroquois traveler who has been sent to France on a kind of recognizance mission sends letters back to a friend who has remained in Canada.[22] Like Lahontan's Adario, Maubert's Igli questions features of French society such as the authoritarianism of church and monarchy and the subservience with which the French obey rulers and

---

22. Maubert de Gouvest, *Lettres iroquoises*.

rules. A more complex example of the genre is Voltaire's novella *The Ingenu* (1767).[23] I want to pause to consider this text for a few moments because it illustrates a somewhat different take on the "primitive" traveler paradigm. Whereas Rousseau, Lahontan, and Maubert de Gouvest take the perspective of the Amerindian other as the point of departure for their critique of modern European society, Voltaire subtly reclaims the savage critique of civilization as a process of enlightened self-critique.

The Ingenu is about a Huron traveler who, after arriving in France, finds himself embroiled in a series of confrontations with both spiritual and temporal authorities. By adopting the perspective of an "ingenuous" traveler guided by natural law and reason, Voltaire is able to highlight the absurdity of quarrels waged within the Roman Catholic Church, notably the quarrel between Jesuits and Jansenists, and to denounce the ravages of religious intolerance, his chief philosophical preoccupation in the 1760s.[24] The fact that the Huron is unversed in the ways of power also allows Voltaire to expose rampant corruption at the court of Versailles. Though Voltaire, unlike Lahontan and Maubert, holds back from attacking royal power itself, he seizes the opportunity to denounce the chicanery of petty officials and the ambitious machinations of aristocratic ministers.

But the novel's strategy of critical alterity is complicated by the fact that the Huron protagonist is recognized early in the narrative to be the long-lost nephew of the two warmhearted Bretons who are, serendipitously, the first people he meets when he arrives in France (17). In light of this discovery, the Ingenu's many impressive attributes, characteristics ranging from a rosy complexion and muscular physique to exemplary moral character and a prodigious capacity for learning, become, at least in principle, traceable to his French ancestry. It is surely not incidental that, unlike Adario or Igli, and despite his various run-ins with church and court, the Ingenu appears to gain something positive from his time in France. After he is arrested and thrown in the Bastille, he undertakes a rigorous course of study under the supervision of an elderly Jansenist who shares his cell (107–111). This program of reading renders him more reflective and less rash, the implication presumably being that book learning is a valuable complement to the lessons of Mother Nature.

Voltaire's qualified version of the good savage—a protagonist who combines the traits of Lahontan's natural philosopher with European looks and an enthusiasm for books—correlates in many ways with the writer's broader philosophical views. It is consonant, notably, with his play *Alzire*, which I discuss in the previous chapter, and with his response to the anthropological premise of

---

23. Voltaire, *L'ingénu; The Ingenu; or, The Sincere Huron; A True History*. Page numbers in the text refer to the translated edition.

24. During this decade Voltaire waged a vigorous campaign for the rehabilitation of Pierre-Paul Sirven and Jean Calas, two Protestants who had been wrongly convicted of murder.

Rousseau's *Second Discourse*. After reading Rousseau's account of man's social history, Voltaire ran off a scathing letter in which he observed to Rousseau that "no one has devoted so much wit to making us simple as beasts. Reading your work makes me want to walk on all fours." Continuing in the same sarcastic vein he explains that he would unfortunately not be able to run off to join the "savages of Canada" (as we saw earlier, Voltaire presumed Rousseau's savages to be North Americans), because he needed the ministrations of a European doctor, because the savages were at war, and because they had, in any case, long been changed for the worse by their contact with Europeans:

> I can't... set off to join the savages of Canada because the maladies to which I am subject make a European doctor necessary, secondly because those countries are at war, and because the example of our nations has made the savages almost as wicked as us. I will limit myself to being a peaceable savage in the solitude that I have chosen, close to your homeland....[25]

In light of this letter I suggest that Voltaire's take on the "noble savage" subtly separates the philosophical figure of the savage from the Amerindian as anthropological referent. By domesticating his savage protagonist, by depicting him as more Frenchman than Huron, Voltaire implies that the encounter with cultural alterity was not a necessary preliminary to the formulation of cultural critique. This move makes it possible to view the critique of laws and conventions from the standpoint of nature as a homegrown, European tradition rather than as a phenomenon born of the encounter between peoples.

We have seen that Enlightenment philosophical discourses often portray Amerindians as abstract figures, situate them outside of history, and efface the colonial framework within which their culture was observed. We have also seen, in the work of Voltaire, a propensity to domesticate critical alterity by reclaiming the uncivilized viewpoint as a purely European invention.[26] But despite these various tendencies we have also seen that Amerindians occupied a central place in Enlightenment philosophy. Perceived as embodiments of the alterity that resides in nature, they were seen to represent the ideal perspective from which to interrogate the ways of culture. The same could not be said about slaves and slavery. There was no parallel literary tradition in which French society was critiqued from the subordinate position of the slave: no enslaved travelers, no figure of the "noble slave."

Slavery does, as we have seen, play a marginal role in the "savage critique of civilization," since the constraint and artifice of European society was often

---

25. Voltaire, letter to Rousseau, *Correspondence*, 117. See also the article "Luxury," in Voltaire, *Dictionnaire philosophique* (*Philosophical Dictionary*).

26. Diderot plays with this idea in a somewhat different way in *Supplément au Voyage de Bougainville* (1772), where he casts doubt on the authenticity of the critical discourse of the savage by suggesting that it is a construction of European philosophy. See *Supplement to Bougainville's Voyage*, translated by Jacques Barzun and Ralph H. Bowen, 192. References in the text are to this edition.

denounced as a form of servitude. In Lahontan's *Dialogues of a Savage,* for example, the Huron traveler Adario states of monarchy that: "We ... [are] born free and joint Brethren, who are all equally masters, whereas you are all slaves to one man" (124). And with regard to Europeans' obsession with social decorum, he asserts that "you prefer slavery to liberty" (2:150).[27] These references are, however, abstract and metaphorical, and they should not be read as direct references to colonial chattel slavery.

Every so often the political metaphor of slavery falls away, and slavery of a more literal kind comes into view. After he has railed for several pages against the French preoccupation with private property, Adario suddenly announces that his conversation with Lahontan will have to end for the day because his "slave" has come to guide him home. Though there would seem to be a significant contradiction between Adario's discourse and his practice, neither character passes comment. For a fleeting moment Native Americans are shown to participate in regimes of hierarchy that overlap with those ascribed to Europeans, a revelation that complicates the schema on which the "good savage" is held up as the absolute other of the corrupt European. But as in many other works of the period, the metaphor of political subordination largely overshadows the reference to literal slavery.

Native Americans and African Americans in Chateaubriand

Though the period studied in this book concludes with the era of the French and Haitian revolutions, in the last two sections of this chapter I consider representations of Amerindians and enslaved Africans and the framing of cultural/ racial diversity in works by two French writers of the early to mid-nineteenth century. The purpose of this foray into a later period is to show how representational patterns established in seventeenth- and eighteenth-century literature were carried forward into later traditions of thought. In the wake of the French, Haitian, and American revolutions, writers could no longer portray the encounter between natives and Europeans as the defining reality of America. Instead, I show, they translated the trope of colonial encounter into a new Romantic idiom of belatedness, lost innocence, and exile. I explore this reframing in the work of the two most prominent nineteenth-century French observers of North America: François-René de Chateaubriand and Alexis de Tocqueville. This choice of writers is to an extent preordained, for as Dominique Jullien has observed, the main topoi of nineteenth- and twentieth-century French writing on America crystallized in their work.[28] Chateaubriand's and Tocqueville's

27. Though Lahontan alludes to the Amerindian practice of enslaving prisoners of war at several points in both *New Voyages* and *Dialogues,* the recognition that Hurons possessed slaves does not prevent him from portraying them as exponents of liberty and equality.

28. Jullien, *Récits du nouveau monde.*

descriptions of America have been discussed widely, and from a range of perspectives, but they have rarely been considered together, and with regard to what they reveal about the construction of racial and cultural diversity. Reading Tocqueville and Chateaubriand together I show how earlier traditions of writing on slavery and indigeneity, race and culture, were carried forward and adapted to the new political and cultural circumstances of the postrevolutionary Atlantic world.

In 1791, with the political situation in France becoming increasingly turbulent, the young François de Chateaubriand embarked on a six-month visit to the United States. This journey would provide the foundation for a series of interconnected texts. The best known of these works, *Atala; ou, Les amours de deux sauvages dans le désert* (*Atala; or The Love of Two Savages in the Desert*) and *René*, are generally read as novellas, but they were originally written as episodes of the monumental *Génie du christianisme* (*Spirit of Christianity*) (1802).[29] Published ahead of the rest of the *Génie*, *Atala* won wide acclaim and launched Chateaubriand's career on the European literary scene. In narrative terms it is a prequel to *René:* though the action is set in an earlier period, the story's narrator and main protagonist, the Natchez Indian Chactas, recounts the events of his life after the young French traveler René has told his story. *Les Natchez* (The Natchez), a lengthy prose epic, picks up where the narrative of *René* leaves off.[30] Chateaubriand later returned to the subject of America in a nonfictional genre in *Voyage en Amérique* (Voyage to America), a text that is part travelogue, part ethnographic description of Native American customs.[31] And finally, he revisited both his American odyssey and the pages that he had devoted to it in his autobiographical monument, *Mémoires d'outre-tombe* (Memoirs from beyond the Tomb), published posthumously in 1848–50.[32]

Though Chateaubriand was by no means indifferent to the United States as a dynamic new nation—in one famous, though probably fictitious episode he claims to have met George Washington—the main focus of his writing on the young nation was not its political culture or life in bustling cities such as Boston and Philadelphia, but rather what might be called "Native America," that is, the continent's flora, fauna, and above all its indigenous population.[33] His writing on these subjects is strongly inflected by a spiritual vision. In the decade between the 1791 voyage and the publication of *Atala*, Chateaubriand

---

29. Chateaubriand, *Atala; Génie du christianisme*. References in the text are to the following edition: *Atala; René*, translated by Irving Putter.
30. Chateaubriand worked intermittently on *Les Natchez* for many years. It appeared for the first time in the first edition of his *Oeuvres complètes*.
31. *Voyage to America* also first appeared in 1827 in the first edition of the *Oeuvres complètes*.
32. Chateaubriand, *Mémoires d'outre-tombe*. The chapters bearing on the United States were composed in 1822. Translations in the text are my own.
33. The meeting with Washington is recounted in *Voyage*, 1:92–95 and *Mémoires*, 411–17.

embraced Christianity and assigned himself the mission of bringing its inherent poetry to light. The virgin forests of Louisiana and the sublime majesty of the Niagara Falls are portrayed in his work as vestiges of divine creation. Correspondingly, Chateaubriand depicts the human inhabitants of these landscapes as poetic, almost ethereal figures. Several of them are also portrayed as converts to Christianity. Like the Native American figures of Enlightenment philosophy, Chateaubriand's Native Americans live in harmony with nature. But the natural world that they inhabit is one that is thoroughly infused with the presence of the divine.

Throughout his writing on America Chateaubriand represents himself as a what Ali Behdad has called a "belated traveler": a visitor who has arrived too late to encounter the pristine natural environment discovered by earlier voyagers but just in time to catch the last glimmerings of an originary splendor.[34] This stance is illustrated in a famous episode in which Chateaubriand describes his first encounter with indigenous people, a passage that appears in different versions in both *Voyage to America* and *Memoirs from beyond the Tomb*. Chateaubriand recalls that while he found the appearance of Native Americans to be suitably exotic, the impact of their alterity was considerably attenuated by the activity in which they were engaged, namely, a performance of French country dancing under the direction of a wigged and powdered maestro named M. Violet. Amused, but also disconcerted by this episode, Chateaubriand exclaims, "Was it not devastating for a disciple of Rousseau to be introduced to the savage life by a ball?"[35] The savages of late eighteenth-century America, he is forced to admit, were not the same people that had been described by Rousseau.

The transformative impact of colonization is addressed most directly in *Voyage to America*, a two-part work in which Chateaubriand first retraces his own itinerary, then offers a long description of American "natural history" and "the customs of the savages." This description is heavily indebted to a number of ethnographic sources, notably Antoine-Simon Le Page du Pratz's *Histoire de la Louisiane* (History of Louisiana) (1758), and Cornelius De Pauw's *Recherches philosophiques sur les Américains* (Philosophical Research on the Americans) (1768–70).[36] Since De Pauw's ideas marked a major transition in the European representation of Native North Americans, I want to consider for a moment how Chateaubriand's writing aligns with this broad shift.

As Philippe Roger explains in a history of French anti-Americanism, the Dutch writer De Pauw's *Philosophical Research on the Americans* had a

---

34. Behdad, *Belated Travelers*.

35. *Mémoires*, 427–28; *Voyage*, 103. This episode also figures in Chateaubriand's Middle Eastern travel narrative, *Itinéraire de Paris à Jérusalem* (1811).

36. Le Page du Pratz, *Histoire de la Louisiane*. Le Page du Pratz wrote extensively about the Natchez, who are central to Chateaubriand's American oeuvre. De Pauw, *Recherches philosophiques sur les Américains*.

transformative impact on European images of Native North Americans.[37] De Pauw pioneered a move away from the positive archetype of the "noble savage" toward a much more negative image of the "degenerate savage." This shift, which was grounded in the claim that America's climate could bring forth only degenerate species and races, was interwoven with new theories of human diversity crystallizing in the 1760s–80s, notably the ideas of Buffon. Chateaubriand's writing reflects the impact of De Pauw's depreciation of Native Americans, but it does so in a somewhat oblique way. That is to say, Chateaubriand picks up on the claim that Native Americans are a degenerate people, but he interprets degeneracy, or perhaps more properly degeneration, not as an effect of climate or race, but rather as a historical condition resulting from contact with Europeans.

The second part of *Voyage to America* opens with a detailed ethnographic tableau of Native American marriage and funeral rites, harvesting techniques, celebrations, hunting parties, and warfare. But having presented this sketch of Native American "culture," Chateaubriand rather unexpectedly shifts gear and, in a final section titled "The Present State of the North American Savages," announces that the customs that he has just painstakingly described are, to all intents and purposes, relics of the past:

> If I presented this tableau of savage America to the reader as the faithful image of what exists today I would be deceiving the reader; I have painted what was rather than what is. One doubtless still finds some traits of the Indian character among the wandering tribes of the new world; but the greater part of their mores, the originality of their customs, the primitive form of their governments, in short the American spirit, has disappeared. (2:381–82)

Having submitted that authentic Amerindian culture had all but vanished, Chateaubriand concludes with resignation that, "having recounted the past, it remains for me to complete my work by sketching out the present" (2:382).

Chateaubriand finds great deal less to say about the present than about the colorful customs and rituals of the past. In a brief and depressing analysis, he sketches a bleak picture of the corrosive impact of contact with Europeans on Native American culture. Cataloging an array of interrelated problems, he points to alcohol addiction, the accumulation of debt, and rapid depopulation as both causes and symptoms of degeneracy (2:389).

The effect of contact that perhaps most disturbs Chateaubriand, however, is the tendency toward cultural hybridization. He bemoans the genesis of what he sees as incoherent religious syncretisms (2:391),[38] and speaks scathingly

---

37. Roger, *L'ennemi américain*, 16–19.
38. See also Chateaubriand, *Mémoires*, 453.

about métis: biracial individuals who to his mind embodied not the productive mixing of cultures but rather the combined vices of European and indigenous culture.[39] Approaching culture in the manner outlined earlier in this chapter— that is, as a self-contained system—Chateaubriand takes a negative view of hybridization as a deleterious infraction of cultural purity.

The transition from ethnography to historical and sociological analysis that occurs at the end of *Voyage* reflects a wider bifurcation in Chateaubriand's writing on Native Americans. Some passages in Chateaubriand express dismay about the degraded condition of Amerindians, while others promote a nostalgic image of their free spirit and noble bearing. But even in this second kind of passage, Chateaubriand almost invariably positions himself, or his narrator, as the last witness to a world that is rapidly disappearing.[40] At the same time that he paints a poetic portrait of the free-spirited nomads of the American wilderness, he also gestures to the prospect of change looming on the horizon. Chateaubriand's nomads are always on the verge of becoming exiles: victims of European expansionism forced to move elsewhere, usually toward the west, in search of new lands.

Perhaps the most famous example of this form of writing is the epilogue to *Atala*. Narrated by a traveler who seems to represent Chateaubriand himself, this episode recounts a meeting with a party of Natchez Indians fleeing the onslaught of French and British settlers. Among the few possessions that they carry with them are the remains of their ancestors, including those of the narrative's star-crossed protagonists, Chactas and Atala. The narrator befriends a young couple whose infant son has died as a result of the rigors of the journey. (This is the scene pictorialized in Eugène Delacroix's well-known painting *The Natchez* [1823–35], which depicts a man and a woman resting beside a lake, the father cradling a baby, while the mother looks sorrowfully on.[41]) Nomadism is a central theme of *Atala*, which depicts not only the mobile lifestyle of some Native American peoples but also the restless wanderings of individuals such as Chactas and René. But the epilogue sounds a new note in its representation of enforced exile. For the refugees camped at Niagara Falls, exile is not a customary practice or a personal disposition but an irreversible historical predicament, a fate becoming increasingly prevalent in the early nineteenth century. In a move with enormous resonance for French Romanticism, Chateaubriand's narrator identifies with these exiles, drawing an analogy between the plight of the Native Americans and the

39. Chateaubriand, *Voyage*, 396–97; *Mémoires*, 453–54.

40. Chateaubriand's nostalgia is reinforced by the fact that he wrote about his travels in America over a period of several decades, during which time the continent changed dramatically. In *Mémoires d'outre-tombe* he notes to this effect that "if I were to see the United States again today, I would no longer recognize them: where I left forests I would find cultivated fields" (489).

41. *Atala*'s cultural impact is reflected in the fact that it also inspired a second well-known Romantic painting: Anne-Louis Girodet's *Atala au tombeau* (The Tomb of Atala) (1808).

impact that the French Revolution had exercised on his life: "Hapless Indians whom I have seen wandering in the wildernesses of the new world...you who showed me hospitality in the midst of your misery, today I could not return your kindness, for like you I wander at the mercy of men, and less fortunate than you in my exile, I have not brought with me the bones of my fathers" (82).

Americans of African descent occupy a far more circumscribed place than the continent's indigenous peoples in Chateaubriand's writing on America. Indeed Chateaubriand refers to slaves and to slavery in only in a few isolated passages. In both *Voyage* and *Memoirs* Chateaubriand recalls that the first person he met when he set foot in the United States was a beautiful young black girl.[42] In *Memoirs* he points to the irony of being met in the land of liberty by a slave: "It was a slave who received me in the land of liberty" (405), he exclaims. But Chateaubriand does not take this encounter as an opportunity to elaborate further on the problem of American slavery. Nor does he co-opt this attractive figure as the model for a fictional heroine, in the way that, according to his own account, he based characters including Atala and Céluta on Native American girls whom he met during his travels.

In one episode of *Voyage to America* Chateaubriand recalls feeling inspired by the solitude and pristine beauty of the natural environment of the Kentucky wilderness. This splendor moves him to intone a Rousseauist hymn to man's primitive freedom: "Primitive freedom, I discover you again at last! I move like the bird that flies before me....Run and enclose yourselves in your cities, submit to your petty laws; earn your bread with the sweat of your brow ...: I will wander in my solitary wilderness...I will be as free as nature" (133–34). But as he brings this poetic exclamation to an end, Chateaubriand wonders whether, in the future, Kentucky would be transformed into a patchwork of farms and settlements, and whether slaves would one day toil in its fields, beneath a master's whip:

> Will not slaves labor under the whip of their master, in these deserts where man paraded his independence? Will prisons and gibbets not replace the open hut and the tall oak...? Will this rich soil not give rise to new wars? Will Kentucky cease to be the land of blood, and will the buildings of men embellish the banks of the Ohio better than the monuments of nature? (161)

He does not attempt to answer these rhetorical questions. Rather, he leaves the question of slavery hovering in the air, as though he felt unable to examine it further.

42. *Voyage*, 87.

Somewhat revealingly, the same rhetorical technique is used in one other of the small group of passages in which Chateaubriand comments on slavery. Pondering the future of the American union in *Memoirs from beyond the Tomb*, Chateaubriand wonders:

> Will America conserve the form of its government? Will the States not divide? Has a deputy from Virginia not already upheld the thesis of ancient liberty with slaves, the fruit of paganism, against a deputy from Massachusetts who defended the cause of modern liberty without slaves such that Christianity has yielded? (496)

While on balance Chateaubriand seems here to uphold the cause of modern liberty without slaves, his framing of the issues as a series of rhetorical questions is strikingly inconclusive.

In choosing to set his American fictions—*Atala, René,* and *The Natchez*—in the southern United States, Chateaubriand was of course focusing on the very region of the country in which slavery was most prevalent. But while these narratives explore the history of conflict between Europeans and Native Americans, Chateaubriand says very little about the circumstances of the region's enslaved black population. One of the pivotal historical events in the saga of the Natchez is the Natchez Revolt of 1729–31, a rebellion against French colonial rule that was so mercilessly suppressed that the entire Natchez nation was virtually destroyed. The refugees whom the narrator of *Atala* encounters at Niagara Falls are in fact Natchez Indians fleeing the bloodshed that followed this ill-fated uprising. What Chateaubriand does not mention about the revolt, however, is that the Natchez were joined in their insurrection by hundreds of African slaves—rebels who, like the Native Americans, had undertaken to throw off the shackles of French rule.[43]

How do we account for Chateaubriand's lack of engagement with the moral and political issues raised by American slavery? Several factors may have been involved, including, closest to home, the writer's own family history. As Émilienne Leroux notes in her history of Nantes, Chateaubriand's father, René-Auguste, was a well-known slave trader.[44] Perhaps Chateaubriand was reluctant to enter into a discussion that would have resuscitated this chapter of his family's recent past. But Chateaubriand's relative indifference to slavery must also be placed in a wider context, because, as Robin Blackburn explains, it was perfectly consonant with the wider political attitudes of the Restoration.[45] Though the abolition of slavery had emerged as a political cause in the 1790s, in the postrevolutionary era only a small handful of militants continued to emphasize the issue. In *Spirit of Christianity,* a work published at the height of the

43. On the participation of enslaved Africans in the Natchez Revolt, see Midlo Hall, *Africans in Colonial Louisiana.*
44. Leroux, *Histoire d'une ville,* 55.
45. Blackburn, *Overthrow of Colonial Slavery,* 476.

conflict between France and rebel slaves in Saint-Domingue, Chateaubriand writes that the massacre of colonists by the rebels had utterly destroyed public sympathy for their cause. As Blackburn eloquently observes, "Chateaubriand, who made Europe weep for the fate of the Natchez, coldly argued, 'Who will now plead the cause of the blacks, after the crimes they have committed?'"[46]

A third factor may have been Chateaubriand's overall enthusiasm for French colonial ventures. In *Memoirs from beyond the Tomb* he expresses regret over the losses that France had sustained during the Seven Years' and Napoleonic wars, observing that the colonies had provided a useful outlet for population, as well as a valuable market for French goods (456–60). In another passage, included in both *Voyage* and *Memoirs,* he contrasts authoritarian British rule with the kinder and gentler approach of the French missionaries. He in fact goes so far as to suggest that Amerindians had come to miss the French: "Let it be said, to the honor of our country and the glory of our religion, that the Indians were strongly attached to us, and have never ceased to miss us."[47] This idealized account of French colonialism in the Americas of course refers primarily to assimilationist policies pursued in New France. Such nostalgia would no doubt have been more difficult to maintain had Chateaubriand looked more closely into the colonial history of French Louisiana.

But alongside these various factors I think that Chateaubriand's relative indifference to slavery bears of another interpretation, which concerns the extent to which his writing on the Americas was anchored in a grid of topoi and discourses established by earlier French observers. As we have seen, Chateaubriand envisioned America in terms of its natural landscape and native population, and portrayed it as a terrain of encounter between Europeans and indigenous people. His approach differed from that of earlier writers in the sense that he acknowledged and indeed emphasized the gradual transformation of Native American culture as a result of the spread of European and American civilization. Yet despite this acknowledgment of change, Chateaubriand cultivated the memory of the past in his description of the present, coating his account of "Native America" with a layer of nostalgia. Slaves, as a nonnative people, remained as marginal to Chateaubriand's vision of the Americas as they had been to earlier French travel writing. Unable to consider their past with nostalgia, or to take a stance in the political debate over their future, Chateaubriand contented himself with fragmentary allusions to these other subjects of Anglo-American domination.

"Minorities" in Tocqueville

In closing this chapter I turn to a nineteenth-century French description of North America that is more overtly political in nature: Alexis de Tocqueville's

---

46. Ibid.
47. *Memoirs,* 453; *Voyage,* 2:391.

De la démocratie en Amérique (*Democracy in America*), a monumental account of U.S. politics and society published in two parts in 1835 and 1840.[48] A classic of modern political thought, *Democracy in America* was the fruit of Tocqueville's eighteen-month sojourn in the United States in 1831–32. Unlike Chateaubriand, who dwells nostalgically on the remnants of precolonial North America, Tocqueville's main concern lies in describing and analyzing the dynamics of the United States as a modern urban society.

Native and African Americans do not figure at all in this description until the closing chapter of part 1. In order to justify this deferral and his treatment of these populations as a separate social group, Tocqueville explains that his primary concern was to describe democracy in the United States, a social and political order that did not include either Native Americans or enslaved or free blacks (316). One way of interpreting this gesture would be to say that Tocqueville proposes that democracy exists for those who are included in the democratic process. On this reading the exclusion of certain groups represents, not an internal flaw in the system, but rather the outer limit of democracy's jurisdiction.

This said, Tocqueville's decision to examine Native and African Americans apart from the mainstream of society but in relation to each other is also one of the most politically innovative aspects of the text. Whereas previous French chroniclers had largely dwelled on the plight of "natives" and ignored that of slaves, Tocqueville considers the history and future prospects of the two groups conjointly, acknowledging parallels in their experience as victims of European expansion. Using the contemporary-sounding terms "opprimés" and "oppresseurs" (oppressed/oppressors), he lays the groundwork for the conceptualization of groups subject to oppression and marginalization as "minority" populations.

Tocqueville pairs African and Native Americans on the basis of their common disenfranchisement, but he also underscores what he considers to be essential differences between the two groups. He states, in fact, that "these two unlucky races have neither birth, physique, language nor mores in common" (317). Like previous observers, Tocqueville describes Native Americans in terms of their free spirit. Yet rather than viewing this instinct as a positive trait, he interprets it as a fatal incapacity to adapt to new conditions. Influenced, no doubt, by De Pauw's depreciation of Native American culture, he argues that Native Americans found it impossible to live successfully alongside Europeans, not only because they were overwhelmed by the negative effects of contact, but also because of their fatal need for autonomy. Tocqueville certainly does not deny that Native Americans had suffered at the hands of European settlers—he states in one passage that blaming their dwindling numbers on famine rather than on deliberate persecution amounted to a abrogation of moral responsibility— but by focusing on their failure to adapt, he subtly shifts the emphasis that

---

48. Tocqueville, *Democracy in America,* translated by George Lawrence.

Chateaubriand had placed on dispossession onto the role of cultural dispositions. In this connection he emphasizes the tendency of indigenous peoples to overidentify with their cultural heritage, that is to say, to live in the past rather than contending with the circumstances of the present. "The pretended nobility of his origin fills the whole imagination of the Indian," Tocqueville writes. "He lives and dies amid these proud dreams" (319). In thinking about the "blame the victim" scenario toward which Tocqueville's analysis seems to veer here, it is perhaps worth asking to what extent his claim that Native Americans overidentified with their cultural heritage continued a long tradition of writing in which Amerindians had been viewed as living embodiments of cultural traditions, rather than as communities responding to rapidly changing conditions.

In a passage that strongly echoes Chateaubriand's epilogue to *Atala,* Tocqueville recalls an encounter with a group of Iroquois who were preparing to cross the Mississippi at Memphis. He states, with what for him is heightened emotion, that the image of their exile had haunted him ever since:

> At the end of the year 1831 I was on the left bank of the Mississippi, at the place the Europeans called Memphis. While I was there a numerous band of Choctaws (or Chactas as they are called by the French of Louisiana) arrived; these savages were leaving their country and seeking to pass over to the right bank of the Mississippi, where they hoped to find an asylum promised to them by the American government. It was then the depths of winter, and that year the cold was exceptionally severe; the snow was hard on the ground, and huge masses of ice drifted on the river. The Indians brought their families with them; there were among them the wounded, the sick, newborn babies, and the old men on the point of death. They had neither tents nor wagons, but only some provisions and weapons. I saw them embark to cross the great river, and the sight will never fade from my memory. (324)

But if this passage reprises many elements of Chateaubriand's account of the exile of the Natchez, there are also significant differences in the way that Chateaubriand and Tocqueville envisaged the forced migration of Native Americans. Though both writers viewed this displacement as a kind of fall into history, for Tocqueville this fall also coincided, for all intents and purposes, with the end of Native American history. He thus writes in one passage that "the ills that I have described are great, and I must add that they seem to me irremediable. I think that the Indian race is doomed to perish, and . . . that on the day when the Europeans shall be established on the coasts of the Pacific Ocean, it will cease to exist" (326). Whereas Chateaubriand identifies with Native Americans on the basis of a common experience of disinheritance, Tocqueville looks on their predicament with sympathy but views their territorial dispossession as a preliminary to outright annihilation. Obviously Tocqueville's pessimistic assessment can be ascribed to the fact that he visited America a full four decades after Chateaubriand. But I think that it is also consonant with his overall vision of Native Americans as a prehistoric people who, being defined by cultural heritage, could have no future in the modern world.

If, in Tocqueville's schema, Native Americans inhabited the "extreme edge of freedom," African Americans, by contrast, occupied the "ultimate limits of slavery" (318). Correspondingly, whereas Native Americans clung to the traditions of their past, black Americans had lost contact with, or were ashamed of, their cultural origins. Whereas one group was defined by its cultural traditions, the other manifested an extreme form of deculturation. Caught between two peoples—sold by Africans, repudiated by white Americans—African Americans, Tocqueville argued, had no direct link to Africa and no social or political stake in the new United States (317).

Tocqueville rejects outright the premise of proposals such as the scheme to resettle emancipated slaves in Liberia. He argues that after two centuries in the Americas, the project of a "return" to Africa had little chance of success (358–59). In his eyes the future of black Americans would inevitably remain intertwined with that of the continent's white population: "The two races are bound one to the other without mingling," he writes. "It is equally difficult for them to separate completely or to unite" (340). For Tocqueville this future coexistence of white and black Americans was one of the greatest dangers facing the United States: "The most formidable evil threatening the future of the United States is the presence of the blacks on their soil" (340). In the pages following this statement—which could be interpreted to mean either that the United States faced a great danger or in a more partisan sense that its white population was endangered—he proceeds to explore several potential scenarios of conflict. These forecasts include the total collapse of the union—a rupture between northern and southern states—and a civil war in the South pitting whites against blacks (357–61).[49]

Although, as we have seen, Tocqueville generally differentiates the status of Native Americans from that of African Americans, the two groups are brought together in his scattered references to racial mixing. In his discussions of both métis and mulattoes Tocqueville vacillates over whether mixed-race people are valuable intermediaries who have the capacity to defuse polarizing racial tensions or the degraded offshoots of a deleterious process of cultural and biological adulteration.

In *Quinze jours dans le désert* (Fifteen Days in the Desert), a posthumously published travel narrative written in conjunction with *Democracy,* Tocqueville describes a journey that he made across Lake Erie to Michigan, the frontier

---

49. While Tocqueville is deeply critical of European or Euro-American mistreatment of Native and African Americans, he also claims in a number of passages that Europeans are morally and intellectually superior to Africans and Amerindians. At certain points in the text these two perspectives collide—the passage in which he portrays the presence of blacks in the United States as a danger being a case in point—generating interpretative questions.

territory of the 1820s–30s, with the purpose of encountering Native Americans.[50] He explains that having come to America with his head full of James Fenimore Cooper and Chateaubriand, he was disappointed to discover that Native Americans were not strong, healthy, and free, but rather short and puny (361). He also recalls feeling dismayed by their color: they were not copper colored, as he had expected, but rather the same deep bronze color as mulattoes. Drawing an implied connection, not only between métis and mulattoes, but also between biological and cultural mixing, he adds, "Their physique announced the profound depravation that only a long abuse of the comforts of civilization can confer" (ibid.).

At Saginaw, which marked the frontier between the old America and the new, Tocqueville came upon the solitary cabin of a métis. Both the location and the structure of this dwelling, a merger between a wigwam and a hut, reflected the cultural "in-betweenness" of its mixed-race occupant, and Tocqueville seizes the opportunity to offer some general reflections on the subject of métissage. What he has to say on this subject is overwhelmingly negative. "The images of the world reflected in his crude brain," he writes of the métis, "appear to him as an impenetrable chaos. . . . His tastes are in contradiction with his ideas, his opinions with his morals" (404). Later he adds that "he prays to two altars: he believes in the Savior of the world and in the amulets of the jongleur" (405).

Interestingly, however, métis receive a somewhat more favorable treatment in *Democracy in America*. In Tocqueville's discussion of the Cherokee nation, the one Native American group that he considered to have successfully adapted to the European presence, métis are depicted as natural mediators between Amerindian and European cultures, and Tocqueville regrets in a footnote that there were not more of them in the United States (328–29).

It is instructive to compare this observation with a parallel paragraph concerning mulattoes in which Tocqueville writes that one solution to the dangerous marginality of blacks in America would be a thoroughgoing mixing of blood.[51] He notes that in regions where there are many mulattoes, the fusion of white and black races is less difficult, and reminds his readers that he had previously characterized métis as the mediating link between Europeans and Native Americans (356). Continuing in this optimistic spirit, he observes that "there are parts of the United States where European and Negro blood are so crossed that one cannot find a man who is either completely white or completely black" (356). Having said this, however, Tocqueville proceeds to

---

50. *Voyage au Lac Onéida: Quinze jours dans le désert*. This narrative was first published in the *Revue des deux mondes* in 1860.

51. The idea that a mingling of blood could bring an end to racial prejudice and tensions is contemplated more seriously (and in a more positive light) by Abbé Grégoire, one of the few prominent members of the Société des amis des noirs to survive the Revolution. See Gregoire, *De la littérature des nègres*.

claim in the very next paragraph that "of all Europeans, the English have least mingled their blood with that of Negroes," adding that although there were a few mulattoes in the South, there were fewer mixed-race people in the United States than in any other European colony (357).

In the ensuing pages, which evoke the future potential for a violent conflict either between North and South or between white and black Americans, Tocqueville once again changes course. Positioning southern Americans between whites and blacks, he asks, "Can one for a moment suppose that the southern American, situated as he will always be between the white man, with all his physical and moral superiority, and the black, would ever dream of mingling with the latter?" (357). While the point that Tocqueville is trying to make with this rhetorical question is fairly clear—white southerners felt inferior in relation to northerners and so defensively reinforced distinctions between themselves and the subordinate blacks—the way he phrases it has the apparently unintended effect of erasing the racial boundaries that white southerners are said to uphold. In sum, Tocqueville claims, at different points, that there were many or that there were few mulattoes in the United States, and proposes that the group most averse to miscegenation, southern whites, was itself, like mulattoes, an intermediate group situated precariously in the divide between white and black races!

Though the inconsistencies of this account can perhaps be ascribed to anxiety about miscegenation (we are pretty far here from the "race-blind" politics of intermarriage once contemplated in New France), I would argue, once again, that they also reflect important aspects of the legacy of French writing on the Americas. We have observed that seventeenth- and eighteenth-century French writers approached America less as the site of a developing colonial society than as a zone of encounter between European civilization and a precolonial or "native" culture. Africans and their descendants were underrepresented in this tradition both because they personified the harsh realities of slavery and because they embodied processes of métissage and creolization. Operating within this tradition of thought, Tocqueville not only laments the mistreatment of Native Americans by European Americans, but also regrets the adulteration of indigenous culture. Correspondingly, in his discussion of enslaved and free blacks—one of the first sustained representations of this group by a French writer—he struggles to situate African Americans in relation to the new nation's white population. His alternate affirmations and denials of the effects of métissage unintentionally gesture toward the fluidity of cultural boundaries in "postcolonial" North America, a mobility that he, like many previous and subsequent observers, was reluctant to acknowledge.

PART III

LIBERTY, EQUALITY, ECONOMY

6

Colonial Political Economy

At the beginning of Voltaire's 1768 tale, *L'homme aux quarante écus* (The Man with Forty Crowns), an elderly man explains to the narrator (the eponymous "man with forty crowns") that if France was less wealthy than it had been in the past, it was because "the land is not so well tended...there is a shortage of labor, and since day laborers now cost more than they used to, some colonists have let land they inherited lie fallow."[1] The old man blames France's stagnant economy on the nation's growing dependence on costly foreign luxuries. "A smelly powder from America; coffee; tea; chocolate, co-chineal, indigo...cost us more than sixty million a year," he complains (2). The narrator soon has an opportunity to test one possible remedy to these economic woes. A new land-based system of taxation is introduced, and since he is a landowner, he is required to double his contribution to the royal coffers. Unable to pay his dues, he is carted off to jail. On his release some time later, he encounters a ruddy, well-fed man with an opulent carriage and a suite of lackeys. They fall into conversation, and the man explains that although he has an income of four hundred thousand crowns a year—revenue from his investments in Cadiz (the America trade) and Surat (the India trade)—he pays no taxes at all, because he is not a landowner. Smoothing over this seeming injustice with a little economic theory, the well-off man opines that "if the Minister of Finance asked me to help the motherland, he would be an imbecile who doesn't know how to calculate....Because everything comes from land. Money and bank notes are nothing but tokens of exchange" (6–7).

1. Voltaire, *L'homme aux quarante écus*, 1.

I recap this story here because it concisely illustrates two important aspects of the development of French philosophy in the second half of the eighteenth century. The first is the rising importance of economic theory as a medium of philosophical reflection. *The Man with Forty Crowns* can be read as a late 1760s version of *Candide:* it is written in the same satirical spirit and, like the earlier work, follows the progress of a naive protagonist through a world filled with charlatans and fools. But it is more targeted than *Candide* in its critique of French politics and society. Indeed, it revolves around a single controversial issue: the causes of France's growing economic crisis and potential remedies to the problem. In the exchanges cited above, Voltaire rehearses the economic debates of the late 1760s, paraphrasing and parodying the theories of the "physiocrats," the first French school of liberal economic theory (see below, pages 215–19, for a discussion of physiocracy). Where *Candide* makes light of the tenets of Leibnizian optimism, *The Man with Forty Crowns* takes aim at the physiocratic argument that all wealth derives from agriculture, and that only land-based income should be subject to taxation.

The second important discursive tendency illustrated by Voltaire's story is the new level of attention conferred on colonial agriculture and commerce. The tale's allusions to exotic colonial imports, investments in Cadiz, and colonial land use are far from incidental. To the contrary, they reflect a growing preoccupation with the conduct of colonial trade, and with the impact of this commercial activity on France's troubled economy.

The rise of liberal economic theory and the centrality of colonial affairs to this new school of thought are the subject of the final section of this book. In previous chapters I describe patterns of avoidance and displacement: the diffuse cultural repression of slavery, and the ensuing invisibility of the colonial world. In what follows I describe the circumstances in which, in the late 1760s, silence evolved into discourse, and the colonies and slavery belatedly became topics of representation and debate.

The transition from silence to discourse was to some extent a function of political circumstances. In 1763, at the end of the Seven Years' War, France lost her colonies in Canada and Louisiana to England and Spain, a foreign-policy catastrophe that forced officials and writers to reevaluate the nation's colonial policy. But the establishment of colonization and slavery as subjects of literary and political representation also had a discursive dimension, and it is on these cultural conditions of possibility that I will focus. In this chapter and the next I argue that sustained representation of colonization in genres other than the empirical literature of travel and commerce only became possible in the context of the formulation of abolitionist arguments, and that in France an abolitionist perspective coalesced in conjunction with the rise of liberal economic theory. I propose that there was no sustained representation of the colonies without abolitionism, and no abolitionism (at least in the French context) without the appeal to economic interests that these new theories entailed.

In this chapter I give an overview of the principal stages through which economic deliberation on colonization and slavery evolved, underscoring the extent to which the discussion of colonial questions that took place in the 1770s and 1780s was underpinned by economic arguments. I show how a set of economic questions—including whether colonial commerce was lucrative and for whom; whether independent nations made more-profitable trading partners than colonial dependencies; whether trade barriers and corporate monopolies were beneficial; and whether slave labor was more cost effective than paid labor—shaped the representation of the colonial world in late-eighteenth-century France. Some aspects of the "story" that I relate here have been examined by other scholars. There has been a recent rise of interest in Quesnay and physiocracy on the part of economic historians,[2] and scholars including Malick Ghachem and Doris Garraway have written in interesting ways about the writing on colonial administration produced by members of the colonial/Creole elite in the 1770s and 1780s.[3] My contribution will be to highlight the continuities between these various discourses, and to emphasize the extent to which the debate between mercantilism and liberal political economy that took shape in the second half of the eighteenth century framed the representation of colonial questions.

In the book's final chapter I turn from overtly economic literature to the small corpus of late eighteenth-century fictional works that explore colonial slavery. As previous readers have established, the short stories and novellas of writers such as Saint-Lambert and Germaine de Staël approached the question of slavery from a psychological perspective. My reading of these works however, focuses not on their appeal to sentiment but rather on the incorporation of ideas borrowed from liberal political economy. By highlighting the central place that issues such as free labor and free trade, economic productivity, and agricultural improvement occupy in these texts, I demonstrate the close relationship between sentimental abolitionism and economic abolitionism.

Whereas the previous parts of this book point to patterns of avoidance and displacement, in this final section I show that from the late 1760s to the Revolution, slavery, along with other aspects of colonial policy and administration, was explored in a variety of public contexts and literary genres. Yet I also argue that while colonization was no longer a *repressed* cultural issue, it was a topic framed, and to some extent overshadowed, by adjacent concerns, notably the agenda of liberal economic theory. Many late Enlightenment French thinkers

---

2. A new critical edition of Quesnay's works was published in 2005 under the direction of economic historians Christine Théré, Loïc Charles, and Jean-Claude Perrot. Quesnay, *Oeuvres*.
3. Garraway, *Libertine Colony*, 218–92; Ghachem, "Age of the Code Noir."

recognized slavery to be an acute moral and political problem. Their articulation of this problem, and the solutions that they proposed to it, however, were couched less in terms of human rights than in the language of productivity, property, and economic growth. The fact that the first major critical response to slavery was articulated in economic terms is perhaps not surprising. Although colonial slavery clearly had important political, cultural, and psychological dimensions, it existed first and foremost as a system of economic exploitation. As a primarily economic phenomenon, slavery called for an economic response. The economic critique of slavery, however, carried significant limitations. Most significantly, it produced proposals for abolition and visions of the postslavery order in which protection of the colonies' economic viability was prioritized over the enactment of social justice.

Colonial Political Economy

In a book published in 1972, the historian Jean Tarrade observed that most histories of Old Regime colonialism had focused either on the military history of conquest or on the social history of plantations. Other aspects of colonization, for example, the laws and policies under which the colonies were administered and the body of economic theory that informed these laws, had largely been neglected.[4] Much has changed in the field of colonial history since 1972, but Tarrade's observation still holds true to the extent that relatively little attention has been devoted to the substantial economic literature on the colonies produced between the late 1750s and the Revolution.

Until the 1750s, French commercial policy was dominated by a body of ideas that had been formulated in the mid-seventeenth century. This set of principles, which was known as the *système mercantile* (mercantile system), rested on the argument that a nation's prosperity derives from its ability to achieve a positive balance of external trade and as a result to accumulate a large reserve of gold and silver. Once a nation had achieved this objective, the focus shifted to defending lucrative markets against foreign competitors. On the mercantilist model, trade was essentially understood as a zero-sum game in which rival nations competed against each other to control the flow of capital.[5]

Mercantilism was implemented through an extensive body of commercial laws, perhaps the most important of which was the 1727 edict known as the *Exclusif* (Exclusive), a statute that decreed that France's colonies could engage in trade only with France. The mercantile system also involved a high level of regulation of domestic manufacturing and industry. Laws dictated which raw materials and chemical agents could be used in the manufacture of a given product, leaving little scope for experimentation. During the ascendancy of

4. Tarrade, *Le commerce colonial*, 1:8.
5. On mercantilism and global commerce, see Wallerstein, *Mercantilism*.

Colbert in the 1660s–80s, France prioritized the manufacture of luxury goods. To maintain the highest standards quality controls were strictly enforced, largely under the auspices of the nation's official trade guilds, or *jurandes*.

In the second half of the eighteenth century French thinkers began to question mercantilism and the matrix of practices and laws that were associated with it. A new cohort of thinkers who called themselves *économistes* (economists) argued that wealth should be measured, not according to the quantity of bullion stored in the national treasury, or with regard to narrow criteria such as the positive balance of trade, but rather from the perspective of the production, circulation, and consumption of goods.[6] Although the *économistes* did not stop thinking in terms of national interest, they changed the ways in which this interest was defined. Rather than considering the nation to be coextensive with the state—which effectively meant the crown, since in Old Regime France public finance was amalgamated with the royal budget—they approached it as a community of private individuals engaged in processes of production, exchange, and consumption that were overseen and regulated by the state. These arguments betokened not a minor adjustment of principles but rather a profound paradigm shift, a widening of the conceptual field to encompass not only trade, money, and production but also practices of consumption and the relationship between wealth and the nature of government. As the title of Pierre-Samuel Dupont de Nemours's 1767 work, *De l'origine et des progrès d'une science nouvelle* (On the Origin and Progress of a New Science) indicates, economic theory was a "new science," an emergent discipline with its own methodology and vocabulary. Like all new and dynamic fields, it attracted thinkers and generated texts. According to Christine Théré, in the 1750s publication on economic issues increased fourfold in relation to previous decades.[7]

The rise of economic liberalism was historically and conceptually intertwined with the rise of political liberalism. These two sets of principles were, however, not entirely interchangeable. The political viewpoints of leading eighteenth-century economists ranged across a wide ideological spectrum. Some, for instance François Quesnay, the leader of the physiocratic circle, favored the enlightened exercise of absolute power. Others, including the Marquis de Condorcet, placed greater emphasis on individual freedoms and rights. Some upheld the rights of property owners, others the claims of those disadvantaged by the existing system. As Emma Rothschild writes of the two prominent economic liberalizers whom she studies in her book *Economic Sentiments,* one—Adam Smith—is usually regarded as an "economic conservative," while

---

6. As Catherine Larrère observes, these thinkers have often been lumped together as members of a single school, the "physiocrats." In reality, many did not identify with the economic circle associated with Quesnay. See *L'invention de l'économie,* 5.

7. Théré, "L'édition économique," 60.

the other—Condorcet—is widely perceived as a "utopian universalist."[8] As we shall see, one of the domains in which these political divergences came to the fore was these thinkers' approach to colonial issues.

When the *économistes* contemplated the colonies, what they saw was a system of cumbersome trade restrictions and commercial monopolies that stifled competition and inhibited individual enterprise. They also found the colonies' agricultural system to be outdated, and speculated that if it were rationalized, productivity could be dramatically improved. Between 1757 and 1794 French liberal economists picked apart the premises of what Pierre Dockès has called the "paradigme sucrier" (the sugar paradigm), the long-established view that sugar could only be produced on tropical islands, by African slaves, as a monoculture.[9]

The *économistes'* arguments against protectionism and monopolies and in favor of agricultural reform pulled in a variety of political directions. Criticism of trade restrictions and tariffs was sometimes allied with championship of the rights of planters, a group that resented the Exclusive because it prevented them from doing business on their own terms.[10] In other cases, however, arguments for free trade and free labor were accompanied by calls for the abolition of slavery.

The abolitionist arguments that gained momentum in Britain, France, and North America in the 1770s were guided by two main currents of thought. One was the principle of brotherly love and Christian charity propounded by American and British evangelical Protestants, notably the Quaker sect. The other was a more secular perspective grounded in philosophical ideas, the viewpoint that was dominant in France. Previous considerations of these philosophical arguments have tended to emphasize the role played by the theory of individual human rights, a tradition rightly viewed as one of the main contributions of Enlightenment thought. In her 2007 book, *Inventing Human Rights,* for example, Lynn Hunt represents the campaign for the abolition of slavery waged by the Society of the Friends of Blacks as one arm of a broader revolutionary movement to recognize and secure the rights of marginalized or oppressed groups.[11] But while this narrative is not without historical foundation, a degree of caution is warranted here. When we look closely at the prerevolutionary and revolutionary texts in which colonial slavery is debated, we find that the dominant discursive framework was not the philosophy of rights but rather liberal economic theory (though it would be true to say that arguments

---

8. Rothschild, *Economic Sentiments,* 2.

9. Dockès, "Le paradigme sucrier."

10. The *économistes* were strongly influenced by the Enlightenment tradition of concern for individual property rights, including the right of each person to own things touched by his labor, a perspective first set forth by John Locke in *Second Treatise of Civil Government* (1690), chapter 5.

11. Hunt, *Inventing Human Rights.*

about productivity and profit were often interwoven with moral and political claims). As we shall see, these economic bearings were strongly reflected in the kind of abolitionist proposals that French antislavery advocates formulated. Because they were as preoccupied with the maintenance of public order and the continued viability of the colonial economy as with the protection of individual rights, they typically called for gradual abolition, or for emancipation deferred to a safely distant future. They also tended to accept unquestioningly that in the aftermath of abolition, colonial society would continue to function more or less as before; in other words, that it would be divided between a class of owner-entrepreneurs and a class of "free" black laborers, in essence a new, racially defined colonial underclass.[12]

A final implication of the economic anchorage of French abolitionism was that many antislavery writers not only supported the continued existence of plantation colonies but also favored further colonial expansion. A number of prominent antislavery advocates called for the establishment of new agricultural colonies in Asia and Africa. They argued that the free workers of these new settlements would be more productive than slaves and that they would provide an important market for French manufactured goods. These arguments created the foundations for the liberal colonial ideology that took root in France in the mid-nineteenth century, a doctrine of benevolent colonialism in which the creation of new consumers was aligned with the tenets of the civilizing mission.[13]

In *Enlightenment against Empire* political theorist Sankar Muthu argues that political thinkers of the late eighteenth and early nineteenth century not only criticized colonial policy in the manner of precursors such as Bartolomé de Las Casas, but also went a step further by calling the entire imperial project into question.[14] For Muthu the rise of this "anticolonial" perspective was interwoven with a late-eighteenth-century shift in anthropological representation. Whereas thinkers from Montaigne to Rousseau portrayed "native" or "savage" peoples as uncivilized, uncorrupted, and in other ways fundamentally different from contemporary Europeans—descriptions that elicited sympathy for extra-European peoples but also opened the door for their dehumanization and exploitation—Diderot, Kant, and Herder tried to show that all peoples

---

12. This vision of the postabolition order still informed the thinking of Victor Schoelcher, the main metropolitan architect of the 1848 decree of abolition. In writings of the 1830s Schoelcher commented, for instance, that in the wake of emancipation blacks would be more contented, population would increase, and agriculture would be improved. Taking a position previously adopted by Dupont de Nemours, he also claims that one free worker is equal to five slaves. Even in the report preparing the decree of emancipation presented to the minister of the navy in 1848, Schoelcher emphasized that after emancipation blacks would return to their labors. See *Esclavage et colonisation*, 47, 145.

13. On colonial ideology in the mid-nineteenth century, see Pitts, *Turn to Empire*.

14. Muthu, *Enlightenment against Empire*, 4.

engage in the production of culture, a perspective that fostered identification among different cultural groups (8). Muthu suggests that the recognition of shared cultural agency allowed the very principle of colonial rule to be called into question (98–100).

I agree with Muthu's claim that viewing other human groups as producers of culture rather than as products of nature played an important role in the genealogy of opposition to slavery and other forms of colonial exploitation. I am less convinced, however, by his claim that Diderot, or other late Enlightenment thinkers, embraced an overtly anti-imperialist philosophy. As we will see in more detail later on, thinkers such as Diderot and Condorcet denounced many aspects of colonial rule. They abhorred the violence of conquest, the barbaric treatment of indigenous people, the ruthless pursuit of commercial supremacy, and the practice of slavery. But the question remains whether these critiques betokened a full-fledged anti-imperialist perspective or rather, as I propose, an immanent critique of commercial and colonial practices. One factor behind this difference of interpretation concerns the corpus on which judgments are based. As we have seen, Muthu's account of late Enlightenment perspectives on colonization is anchored in readings of philosophical anthropology and political theory. From my perspective it is also necessary to consider the intellectual tradition within which colonization was most widely debated in the latter part of the eighteenth century, that is to say, the discourse that I designate in this chapter as "colonial political economy."

The Problem of the Spanish Economy

The first stirrings of colonial political economy can be traced to the 1730s and 1740s, when a small handful of thinkers began to formulate ideas that departed from the prevailing mercantilist orthodoxy. Influenced by philosophical currents emanating from England, as well as by a variety of political and economic factors, including France's sluggish economy and a series of setbacks and crises in the colonial arena—not least the collapse, in 1721, of a massive colonial investment scheme set up by John Law, a Scottish banker who served as financial adviser to the regent—these thinkers began to question some of the principles under which the colonies had been governed since their formation in the mid-1600s. They sketched out what could be called a neomercantilist philosophy, a position rooted in established doctrine, but which in certain respects paved the way for subsequent developments in colonial political economy.

Mercantilist doctrine held that colonies existed in order to meet the needs of the metropole, and that their primary role was that of generating surplus revenue by producing export goods. Considered as outposts of national commerce, the colonies were declared off-limits to the merchants of foreign nations. Here, for example, is Montesquieu summarizing the mercantilist position in *Spirit of Law:*

The purpose of these colonies is to trade on more advantageous conditions than could otherwise be done with neighboring peoples, with whom all advantages are reciprocal. It has been established that the metropole alone shall trade in the colonies, and for good reason, because the design of the settlement was the extension of commerce, not the foundation of a city or a new empire. (391)

Laws introduced by Colbert in the 1660s and reinforced by the Exclusive specified that the colonies could only import goods that were made in France and transported on French vessels, and that they could only export goods to France on French ships. These restrictions were popular with French merchants but disputed by colonial planters, who aspired to sell sugar and other agricultural commodities on the open market. Planters also coveted the right to purchase provisions from Dutch and English merchants and from England's North American colonies, a right that would have been particularly beneficial in wartime, when naval blockades often prevented French merchantmen from reaching the colonies.[15]

Another aspect of the mercantilist commercial apparatus was the state's delegation of power to monopoly trading companies, notably the behemoth Compagnie des Indes, which enjoyed exclusive rights over several sectors of colonial trade. Born in 1719 of a merger between several earlier companies, the Compagnie went bankrupt in 1721 after Law's integrated system of banking and colonial investment came crashing down. It was subsequently reorganized, and granted fresh privileges over trade with the East.[16] In the West Indies, where individual merchants could conduct trade more easily (the distances involved were shorter, and there were established French ports), the Compagnie lost its exclusive rights in 1727, though it continued to exercise a monopoly on trade in certain parts of the African coast.

It is perhaps not surprising that one of the first French thinkers to question these arrangements was a former secretary to John Law. In 1734 Jean-François Melon published *Essai politique sur le commerce* (Political Essay on Commerce), a work that was to have an important influence on subsequent "neomercantilist" thinkers, including Montesquieu and François Véron de Forbonnais. Melon's *Political Essay* was a pioneering work in several regards. I will highlight two areas of innovation that bear on colonial commerce. One is

15. Another source of contention was the fact that, by letters patent of 1717, colonial commerce was restricted to thirteen French ports. As a result of pressure from the ports excluded from these lucrative arrangements, an additional seven cities were included in 1763, and in 1784 commerce was opened to all ports with the capacity to receive large ships. See Tarrade, *Le commerce colonial*, 1:89–90.

16. The company's monopoly over the East India trade lasted until the company itself was dissolved in 1770. Fresh privileges were accorded in 1787, when the company was reborn under the name Compagnie des Indes orientales et de la Chine. This monopoly was rescinded by the Constituent Assembly in 1791. On the history of the Compagnie, see Le Bouëdec, Haudrère, and Mézin, *Les compagnies des Indes.*

Melon's natalist-inspired critique of the Spanish colonization of the Americas, the other his vision for the reform of slavery.

As Law's former secretary and an enthusiastic supporter of colonial ventures, Melon seems to have felt compelled to engage with a question that had begun to preoccupy several French thinkers in the 1720s and 1730s: why Spain's economy seemed to have declined rather than thrived in the wake of the conquest of the Americas. Melon's conclusion on this point is that the massive influx of gold and silver that followed the conquest had created the conditions for spiraling inflation. Although mercantilism held that a large supply of gold and silver was always beneficial, Melon contended that this was not the case. A second argument made by Melon was that the establishment of colonies had depleted a population already weakened by the expulsion of Jews and Muslims. He hypothesized that this demographic decline had undermined Spain's domestic agriculture and manufacturing industries.

On the basis of these two points, readers are left to draw the conclusion that population is as essential to economic growth as amassing gold and silver. Among the influential readers who did draw this conclusion was Montesquieu, who reprised the essentials of Melon's analysis of the decline of the Spanish economy in *Spirit of Law,* and the Marquis de Mirabeau, who formulated a natalist critique of French colonial policy in *L'ami des hommes* (The Friend of Mankind) (1757).

In a later section of *Political Essay,* Melon turns to the issue of colonial slavery. Though he does not question the fundamental legitimacy of the institution, he does clearly feel that it raised moral questions. As one of the first French writers (other than travel writers) to examine colonial slavery, Melon struggled to locate the right perspective from which to approach it. After making the clumsily circular assertion that since slavery is practiced in the colonies, it must be morally legitimate, Melon ponders whether it would also be legitimate to introduce slavery in continental Europe. He argues that although, as a general rule, it is acceptable to injure one person if many others benefit, there are cases in which this maxim should not be applied. He speculates that in the case of slavery the transfer of one individual's property to another would create social and economic instability. He adds that this kind of disorder is characteristic of Oriental despotism, that it is indeed what makes Oriental government unpalatable to Europeans. In the end Melon concludes that transactions that are overwhelmingly advantageous to the state, as opposed to particular citizens, justify unequal treatment, and that is the case for colonial slavery (though not for self-destructive Oriental despotism). He nonetheless seems dissatisfied with this explanation because, by way of an afterthought, he observes that equality is in any event fundamentally a chimera, and that the workings of the state, like those of the Supreme Being, are impossible to apprehend in their entirety.

If Melon considered slavery in a colonial setting to be fundamentally legitimate, he nonetheless also felt that it should be reformed. He comments favorably on the 1685 and 1724 *Black Codes,* characterizing them as forward-looking restraints on the power of slave owners, and suggests that further legislation of the kind would also be beneficial. In the colonial order of the future imagined by Melon, slaves would acquire certain rights and benefits, notably the right to "retire" with a modest stipend when they reached old age, and the right to leave a cruel master (Melon compares this to the option to end the "indissoluble bond of matrimony," a strange comparison when we consider that divorce was not authorized in Old Regime France, but one that highlights the "domestic" grid through which Melon imagined slavery.) In this new dispensation, slave owners would be responsible for educating the children of their slaves, and in order to encourage population growth, one in every three children born to an enslaved woman would be emancipated.

It is hard to know what to make of these proposals. It is difficult, for example, to square the idea of giving slaves a pension when they reached old age with the fact that the average life expectancy of a slave in a Caribbean plantation colony at this time is often calculated to have been around seven or eight years.[17] A further layer of complexity is added by the fact that the enslaved people for whom Melon imagines this colonial welfare state are *not* the slaves of African descent who constituted the vast majority of the enslaved population in the 1730s. Melon argues that slaves should not be imported from Africa because this practice led to racial mixing and to the formation of a new race of "deformed" mulattoes. Although it is not clear exactly what Melon *is* suggesting, we can perhaps surmise that although he pronounced himself against the extension of slavery to the metropole, he favored creating a white colonial underclass, governed by paternalistic laws yet enjoying material advantages that were unavailable to laborers in France. (One model for Melon may perhaps have been the *engagés*.)

The idea that Europeans could be enslaved in conditions more favorable than those experienced by French workers had a significant afterlife in French social thought. Later in the century Pierre-Victor de Malouet, a defender of slavery whose ideas are discussed below, favorably compared the lot of slaves to the circumstances of the French working class.[18] Taking this idea to its conclusion, an anonymous 1797 manuscript discovered and published by Myriam Cottias and Arlette Farge called for the extension of slavery to the metropole as a remedy to the spread of poverty and delinquency.[19] The idea that French laborers might react positively to the option of enslavement reflects, I think, a mix of political impulses. Proponents of this idea were acknowledging the

17. This is, for example, the statistic given by the Gilder Lehrman Center for the Study of Slavery at Yale University in its online materials. See: http://www.yale.edu/glc/citizens/trade/page2.html.

18. Malouet, *Mémoire sur l'esclavage des nègres*. References below in the text are to this edition.

19. Cottias and Farge, *De la nécéssité d'adopter l'esclavage en France*. On Melon and slavery, see also 43–46, above.

extreme poverty that many French workers endured. But at the same time, they were understating the extreme conditions of colonial slavery. Proposals for a form of benevolent "white slavery" in fact share common ground with the orientalization of slavery described in the first section of this book. In both cases slavery was associated with a population other than Africans, and its image was softened such that it appeared to be a recuperable institution.

Several of Melon's ideas are reprised in Montesquieu's *Spirit of Law*, the work that was viewed both by contemporaries and thinkers of the following generation as the first major discussion of colonization and as a founding text of the new "economic science."[20] As we saw earlier, *Spirit of Law* establishes the basic tenets of mercantilist doctrine, foremost among them the principle that the colonies existed for the benefit of the metropole. In other passages, however, Montesquieu departs from the mercantilist position in important ways. Distilling arguments that he first formulated in an unpublished text titled *Considérations sur les richesses de l'Espagne* (Considerations on the Wealth of Spain), he argues that gold and silver are not wealth but signs of wealth, and that when these signs exist in excessive quantities, as happened in seventeenth-century Spain, they obliterate the referent that they are supposed to represent: "Gold and silver are a fiction or a sign of wealth. These signs are extremely durable, and by nature little subject to decay. But the more they are multiplied, the more they lose their value, because they represent fewer things" (393).[21] This distinction between money and the wealth that it represents was to pave the way for the views of the *économistes*, who similarly distinguished the accumulation of gold and silver from the generation of wealth.[22]

Another argument made by Montesquieu (again following Melon) is that the establishment of colonies had led to depopulation, and that the decline of Spain's population had resulted in economic stagnation. In the following passage of *Persian Letters* these various ideas come together, with Montesquieu depicting colonial conquest as the futile pursuit of empty wealth, and portraying America as an empty desert that consumes African lives:

> What is so strange is that this same America, which each year receives so many new inhabitants, is itself unpopulated, and does not profit from Africa's relentless

20. In 1759 the young physiocrat Dupont de Nemours traced his generation's obsession with "economic science" back to Montesquieu's magnum opus. See *Journal de commerce*, April 1759, 85–86.

21. This argument is developed further in book 22, which is devoted to the nature of money. For a fuller discussion of Montesquieu's writing on the impact of colonial expansion on Spain's economy, see my essay, "Exotic Economies."

22. In *Les mots et les choses* Michel Foucault characterizes Montesquieu as a thinker of the "classical age" who approached the representational status of money in terms of the correspondence between signs and things. By contrast, he identifies the *économistes*, who viewed money as one component of a dynamic cycle of production and consumption, as proponents of a "modern" theory of the sign. See *Les mots*, 14–15, 177–213.

losses. These slaves, transported into a different climate, die there by the thousand: the work in the mines, where both natives and foreigners are employed, the pestilential gases emanating from the mines, and mercury, which the miners are obliged to use all the time, destroy them beyond hope. Nothing can be more outrageous than to cause the death of an incalculable number of men in order to remove gold and silver from the depths of the earth; these metals are in themselves completely useless, and are only seen as wealth because they have been chosen as its symbols. (159)

Montesquieu's thesis that colonization leads to depopulation was rapidly established as orthodoxy. It remained unchallenged until the late nineteenth century (i.e., the expansionist years of the Third Republic), when the Société de géographie, a prominent "think tank" on colonial matters, published an essay that reexamined this question.[23] The author of this report argued that since Britain counted seven colonial subjects for every metropolitan subject, the establishment of overseas colonies could scarcely be said to have a depopulating effect. He concluded, to the contrary, that empire supplied not only goods but also men, including a valuable cohort of military auxiliaries (124).

The last figure in the trio of neomercantilist thinkers whose ideas I want to consider is François Véron de Forbonnais, an economic theorist who came to prominence in the early 1750s when he was named economic adviser to the reform-minded *contrôleur général des finances* (controller-general/minister of finance), Étienne de Silhouette. Forbonnais was steeped in French and English mercantilist theory, but his views on colonial issues were also informed by knowledge of a more practical kind: his experience managing a family business in Nantes, the leading port of the French slave trade. In addition to writing several widely read works on the history of French public finance,[24] Forbonnais authored one of the most visible midcentury discussions of colonial issues, the *Encyclopedia* article "Colony" (volume 3, 1753).[25]

From its opening lines, "Colony" espouses the tenets of mercantilist theory:

Since these colonies [of the Americas] have been established solely for the benefit of the metropole, it follows:

1. That they must be directly dependent upon it, and consequently under its protection.
2. That the founders of the colony must have a monopoly on trade there....

23. Girardet, *Le nationalisme français.* Some skepticism about the linkage between colonization and depopulation was voiced as early as 1770. See, for example, Raynal, *Histoire des deux Indes* 6:279–80.

24. These are *Éléments du commerce* and *Recherches et considérations sur les finances de France.*

25. Forbonnais also wrote the *Encyclopedia* article "Commerce" (volume 3, 1753), which overlaps with "Colony" on many points.

If the *colony* undertakes trade with foreigners, or consumes foreign goods, the amount of this trade and these goods is like a theft against the metropole.

But while Forbonnais upholds national protection, he is critical of the commercial monopolies that the state awarded to trading companies. He proposes that competition and the even distribution of land were preconditions for population growth, which he portrays as a prerequisite for increasing wealth:

> Estates must be divided equally among the children, so that the distribution of family fortunes can support a greater number of inhabitants; and commercial competition must be firmly established, because the ambitions of merchants will lead them to offer more loans to farmers against their crops than the companies would, being monopolistic and consequently in a position to dictate the price of goods as well as the term of payments.

Like Melon and Montesquieu, Forbonnais advances a critique of established colonial policy framed in terms of the need to encourage economic growth by increasing population. Unsurprisingly, at the end of the article, he directs his readers to the works of his two fellow neomercantilists. Unlike Melon and Montesquieu, Forbonnais does not include the issue of slavery in his discussion of colonial population; "Colony" is in fact one of the more glaring examples of an *Encyclopedia* article in which we expect to encounter a reflection on slavery but don't.[26]

Colonial Natalism

The critique of colonial practice from the perspective of its impact on population is developed more fully in *The Friend of Mankind* (1757), a long, digressive, but rhetorically brilliant essay that was one of the most widely read books of the eighteenth century. Its author, Victor de Riquetti, Marquis de Mirabeau, has been somewhat overshadowed by his illustrious son, the revolutionary orator Honoré Gabriel de Mirabeau, but he was in his own day a celebrity figure, hailed in France and abroad as "the friend of mankind." Mirabeau is often branded as a physiocrat because in 1758 he joined the small circle of agrarian thinkers and economic reformers clustered around François Quesnay. But the first and most widely read version of *Friend of Mankind* was written before this encounter, and it reflects rather the ideas of the previous generation of neomercantilist thinkers.[27] Notably, Mirabeau expanded Montesquieu and

---

26. Forbonnais does briefly refer to slavery in *Éléments du commerce*, where he says that slaves were necessary to the agricultural prosperity of the colonies.

27. After joining Quesnay's circle Mirabeau added material to *Friend of Mankind* that reflects Quesnay's emphasis on land as the source of wealth.

Forbonnais's ideas on population into a full-blown model of prosperity that ties the economic vitality of a nation to the size of its population.

As my discussion of Montesquieu and Forbonnais has suggested, French thinkers of the mid-eighteenth century were deeply concerned with the subject of falling population. In a study devoted to this preoccupation, Carol Blum argues that if "depopulation anxiety" was so widespread in France, it was not so much because population was falling or stagnant, as because it served a number of philosophical causes and intersected with some of the major moral and political debates of the day.[28] One of these debates was the long-running controversy regarding the economic and social effects of the consumption of luxury goods. The "luxury debate" was a multilayered European quarrel with roots in Bernard de Mandeville's celebrated *Fable of the Bees* (1729). In France supporters of the mercantilist policy of promoting the manufacture of luxury goods squared off against the followers of François Fénelon, the austere archbishop of Cambrai, who attacked luxury on the basis of Christian doctrine.[29] Melon and other neomercantilists took a midway position, defending luxury in moderation as a stimulant to economic growth. Mirabeau, on the other hand, opened up a new vector in the debate by siding with the antiluxury camp on socioeconomic rather than moral/religious grounds. In a series of arguments that were subsequently adopted by Quesnay, Mirabeau portrayed luxury as an agent of social inequality and by extension as a cause of depopulation and economic stagnation.

In one chapter of *Friend of Mankind* (volume 3, chapter 7), Mirabeau applies his thinking about luxury, inequality, and depopulation to the colonial universe. He took a keen interest in colonial affairs because, during the time that he was writing *Friend to Mankind*, his brother, Jean-Antoine-Joseph de Mirabeau, was serving as the governor of Martinique (1753–57). In letters to his brother, Jean-Antoine criticized many aspects of colonial society and administration. Victor, in turn, incorporated some of these critiques into his discussion of colonial political economy. For example, Mirabeau asserts that the "true strength" of France's colonies, which he identifies as agriculture and population, had been neglected in favor of an exclusive focus on trade.[30] Correspondingly, he objects vigorously to the exchange of domestic agricultural products such as flour and wine for tropical commodities such as coffee and sugar, which he dismisses as luxury goods of secondary utility (3:196–97). Perhaps unsurprisingly, the overseas possessions that Mirabeau valued most highly were France's territorial colonies, Canada and Louisiana (he goes so far

---

28. Blum, *Strength in Numbers.*

29. On luxury and the luxury debate in the eighteenth century, see Berry, *Idea of Luxury;* Berg and Eger, *Luxury in the Eighteenth Century;* Shovlin, *Political Economy of Virtue;* and Jennings, "Debate about Luxury."

30. Mirabeau, *L'Ami des hommes, ou traité de la population,* 3:179.

as to argue that France should attempt to win back Acadia, which it had lost to Britain in 1713).

Friend to Mankind also broaches the difficult subject of colonial slavery. In passages that suggest the influence of Jean-Antoine, Mirabeau criticizes the luxurious and indolent lifestyle of wealthy Creoles, whose reliance on slave labor led them to neglect their plantations. In rhetoric that anticipates physiocratic discourse, he also criticizes slave labor as an affront to the dignity of agriculture. Finally, as one might expect, Mirabeau claims that slavery was detrimental from the standpoint of population. He observes that the colonies' African population was decimated by the abject poverty in which it was forced to live and, like a few other observers of the colonial society, claims that women often aborted pregnancies rather than bear a child in such harsh conditions (3:205).

Because he took these positions, Mirabeau is often hailed as a critic of slavery and an enemy of racial prejudice: a "friend of mankind" in the most universal sense of the expression. In reality, his thinking on race and slavery was fraught with ambivalence. In one passage, for example, Mirabeau suggests that if the rigors of slavery were relaxed, masters would welcome slaves into their households. Yet rather than looking on this prospect with enthusiasm, he worries that it would result in the growth of the colonies' mixed-race population and warns that a new cohort of "métis" would take over the liberal professions, leaving lower-class whites to sink into decline (3:205). In another, he characterizes the gap between blacks and whites as an unbridgeable divide: "The slaves in our American colonies are a race apart, distinct and separate from our species by the most indelible trait, that is to say color" (3:204). As if to underscore these differences, he depicts slaves as "brutish" and alien— "They arrive either brutish or endowed with an instinct that is foreign to us" (178)—and claims that they are fundamentally incapable of industry (3:204). If these passages are anything to go by, Mirabeau's opposition to slavery had as much to do with racism and fear of métissage as with enlightened thinking about wealth and population. These underlying concerns did not, in any case, lead Mirabeau to call (à la Melon) for the termination of the African slave trade. Rather, applying laissez-faire logic in reverse, he argues that if slavery were subject to rigorous regulations, it would quickly die out.

A few elements of Mirabeau's demographic approach to colonial political economy were reprised by Étienne Noël Damilaville in the *Encyclopedia* article "Population" (volume 12, 1765). Like Mirabeau, Damilaville represents luxury and the social inequality with which it is associated as causes of depopulation and champions agriculture as an agent of population growth. He also connects slavery with inequality and despotism, arguing that slavery, like luxury, impeded demographic growth. Synthesizing and expanding claims made by Montesquieu and Mirabeau, Damilaville claims that long sea voyages and exposure to different climates and diseases decimated the numbers of European migrants, while Africans transported to Caribbean plantations perished in large numbers as a result of abusive treatment. Colonial slavery was detrimental, Damilaville seems to say, because it was a vast drain on the world's population. Above I mentioned that the subject of slavery is often absent from the *Encyclopedia* articles in which one expects to encounter it. At first glance "Population" appears to be a case of the opposite scenario. That is to say, one of the *Encyclopedia's* longest treatments of colonial slavery appears in an article in which we would not necessarily expect to find it. But this is actually not, as Yves Bénot suggests, yet another case of thematic displacement.[31] Rather, by 1765, the field of political economy, a genre of writing in which the question of population occupied a central place, had become the primary discursive context within which the colonies and slavery were discussed.

Colonial Physiocracy

If the rise of economic liberalism in England is associated first and foremost with Adam Smith, in the French context it is most often associated with the theories of the "physiocratic" school or movement. There is, indeed, a tendency to conflate eighteenth-century French economic liberalism with physiocracy, though in reality this philosophy was only the first avatar of an intellectual tradition that assumed many different forms between the late 1750s and the years of the Revolution. Like many first versions of an idea, physiocracy is a rather extreme and dogmatic philosophical statement. Subsequent thinkers would bring nuance to the arguments of liberal political economy, and reject outright some of its more radical ideas.

The "physiocrats" were a small group of like-minded thinkers clustered around the medical doctor turned economic theorist, François Quesnay.[32] Quesnay began to develop an interest in economic questions in the mid-1750s. He wrote articles on agriculture and the grain trade for the *Encyclopedia,* and later authored a number of dense economic treatises, including *Tableau économique* (1758), one of the first works to incorporate such appurtenances of modern economic theory as diagrams and statistical charts.[33] Quesnay's leadership of a group of thinkers that included Mirabeau—whom Quesnay is often said to have "converted" from natalism to physiocracy—was not just a matter of intellectual stature. As personal physician to Madame de

---

31. Bénot, *Diderot,* 169.
32. The term "physiocracy" appears to have first been used by Abbé Baudeau in the journal *Ephémérides du citoyen* in 1757. Mirabeau tried to recruit Rousseau to Quesnay's circle in the late 1750s. Beyond the obvious personality factor—Rousseau was simply not a "recruitable" individual—Rousseau and Quesnay's political ideas were quite divergent. Quesnay favored a noninterventionist, enlightened despotism, whereas Rousseau advocated a republican model with democratic and populist elements.
33. Quesnay, *Tableau économique.*

Pompadour, he occupied an apartment at Versailles and enjoyed an unusual degree of access to the leading figures of the court. Quesnay's collaborators also benefited from this access, which afforded them what for the period was a rare opportunity to influence high-placed government officials.

As the term physiocracy implies, Quesnay and his collaborators believed that government should be guided by the laws of nature. What they meant by this was that the state should allow nature to run its course and should intervene as little as possible in the affairs of private citizens. One area in which the physiocrats wanted the state to step back was the nation's commercial policy. Taking a laissez-faire stance on trade, they called for France's convoluted system of domestic and external trade barriers and tariffs to be dismantled.

But Quesnay and his circle were, on the whole, less preoccupied with trade than their mercantilist and neomercantilist predecessors. Their main interest lay in land and agriculture, which they viewed as the cornerstone of the national economy. In the *Encyclopedia* article "Farmers" (volume 6, 1756), Quesnay advocated wide-ranging agrarian reforms and called for increased research into the improvement of farming methods. The physiocrats' enthusiasm for nature and agriculture and concomitant distaste for urban environments obviously bears comparison with the thought of Rousseau, and indeed Mirabeau and Quesnay seem to have tried to recruit Rousseau to their circle at one juncture. Richard Grove has suggested that although Rousseau's "primitivism" is often viewed as a pre-environmentalist outlook, a forerunner of a perspective that solidified in Romanticism, in reality "Rousseau...was much more sharply and directly connected with a fully developed and practically oriented environmentalism."[34] He is alluding to the work of naturalists and horticulturalists who had close ties to Quesnay's circle, figures such as Pierre Poivre and Rousseau's friend and disciple Jacques-Henri Bernardin de Saint-Pierre. As I discuss below, both of these writers were influenced by their experience of colonial agriculture, and their work stands as an illustration of the "cross-pollination" of metropolitan and colonial ideas.

One of the physiocrats' signature ideas was the proposal to put an end to the wasteful practice of tax farming (the sale of the right to collect taxes to individuals known as "tax farmers," who were allowed to skim off a portion of the revenue) by replacing the nation's complex array of taxes with an "impôt unique": a single tax levied on revenue generated from agriculture. Since they believed that only land was truly productive, it stood to rights that only the income earned from agriculture should be subject to taxation. The physiocrats' proposal for a "flat tax" was highly controversial, not least because it would have put an end to one of the key privileges of the aristocracy: exemption from taxation. It was criticized and mocked from many quarters, including,

34. Grove, *Green Imperialism*, 224.

as we have seen, by Voltaire in *The Man with Forty Crowns*. Highlighting the potential flaws of Quesnay's system, Voltaire imagines a scenario in which an impoverished landowner is forced to shoulder the entire national tax burden, while a rich merchant who has amassed a considerable fortune in colonial ventures is given a free ride.

Though Quesnay himself did not write extensively about colonial economics, he did produce one important position piece on the subject, an essay titled *Remarques sur l'opinion de l'auteur de "l'Esprit des lois" concernant les colonies* (Remarks on the Opinion of the Author of the *Spirit of Laws* concerning Colonies), which was published in 1766 in the *Journal d'agriculture* (Journal of Agriculture).[35] Recognizing Montesquieu as the leading French authority on colonial economics, Quesnay undertook in this piece to analyze and challenge a presentation of the subject that he considered to be permeated with outdated mercantilist ideas. In essence, what he tried to show was that if, as Montesquieu had claimed, colonies existed for the benefit of the nation and to expand the nation's commercial base, then the restrictions associated with mercantilism represented a flagrant violation of this principle. He argues that although the Exclusive was designed to protect the nation's colonial markets, its real effects were to inflate production costs and lower commodity values. In place of the existing regime he calls for the institution of a system in which different nations, each with an abundant supply of goods of diverse kinds, engaged openly in trade. Quesnay also addresses the effects of trade policy on agriculture. He suggests that low prices translated into limited investment in agriculture, with the result that only the most fertile colonial land was cultivated. In the essay's closing paragraph, Quesnay observes condescendingly that if Montesquieu (who had died in 1754) had failed to appreciate these points, it was because he had not been exposed to recent developments in economic theory. The implication of this parting shot is clear: economic thought had evolved in decisive ways, and there was no point in looking to past masters to settle economic questions.

The physiocrat who took the keenest interest in colonial affairs was Pierre-Paul Le Mercier de la Rivière, a member of Quesnay's inner circle who was also one of the few Enlightenment thinkers with direct experience of the colonial world. From 1759 to 1764 Le Mercier held the post of *intendant* (civil administrator) of the Windward Islands (Martinique, Guadeloupe, and other French territories in the Lesser Antilles). His tenure coincided with the Seven Years' War, a conflict during which first Guadeloupe, then Martinique was occupied by British troops, and which created a deep economic crisis in the colonies. An energetic administrator, Le Mercier did his best to attenuate these economic problems, notably by establishing a small colonial bank, the capital of which

---

35. Quesnay, "Remarques sur l'opinion."

was drawn in part from his personal fortune.[36] He also successfully negotiated freedom of commerce in the French islands for the duration of the war, a relaxation that was to pave the way for future commercial reforms, particularly the replacement of the Exclusive with a somewhat less rigorous regime known as the *Exclusif mitigé* (Mitigated Exclusive) in 1767.[37] Though Le Mercier was recalled to France in 1764, he remained an important figure in colonial affairs and participated in several commissions charged with amending colonial legislation.[38]

In 1762 Le Mercier submitted a tract titled *Mémoire sur la Martinique* (Memoir on Martinique) to the most powerful figure in French foreign affairs, the Duc de Choiseul, who, between 1761 and 1766, concurrently held the offices of minister of foreign affairs, the navy, and war.[39] In addition to justifying Le Mercier's sometimes-controversial actions as *intendant*, the *Memoir* offered a detailed account of the economic predicament of the colonies in the aftermath of the Seven Years' War.[40] According to Robin Blackburn, this document had an important impact on Choiseul and helped pave the way for the Mitigated Exclusive.

Memoir first gives a pessimistic overview of the state of Martinique's economy, then proceeds to explore the main causes of these economic problems. Le Mercier identifies these as the subdivision of plantations among multiple heirs, and the perennial shortage of slave labor. He also makes a number of recommendations, arguing, for example, for the prohibition of further subdivisions (2:119–23), free trade in critical areas such as grain, wood, and slaves (2:123–25), and the cultivation of the islands' less fertile lands (2:141). In each of these ideas we can hear echoes of proposals formulated in relation to metropolitan France by Quesnay and other physiocrats.

Memoir on Martinique represents slavery as a necessary component of plantation agriculture. Indeed, it goes so far as to suggest that the liberalization of the slave trade would help to revive the colonies' flagging economies. In a later period, the 1780s, Le Mercier would become involved in a number of initiatives to reform slavery with a view to increasing productivity. Unlike *économistes* of the following generation, however, he never called for the

---

36. See *Le Mercier de la Rivière*, 1:38. Louis-Philippe May, editor of this edition, notes that Le Mercier was never fully reimbursed for this loan.

37. Under this new regime, which survived with some variation until 1786, the Antilles were permitted to purchase goods that France could not supply from foreign powers, and allowed to sell rum and tafia (a sugar syrup) directly to Britain's North American colonies. See Tarrade, *Le commerce colonial*, 1:88–91 and 2:176–99.

38. In the 1760s–70s Le Mercier served on the Comité de législation des colonies, a colonial advisory board established by the Duc de Choiseul. In 1782 a new minister of the navy, the Duc de Castries, asked him to draft a report on the budgets of the colonies, a mission that took him back to the Antilles.

39. Blackburn, *Making of New World Slavery*, 446.

40. Le Mercier de la Rivière, *Mémoire sur la Martinique*, in *Le Mercier de la Rivière*, 2:106–07.

emancipation of the workforce. Rather, caught between the assumptions of the past (that sugar could not be produced without slaves) and the emergent perspective that freedoms of all kinds would enhance productivity, he called in a more limited way for the deregulation of the slave trade and for reforms to the practice of slavery.

Reforming Empire

Le Mercier's memoir on Martinique circulated in an atmosphere of mounting concern about colonial affairs. The main cause of this anxiety was the loss of France's territories in North America, as well as its foothold in India, at the end of the Seven Years' War. But there were also other major problems, notably the financial predicament of the behemoth Compagnie des Indes, which in various avatars had held a monopoly on the Eastern trade since 1664. Crippled by debts incurred in India during the Seven Years' War, the company received sizable subsidies from the crown, and was kept afloat by means of yearly public lotteries.

In the aftermath of 1763, attempts of various kinds were made to address this multifaceted crisis. Under the leadership of Choiseul, France launched a number of compensatory colonial ventures. One was the acquisition/repurchase of several trading posts in west Africa, including Dakar, the future cornerstone of French Senegal. Another was the disastrous Kourou expedition: an attempt to build up the small French settlement in Guiana as a predominantly white settler colony. This ill-thought-out scheme ended in catastrophe, with most of the would-be colonists succumbing to tropical diseases.[41] Changes were also made with regard to the Company of the Indies. Following a concerted campaign by the partisans of free trade, the company's commercial privileges in the East Indies were suspended in 1769.[42] Finally, the years after 1763 were a time in which thinkers articulated new ideas and, at least intermittently, found government officials willing to listen to them. Many proposals for the reform of colonial policy and administration circulated in this period. Most, as we shall see, were marked in some way by the tenets of economic liberalism. The following few paragraphs consider several key examples of this merger between colonial

41. The Kourou mission was led by Étienne-François Turgot, the older brother of the economist and future controller-general Anne-Robert-Jacques Turgot. The settlers recruited for the resettlement scheme, principally peasants from Alsace and Lorraine, arrived in Guiana in the middle of the rainy season. Within a year twelve thousand had succumbed to malaria and other diseases. Despite its failure, the Kourou enterprise inspired a number of later schemes to develop Guiana as a settler rather than a slave colony, projects that reflected not only the growing difficulty of provisioning the colonies with slaves but also a growing enthusiasm for agriculture and increasing aversion to slavery.

42. The most important philosophical statement of the argument for the suspension of the company's privileges was Abbé Morellet's *Mémoire sur la situation actuelle de la Compagnie des Indes*.

reform and economic theory. Schemes that sought to apply the new currents of eighteenth-century science and philosophy to colonial administration have been variously characterized as experiments in "enlightened" (Vaughan) or "scientific" (McClellan) colonialism. I will highlight the economic currents of these initiatives to rationalize colonial practice.

Pierre Poivre, a well-traveled former employee of the East India Company and president of the agricultural society of Lyons, came to Choiseul's attention after delivering a series of public lectures on botany and horticulture. The minister was on the lookout for new, reform-minded administrators, and Poivre fit the bill. In 1767 he was appointed to take over the civil administration of the Indian Ocean colony of Île de France, which three years earlier had been retroceded from the Company of the Indies to the crown. In stepping into this new role, Poivre was charged with carrying out a number of official directives. These included balancing the interests of the colony's various social groups, conducting an official census, expanding the island's agricultural base to include cloves and nutmeg (with the subsidiary goal of breaking into the lucrative Dutch spice trade), and arresting the soil erosion and desiccation that Poivre had identified in his lectures as a negative consequence of plantation agriculture.[43]

In the early 1760s, Poivre had come under the sway of the physiocratic ideas of Quesnay, and his inaugural address to the colonists of Île de France resonated with the doctrines of this school. Ruffling the feathers of wealthy colonists, Poivre addressed the need for a shift from commercial or plantation to sustenance agriculture, and called for changes in the methods by which land was cleared for planting.[44] On the social level he portrayed the consumption of luxury goods as a cause of inequality and corruption.[45] Poivre also made controversial statements about the use of slave labor. He claimed that free labor would be more productive than slave labor, though he reluctantly conceded that slavery would continue to exist as it was accepted under French law and had to content himself with emphasizing that under his administration slavery would be strictly regulated. Ironically, the various social and environmental reforms implemented by Poivre appear to have contributed to an expansion rather than an attenuation of slavery in the colony. According to Megan Vaughan, the number of enslaved in Île de France rose from fifteen thousand to twenty thousand during the five years of his administration.[46] In this instance, the advent of "enlightened colonialism," the effort to rationalize colonial practice, seems to have led to the consolidation of the regime of slavery.

During Poivre's tenure in Île de France a number of forward-looking natural scientists visited the colony. Among these visitors were the botanist Philibert

43. Grove, *Green Imperialism*, 198.
44. Ibid., 201–4.
45. Vaughan, *Creating the Creole Island*, 69.
46. Ibid.

Commerson, who arrived in Île de France after accompanying Antoine de Bougainville on his voyage around the world, and Bernardin de Saint-Pierre, who honed his skills as a botanist while fulfilling official duties as a colonial engineer. Both Bernardin and Poivre later produced travel narratives that include descriptions of Île de France. Bernardin, who had early exposure to the colonial world, having spent a portion of his youth in Martinique, wrote about Île de France in *Voyage to the Island of Mauritius* (1773), and in his later best-selling novel, *Paul and Virginia* (1788). In these works, as in Poivre's *Voyages d'un philosophe* (Travels of a Philosopher) (1768), Île de France is examined from a perspective inflected with Enlightenment sensibility and shaped by an interest in the natural environment.[47]

As Richard H. Grove explains in *Green Imperialism*, Poivre and the naturalists who gathered around him had the opportunity to observe at close quarters the impact of plantation agriculture on a sensitive island ecosystem. Armed with their experience, they brought a new ecological consciousness to the period's thinking about colonization and global commerce.[48] In Poivre's travel writing environmentalism intersects with the agrarian economics of physiocracy. In *Voyages d'un philosophe*, for example, Poivre asserts, following Quesnay, that wealth derives from agriculture, and that agriculture thrives when governments follow the dictates of nature (*Voyages*, 5–6, 63). He points to China as an example of what enlightened government can do for agriculture and by extension for national prosperity (*Voyages*, 108–22). This enthusiasm for China translates Poivre's admiration for a country he had visited earlier in life as a young Jesuit missionary, but it is perhaps not incidental that Quesnay had also written admiringly of Chinese agrarianism.[49] Last, with its laissez-faire stance on commerce, *Voyages* takes a number of digs at the Company of the Indies. Among the many criticisms that Poivre directs against his former employer is that during its oversight of France's Indian Ocean colonies it had focused exclusively on trade, neglecting agricultural policy and turning a blind eye to the ecological devastation of the islands.

Other reform-minded discussions of colonial policy issued from the colonial administration and Creole elite of France's most populous and prosperous colony, Saint-Domingue. In the 1770s and 1780s a number of Creole lawyers and magistrates wrote descriptions of the colony that were attached to proposals for administrative reforms. These documents bespeak the desire of the white Creole elite to have a voice in the administration of their own affairs. They are also testaments to the growing sophistication of colonial society

---

47. Poivre, *Voyages d'un philosophe; Travels of a Philosopher.*
48. Grove, *Green Imperialism*, 168–263.
49. Quesnay offers an enthusiastic appreciation of China in *Despotisme de la Chine* (1767). As Richard Grove notes, it is reductive to see Poivre as a thinker influenced solely by the currents of European thought, as he was also indebted to Chinese, Zoroastrian, and Indian ideas (Grove, *Green Imperialism*, 168–69).

in the late eighteenth century. To borrow an expression used by Gene Ogle, these texts, in which colonial policy and administration are subjected to a rigorous critique couched in the language of "reason" and "justice," can be read as traces of a burgeoning "colonial Enlightenment."[50]

Perhaps the most far-reaching reform proposal by a writer based in Saint-Domingue was *Considérations sur l'état présent de la colonie française de Saint-Domingue, ouvrage politique et législatif* (Considerations on the Present State of the French Colony of Saint-Domingue) (1776–77) by Michel René Hilliard d'Auberteuil, a lawyer who lived and practiced in the colony for several decades.[51] The *Considerations* vigorously criticized almost every aspect of colonial policy and administration, and though well received by fellow reformers, including Le Mercier de la Rivière, it was quickly suppressed by the colonial authorities.[52] Gene Ogle suggests that *Considerations* was composed in the spirit of Montesquieu, Rousseau, and Raynal (44). Though I think that this characterization is fair, I would propose that the philosophical tradition within which Hilliard d'Auberteuil operates can be described in more specific terms as that of the liberal critique of mercantilism. Like liberal economists in the metropole, Hilliard d'Auberteuil objected to the constraints that the Mitigated Exclusive imposed on trade and insisted that these restrictions had a negative impact on the colonial economy. He also argued for a readjustment of the one-sided relationship between metropole and colony, calling, for example, for the creation of an autonomous colonial magistrature.[53]

As several recent scholars have noted, Hilliard d'Auberteuil also had much to say about race and slavery. He was deeply preoccupied with the growing economic power and social prestige of the colony's free people of color and proposed trying to rein them in by imposing a rigid racial distinction between whites and "mulattoes."[54] Following in the footsteps of several previous Enlightenment thinkers, Hilliard d'Auberteuil condemned the institution of slavery in principle, while justifying it in practice (1:130–32). Slavery was necessary to the colonial economy, he argued, and also beneficial for Africans, who were rescued from lives of ignorance and despotism. Like other aspects of colonial society, however, Hilliard d'Auberteuil felt that slavery needed to be reformed. He argued for reforms on humanitarian grounds, while also observing that

---

50. Ogle, "'Eternal Power of Reason.'"

51. Hilliard d'Auberteuil, *Considérations sur l'état*.

52. Though commissioned by the Ministry of the Navy, Hilliard d'Auberteuil's report was suppressed because its frank assessment of the colonial administration enraged Saint-Domingue's civil administrator. See Ogle, "'Eternal Power of Reason,'" 37–40.

53. See ibid., 35, 40.

54. On Hilliard d'Auberteuil, the free people of color, and the management of race, see Ogle, "'Eternal Power of Reason'"; Dayan, *Haiti*, 203; Garraway, *Libertine Colony*, 218–26; and Fabella, "'Empire Founded on Libertinage.'"

improvements to slaves' working and living conditions would be likely to increase productivity (1:132–41).

A second example of Creole reform writing is Émilien Petit's *Traité sur le gouvernement des esclaves* (Treatise on the Government of Slaves) (1777).[55] The *Treatise*'s author, a judge who served on one of Saint-Domingue's two high courts, had previously been invited by the Ministry of the Navy to draw up a colonial legal code. In his discussion of slavery, he offers a detailed overview of the conditions in which slaves lived and worked in Saint-Domingue, and undertakes a comparative analysis of the various European laws bearing on the management of slaves.

Petit was by no means as harsh a critic of the colonial regime as Hilliard d'Auberteuil. For the most part, he contented himself with describing the status quo in minute detail, though he did make a few minor suggestions for adjustments and improvements. If Petit is aligned with the spirit of Enlightenment philosophy, it is less because of what he says than because of the ways in which he says it. His exhaustive approach to the description of colonial laws and practices resonates with the great classificatory projects of the age, and as Malick Ghachem, who has devoted several interesting articles to Creole administrative proposals, observes, the very labeling of a discussion of slavery as a treatise on "government" situates Petit's commentary within the wider discourse of political economy.[56]

Ghachem sees the proposals to reform colonial administration and improve the management of labor penned by Creole authors in the 1770s–80s as extensions of the mercantilist doctrine of exercising control over every aspect of colonial affairs. But although control was certainly an important concern for writers such as Petit and Hilliard d'Auberteuil, it seems to me that this interpretation misses a key dimension of the intellectual foundations of a work such as *Considerations*. As colonial reform proposals typically tied the need for change to processes of liberalization and decentralization, the reforming impulse of this cohort of writers is better described as a departure from the mercantile system than as a continuation or reinforcement of it.

The calls for liberalization and reform issued in these works did not go unheeded. As in the 1760s, when Le Mercier's *Memoir* spurred Choiseul to implement commercial reforms, so in the 1770s and 1780s reform proposals authored by Creole administrators helped convince government officials that changes of various kinds were warranted. Decentralizing measures implemented in the 1780s initiated the recognition of colonists as a distinct political constituency. In 1786 the Mitigated Exclusive was superseded by the Traité de commerce, or Anglo-French Commercial Treaty, an agreement that liberalized

---

55. Petit, *Traité sur le gouvernement*.
56. Ghachem, "Age of the Code Noir," 68.

trade between France and Britain.[57] And in 1784, the *Black Code* was amended in a number of ways. Under the terms of the revised *Code,* each plantation was required to have its own "clinic," and limits were placed on the length of the workday and on the number of lashes that could be administered as a form of punishment. The role of overseers, who were often accused of brutality, was also more clearly defined. They were required, for example, to send their employers monthly registers recording the birth and death of slaves. Finally, slave owners were enjoined to allow their slaves to tend "provision grounds," so that they could grow their own food and supplement their official rations.[58] One objective of these reforms was to humanize the practice of slavery. Another was to improve colonial productivity: to "produce in the colonies the greatest revenue possible by means of good management, and to increase the black population by humane conditions, better nourishment, and by not harassing them constantly with barbaric treatment and excessive work," as one colonial commentator observed at the time.[59]

The Cost of Slavery

In a data analysis of eighteenth-century economic literature produced by the Institut national d'études démographiques (INED), Philippe Steiner shows that it was only after 1770 that discussion of the economic impact of slavery began in earnest.[60] Of the thirty-eight references to slavery that appeared in economic works between 1750 and 1789, 20 percent occurred in works written between 1770 and 1780, while 75 percent were in works written after 1780. Clearly, in the 1770s–80s French thinkers were beginning to consider slavery in new ways and, for the first time, to seriously question its economic benefits.

Steiner attributes the surge of economic writing on slavery that occurred in the late eighteenth century to the fact that in previous decades slavery was so "familiar" that its cost-effectiveness appeared to be self-evident.[61] I am not convinced by this thesis, which to me seems to overstate the degree to which French writers were aware of colonial practices, and to overlook the cultural

---

57. The signing of the Traité de commerce was precipitated by fiscal crises in both England and France, but it was also shaped by the arguments of the *économistes,* notably Dupont de Nemours. On the treaty, see Henderson, "Anglo-French Commercial Treaty of 1786." On Dupont's role as an advocate for the treaty, see Labrouquère, "Les idées coloniales," 128.

58. On provision grounds, see Berlin and Morgan, *Slaves' Economy,* 72–73. Provision grounds were forbidden by the articles of the 1685 *Black Code* because owners often forced slaves to produce all of their own food.

59. This passage, cited by Louis-Philippe May (*Le Mercier de la Rivière,* 1:121), is drawn from the deliberations on the reform of the *Black Code* conducted in the Conseil du Cap, an advisory body representing the interests of Saint-Domingue planters.

60. Steiner, "L'esclavage."

61. Ibid., 166.

censorship to which slavery was subject. Steiner's interpretation also raises the question of what happened after 1770 to defamiliarize slavery to the point that silence exploded into discourse.

I want to propose a different hypothesis, which is that the shift that occurred in the 1770s resulted from a combination of historical and cultural factors that included the defeat of 1763, the rethinking of colonial affairs to which this military debacle gave rise, and the expansion and refinement of economic philosophy. Before the emergence of liberal political economy, slavery was considered morally problematic but economically beneficial, an equation that led to cultural repression, and the displacement of the issue onto adjacent concerns. In the 1760s and 1770s, by contrast, not only the morality but also the economic benefits of slavery were called into question, a convergence that gave rise to discourse and debate.

There was also, I think, a further dimension to the outpouring of economic reflection on slavery that occurred in France in the late eighteenth century, and this was that beginning in the 1760s, economic discourses, like other branches of Enlightenment social and political thought, gradually became less abstract and more attuned to the specific concerns of the moment. In the field of economics this process was given significant impetus by the actions of Vincent de Gournay, mentor of the liberal economist Turgot, and the man usually credited with coining the expression *laissez-faire*. During his tenure as *intendant du commerce*, Gournay took the unprecedented decision to open up the records of public finance. As a result of this declassification, economists enjoyed a greater level of access to economic facts and figures than ever before and were able to comment in concrete terms on policies and their effects.

One place in which the impact of declassification of public finance on economic thought could be clearly observed was the economic journal *Éphémérides du citoyen* (Citizen's Almanac), founded in 1765 by the Abbé Baudeau. Instead of publishing abstract philosophical meditations on questions of political economy, *Éphémérides* published specialized, well-documented articles on focused economic topics. Not incidentally, it was in the pages of this journal that detailed calculations of the financial implications of slavery first appeared.

The founder of *Éphémérides,* Abbé Baudeau, was "converted" to physiocracy from mercantilism by Dupont de Nemours in 1766. Shortly after this change of perspective he authored two long articles on the subject of the colonies. The first of these pieces, "Des colonies françaises aux Indes occidentales" (On the French Colonies in the West Indies),[62] opens with a by now familiar move. Baudeau denounces slavery as morally offensive, then proceeds to justify it on the grounds that Africans lived under despotic regimes. (As we have observed,

---

62. *Éphémérides,* 1766, no. 5.

Hilliard d'Auberteuil, writing ten years later, followed exactly the same line of reasoning.) But having made these opening moves, Baudeau takes a step back and, striking out in a new direction, suggests that the time had come for the creation of a new kind of colonial order, a regime in which tropical crops were cultivated in Africa by free African workers rather than on Caribbean islands, and in conjunction with this proposal, he calls for the abolition of slavery. The convergence of these ideas illustrates a point that Christopher Miller makes about abolitionism, which is that emancipation finally became a viable idea when the irony of a system that moved slaves around the world to grow crops that could have been grown in Africa finally became apparent.[63]

But Bandeau's plan for abolition was, to say the least, a circumspect one. Slaves were to be freed at age twenty but they would be required to remain with their masters and to work for wages for another five years. It was no doubt because of its extreme caution that this plan was reiterated, with minor variations, in a number of subsequent works, including Baron de Bessner's *De l'esclavage des nègres* (On Black Slavery) (1774); the third edition of Raynal's *History of the Two Indies* (1780); and Condorcet's *Réflexions sur l'esclavage des nègres* (*Reflections on Black Slavery*) (1781).[64]

In a subsequent issue of *Éphémérides* (1766, no. 9) an unnamed "American" (i.e., Creole) correspondent took issue with Baudeau's arguments in favor of the abolition of slavery. Baudeau responded in turn by stating, rather vaguely, that the example of savages in the state of nature shows that men must remain in control of their own subsistence (1766, no. 10). Following this inconclusive exchange, the subject of slavery disappeared from the pages of the journal for several years. It resurfaced at the start of the 1770s, after the editorship of the journal passed from Baudeau to Dupont de Nemours, the member of the physiocratic circle who took the firmest stand against slavery.

In 1769–70 Dupont published in *Éphémérides* the most important work of French economic liberalism produced in this period, Anne-Robert-Jacques Turgot's *Réflexions sur la formation et la distribution des richesses* (Reflections on the Formation and Distribution of Wealth).[65] Turgot, who was Dupont's mentor (as well as Condorcet's) was the most accomplished French economic thinker of his age. His theories in several key areas anticipated the insights of Adam Smith.[66] He was also the most politically powerful figure among the *économistes*. In 1774 he was appointed by Louis XVI to the office of controller-general. This appointment was an enormous coup for the circle of the philosophes because it was the first time that a thinker whom they viewed

63. Miller, *French Atlantic Triangle*, 23.

64. Bessner, *De l'esclavage;* Raynal, *Histoire politique;* Condorcet, *Réflexions sur l'esclavage.*

65. Turgot, *Réflexions*. Reprinted in *Éphémérides du citoyen*, 1769, nos. 11–12; and 1770, no. 1. References in text are to the 1788 edition, my translation.

66. One of the areas in which Turgot anticipated Smith was the theory of the division of labor (see *Reflections* 2–5, 11–15).

as one of their own was given a significant role in government. It also testified to the unique status of political economy as an interface between the sphere of government and the world of the Enlightenment.[67]

Slavery is not one of the central topics of discussion of *Reflections on the Formation and Distribution of Wealth*. It comes up only as a peripheral issue, in conjunction with questions of property and labor, and for the most part it is treated in the same abstract way as in Montesquieu or Rousseau. However, *Reflections* does include a short passage in which Turgot leaves the plane of abstraction to consider slavery in the concrete context of the colonies. Having first raised the subject of slavery and its destabilizing effects in a broad historical sense, Turgot turns to the specific case of the contemporary slave trade and acknowledges its disruptive effects on African society: "This plunder and this commerce still reign in all their horror on the Guinea coast, where Europeans foment it by going to buy slaves to labor in their American colonies" (26). He also notes in a more economic vein that slave labor is essentially counterproductive. In order to make slaves productive, colonists were forced to work them too hard, and as a result many died and had to be replaced, Turgot explains. Having made these points, however, he slides back into an abstract register that is reminiscent of Grotius. Apparently losing sight of the fact that slavery still existed in the colonial world, he suggests that it had never proved possible to capture a sufficient number of "prisoners" to serve as slaves, and states that the peace treaties among nations had conspired to put an end to the institution (28).

When Dupont brought Turgot's *Reflections* to print in 1769, he took a number of liberties with the text, adding a number of embellishments that its astute author did not fail to notice. One of the principal areas in which Dupont made changes was Turgot's discussion of the cost-effectiveness of slavery. Here is Turgot commenting on these changes in a letter of February 20, 1770:

> I will limit myself to telling you straightforwardly that: 1) it can in no way be deduced from what I say that slavery has been good for any society, even in its infancy. As to individuals who own slaves, that is another matter. I wish very much that your claim that slavery never benefits anyone were right, for it is an abominable injustice, but I fear that you are wrong, and that this injustice is sometimes useful to the person who commits it. The human race is not so fortunate that injustice is always punished right away.... Sometimes remorse outweighs benefits that result from injustice, but when injustice is not acknowledged by public opinion, it does not excite remorse.... I do not believe...that in societies where slavery is established, masters have any scruples about owning slaves. It is therefore incontestable that injustice is often useful to whoever commits it, and that slavery is no exception to this rule.[68]

67. On Turgot's stormy tenure as controller-general, see Baker, *Inventing the French Revolution*, 112.
68. *Oeuvres de Turgot*, 3:337–39.

Writing in a characteristically precise and matter-of-fact style, Turgot suggested to Dupont that although slavery was morally reprehensible and unprofitable for the state, it might hold advantages for individual investors. Dupont, as we shall see, was not persuaded by this claim, and he quickly set about proving his mentor wrong.[69]

Dupont published his response to Turgot in the pages of *Éphémérides* (1771, no. 6). He clearly intended to make a major statement on the subject of slavery because he prefaced his discussion with a reproduction of the Marquis de Saint-Lambert's short story "Ziméo" (1769), a fictional account of a slave revolt in Jamaica that had recently been published to considerable acclaim. Dupont observes that whereas Saint-Lambert, as a poet, had the power to move hearts, he, as a specialist in economic theory, could make a different kind of contribution (216).[70]

Dupont opens his discussion with the blanket statement that if the cost of abolition were giving up sugar, then sugar would have to be renounced. This firm moral stand, however, prefaces a long attempt to show that a sacrifice of this kind was unnecessary. Though Dupont states categorically that ethics trump economics, he obviously felt that in order to sway opinion, moral reasoning had to be combined with economic calculation. There is, of course, a rather fine line between concluding that material persuasions are necessary to convince people to support a cause and embracing them as a reason for action. Rather like the "supplement" as analyzed by Jacques Derrida, Dupont's recourse to economic reasoning can be seen either to bring an additional element to a moral argument that is already complete, or to remedy an insufficiency within it.[71] As we shall see, the question of the relationship between moral and economic arguments for abolition is by no means an abstract one, since the nature of the arguments that were made had a direct impact on the way in which the process of emancipation came to be envisaged.

The basic premise of Dupont's argument is, somewhat ironically, one that he borrowed from Turgot, namely, the idea that, far from being "free," slave labor entailed many hidden costs. These expenses included the capital required to purchase slaves, the cost of replacing those who had died or run away, and the expenses associated with feeding and clothing slaves and caring for them

69. Evidence from other sources suggests that Turgot felt a strong moral opposition to slavery. In a letter of 1769 he complains that Dupont had written enthusiastically about Virginia in *Éphémérides* despite the colony's dependence on slave labor. And in his eulogistic biography of Turgot, Condorcet claims that, during his brief tenure as minister of the navy and the colonies, Turgot declined the honor of having a slave ship named after him, a tribute that other officials of the period had accepted complacently. See Condorcet, *Vie de M. Turgot*.

70. In a subsequent volume (1771, no. 8), Dupont discusses another abolitionist fiction, Jean-François Butini's *African Letters*. I discuss both works in chapter 7.

71. Derrida discusses the supplement's undecidable logic in his reading of Rousseau in *On Grammatology*.

during illness. Dupont also comments on the cost of repairing tools, often mishandled and abused by unwilling workers. After providing rough figures for each of these expenses, he finally concludes that the cost per day of slave labor was twenty-eight sous, a sum that he claims many French peasants would be glad to earn (235–36). These figures were later contested by Turgot but endorsed by Condorcet.[72]

Having presented his calculations of the daily cost of slavery, Dupont moves on to other lines of argument. Mobilizing laissez-faire theory and physiocratic agrarianism, he claims that free workers would be twice as productive as slaves, and, therefore, that it would be reasonable to pay them twice as much. He also notes that sugar was native to Africa and could be grown there by free workers more efficiently and more cheaply than on Caribbean plantations (243). Finally, channeling the period's nascent environmentalism, he argues that the soil of the Antillean colonies had been exhausted by decades of sugar production and needed to be turned over to other uses.

In a later issue of *Éphémérides* (1771, no. 12), Dupont published a response to a set of comments that had been sent to the journal by an unnamed "navigator," presumably a euphemism for a slave trader. This anonymous writer seconds Dupont's laissez-faire position, arguing, for example, that if indigo and coffee were cultivated by free men, they would be produced and consumed more widely, and as a result, prices would fall and profits would rise. He also proposes that Dupont's analysis of the hidden costs of slavery could be extended to the slave trade. He claims that the *traite* was much less profitable for merchants than people generally imagined, and provides a set of figures to prove his case. These calculations are followed by a detailed and unvarnished account of the conduct of the *traite*, in the course of which the author bemoans the depopulating effects of slavery both on Africa and on the maritime communities of Europe. Curiously, however, Dupont's interlocutor ends his letter by stating, in a rather unexpected twist, that it would nonetheless be impossible to abolish the slave trade, giving the often-cited reason that Europeans could not work productively in tropical climates. Shying away from abolition, Dupont's interlocutor argues that slavery should be reformed and that measures should be taken to increase the population of Creole slaves.

In a brief coda to the "navigator's" letter, Dupont promised to respond in the next volume, adding that he hoped to see slavery abolished in his lifetime. Why did he never reply? Though it is impossible to answer this question with certainty, it is tempting to suggest that he understood, at least on some level, that claims about whether slave or free labor was more productive or more profitable were ultimately inconclusive and could be marshaled in support of divergent positions.

---

72. Condorcet, *Réflexions sur l'esclavage*, 19–20.

Dupont did, as he hoped, live to see the abolition of slavery. He lived until 1817, long enough to see the abolition of slavery by the Convention in 1794, but also its restoration under Napoleon in 1802. His own life also took a sinuous path. Having narrowly escaped the guillotine, he left France for the United States, and as a lieutenant of Thomas Jefferson helped to negotiate the Louisiana Purchase of 1803. His son, Éleuthère, became a major figure in U.S. industrial capitalism and was the founder of the DuPont chemical company.

Éphémérides contains one final passage in which Dupont brings up the issue of slavery: his review of the Abbé Raynal's multivolume *Political and Philosophical History of the Commerce and Establishments of Europeans in the Two Indies*. This review is by no means enthusiastic. It points to many inconsistencies in the text, notably with regard to its treatment of slavery. At one moment slavery is portrayed as a moral scourge, Dupont observes, while at another it is deemed beneficial and useful. He adds that slavery is not the only issue on which *History of the Two Indies* lays out contradictory positions. It is equally inconsistent, he finds, on the subject of monopoly trading companies and on the benefits that can be derived from colonies (1771, no. 11, 183–84). Dupont was not the only economist who held *History of the Two Indies* in low esteem. In a letter to his mentee Turgot similarly objects to the text's many paradoxes and endless digressions.[73] In the following section I consider the apparent contradictions in this work, which did more than any other to establish colonization as a topic of political and philosophical discourse.

Political Economy in *History of the Two Indies*

History of the Two Indies was published in three different editions, in 1770, 1774, and 1780.[74] As Robert Darnton has shown, it figured among the list of "forbidden best-sellers" of the second half of the eighteenth century, its public condemnation in 1781 only increasing its circulation.[75] As the text's long, unwieldy title suggests, it is what today is called an "interdisciplinary" work. It explored a broad range of issues and brought together subjects that had not previously been considered in the same framework. By linking together commerce and navigation, the East and West Indies, political and philosophical reflection, *History of the Two Indies* indeed played an important role in constituting the discursive entity that we now call "colonialism."

Though it was published under the name of its editor, Guillaume-Thomas Raynal, *History of the Two Indies* was the work of many hands, and as such, like its precursor the *Encyclopedia*, it has a polyphonic quality. Passionate critiques of conquest and slavery are juxtaposed with passages that suggest the more

---

73. Letter of July 14, 1772, *Oeuvres de Turgot*, 3:576.
74. References are to the 1780 edition listed in "Works Cited." Raynal, *Histoire politique*.
75. Darnton, *Forbidden Best-Sellers*, 61–63.

matter-of-fact perspective of a well-informed administrator. Michèle Duchet has claimed that the project of writing a history of European colonialism was suggested to Raynal by a high-placed official at the Ministry of the Navy.[76] Certainly, many passages are written in the kind of neutral but reform-minded tone that this kind of official encouragement would invite. Because of these divergences, it is impossible to reduce *History of the Two Indies*'s presentation of any topic to a single, univocal position. The process of interpretation is further complicated by the existence of three different editions. Though each version is distinct, the editions overlap considerably. In the "final" edition of 1780, for example, freshly contributed material, including seven hundred pages written by Diderot, is juxtaposed with passages retained from the 1770 and 1774 editions.[77]

Yves Bénot has described Diderot's participation in *History of the Two Indies* as the culmination of a lifetime spent in defiance of despotism and injustice.[78] While I would not necessarily want to disagree with this characterization of Diderot's career, I think it is important to note that before his involvement with *History of the Two Indies,* Diderot wrote very little on issues relating to colonization. The year 1770 indeed marked something of a watershed in Diderot's intellectual biography. Prior to this time Diderot was primarily concerned with "domestic" social and political issues. Afterward he thought in more-global terms. In addition to his contributions to *History of the Two Indies,* Diderot explored questions bearing on colonization and global commerce in *Supplement to Bougainville's Voyage* (1772) and touched on the conduct and respective rights of masters and slaves in *Essai sur les règnes de Claude et de Néron* (Essay on the Reigns of Claudius and Nero) (1782). He even returned to one of his early works, the libertine Oriental novel *Bijoux indiscrets* (1748), a narrative that he had at one time dismissed as a piece of youthful folly, and added two new chapters, additions that were written concurrently with *Supplement to Bougainville's Voyage* and that share both its anthropological orientation and its concern with the long-term effects of travel and exploration.[79] As we have seen, this intellectual trajectory was by no means limited to Diderot. Rather, the entire field of French political thought underwent a process of globalization in the 1770s–80s, an intellectual expansion of which *History of the Two Indies* was both a symptom and a catalyst.

History of the Two Indies also illustrates a second intellectual trend of the closing decades of the eighteenth century: the diffusion of liberal economic

76. Duchet, *Anthropologie et histoire,* 173–76.

77. Research on Diderot's papers in the Fonds Vandeul and philological studies of the text have made it possible, in many cases, to determine which passages the philosopher contributed. See Duchet, *Diderot.*

78. Bénot, *Diderot,* 63–65.

79. These chapters circulated in manuscript form in the 1770s. They were first incorporated into the *Bijoux indiscrets* by Diderot's friend and editor Naigeon in 1798. In this edition they are titled "Le rêve de Mangogul" and "Des voyageurs" and numbered chapters 16 and 18. See *Les bijoux indiscrets* in *Oeuvres de Diderot,* 2:199–216.

theory beyond a narrow circle of specialists to a wider group of thinkers. Though Raynal and his collaborators were not "scientific" economists in the mold of Turgot or Dupont, *History of the Two Indies* reads as a popular re-hashing of contemporary economic philosophy. Its contributors channeled liberal economic theory, applying its principal insights to colonial contexts and questions.[80] Many passages of *History of the Two Indies* take issue with doc-trines associated with mercantilism, notably protectionist trade policies and the privileges accorded to monopoly companies. Others assert that slavery was economically counterproductive.

In the following paragraphs I consider how liberal economic theory in-formed two key sections of *History of the Two Indies:* the discussion of the East India trade in book 4, and the discussion of colonial slavery in book 11. But before turning to these passages, I need to comment briefly on my approach to the text. As noted above, *History of the Two Indies* presents scholarly readers with a number of philological challenges. In response to these complexities, some readers have limited their observations to the "final" 1780 edition, while many others have focused on the contributions of Diderot, which can be iden-tified thanks to the painstaking scholarship of Michèle Duchet.[81] Though I do not want to suggest that these approaches are illegitimate, they do reflect a number of critical assumptions. The exclusive focus on Diderot, for one thing, implies that the narrative sequence in which the passages that he contributed occur is more or less irrelevant. Though critical studies of Diderot have under-scored the dialogical or polyphonic quality of his writing, this reading practice seems, quite strikingly, to pull in the opposite direction by privileging singular authorship over dialogue and over questions of reading and reception.[82] Given these philological concerns, I have decided to approach *History of the Two In-dies* in a somewhat different manner and to consider it less as work that show-cases the radicalism of Diderot than as a repository of the varied attitudes to commerce and colonization circulating in late eighteenth-century France. As a result, while I have specific things to say about the contributions of Diderot, I try to situate these passages in their textual context, relating them to the argu-ments and ideas with which they are juxtaposed.

80. On the representation of commerce in *History of the Two Indies,* see Terjanian, "'Doux commerce' and Its Discontents."

81. Diderot was most involved in the production of the third edition of 1780, but he also made significant contributions to the 1774 edition and, as Gianluigi Goggi has shown, played a role in the compilation of the 1770 edition. See Goggi, "La collaboration de Diderot." For an analysis of the passages contributed by Diderot, see Duchet, *Diderot.*

82. Among the readings that approach *History of the Two Indies* primarily from the perspective of Diderot's views and radicalizing additions, I would include Bénot, *Diderot;* Muthu, *Enlighten-ment against Empire;* Aravamudan, *Tropicopolitans;* Goggi, *Diderot;* and Agnani, "Doux Com-merce, Douce Colonisation." See also Lüsebrink and Strugnell's introduction to *L'Histoire des deux Indes,* 5.

Book 4 of *History of the Two Indies,* which examines the European presence in India, is largely devoted to a critique of the stranglehold that the Company of the Indies, whose privileges had been suspended in 1769, had exercised on the Eastern trade. The company, and its even larger and more powerful British counterpart, are blamed not only for impeding the free flow of commerce but also for engaging in a violent struggle for domination. In the 1774 and 1780 editions this line of critical thinking is developed further, as the contributors ponder France's place in India in the wake of the Seven Years' War. Considering that France had been kicked out of India in 1763, *History of the Two Indies* sounds a surprisingly optimistic note about her future in the subcontinent. What underpins this optimism is the claim that the rival British Empire had become overextended and was therefore vulnerable. Following up on its critique of aggressive trade monopolies, *History of the Two Indies* argues that France could target this vulnerability by pursuing a commercial policy that was benevolent and cosmopolitan. By differentiating itself from the monopolistic and authoritarian British East India Company, it is suggested, France could ingratiate itself with the Indian population, which was likely to be receptive to a change of regime and might welcome a French attack as an act of liberation.[83]

In a passage by Diderot that is included in both the 1774 and 1780 editions, a note of caution is introduced into this optimistic scenario.[84] Apparently concerned that an attempt to dislodge the British from India would deteriorate into a process of reconquest, Diderot warns ominously that "this prosperity would end in catastrophes if overweening ambition caused them to pillage, to ravage, to oppress. . . . To conquer and to spoliate with violence are the same thing. The spoliator and the man of violence are always odious" (2:550). Rehearsing the tenets of the trade philosophy known as "le doux commerce" (sweet/ gentle commerce)—the view, associated in particular with Montesquieu, that trade is the foundation of a beneficial cosmopolitanism—Diderot underlines the importance of abiding by contracts, providing high-quality merchandise, respecting property and liberty, and tolerating other people's cultural customs (2:550–53).[85] He gestures, in other words, both to the importance of observing proper comportment in the conduct of transcontinental trade and to the

83. *Histoire des deux Indes,* 2:549. References in the text to the 1774 edition are to Raynal, *Histoire philosophique.* For the passage in question see 2:180–82. *History of the Two Indies's* optimistic assessment of France's prospects in India contrasts with Morellet's lucid assessment that if Indians were able to overthrow the British, they would scarcely allow another European power to take their place (*Mémoire sur la situation,* 155).

84. On the identification of these passages, see Duchet, *Diderot,* 70.

85. In *Spirit of Law* Montesquieu writes that "commerce cures destructive prejudices, and it is an almost general rule that everywhere there are gentle mores, there is commerce and that everywhere there is commerce there are gentle mores" (338). The philosophy of "doux commerce" is discussed in detail in Albert O. Hirschman's classic study, *Passions and Interests.*

need to avoid the kind of economic disappropriation and cultural domination that global commerce and/or colonial ventures all too often entailed.

Sankar Muthu has suggested that Diderot emphasized the distinction between benevolent commerce and conquest because he was fundamentally opposed to the latter. As noted earlier, I am not convinced that Diderot was, in such clear-cut terms, an anti-imperialist thinker. The passage cited above shows that Diderot was concerned by the propensity of international commerce to degenerate into violent conquest, but I am not convinced that this implies opposition to colonization per se. It is instructive in this regard to consider what Diderot goes on to say in the next few sentences. Having rejected acts of conquest, Diderot observes that the best way to achieve peaceful relations with the indigenous population would be to dispatch shiploads of young men and women to India with the purpose of encouraging intermarriage. "Increase not only productions, but also agriculture, consumers, and with them all kinds of industry" (2:554), he enjoins, mobilizing the natalist and agrarian ideas of Mirabeau and the physiocrats. Far from rejecting the principle of further global expansion, what Diderot seems to advocate in this passage is the reinvention of colonialism as a mechanism for the opening up of markets and the intermingling of populations. That what Diderot was entertaining was a liberalized theory of colonial expansion is confirmed in the following passages, in which a future of harmonious intercultural relations is imagined using a colonial vocabulary of "colonists" and "settlements," "subjects" and "natives."

The fragile boundary between conquest and commerce is also at issue in book 6, the first volume devoted to the European presence in the Americas. In all three editions this examination opens with a diatribe against the brutality of the conquistadors and the destruction of indigenous cultures that their arrival in the Americas had entailed. In the 1780 edition, Diderot brought a new level of pathos to this invective by lamenting, "Their race is no more. I must stop here for a moment. My eyes are filling with tears and I can no longer see what I am writing" (3:366). Toward the middle of the volume, however, the tone changes, as the critical account of conquest gives way to a favorable discussion of the material benefits that commerce with and colonization of the Americas had brought to Europe. In all three editions, the critique of colonial brutality transitions to an enthusiastic account of indigo, vanilla, and cochineal, and, later in the text, logwood, brazilwood, and tortoiseshell. The various manufacturing applications of these products are discussed, and production figures supplied. In a strongly nationalistic passage inserted in the 1780 edition, the act of international industrial espionage perpetrated by Nicolas Joseph Thiéry de Menonville, a French botanist who traveled to Mexico, discovered the secret of cochineal production, and imported samples to Saint-Domingue, is recounted effusively. "This rich crop [that] until now has been grown only to the profit of Spain, M. Thiery, a French botanist, braving more dangers than one can imagine, removed it from Oaxaca itself and transplanted it to

Saint-Domingue" (3:475), the author exclaims with satisfaction.[86] The sequence of passages devoted to tropical commodities concludes with an emotional celebration of (colonial) commerce as a medium of intercultural contact:

> May this kind of agriculture, as well as others, spread further and occupy new nations. What? Are we not all brothers? Children of the same father? ...Must I traverse the prosperity of my fellow man because nature has placed a river or a mountain between him and me? (3:476)

In several respects, then, book 6 follows a trajectory similar to that of book 4. In both volumes commerce that entails violent conquest—for example, the relentless pursuit of gold by the conquistadors—is harshly criticized, while peaceful commerce, particularly commerce involving agriculture, is contemplated enthusiastically. The potential of this kind of commerce to have a positive impact is indeed considered so great that borders are imagined to recede, as the particularism of nations and cultures is transcended by the universality of commerce.

The section of *History of the Two Indies* in which Diderot comes closest to articulating an overtly anti-imperialist philosophy is a chapter appended to book 8 in the 1780 edition. Here Diderot considers the circumstances under which it was legitimate to found colonies. Reprising arguments presented by Étienne-Noël Damilaville in the *Encyclopedia* article "Population" (volume 13, 1766), Diderot argues that the right to colonize should be limited to cases in which land is deserted or partially deserted. How does this rigorous interpretation of the right to colonize accommodate Diderot's arguments in favor of cultural and biological fusion? The answer, I think, is that Diderot gets past the strictures that he himself, following Damilaville, places on colonization by blurring the boundary between colonization and global commerce. In his calls for commercial exchanges in which trade barriers are removed and populations conjoined, he seems to envisage a new postcolonial, and indeed postnational, order in which the colonization of one group by another is rendered a de facto impossibility. The mechanism that allows for the emergence of this new order, however, is all too familiar, for it is the process of sending European, or more specifically French, subjects out across the globe to inhabit other regions.

An instructive comparison can be drawn between what Diderot has to say about métissage and intercultural relationships in *History of the Two Indies* with the ideas elaborated in *Supplement to Bougainville's Voyage,* a work from the same period that, at least on a first reading, appears to articulate an overtly anticolonial perspective. In *Supplement*—a philosophical response to the navigator

---

86. On Menonville's act of international industrial espionage see chapter 3, 109–10. Menonville wrote about his voyage and cochineal in his 1787 *Traité de la culture du nopal.*

Louis-Antoine de Bougainville's recently published account of his circumnavigation of the globe—Diderot voices skepticism about the aims and effects of European colonial expansion through the intermediary of two Tahitian protagonists, a "Vieillard," or elder, and a younger man named Orou.[87] In a long diatribe uttered as Bougainville is about to depart from Tahiti, the Old Man claims that more Europeans would inevitably follow in the wake of the explorer and warns his countrymen that before long Europeans would begin to exploit and perhaps even enslave Tahitians (187). But the text is concerned not only with exposing the bad intentions and practices associated with European colonization but also with contesting the assumption of European superiority. In a reworking of Rousseau it is suggested that societies that draw their principles from nature (Tahiti providing the key example) may in some key respects be considered superior to European society. Through the speeches and dialogues of his various protagonists Diderot observes, specifically, that whereas Tahitians attribute positive meanings to sexual relations, and engage in them frankly and openly, Europeans encumber them with contradictory moral interpretations, leading to embarrassment and shame.

What complicates this schema, however—and this is one of the points that differentiates Diderot's affirmation of nature from Rousseau's—is that Tahitians' wholehearted embrace of sexuality is grounded in principles of social utility. Sex is deemed to be good, not only because it is natural, but also because it gives rise to population and allows for the renewal of the labor force. Coming close to the theory of "human capital" set forth by Mirabeau, Orou implies that in Tahitian culture men embody a form of value equivalent to money (225). The upshot of this is that if Tahiti can, at least in certain respects, be deemed superior to Europe, it is not just because it is closer to nature but also because it is, from an economic standpoint, a more rational society.

A second point to be made about the perspective on colonization articulated in *Supplement* is that the positive view of cultural mixing and "miscegenation" that makes an appearance in *History of the Two Indies* also surfaces here. Though the Old Man castigates Europeans for bringing syphilis to Tahiti, deploying a metaphor of intercultural contagion that, since Montesquieu's *Persian Letters,* had figured the wider contamination of colonial contact, Orou suggests that Tahitians had in fact actively encouraged their women to have relations with the European visitors (211).[88] He explains that rather than badgering their French visitors for goods or money, the Tahitians had decided to "tax" them by using them to produce more children than would otherwise have been possible. He explains that one reason for this decision was that

---

87. Diderot, *Supplement to Bougainville's Voyage;* Bougainville, *Voyage autour du monde.*

88. In *Persian Letters* Montesquieu writes tacitly of the effects of syphilis in Europe that "owing to a misfortune that would be more appropriately called divine justice, the destroyers are destroying themselves, and decaying further every day" (163).

although Tahitians considered themselves healthier and more vigorous than Europeans, they thought Europeans were more intelligent, and believed that they would benefit from mixing with a "race superior to ours" (212).

Orou's endorsement of "miscegenation," along with the natalist/economic subtext that underpins much of what Diderot's Tahitians have to say, introduces a degree of complexity into *Supplement*'s anticolonial stance. This complexity is illuminated when we read the text alongside *History of the Two Indies*, a work that it references directly on several occasions, as if, in the mode of the cross-references of the *Encyclopedia*, to direct readers' attention to the thematic overlaps. Both texts channel the theories of political economy that were circulating in France in the 1770s and 1780s, notably the natalist current that passed from Mirabeau into the discourse of physiocracy. Given this convergence, I suggest that we can read the trope of racial mixing that occurs in this dialogue and in the passage of *History of the Two Indies* discussed above as an interface for the harmonious conjunction of Tahitian natalism and French economic liberalism. In both of these interwoven works, Diderot opposes colonial violence but endorses forms of transcontinental expansion that promote production and reproduction. This combination of ideas would come to occupy a central place in French colonial ideology in the following century, when colonization in Algeria and sub-Saharan Africa was aligned with the forces of market capitalism and the policy of intermarriage was reinvented as the doctrine of cultural assimilation.

The last section of *History of the Two Indies* that I would like to consider is the discussion of colonial slavery that appears in book 11. All three editions offer detailed descriptions of the regions of Africa from which slaves were imported, explain the history and conduct of the slave trade, and touch on certain features of the practice of slavery in the colonies. This account alternates between description and polemic, and between calls for the reform of the system and demands for its outright abolition.

These discursive shifts are interwoven with the use of the formal device of apostrophe to simulate address to the populations most immediately involved in slavery: on the one hand colonial planters/officials, and on the other the enslaved. As Michel Delon has observed, *History of the Two Indies* abounds in apostrophes that address both colonial elites and those who have suffered privations as a result of colonization.[89] These addresses, however, are far from symmetrical: whereas indigenous peoples and enslaved Africans were unlikely ever to read the words addressed to them, probate inventories and other archival sources show that *History of the Two Indies* enjoyed a wide readership among colonial planters.[90] Passages such as the sequence devoted to slavery and abolition must consequently be read both as a message addressed in real

89. Delon, "L'appel au lecteur."
90. On *History of the Two Indies*'s colonial readership, see Racault, "L'effet exotique," 119–20.

time to planters and colonial officials and as a kind of latent political discourse anticipating a future world in which both colonizer and colonized would share access to the written word.[91]

Following a lengthy passage in which reforms to the institution of slavery are advocated on both humanitarian and economic grounds, the text changes gear and contemplates the possibility of outright emancipation. A passage that Diderot added to the 1780 edition paves the way for this transition by noting that although the previous century had been characterized by its hatred of persecution and intolerance, scarcely a tear had been shed over the plight of the colonial slave:

> For more than a century the soundest, the most sublime maxims of morality have resounded in Europe. The brotherhood of all men has been established in the most touching ways in immortal writings. We despise the civil or religious outrages of our cruel ancestors and we turn our eyes away from these centuries of horror and blood. We lend our succor and our pity to those of our neighbors whom Barbary has bound with chains. Even imaginary misfortunes draw tears from us in the silence of our study, and above all at the theater. Only the fatal destiny of black men fails to interest us... the torment of a people to whom we owe our pleasures never touches our hearts. (6:167–8)

The proposals for emancipation that follow this lucid passage unfold in three different stages, with some variation among the three editions. The first set of arguments, presented in all three editions, though particularly in the 1774 and 1780 texts, are targeted proposals for reform. *History of the Two Indies* advocates improvements to slaves' living conditions, including better housing, improved nourishment, and a lighter workload (6:178). The reasons given for implementing these changes are both moral and economic: "For slavery to be made useful, it must at least be made mild... it is in the master's interest that the slave should wish to live" (6:177). It is also argued, once again largely on economic grounds, that as slaves born in the colonies were more resilient and more productive than those newly arrived from Africa, measures should be taken to increase the Creole population.

These paragraphs are followed (again in all three editions) by the observation that reform is not enough. "It is appropriate to look higher," it is stated; "let us prove in advance that no reasons of state justify slavery" (6:186). In a passage that echoes Montesquieu's chapter on the Atlantic slave trade in *Spirit of Law*, the author entertains various arguments that might be made against the abolition of slavery, then proceeds to refute them one by one. Among the counterarguments that are cited in this context are: the vicious and deceitful

---

91. In a famous passage of book 2, Diderot acknowledges these asymmetrical conditions of literacy and address. After urging the Hottentots of the Cape of Good Hope to flee from Dutch colonists, and even to attack them, he turns to his European readers and observes that no Hottentot will ever read his words (1:258–59).

nature of Africans (it is agreed that Africans have many vices, but this propensity is attributed to the conditions imposed by slavery); the claim that slaves are happier in the colonies than in Africa (a claim said to be belied by their efforts to escape); and the argument that enslavement provides a good opportunity for conversion (slavery is declared to be unchristian).

In the 1780 edition the process of emancipation is considered in greater detail. It is argued that slaves should be freed gradually rather than immediately, as they might otherwise do themselves harm. *History of the Two Indies* in fact reprises the proposal for staggered abolition laid out by Abbé Baudeau. According to this plan, we recall, slaves were to be freed in their twentieth year but were required to perform paid labor for their former masters for an additional five years.

Though this proposal may strike us as being, among other things, absurdly convoluted and difficult to implement, similar provisions were included in the British Abolition of Slavery Act of 1833. Under the terms of a system known as the "apprenticeship," freed slaves were required to work for their former masters for four and a half days each week. As Emma Rothschild notes, the apprenticeship was abandoned in 1838, not on moral grounds or because of documented cases of abuse, but on the basis of new economic arguments that linked the productivity of workers to the receipt of wages and the prospect of owning property (105–7).

Profitability is also an issue raised in *History of the Two Indies.* On the question whether it is more profitable to use free or enslaved workers, the text falls somewhere between Turgot and Dupont. Like Turgot, it argues that paying free workers would cost planters more than paying for slaves. Like Dupont, it finds that free workers would be more productive, and that a larger and wealthier colonial population would signify more consumers for metropolitan goods (6:208).

The doctrine of staggered emancipation is not the only model of abolition advocated in *History of the Two Indies.* In both 1774 and 1780 editions, passages contributed by Diderot assert that emancipation should occur immediately and propose that if Europeans did not quickly put an end to slavery, slaves would undertake to free themselves. In the 1774 edition Diderot famously foretells the coming of a black "Spartacus" who would avenge the oppression of his people by initiating a violent insurrection:

> The blacks lack only a leader courageous enough to lead them to vengeance and carnage.
>   Where is he this great man...? He will appear, let us not doubt it, he will reveal himself, he will raise the sacred standard of liberty. (6:221).

This rousing speech reworks a passage that appears in Louis-Sébastien Mercier's futurist utopia, *L'an deux mille quatre cent quarante, rêve s'il en fut jamais* (*The Year Two Thousand Four Hundred and Forty: Dream if There Ever*

Was One) (1771). The narrator of Mercier's story awakens in the Paris of the future and finds that the evils of Old Regime society have miraculously been corrected. During a tour of the city he comes upon a statue erected in memory of the black "avenger" who had achieved the overthrow of slavery.

In the 1780 edition Diderot added a new twist to his prophesy of a black insurrection by issuing what is effectively a warning to his readers, particularly the members of the colonial elite. With the coming of a black leader, he submits, "The Black Code will disappear; how terrible the White Code will be, if the victor consults only the right of reprisal" (6:185).

Diderot's "black avenger" speech is generally represented as a passage that sounds the final note in a sequence of less radical meditations on slavery and emancipation. While this characterization is accurate—the reference to a black avenger or a white code does come at the end of a long discussion of slavery, and it does introduce a note of urgency into a discussion marked by ambivalence and caution—there is more to be said about how Diderot's additions are incorporated into the text. It is important to note, for example, that this rousing passage does not mark the end of book 11, or even the end of a chapter. Rather, in all three editions, there is a seamless transition from the subject of emancipation to a discussion of the various valuable commodities that Europeans derived from the Americas, a list that includes not only sugar and cotton, but also—and perhaps surprisingly, given the tenor of the preceding passage—white Creoles. Though in the second half of the eighteenth century white Creole populations were often depicted negatively as degenerate or corrupt, in this passage they are praised for their robust physical health and dynamic spirit.[92] "If a happy revolution ever occurs in the world it will come from America," the author declares (6:272).[93] The reason given for this vitality is that Creoles represent a blend of European and American "families" and "races." Strikingly, though the author deplores white Creoles' immersion in slavery, and criticizes Creole men for their affairs with "negresses," salutary racial mixing is represented here as the product of intermarriage among "whites." (6:268).

Diderot's black Spartacus speech is unquestionably a text of great power. One can certainly understand why, in his classic study of the Haitian Revolution, *The Black Jacobins*, C. L. R. James felt moved to claim that the figure of a black Spartacus had inspired Toussaint Louverture.[94] Reinserting the speech into its full textual context does not diminish its eloquence. It does, however, affect the way in which we imagine it to have been read by eighteenth-century readers. In book 11, as in book 6, the transition from vehement condemnation of colonial abuse to enthusiastic appreciation of tropical commodities seems

---

92. Cornelius De Pauw and Buffon both claimed that Europeans exposed to the unhealthy climate of the Americas were subject to moral and physical degeneration. See chapter 5, 185–86.
93. In the 1780 edition see 6:262–82.
94. James, *Black Jacobins*, 24–25.

to combine the threat of a penalty with the promise of a reward. That is to say, Europeans are first castigated for the worst aspects of colonization, then warned of the danger of slave revolts and reminded of the benefits that a reformed colonial system would enable them to maintain.

The section of *History of the Two Indies* in which the influence of liberal economic theory is most clearly in evidence is the closing discourse of book 19, added in 1780. This discourse was principally authored by Alexandre Deleyre, though Diderot probably had a hand in it too.[95] Embracing standard liberal positions on issues such as commerce, luxury, and population, Deleyre champions free trade as a peaceful alternative to war, criticizes protectionism and commercial monopolies (10:258–59), and decries luxury as a corrupting influence that led to depopulation (10:244; 10:333). He calls for an end to monopolies, restrictions, and trade barriers, and for the replacement of these pernicious obstacles with a "system of general and unlimited freedom" in which weaker, poorer nations would be able to compete with more-powerful states (10:277).

Many of the ideas voiced in the closing discourse reflect a specifically physiocratic point of view. It is argued, for example, that "commerce, which flows naturally from agriculture, returns to it by the direction of its circulation" (10:279). Trading nations may enjoy the "fruits" of commerce, but only nations that encourage agriculture own the "tree" (10:279). In light of these claims the discovery of America is portrayed as a stimulus to European agriculture that led not only to the cultivation of tropical crops but also to the emergence of a vast new market for European grain. Deleyre also echoes the physiocrats by arguing that arbitrary taxes had impeded agricultural development. He likens the existing system of tax farming to Oriental despotism and recommends that it should be replaced with a simple land tax along the lines proposed by Quesnay. In the same vein he argues that governments should protect and encourage farmers, privileging agriculture over "the arts of luxury," meaning manufacture and commerce, because income earned from land is the cornerstone of every economy (10:296).

In the very last paragraph of the 1780 edition the negative and positive effects of the European discovery of the Americas are placed in the balance, and it is concluded, with reference to the violence and depredation that followed this event, that these effects had primarily been negative. Yet as we have just seen, this judgment comes at the end of a long passage in which the advantages of colonial commerce and agriculture are described most enthusiastically, and as such it appears to be more than a little contrived.

To sum up, I think that the following points can be made. Following a pattern that I describe in the middle section of this book, the contributors to

95. On Deleyre's contribution to *History of the Two Indies,* see Benot, "Deleyre."

History of the Two Indies, including Diderot, vigorously denounce the destruction of indigenous cultures that ensued from European expansionism (recall, for instance, Diderot's claim that at the memory of this sacrifice his eyes filled with tears), yet for various reasons, including the perceived economic and material benefits of the colonial system, they are less forthright about attacking other aspects of empire. The contributors look critically on intercultural encounters governed by the rules of the mercantile system, namely, trade restrictions and monopolies, practices perceived as entailing greed and violence. By contrast, relationships conducted in accordance with the principles of free trade are endorsed for their capacity to expand trade and agriculture and demolish cultural barriers.

One implication of this discursive framework is that the question of the fundamental legitimacy of colonization is largely subordinated to the interpretation of the commercial/economic principles that governed intercultural encounters. Like several other metropolitan and Creole writers of the 1760s–80s, the contributors to the *History of the Two Indies* rejected certain aspects of the colonial order, while imagining the emergence of a new and improved system in which protectionism would be replaced by open competition, monopolies would be dismantled, and slavery would be either reformed or abolished.

Rationalizing Abolition: Condorcet's *Reflections on Black Slavery*

In the late 1780s–early 1790s, against the backdrop of revolution in both metropole and colonies, colonization and slavery at last become hotly debated political topics. In this section I consider several works that illustrate this belated topicality: meditations on slavery and emancipation that spoke to the political zeitgeist while also channeling the arguments of liberal economic thought.

The Marquis de Condorcet's *Reflections on Black Slavery* was the first work by a French author devoted entirely to the argument for abolition. First published in 1781 to little fanfare, the book was published again in 1788 in a revised and expanded edition.[96] What precipitated this republication was the emergence of slavery as an object of public scrutiny. The creation of the Society of the Friends of Blacks in February 1788, and the looming debate over whether colonial planters and/or free people of color would be given a political voice under the auspices of the French Revolution, gave the colonial world a much higher profile than it had previously enjoyed.

The *Reflections'* polymathic author, the Marquis de Condorcet, was an expert in the field of mathematical probability, as well as a gifted political philosopher. Though he did not specialize in economic theory in the manner of Turgot

---

96. References in the text are to Condorcet, *Réflexions sur l'esclavage.*

and Adam Smith, Condorcet nonetheless contributed a considerable body of writing on economic topics. All of Condorcet's economic works are strongly marked by the liberal theories of the period. His early writings, for example, include the *Encyclopedia* articles "Monopole" and "Monopoliste" (volume 10, 1765), both diatribes against commercial privileges and in favor of free trade. In the mid-1770s, when Turgot was appointed controller-general, he invited Condorcet to serve under him as inspector-general of the mint. In this capacity Condorcet wrote two long pieces on the topic of the liberalization of the grain trade, a measure that Turgot implemented, amid much controversy, in 1774.[97] *Reflections on Black Slavery* is not an overtly economic text, but as we shall see, it is a work that accords an important place to economic questions and applies arguments about commerce, freedom, and prosperity that Condorcet had explored in other contexts to the issue of colonial slavery.

Borrowing a device used by Montesquieu and other Enlightenment writers, Condorcet writes in the name of a fictional persona, a Swiss pastor named Jacob Schwartz (in English, "Jacob Black"). As Joseph Jurt has observed, Condorcet's adoption of this "black mask" can be read as a gesture toward the complexities of writing in the name of the other or in favor of another's cause.[98] But there is another dimension to Condorcet's use of this persona. By portraying himself as a Swiss pastor, he implicitly aligned himself with the abolitionist tradition of evangelical Protestantism, rather than with the secular philosophical perspective that was dominant in France.[99] This posture is, however, not kept up for long, for almost immediately Condorcet's narrator begins to forget brotherly love and to speak the language of natural rights and material benefits.

In the first few sections of the text, Condorcet situates the problem of slavery in relation to one of the key discourses of Enlightenment philosophy: the recognition and protection of property rights. Slavery is described as a crime worse than theft because "one deprives the slave not only of all his property, but also of the capacity to acquire it and the ownership of his time and strength" (7). Slavery represents a double act of larceny, Condorcet suggests, since the slave loses ownership, not only of himself, but also of all his potential possessions. Condorcet notes that whereas theft is typically the last resort of the weak, slavery is a kind of theft perpetrated by the strong. Dealing a sideways blow to the arguments of Grotius and his followers, he also observes that the illegality of this theft had often been cloaked by the mantle of conquest, that is to say,

97. Condorcet, *Lettres sur le commerce des grains* (Letters on the Grain Trade), *Réflexions sur le commerce des blés* (Reflections on the Wheat Trade).

98. Jurt, "Condorcet."

99. Although most of the leading members of the Society of the Friends of Blacks approached slavery from a perspective grounded in the philosophy of property and rights and in laissez-faire economics, one leading figure, the Abbé Grégoire, rejected slavery from the perspective of Christian universalism. On Grégoire and abolition, see Sepinwall, *Abbé Grégoire*.

portrayed as an act of war rather than as one of illegal brigandage. Turning to the responsibilities of the state, Condorcet argues that governments are supposed to protect individual rights and may only abrogate them when the safety or survival of an individual is at stake, as, for example, in the case of minors (14). Later in the text this argument is brought back to justify the deferral of abolition on the grounds that slaves (who are implicitly likened to children) would injure themselves if they were suddenly given unlimited freedom (24–25).

Much like Dupont, Condorcet asserts that slavery should be abolished because it violates individual rights, and not for reasons relating to profit or loss, yet nonetheless seems to find it impossible to separate these two perspectives. "The prosperity of commerce, the wealth of the nation, cannot be placed in the balance with justice," he writes, before going on to show that slavery was fundamentally opposed to France's commercial interests (15–16).

In this demonstration, Condorcet presents a series of arguments to show that slavery was neither necessary nor beneficial to colonial economies. Against the claim that the special nature of tropical agriculture mandated slave labor, he argues for changes in the mode of production, notably the increased specialization of labor advocated by Smith and Turgot (17). And with respect to the claim that Europeans could not work productively in the tropics, he argues, paraphrasing Mirabeau, that if vast plantations were replaced by small farms, a new "race" of white workers would quickly be formed. In other passages, taking a somewhat different approach, Condorcet argues that even if blacks were necessary to colonial agriculture, it was not necessary for them to be enslaved. Contesting the widespread claim that Africans had to be forced to work because they were constitutionally lazy, he advances another key tenet of liberal economic theory: that after meeting the needs of subsistence, all free people will work to improve their lot.

In a passage that loosely follows Dupont, whose calculations are cited in a footnote, and that borrows its vocabulary from Quesnay, Condorcet observes that when planters claimed that slave labor generated more wealth than free labor, they were failing to differentiate between the *produit net* (net product) and the *produit réel* or *brut* (gross product) (18–21).[100] He argues that although slave labor increased the net product because production costs were minimal, the gross product was low because slaves were not productive workers. Slavery, in other words, increased revenue but not productivity, benefiting owners but not the state. (As noted earlier, Dupont used the same argument to reach the somewhat different conclusion that slavery was not even profitable for slave owners.)

Condorcet calls for an immediate ban on the slave trade, both on moral grounds and for economic reasons. He argues that compensating for attrition

---

100. The distinction between net and gross product was one that Quesnay had introduced.

in the workforce by importing new slaves from Africa was not economically sound, and that it would make more sense to try to improve conditions in the colonies (20). He also states categorically that slavery itself should be abolished, and that owners had no right whatsoever to receive compensation. His views on this issue are, however, more complex than they at first appear, because when it comes to laying out a plan for abolition, Condorcet is as tentative as Baudeau, Bessner, and Dupont. Indeed, if abolition had been implemented in the manner outlined in the *Reflections,* planters would have had little cause to claim compensation, because their losses would have been very minimal.

Guided, perhaps, by his expertise in the field of probability, Condorcet lays out a plan for abolition that is replete with intricate subclauses and fallback provisions. Citing the need to maintain public order, he claims, first of all, that "blacks must at first be subject to severe discipline, regulated by laws" (24). Having established the state's right to impose "severe discipline" on recently freed slaves, he proceeds to outline a plan for staggered emancipation. Mixed-race people born on plantations would be freed, not at birth—because masters might be tempted to abort pregnancies that did not benefit them—but at age thirty-five. Enslaved people who were under fifteen at the time of abolition would be freed at age forty, those who were over fifteen at age fifty (29–30). In Condorcet's plan, slavery was to be dramatically reduced within forty years and ended altogether within seventy. Is it coincidental that abolition finally occurred in 1848, almost seventy years after the first publication of *Reflections?*

Reflections on Black Slavery was by no means Condorcet's final word on the subject of slavery and abolition. In January 1789, he assumed the position of president of the Society of the Friends of Blacks, and in this capacity delivered speeches before the Constituent Assembly and contributed essays to political journals.[101] As a detailed discussion of revolutionary debates on slavery and the colonies lies beyond the scope of this book, I will not address these various pieces here.[102] Instead, I want to turn to a work that one of the period's chief opponents of abolition wrote in response to the *Reflections:* Baron Pierre-Victor de Malouet's *Mémoire sur l'esclavage des nègres* (Treatise on Black Slavery) (1788).

Malouet was a high naval official who served as an administrator in Saint-Domingue from 1767 to 1774, and later led an expedition to reestablish the struggling French colony in Guiana. In the 1770s–80s he authored several memoranda on colonial affairs, including a reform proposal titled *Essai sur*

---

101. Condorcet's revolutionary addresses on slavery are gathered at the end of the edition of *Reflections* cited in the text.

102. On these debates, see, for example, Bénot, "Condorcet journaliste"; Dorigny and Gainot, *La Société des amis des noirs;* Dorigny, *Les abolitions de l'esclavage;* Williams, *Condorcet and Modernity.*

l'administration de Saint Domingue (Essay on the Administration of Saint Domingue) (1785).[103] During his tenure in Saint-Domingue, he married a Creole heiress and as a result became a slave owner and member of the planter class. Given his biography, it is unsurprising that in 1789 Malouet decided to ally himself with the newly formed Club Massiac, the proslavery lobby formed to combat the influence of the Society of the Friends of Blacks.[104] He participated actively in the debates on colonial issues conducted in the National Assembly between 1789 and 1791, and during the directorate published an essay on the probable future of France's colonies in the aftermath of the Revolution.

Like *Reflections on Black Slavery*, Malouet's *Treatise* was published twice. It appeared first in 1775, in the context of the increased reflection on colonial affairs discussed earlier in this chapter. It was republished in 1788, in the wake of the founding of the Society of the Friends of Blacks and in response to the republication of Condorcet's abolitionist tract. The revised second edition included a set of "New Observations" in which Malouet responded directly to Condorcet's arguments, and in a sense to the entire tradition of liberal thinking on colonial affairs.[105]

After a sarcastic expression of admiration for the noble intentions of the philosophes, Malouet expresses concern that their ideas, if implemented, would lead to total chaos. He indeed insinuates that if a philosopher had to run the colonies, he would soon discover that translating *bienfaisance* into legislation is no easy matter (72). Highlighting his own informed perspective as an experienced colonial administrator, Malouet lays out what is basically a mercantilist response to liberal doctrine.

Malouet was by no means opposed to the idea that slavery should be reformed: he in fact reproduces a legislative proposal advocating reforms that he had drawn up in 1779 (85). However, he rejects outright the idea that slavery should be abolished, claiming that an act of this nature would be extremely detrimental to France's already troubled economy. Contra Quesnay and Mirabeau, he asserts that great empires thrive on luxury, not abstinence, and that coffee and sugar, which could be cultivated only in tropical colonies by slaves, had become necessary to France (27). On the question of trade and surpluses, Malouet takes the traditional mercantilist line that without supplementary revenue from its colonies France would have to draw on other income to purchase goods from abroad, and that in the absence of the Exclusive, French farmers and manufacturers would have to find new outlets for their goods (66–69). A

---

103. *Essay on the Administration of Saint Domingue* was published under the name of Raynal, a figure associated with colonial affairs but not actively engaged in colonial administration.

104. Malouet emigrated in 1793 but returned to France after the Revolution to serve under Napoleon and Louis XVIII.

105. Malouet, *Mémoire sur l'esclavage des nègres*.

"slice of the pie" thinker rather than a theorist of wealth as growth, Malouet argues that giving up slavery and the Exclusive would mean a decrease in revenue and a shrinking balance of trade, consequences for which he finds it impossible to see an upside.

Malouet compares the bond between masters and slaves with the relationship between landowners and subsistence workers (32–33). He suggests that slaves were better off than French laborers because they were given regular nourishment, and because their children received an education (36–37). Offering a highly idealized portrait of the Caribbean *habitation* as a nurturing environment in which singing and dancing were encouraged, he raises the question that Jean-François Melon had explored in the 1730s, and which would be examined again in 1797 by the author of the anonymous pamphlet discussed earlier: whether a form of serfdom should be reintroduced in France. Like Melon, Malouet finds, in the end, that this step would weaken property rights and undermine the stability that such protections brought to the nation. Concluding that slavery should be limited to offshore sites, he characterizes the colonies as an exceptional environment in which individuals who were already enslaved in their African birth lands were given a better life (52–53).[106]

Though Condorcet and Malouet embodied contrasting perspectives on abolition and represented rival political factions—the Society of the Friends of Blacks on the one hand, the Club Massiac on the other—they both operated within a discursive field that was structured around economic arguments, and in which other forms of argument, such as humanitarian concerns or the recognition of individual rights, were invariably inflected with economic ideas. Both writers were acutely aware of the set of claims that the other side had laid out in defense of its position—that Europeans could not be productive in tropical environments, that free labor was more productive than slave labor, that emancipation would create new consumers, and that emancipation would lead to utter chaos—and each sought to refute the other side's arguments. In these exchanges between pro- and antislavery writers, liberals and mercantilists, the abstract meditations of the past crystallized into a focused and concrete debate in which the social, political, and economic implications of slavery were identified and examined.

Brissot and the "Human Rights" Perspective

In February 1788 the lawyer, liberal journalist, and future leader of the Girondist faction, Jacques-Pierre Brissot de Warville, in tandem with Étienne Clavière, a Genevan democrat, founded the Society of the Friends of Blacks.

---

106. One of Malouet's concerns about abolition was that it would lead to an undesirable rise in métissage (60). We recall that the same fear led Mirabeau to make the opposite argument: that the African slave trade should be suppressed.

With the creation of this body, the antislavery writing of the 1770s and 1780s was translated into a concrete political movement with a legislative agenda. As has often been noted, Brissot and Clavière were inspired, not only by the tradition of French antislavery writing, but also by the English abolitionist movement. Both men lived in exile in England in the 1780s, and during this time they met Thomas Clarkson and Granville Sharpe, who urged them to establish a parallel movement in France.[107] Brissot's strong ties to England would later became a factor in his political downfall, since after the two nations went to war in 1793, he was often accused of disloyalty and espionage by his Jacobin rivals.

Brissot's published writings on slavery are distinguished by the fact that they defer less to economic reasoning than other antislavery works of the period. I would say, in fact, that of all prerevolutionary and revolutionary-era French antislavery writers, Brissot came closest to articulating the "human rights" perspective that Lynn Hunt attributes to the abolitionist movement. When he called for abolition, Brissot, for the most part, alluded to freedom, humanity, and rights, and left profit and productivity out of the equation. In only one work, *Mémoire sur les noirs de l'Amérique septentrionale* (Memoir on the Blacks of North America), does Brissot come close to arguing for abolition on economic grounds (he contrasts the prosperous, productive free states of the North with the run-down, underproductive slave states of the South, anticipating the commentaries of Tocqueville [40]).[108]

What was the impact of identifying abolition as a moral imperative without, at the same time, presenting an economic rationale? One palpable effect is that it seems to have moved Brissot to call for slavery to be abolished immediately rather than in the remote future. In the *Discourse* that he pronounced at the inaugural meeting of the Society of the Friends of Blacks, Brissot stated that emancipation should be more or less immediate. Adopting a relatively pure form of the liberal stance that freedom is the root of all positive change, he argued that deferral for social and economic reasons would inevitably be counterproductive (6).

Brissot's "human rights" perspective also seems to have had an impact on the way in which he envisioned the postslavery order. In a work devoted to France and America, a text rather verbosely titled *Examen critique des voyages dans l'Amérique Septentrionale, de M. le Marquis de Chastellux; ou, Lettre à M. le Marquis de Chastellux, dans laquelle on réfute principalement ses opinions sur les Quakers, sur les nègres, sur le peuple, et sur l'homme* (Critical Examination of

---

107. Brissot titled his speech for the inaugural meeting of the Society of the Friends of Blacks "Discours sur la nécessité d'établir à Paris une société pour concourir, avec celle de Londres, à l'abolition de la traite et de l'esclavage des nègres" (Discourse on the Need to Establish in Paris a Society to Collaborate, with that of London, on the Abolition of the Slave Trade and Black Slavery).

108. Brissot, *Mémoire sur les noirs de l'Amérique septentrionale* (Paris, 1789).

the Voyage to North America of M. le Marquis de Chastellux; or, Letter to M. le Marquis de Chastellux, in which are principally refuted his Opinions on the Quakers, on Negroes, on the People, and on Man), Brissot took a previous French traveler to task for making derogatory remarks about American Quakers and blacks.[109] In a series of objections that could have been leveled against a number of the *antislavery* advocates considered in this chapter, Brissot observes that it is highly problematic to call for reform and kind treatment in one breath while asserting in the next that blacks are fundamentally different from whites—for example that they are less sensitive to suffering (88). Pointing to a widespread tendency to substitute effect for cause, Brissot argues that social and intellectual differences between blacks and whites were the result of slavery, not its cause, and would rapidly disappear in the wake of emancipation. Whereas many other antislavery writers of the period looked forward to the rapid transformation of the slave labor force into a separate and unequal class of laborers, Brissot envisioned an attenuation of differences and the amelioration of the social condition of blacks as a result of education.

As we have seen throughout this chapter, the humanitarian perspective that we encounter in the writings of Brissot was far from being the primary mode in which abolition was advocated in the latter part of the eighteenth century. Instead, a market-oriented perspective grounded in economic theory dominated the field, yielding cautious proposals for emancipation and hierarchical visions of the future of colonial society.

From Abolitionism to Abolition

The decree of abolition issued by the Convention in 1794 was less the culmination of the opposition to slavery that coalesced in France in the 1770s and 1780s than an emergency measure precipitated by the political crisis unfolding in Saint-Domingue. Though French activists fought for emancipation before and during the Revolution, the pace of their activism was slow, and as Mercier and Diderot had predicted, it was ultimately the slaves themselves who seized the initiative and, as Laurent Dubois has put it, brought a true universality to the idea of human rights.[110]

Though the establishment of the Society of the Friends of Blacks and the Club Massiac seemed to set the stage for a major public debate over slavery, this standoff never fully materialized. This was in part because the Club Massiac managed to block discussion of slavery in the National Assembly by

---

109. Brissot, *Examen critique des voyages*. The Marquis de Chastellux was a military officer and philosopher influenced by liberal economic ideas who participated in the American War of Independence and later wrote a travel narrative based on his experiences. See Chastellux, *Voyages de M. le Marquis de Chastellux*.

110. Dubois, "La république métissée," 22. See also *Colony of Citizens*.

engineering the creation of a committee that controlled discussion of colonial matters.[111] But it was also because the debate over slavery was largely displaced onto a related but subsidiary issue: the political rights of free people of color. As several scholars have observed, the society's strong commitment to the cause of free people of color was at the end of the day rather questionable. Many members of this constituency were slave owners, most were not opposed to slavery, and one of the main reasons adduced for giving them rights was that this measure would help forestall slave insurgencies. Acceptance of the voting rights of free people of color was indeed given a major impetus by a speech delivered by Julien Raimond—a delegate sent from Saint-Domingue to represent the interests of the free people of color—to the effect that as property owners, free people of color had no interest in securing the freedom of slaves. Property and public order, rather than fundamental human rights, emerged as the chief concerns of the day.[112]

Lacking a clear direction, the society slowly faded over the winter of 1791–92, and in the following years several of the society's most prominent members fell victim to the Terror. In the new, more conservative political atmosphere of the directory, the society was reconvened under the expanded title Société des amis des noirs et des colonies (Society of Friends of Blacks and the Colonies), a name change calculated to convey that although it was an antislavery and pro-black movement, it was not an anticolonial lobby.[113] The research of Marcel Dorigny and Bernard Gainot has shown that only eleven of the ninety-two members were veterans of the first society, and that many members of the reformed society were colonial planters.[114]

Some years ago the historian Daniel Resnick argued that the society, and by extension key members such as Brissot and Condorcet, failed in their efforts to spread antislavery ideas because they made their case on the basis of moral arguments and failed to incorporate economic perspectives that would have appealed to a broader constituency.[115] Obviously, I would argue that the opposite was true. Not only was economic reasoning a major focus of French antislavery writing, but moral and political arguments, when presented, were usually interwoven with economic claims. I would perhaps not go so far as to suggest that the economic emphasis of antislavery writing was responsible for the miscarriage of the cause. Like Resnick, I think that since colonial slavery was largely economic it was perhaps strategically important for it to be refuted or at least questioned in economic terms. But it is also clear that this approach had limitations. Economic reasoning supported visions of abolition and of the

111. See Dorigny, *Les abolitions de l'esclavage*, 13.
112. On the political failings of the society, see Bénot, "La question coloniale."
113. Dorigny and Gainot, *La Société des amis des noirs*, 312.
114. Ibid., 308–15.
115. Resnick, "*Société des amis des noirs*," 566–67.

postslavery order that detracted from the urgency of the cause. By underwriting their moral arguments with economic claims, abolitionists diluted their ethical position, translating what should have been a categorical imperative into a field of calculation.

The economic arguments made about slavery were, at the end of the day, hard to prove. In different hands, as we have seen, the same arguments and calculations could be marshaled to support different points. Though they shared the same basic economic assumptions, Turgot, Dupont, and Condorcet disagreed over whether slavery was ever profitable and for whom.

These debates, as Philippe Steiner has shown, carried over into the nineteenth century, with liberals of various stripes squaring off against the partisans of a revitalized pro-slavery lobby.[116] Jean-Baptiste Say, the leading political economist of the first empire and a noted interpreter of Smith and the French economists, argued in the first edition of his *Traité d'économie politique* (Treatise of Political Economy) (1803) that slavery was less expensive than paid labor but morally wrong. He also observed that from an economic perspective it would make more sense to grow sugar in Africa and Egypt, which also happened to be the new targets of French colonial ambition.[117] In the revised 1814 edition of the *Treatise*, however, Say made a volte-face and argued that slavery was in fact less cost-effective than free labor. Clearly the question of the cost-effectiveness of slavery that was first raised by Turgot and Dupont was still perplexing specialists at the end of Napoleon's reign. These questions were in fact never to be resolved in the terms in which they were posed. By the time of abolition in 1848, beet sugar grown in Europe had undercut the market for Caribbean cane sugar, and as a result the economic rationale for plantation slavery had fallen away.

116. Steiner, "L'esclavage chez les économistes," 171–73.
117. Say, *Traité d'économie politique.*

7

Economic Sentiments

How do societies transition from extreme inequality—from acceptance that some groups enjoy political, social, and material advantages of which others are utterly deprived—to the view that these asymmetries are illegitimate because all people enjoy certain fundamental rights? And once this principle has been articulated, what strategies are used to convince all members of society to embrace it? These questions are explored by Lynn Hunt in her 2007 book *Inventing Human Rights,*[1] an account of how the idea of universal human rights crystallized in France and the United States at the end of the eighteenth century. One answer that Hunt provides to these questions is by means of literature, or, more specifically, by means of fiction's special capacity to produce identification with unfamiliar others, to make readers view people from radically different backgrounds as similar to themselves, and as a result to recognize their right to enjoy the same freedoms and legal protections.

The timing of Hunt's book, which is aimed at a general as well as an academic readership, is obviously not incidental. Since the events of September 11, 2001, the United States government has repeatedly been criticized for its failure to respect human rights in the prosecution of the "War on Terror." As if to underscore these failures, Hunt devotes an entire chapter of her book to the history of the prohibition of judicial torture in eighteenth-century France (70–111). Yet the implied contrast between the positive achievements of the Enlightenment and the policies of the George W. Bush administration raises a number of questions. Whether or not we embrace

---

1. Hunt, *Inventing Human Rights.*

a fundamental critique of the Enlightenment in the style of Horkheimer and Adorno, it is evident that the moral and political principles that were enunciated in documents such as the *Declaration of the Rights of Man and Citizen* and the United States' *Declaration of Independence* were never fully enacted.[2] The Enlightenment's "lesson" with regard to human rights is, as such, a mixed one. The principle of universal rights was formulated and in some cases applied, but there were often significant discrepancies between the principle and its extension to all human beings, or between the idea and its implementation. How, in light of these intervals, should we understand the role played by literary fiction?

One of the areas in which the discrepancy between discourse and action was most pronounced was the system of colonial slavery. For Hunt the 1794 decree abolishing slavery ranks alongside the prohibition of torture (1789) and legislation recognizing the rights of Jews (1791) and Protestants (1792) as a key example of the Enlightenment's achievement in establishing the rights of oppressed people (160–67). But this characterization is questionable. We have seen that if the Convention abolished slavery in 1794, it was less because there was a clear political consensus about slaves' rights than because there was no viable alternative. Though some of the legislators who voted for abolition in 1794 would undoubtedly have reached the same decision without the political pressure that resulted from the slave revolt in Saint-Domingue, others would just as certainly have demurred. The fact that slavery, having been reinstated in 1802, continued to exist until 1848 can certainly be seen as evidence of the absence of a decisive political will.

In the years before and during the French Revolution, slavery was examined and denounced in a number of fictional works: the first French fictions that represented the colonial world in depth. Anchored in the sentimental tradition, these plays and stories invited readers to empathize with the enslaved and, correspondingly, to recognize the existence of a shared right to self-determination. They also tapped into another set of arguments for reform, namely, the claims regarding the socioeconomic utility of emancipation discussed in the previous chapter. The economic subtexts of colonial fictions and their complex relationship to the project of empathy for slaves and creating/inciting moral opposition to slavery are the subject of this chapter. I consider why, and to what effect, late eighteenth-century fictions encouraged readers to empathize and as a result universalize, while at the same time tying emancipation to arguments of a pragmatic or contingent nature. I suggest that in the apparent "supplementary" of these two strategies we can discern the interval between the emergent principle of a universal human right to freedom and the political will to implement it.

2. Adorno and Horkheimer, *Dialectic of Enlightenment*.

Sentimental Fictions, Economic Theories

Hunt proposes that the belief that human beings share a fundamental set of rights arises, in large part, from the perception that all people share the same basic emotions, needs, and capacity for agency. When we perceive members of other social or cultural groups as being very different from ourselves, we may feel pity for them when they fall victim to abuses, but we do not identify with them or attempt to put ourselves in their shoes. The shift from pity to empathy, Hunt suggests, was an important precondition for the coalescence of the idea of universal human rights. The perception that other people are like ourselves, even if they are from a different culture or social class, did not, however, arise spontaneously. Hunt credits the eighteenth-century novel, particularly the sentimental novels of writers such as Rousseau and Richardson, with playing a crucial mediating role in this moral revolution (35–69). When readers immersed themselves in *Pamela* or *La nouvelle Héloïse,* Hunt suggests, they stopped thinking about people of other classes and genders as others and came to view them as individuals who were in many ways similar to themselves.

The argument that sentimental fiction paved the way for the formulation of human rights is certainly pertinent to the collection of fictional representations of slavery produced in France at the end of the eighteenth century. Between 1763 and 1796 a substantial corpus of novels and short fictions undertook to portray the experience of people enslaved in France's colonies. These works included Gabriel Mailhol's *Le philosophe nègre* (The Black Philosopher) (1764); Jean-François de Saint-Lambert's "Zimeo" (1769); Louis-Sébastien Mercier's *The Year Two Thousand Four Hundred and Forty: Dream If There Ever Was One* (1771); Jean-François Butini's *African Letters* (1771); Bernardin de Saint-Pierre's *Paul and Virginia* (1788); Joseph La Vallée's *Le nègre comme il y a peu de blancs* (The Negro as There Are Few Whites) (1789); Lecointe-Marsillac's *The More-Lack* (1789); and Germaine de Staël's "Mirza; ou, Lettres d'un Voyageur" ("Mirza; or, Letters of a Traveler") (1795). There were also theatrical depictions of enslaved people, including Olympe de Gouges's play *L'esclavage des noirs* (Black Slavery) (1789). Erick Noël calculates that twelve plays were devoted to colonial experience during the revolutionary years, as opposed to six for the rest of the century (180).[3] In these works, slaves are portrayed, not as faceless victims, but rather as individuals with specific traits of character and defined life experiences. These stories invited readers to empathize with enslaved black people and, correspondingly, contributed to the coalescence of the abolitionist perspective.[4]

---

3. Noël, *Être noir en France,* 180.

4. *The Black Philosopher* constitutes something of a case apart. Published in 1764, a few years before slavery became an object of public discussion, it is considerably less critical of the slave trade than the later narratives with which it is sometimes grouped.

Scholarly readings of "colonial fictions," as Youmna Charara has designated this group of texts, have predominantly emphasized their use of the sentimental register.[5] Critics have explored the strategies by means of which French writers tried to "inhabit" the minds of their black protagonists, often highlighting their failure to transcend European norms. Dimensions of colonial fictions that do not involve the portrayal of individual psychology have received less critical attention. For example, the economic currents that are prevalent in this literature have largely been ignored and are not usually identified as a feature of the genre. In a discussion of Jean-François Butini's *African Letters,* the colonial fiction that makes the most overt use of economic reasoning, Léon-François Hoffmann observes that no one, particularly no colonial planter, was likely to have been persuaded by Butini's efforts to show that free labor would be more profitable than slave labor. He may well be right about this. But when Hoffmann states that these arguments were limited to Butini—"Butini is in any case to my knowledge the only one who made this economic argument"—and that "most readers would not have enjoyed these arid discussions, preferring the pathos of fictional inventions,"[6] he is overlooking a key dimension of colonial fictions as a genre. In fact, almost all colonial fictions of the 1760s–80s deploy arguments grounded in political economy, combining sentimental representations with a more or less heavy dose of "arid" economic reasoning.

Focusing on the sentimental and psychological aspects of colonial fictions disposes us to perceive the relationship between feeling empathy for an enslaved character and assenting to the principle of emancipation as a more or less seamless one. It may also foster a perception that the creation of empathy was a politically effective strategy. Christopher Miller writes of Bernardin de Saint-Pierre's popular novel, *Paul and Virginia,* that "the full impact of the novel is hard to calculate but the sympathy that initially produced reforms [in Mauritius] likely contributed to eventual abolition."[7] But as we attempt to draw the connection between text and law, a number of questions arise. To which act of abolition should we consider *Paul and Virginia* to have contributed? To the emancipation proclamations that the Convention's emissary, Léger-Félicité Sonthonax, issued in Saint-Domingue in 1793: decrees issued in the face of insurrection and under the looming threat of an alliance between rebel slaves and invading British troops? To the decree of 1794, which validated the Saint-Domingue proclamations, and which was overturned by Napoleon in 1802? To the suppression of the French slave trade in 1816 at the

---

5. See, for example, Antoine, *Les écrivains français,* 153–59; Hoffmann, *Le nègre romantique,* 82–98; Massardier-Kenney, "Staël, Translation, and Race"; Reinhardt, *Claims to Memory,* 59–86.

6. Hoffman, *Le nègre romantique,* 85.

7. Miller, *French Atlantic Triangle,* 106. The reforms to which Miller is referring are changes implemented in Île de France as a result of an episode in *Paul and Virginia* depicting the harsh punishment of a Maroon slave who returns to her master.

instigation of the European powers gathered at the Congress of Vienna? Or to the definitive abolition of colonial slavery in 1848? The convoluted history of abolition in France makes it particularly difficult to make direct claims about the impact of literary representations on political processes.

Reading the sentimental facade of colonial fictions in conjunction with their economic subtext, on the other hand, brings the potential interval between sentimental leanings, political commitments, and juridical acts into focus, as we are forced to consider what it means that these works try to show that slavery is wrong through psychological means while at the same time attempting to prove that it is inefficient and unprofitable. Below I consider the discursive tensions of four late eighteenth-century colonial fictions: two written in the late 1760s–70s, when arguments against slavery were first beginning to coalesce, the other two dating from the revolutionary period, when the debate over slavery had become more explicit and more urgent. The first two works are by male writers—Jean François de Saint-Lambert and Jean-François Butini; the second pair are by women—Olympe de Gouges and Germaine de Staël. The role of gender in sentimental abolitionism is an issue that has been raised in a number of scholarly discussions of French antislavery writing. I re-open this question from a somewhat different perspective by considering how liberal economic theory framed the articulation of gender and the elaboration of a feminist abolitionism.

Rereading "Zimeo"

Jean-François de Saint-Lambert's short story "Zimeo," first printed in 1769 in *Les saisons, poème* (The Seasons, a Poem), was the first colonial fiction to seize the imagination of French readers. One sign of its popularity, as Christopher Miller has observed, was that it was reprinted seventeen times between 1769 and 1797 (104). The story's impact has largely been understood in terms of the sympathetic reception of its African hero (it has often been suggested, for example, that Germaine de Staël modeled "Ximéo," the principal male figure of her story "Mirza," on Saint-Lambert's protagonist). I will foreground other aspects of the text and consider how these too foreshadowed later efforts to translate the experience of slavery into narrative form.

In the previous chapter we saw that soon after its publication, "Zimeo" was reproduced in the economic journal *Éphémérides du citoyen* as a preface to Dupont de Nemour's attempt to demonstrate that free labor would be more profitable than slave labor. In his introduction to the story, Dupont underscores the difference between his own rationalistic approach and the moral and psychological perspective adopted in "Zimeo."[8] In a letter reproduced

---

8. *Éphémérides*, 1771, no. 6, 180.

in the text, Saint-Lambert responded to Dupont, agreeing with this characterization of his story: "You show that it is in people's interest not to use slaves," he writes, "I contented myself with showing that it is unjust and barbaric to use them."[9] The distinction between moral and economic reasoning is not, however, entirely borne out by Saint-Lambert's story. Indeed, I would suggest that if Dupont found his calculations to be compatible with Saint-Lambert's sentimental narrative, it was not simply because of their common opposition to slavery, but also because they both approached the question from a perspective informed by liberal theories that associated liberty with productivity.

Rather like Condorcet in *Reflections on Black Slavery*, Saint-Lambert employs a narrator who is neither French nor a philosophe, but rather an English Quaker. This narrator, a man named George Filmer, explains that while on business in Jamaica, he visited the plantation of his friend Paul Wilmouth, also a Quaker by birth. The first few pages of the story offer a detailed account of life on Wilmouth's plantation, portrayed as an orderly environment in which everything is tranquil, neat, and harmonious, and a contrasting depiction of conditions on neighboring plantations where slavery wears a different face (49–50). On Wilmouth's plantation, according to Filmer, slaves were well nourished and well housed. They were only required to work moderate hours, and they had two days a week off to tend their own small plots of land. Looking up to Wilmouth as a "good father," the slaves seemed contented with their lot and did not express a desire for freedom (50). On neighboring plantations, by contrast, slaves were malnourished and abused, and they harbored resentment of their mean-spirited masters.

Filmer recalls that while he was in Jamaica the calm and order of the colony were disrupted when a rebel slave known as John, or Zimeo (the man's African name), led a party of Maroons down from the mountain where they had taken refuge to attack the plantations below. Going from plantation to plantation the Maroons slaughtered the most abusive owners and freed the slaves of others (52). Though many slaves joined the rebel group, those who belonged to Wilmouth remained steadfastly loyal to their master, and even took up arms to defend him from attack. One of Wilmouth's slaves, a young man from the same country as Zimeo, indeed bravely set out to meet the Maroon leader, in an effort to convince him that his master was truly benevolent. Intrigued by this slave's loyalty, Zimeo decides to pay Wilmouth's "good" plantation a visit.

As several critics have noted, the most powerful section of "Zimeo" is the first-person narrative of the Maroon leader. In an oration that may have been influenced by an earlier representation of Maroon speech—the oration of Moses Bom-Saam published by the Abbé Prévost in *For and Against* (1735)—Zimeo

<hr />

9. Ibid., 180–81.

justifies his recourse to violence by telling the story of his life.[10] He tells Filmer, Wilmouth, and an audience of assembled slaves how he, his fiancée Ellaroé, and her father Matomba were tricked by Portuguese merchants into boarding a vessel bound for the New World. Speaking in the voice of Zimeo, Saint-Lambert gives one of the first sustained descriptions in French of the rigors of the Middle Passage. Perhaps because there was no real precedent for this kind of narrative, Saint-Lambert has difficulty finding the appropriate register in which to describe the suffering endured by Africans. In particular, he seems to find it necessary to embellish the story by supplementing accurate details of the conditions aboard slave ships with lurid allusions to cannibalism, and with a dramatic shipboard love scene between Zimeo and Ellaroé (57–58).

It is also striking that what appears to afflict Zimeo most is not enslavement per se or abduction from his birth land but rather the separation from his loved ones that occurred when the slave ship reached the New World. He explains that Ellaroé and her father were sold to a Spanish merchant, while he was sold to an English planter and taken to Jamaica. "This was the moment that changed me," he says, "that gave me this passion for vengeance" (59). Is it possible to infer from this statement that Zimeo could have come to terms with his enslavement had the prospect of never seeing Ellaroé again not pushed him over the edge? This reading seems to be confirmed by what happens immediately afterward. As though responding to Zimeo's lament, a young slave steps forward, accompanied by three people who turn out to be none other than Ellaroé, Matomba, and the child born of Ellaroé and Zimeo's shipboard union. Following this happy reunion, Zimeo and his troop of Maroons quietly retreat back up the mountain. With the principal source of his anger against the colonists removed, the Maroon leader is apparently willing to abandon the course of armed insurrection (60).

As I hope my summary of the story has suggested, Saint-Lambert's narrative is in many respects ambiguous. It is not obvious, for example, why Zimeo initiates a campaign of violence. Is he rising up against slavery? Protesting the behavior of the most abusive masters? Or is his main concern to avenge his painful separation from Ellaroé? Zimeo's account of his suffering certainly positions him as a member of the new breed of sentimental heroes who populated late eighteenth-century literature, rather than as a political leader.

If Zimeo's motives are unclear, then so, too, are the objectives of the campaign of terror in which he and his fellow Maroons participate. Are the Maroons seeking freedom for themselves? For all the colony's slaves? Are they calling for an improvement in slaves' living conditions? Or are they exacting revenge? Catherine Reinhardt has characterized "Zimeo" as the most negative and politically inconclusive of Maroon fictions, the small group of texts,

---

10. Prévost, "Harangue d'un chef nègre," in *Le pour et contre*.

including the speech of Moses Bom Saam as reported by Prévost, Mercier's *The Year...*(1771), and Diderot's rewriting of Mercier in *History of the Two Indies* (1774, 1780), that consider slavery through the figure of the Maroon. Reinhardt notes that instead of portraying his protagonist as a leader engaged in a constructive rebellion, Saint-Lambert focuses primarily on revenge, and as a result, his protagonist comes close to embodying the stereotype of the irrational and bloodthirsty African. She further argues that Zimeo's Maroon community does not embody a satisfying alternative to slavery, and that, unable to construct a new life for himself separate from the world of the plantation, Zimeo "remains enslaved to the anger the whites instilled in him" (67). Though I find Reinhardt's reading to be too categorical, notably with regard to the story's sketch of the community of mountain Maroons, I think that she is right to highlight the political shortcomings of the story.

Is "Zimeo" an antislavery work? Dupont de Nemours, as we have seen, represented it as such in *Éphémérides,* and in the letter in which he replied to Dupont, Saint-Lambert affirmed this interpretation. Further corroboration of this intention can be drawn from the short essay titled "Réflexions sur les nègres" (Reflections on Negroes), which Saint-Lambert appended to the narrative portion of the text (60–63). This essay discusses the distorted ways in which Europeans perceived Africans (an issue that is obviously related to the story's attempt to inspire empathy), and in its final paragraph states firmly that slavery is opposed to natural law. As Youmna Charara observes, however, we should perhaps not assume that because the essay ends with a bold statement against slavery, the narrative also pulls in the same direction.[11] As we have seen, the story, taken by itself, does not communicate a clear abolitionist message. Zimeo frees slaves on certain plantations but otherwise seems more concerned with punishing abusive colonists than with ending the system of slavery. In one passage, Filmer recalls that before Zimeo, his family, and their supporters retreated back up the mountain to the Maroons' hideaway, Ellaroé and Matomba effusively told him and Wilmouth that "they wanted to bear all their lives the name of our slaves" (60). Does this parting statement mean that they wanted to keep their Europeanized slave names, or that, overcome with gratitude, they wanted to continue to view themselves as their benefactors' slaves? The answer is not entirely clear, but in either case the upshot is that Wilmouth and Filmer, who turns out to be the owner of Ellaroé and Matomba, are established as the co-heroes of the story. The ending of the story thus circles back to its point of departure: the idealized description of Wilmouth's harmonious plantation and his paternalistic relationship with his slaves.

11. Charara, *Les fictions coloniales,* 39.

By the late 1760s many English and American Quakers had taken a stand in favor of abolition. Why does Saint-Lambert represent his protagonists as Quakers, without also representing them as advocates for abolition, and indeed why does he choose to represent slave owners as Quakers? There are a number of plausible answers to this question, one of which might be that he wanted to use the moral luster of the sect to portray Wilmouth's benevolent patriarchy in the most favorable possible light. How, in the context of an antislavery narrative, is it possible to confer a heroic appearance on two men who own slaves—in Wilmouth's case, a considerable number of slaves—and who do not seem disposed to free them? The explanation for this seeming anomaly lies in the fact that the story focuses less on the fundamental illegitimacy of slavery than on the contrast between good and bad styles of slave management. In light of this, it is necessary to consider whether "Zimeo" is really a call for the abolition of slavery or rather, in a more limited way, a plea for reform. It is perhaps worth noting in this regard that some of the practices of Wilmouth's plantation that are praised by Filmer—for example, the allocation of small provision gardens—were also advocated in the 1784 reforms to the *Black Code*.[12]

In *French Atlantic Triangle* Christopher Miller gives a ringing endorsement of both "Zimeo" and "Reflections on Negroes" as examples of literary abolitionism. He writes of the latter that, "Saint-Lambert leaves no ambiguity...about the meaning of his tale....He issues a complete moral condemnation of the slave trade and of the stranglehold of slave traders on information about the Atlantic trade system" (104). Though a message of this kind can be read in the "Reflections," in order to extract it Miller has to juxtapose the opening paragraph of the essay, in which Saint-Lambert comments on the prejudiced ways in which Europeans typically viewed Africans, with the closing paragraph, in which he declares slavery to be against natural law, in the process bypassing the two or three pages that fall in between. The points made in these pages are, however, significant. They do not negate the antislavery position to which Miller refers, but they do highlight a parallel dimension of Saint-Lambert's thinking on the Europe-Africa relationship.[13]

In the middle section of "Reflections on Negroes," Saint-Lambert expands on his ideas about the ways in which Europeans perceived Africans. He criticizes the widespread tendency to generalize and the patronizing assumption

12. The practice of encouraging (or obliging) slaves to grow their own food was prohibited by the terms of the *Black Code* of 1685. In the 1784 code, by contrast, the allotment of provision gardens was mandated as a way of allowing slaves to increase their food supply.

13. If Miller overlooks the political shortcomings of "Zimeo" and somewhat exaggerates the political impact of *Paul and Virginia,* it is to some extent because he is preoccupied with the need to respond to the volume *Translating Slavery,* which emphasizes the contribution of women writers to French abolitionism. This debate is discussed at more length below.

of African intellectual inferiority. Substituting a historical argument for these essentializing perspectives, the essay asserts that Africans were not less intelligent than Europeans, but rather had fallen behind them in terms of cultural development. Africans represent the past of Europe, Saint-Lambert claims, what Europe was four hundred years earlier, before the invention of the compass and the printing press (62). The way to close this developmental gap, he argues, would be for Europeans to export their own advanced knowledge to Africa: "Let us bring them our discoveries and our lumières. Will no prince ever establish colonies with such lofty aims? Will we never send apostles of reason and the arts? Will we always be guided by a mercantile and barbaric spirit?" (62). In this exhortation, Saint-Lambert points to Europeans' potential to become advanced and enlightened civilizers and urges them, not to leave Africans to their own devices, but rather to export their knowledge and enlightened values to Africa.

The rhetoric of this passage coincides in several ways with the antislavery arguments made by proponents of liberal economic theory. While expansionism that is guided by mercantilist doctrines is held up for criticism, the idea of enlightened colonial expansion, particularly in the direction of Africa, is enthusiastically embraced. If we reread the narrative portion of "Zimeo" in light of this section of "Reflections on Negroes," and in the context of the discursive currents of the period, Saint-Lambert's account of the orderly plantation presided over by Wilmouth seems to me to read less as an idealized description of a world on the verge of disappearance than as the projection of a future colonial society in which (free) African laborers would contentedly till the soil under the paternalistic supervision of enlightened Europeans.

Earlier I raised the question of whether "Zimeo" is really an antislavery text. Despite the various tensions that I have underlined, I believe that it is, and I also think that its author, Saint-Lambert, genuinely supported the abolition of slavery. At the same time, I think that it is important to acknowledge the specific ways in which "Zimeo" frames the issues of slavery and emancipation. Saint-Lambert's sentimental narrative invited readers to identify, perhaps for the first time, with a character who is an enslaved African, but it did not directly call on them to recognize freedom as a fundamental right. Instead, the text's sentimental register, in combination with its economic subtext, encouraged readers to abhor inhumane treatment and to wish for more-enlightened forms of governance. To put this in another way, readers were not asked to think of emancipation as a preliminary step that would eliminate abuse, but rather to focus on mistreatment and to hope for reforms that would eliminate acute suffering while allowing for the continued existence, if not of slavery, then at least of a benevolent colonial hierarchy in which Europeans governed and instructed Africans while at the same time continuing to benefit from their labor.

Between Sentiment and Economy: Jean-François Butini's *African Letters*

The synergy between liberal economic theory and sentimental fiction that we have observed in "Zimeo" is even more manifest in a work published a few years later, Jean-François Butini's *Lettres africaines* (African Letters) (1771).

Butini was a Genevan magistrate and legal reformer who had previously written a socioeconomic treatise on luxury and produced a French adaptation of *Othello:* projects that in a sense come together in his later novel. Written in epistolary form, *African Letters* tells the story of a group of Africans captured by English slave traders and transported to Jamaica.[14] Like "Zimeo," *African Letters* was referenced by Dupont de Nemours as he made the economic case for abolition in the pages of *Éphémérides du citoyen*.[15] But Dupont makes somewhat different uses of the two narratives. Whereas he draws a contrast between Saint-Lambert's sentimental story and his own economic approach, when he turns to *African Letters* it is to review and corroborate calculations that are presented in the course of the novel.

Like other colonial fictions, *African Letters* sweetens representations of colonial slavery with a romance plot. The epistolary form chosen by Butini had a long association with both philosophical writing and the representation of passion, and both traditions echo in Butini's text. At the center of the story is the love affair between its two heroes, Phédima and Abensar. In depicting the romantic lives of two well-educated Africans, Butini no doubt aimed to show his readers that enslaved Africans experienced the same strong and complex emotions as Europeans. But the dissection of personal feelings often seems to get in the way of the representation of slavery. For example, when Phédima, who has just arrived in Jamaica, is put to work in a sugar mill, she writes to her confidante, Zélime, not about the exhausting and dangerous conditions of the work that she is required to perform, but rather about her sadness over losing a miniature portrait of her beloved Abensar (118–19). Though Phédima's delicate feelings would not be out of place in a French salon, they somewhat deflect attention from the harsh realities of colonial life.

The novel's romance plot is given an intriguing twist when the plantation owner, Sir Darnley, falls in love with Phédima and—with what seems like conspicuous gallantry for a colonial planter—not only proposes marriage but also offers to free her and her entire entourage (124–26). Since Phédima believes Abensar to be dead, she pragmatically accepts. This development illustrates the ambiguities of the merger between romance novel and political manifesto. The

---

14. Butini, *Traité du luxe; Othello.* The fact that Saint-Lambert too wrote an essay on luxury illustrates the deep connections among the luxury debate, the critique of mercantilism, and abolitionism.

15. *Éphémérides*, 1771, no. 8, 68–117.

representation of a marriage between an enslaved African woman and an English planter transgressed both the master-slave hierarchy and the racial order on which it rested. Yet in portraying the triumph of love over slavery, the narrative also effectively subordinated the issue of enslavement and emancipation to the contingencies of an implausible personal relationship.

After Phédima's marriage to Sir Darnley, the colony's slave-labor system comes under attack from two opposed quarters. While Phédima urges her husband to free all of his slaves for both moral and economic reasons (132), Abensar reappears and establishes himself as the leader of a rebellious group of Maroons (141). Though the interplay between abolition and self-emancipation unfolds in a somewhat chaotic way, the juxtaposition of insurrection and abolition is an important move. Whereas many colonial fictions depict only one side of this dynamic—Europeans generously conferring freedom on Africans—*African Letters* imagines slaves freeing themselves and gestures to the connection between slave revolts and Europeans' willingness to contemplate change.

As turmoil begins to take hold of the colony, the novel's plot is suspended for the duration of two letters (25–26), as Sir Darnley and his friend Sir Bevil debate the economic pros and cons of slave labor. Just as Dupont de Nemours claimed that moral arguments were sufficient to condemn slavery, then proceeded to show that slavery was economically unproductive, so Sir Bevil first observes to Sir Darnley that he would scarcely be able to refute the claim that emancipating his slaves was morally right, then hurriedly reassures his friend that he is not going to try to convince him through moral argument. Shifting into an economic register, Sir Bevil sets out to show that emancipation would be in Sir Darnley's personal interest as an entrepreneur, as well as in the interest of the state (132). He argues that free workers are not only more productive than enslaved workers—a claim also made by Dupont—but also that freedom of labor creates favorable conditions for experimentation and creativity (ibid.). Looking beyond abolition, Sir Bevil imagines a new colonial order in which the benevolence of masters would be rewarded by the assiduity of workers, and in which formerly uncultivated land would be converted into productive farms:

> Imagine...that the blacks have been freed...observe how, touched by this unexpected gift, inspired by their gratitude to emulation, guided above all by the hope of gain, they show off the results of their industry. Today they have only hands, then they will have intelligence and eyes. Today most of the land in the interior of the island is condemned to an eternal sterility...then most of this land will be cultivated, because the charms of liberty and the certainty of finding work will keep laborers close to home. (131–32)

Sounding a natalist note, Sir Bevil also argues that abolition would be followed by an increase in the Creole population that would eliminate the exorbitant cost of importing slaves from Africa. Free black Creoles, he claims, would constitute a ready-made workforce requiring neither transportation nor the kind of social reeducation that had to be given to transplanted Africans (133). In a final note, Sir Bevil argues that in the aftermath of emancipation, slaves would be changed from enemies inclined toward revolt into loyal subjects, and above all into significant consumers of the nation's manufactured goods, notably textiles:

> It is not only with their arms that these new subjects would serve their masters, they would also serve them by the useful employment of the fruits of their labor. Observe, and this remark would perhaps be even more striking to you if you were French,...that the passions of Negroes contribute to the utility of this project: clothes are their dominant taste, and a beautiful piece of fabric is a magnet with which you can lead them wherever you want. As a result, the wages, the compensation they received would be devoted to the purchase of the materials, fashions, and manufactured goods of the metropole. (133–34)

Embracing the view that free commerce and free labor promoted the emergence of new markets, Sir Bevil imagines a new contingent of paid workers eager to purchase French textiles. His claim that Africans love finery is one that is made in a number of works of this period.[16] In most cases it is simply a patronizing commentary on Africans' childlike (and apolitical) preoccupations. But Butini's allusion to the French passion for clothes seems to tend in a somewhat different direction to the extent that it establishes a parallel between French sartorial refinement and African taste.

In the second of his two letters, Sir Bevil responds proleptically to the objections that he expects his friend to raise. Chief among these is the fear that if slaves earned wages, the price of colonial commodities would rise, sales would fall, and the whole colonial economy would come toppling down. Sir Bevil responds to this concern by providing a precise set of calculations (the figures that Dupont reviews in *Éphémérides*), a financial analysis that lays out the upside of expanding the number of consumers by growing the population of paid Creole workers. Sir Bevil is forced to acknowledge that this population growth would not occur overnight, and he suggests that in the interim it would be necessary to continue to import workers from Africa, though not in the capacity of slaves. As Youmna Charara observes, whereas many late eighteenth-century abolitionists (particularly in England) envisioned first the abolition of the slave trade and then the phasing out of slavery, Butini rather idiosyncratically imagined this process happening in reverse (88–89).[17]

---

16. See, for example, Moreau de Saint-Méry, *Description topographique*, 1:60, 1:93.

17. The distinction between abolishing the slave trade and abolishing slavery was very pronounced in England, much less so in France. One reason for this difference in emphasis was that the English slave trade was a much larger operation than its French rival. Another was that French thinkers focused more on the economic consequences of abolition than on the humanitarian aspect of the question. Whereas British Protestant evangelicals insisted on the asperities of the

Sir Darnley is apparently convinced by his friend's arguments, because following their exchange of letters he emancipates his slaves. In the aftermath of this act, confusion breaks out. Colonists oppose his action on one side, Maroons fight for the general overthrow of slavery on the other, and in the course of these confrontations, Sir Darnley is killed. His decision to proceed with emancipation, however, is shown not to have been in vain, for in the end, all of the colony's slaves are freed in exchange for the restoration of order. Former slaves are instructed to disperse across the island and are employed "as domestics or laborers" (148). On the romance front, after a decent interval of mourning for Sir Darnley, Phédima and Abensar are married. Interestingly, the reunited couple does not consider returning to Africa. Rather, much as Sir Bevil had predicted, along with the other freed slaves, they choose to remain in the site of their former servitude. As one of the few antislavery writers who tried to imagine what would happen to the colonies after abolition, Butini presumably felt it important to reassure his readers that things would continue much as ever, and to portray freed slaves evolving contentedly into a cohort of low-paid domestics and laborers.

If *African Letters* goes further than "Zimeo," not only in advocating abolition, but also in imagining the future of a colony after emancipation, it is perhaps because Butini's thoroughgoing embrace of economic principles empowered him to write about abolition more directly than Saint-Lambert. By laying out the costs and benefits of abolition so precisely, he proved, at least to his own satisfaction, that this step would be in everyone's interests, and as a result felt few inhibitions about representing emancipation and its aftermath. There is, however, another side to this picture, which is that while Butini represented the abolition of slavery boldly and directly, he also represented it as the cornerstone of a new colonial order. In this new dispensation, African/Creole workers would remain subordinate, functioning not only as producers but also as consumers of European goods.

Slavery and Women's Rights

In the 1780s–90s, two female writers, Olympe de Gouges and Germaine de Staël, produced fictional narratives in which the representation of slavery is interwoven with commentary on the social and political position of women in France. A few decades later, another French woman, Claire de Duras, also wrote a novella in which slavery, race, and gender are bound together as central themes (*Ourika*, 1823). Like many works by eighteenth- and early nineteenth-century French women, these texts quickly faded from view and were for many decades largely forgotten. In the 1980s–90s, however, the marginalization of

---

Middle Passage, French writers approached the subject of slavery from the perspective of rights, property, and economic benefits.

women's writing became an important area of concern for feminist scholars, as critics began to study the mechanisms of exclusion and to rediscover forgotten texts. It was in this intellectual context that in 1994 Gouges's, Staël's, and Duras's writing on race and slavery was republished with accompanying translations in the volume *Translating Slavery: Gender and Race in French Women's Writing, 1783–1823,* edited by Doris Kadish and Françoise Massardier-Kenney. As its title suggests, this volume highlights the relationship between abolitionism and questions of gender. This intersection is presented from a number of different perspectives that include the following main points. The contributors observe that of the relatively small number of women writing in France in this period, several were drawn to the subject of slavery. Correspondingly, they note that a significant proportion of antislavery writing, at least in fictional genres, was authored by women. In interpreting this apparent affinity, they propose that women writers were drawn to this topic because they saw parallels between the status of slaves and their own subordinate condition. Some of the essays also suggest that women writers' social marginality endowed them with an unusual capacity to identify with cultural others, or that as women Staël, Gouges, and Duras were endowed with a cosmopolitan outlook that enabled them to think beyond national, racial, and linguistic boundaries.[18]

In *French Atlantic Triangle* Christopher Miller returns to the corpus of women's antislavery writing presented in *Translating Slavery.* Since his readings respond to this volume, they too are primarily organized around the category of gender. Miller argues that it is problematic to speak of women's particular sensitivity to the plight of slaves when more men than women wrote antislavery fictions (he mentions Mailhol, Saint-Lambert, and Bernardin de Saint-Pierre, among others), when several of these men wrote before women took up the cause, and when the perspectives on slavery and colonization represented in male- and female-authored works are broadly comparable. Miller also suggests that some male writers made the case for abolition more directly and more urgently than their female counterparts (he points in particular to the example of Saint-Lambert) (103) and expresses skepticism toward the claim that women writers were more adept at embracing the cultural characteristics and productions of Africans, and more able to interrogate the dominant values and aesthetic paradigms of European culture. He notes, for example, that the protagonists of Germaine de Staël's story "Mirza" are rendered sympathetic, not on the basis of any distinctively "African" qualities, but because they speak perfect French and conform in various ways to French cultural norms (148–49).

Several of Miller's points about *Translating Slavery* seem to me to be justified. It is certainly the case that male writers as well as women took up the

---

18. Staël is recognized for her role in introducing German Romanticism to France in her book *De l'Allemagne* (On Germany) (1813). She also wrote an essay on translation, "De l'esprit des traductions" (On the Spirit of Translation) (1814).

cause of abolition, and that in some instances they did so at an earlier moment ("Zimeo" was published in 1769, more than two decades before the contributions of Gouges and Staël). On another level, however, I find that Miller understates the discursive connections between abolitionism and the politics of gender to which *Translating Slavery* points.

One point made by several contributors to the volume is that issues bearing on gender occupy a more prominent place in the works of women writers than in those of their male counterparts. They observe, for example, that women writers accorded a more central role to female protagonists—they were able to imagine the enslaved as a woman—and that they depicted social marginality as a function of gender as well as race.

This point is one that has also been made in a slightly different way by the historian Karen Offen. In an essay devoted to the use of slavery as a metaphor for social marginality and political disenfranchisement, "How (and Why) the Analogy of Marriage with Slavery Provided the Springboard for Women's Rights Demands in France, 1640–1848," Offen shows that in revolutionary political discourse women's subaltern status was often portrayed as a form of enslavement.[19] Pamphlets drew analogies between men's absolute authority in marriage and the master-slave relationship, and compared France's elaborate system of arranged marriages and dowries to the transactions of the slave trade. For example, in the postface to her *Déclaration des droits de la femme et de la citoyenne* (*Declaration of the Rights of Woman and Citizeness*) (1791), a provocative reworking of the Declaration of the Rights of Man and Citizen, Olympe de Gouges likened European marital customs to the slave trade, lamenting that woman is "bought like a slave from the coasts of Africa."[20] Conjugal relations were not the only aspect of gender relations that were metaphorized as a form of enslavement. Rather, as Offen demonstrates, references to slavery provided an important "springboard" for the assertion of Frenchwomen's political rights. Gouges, for example, observes in the postface to *Declaration* that having broken free of their chains with women's help, men had become unjust to their companions, whose emancipation remained to be secured.

In the discussion of the antislavery writing of Gouges and Staël that follows I will develop some of the points that have been made in previous discussions of the intersections of abolitionism, feminism, and gender. But I also will take a step back from these arguments by considering how the critical focus on gender has shaped the ways in which these texts have been read. I will argue, for example, that one by-product of this emphasis has been that while scholars

---

19. Offen, "Analogy of Marriage with Slavery." Offen's essay is thorough, but at times it fails to differentiate between allusions to slavery in seventeenth-century romances, where the referent is ancient/biblical/Oriental slavery, and the more specific allusions to the Atlantic slave trade that appear in writing of the 1780s–90s.

20. Gouges, *Oeuvres,* 108.

have produced rich interpretations of the psychological and sentimental dimensions of women's writing on slavery, they have made little of the important place that economic reasoning occupies in this body of writing. In my readings I show that the liberal economic theories that informed the work of Saint-Lambert and Butini were equally central to the writing of Gouges and Staël. In the case of Gouges I argue that what some scholars have viewed as an ambivalent or even opportunistic attitude toward abolition can be contextualized in relation to the broader tendencies of antislavery discourse in this period. In the case of Staël I highlight the important implications of the writer's decision to represent an experimental "postslavery" colony in which the production of sugar has been transferred from the Caribbean to Africa.

A second aspect of these questions that I want to reconsider is the way in which Offen, in particular, articulates the relationship between abolitionism and revolutionary-era feminism. As the title of her long and thorough article on the subject suggests, Offen perceives opposition to slavery as a "springboard" for the formulation of questions relating to women's social and political marginality. I will argue that this springboard also operated in the other direction: that discourses relating to women's social position and rights provided a crucial framework for the critique of slavery. One of the factors that leads Offen to structure her argument the way she does is her perception that, by the 1780s, abolitionism was a well-established political discourse available for feminists to mine. I argue, by contrast, that abolitionism remained in this period a tentative and conditional discourse, and that its association with the question of women's rights lent it additional resonance. This is not to say that women's rights were better established than slaves', or that they were given more serious consideration in revolutionary debates and legislation, a question on which a number of scholars, including Lynn Hunt and Louis Sala-Molins, have commented and drawn different conclusions.[21] Rather, in a more limited sense, I want to show that late eighteenth-century opposition to slavery coalesced in conjunction with discourses that concerned metropolitan France as well as the colonial arena. As I have shown, these discourses included the far-ranging field of political economy. Below I argue that examination of the social and political status of women also provided a context for the examination of slavery. Economic theory, as we have seen, shaped the representation of slavery in important ways. In similar fashion, the projection of a feminist social and political agenda onto the terrain of race and slavery carried significant consequences. It was one thing to claim that Frenchwomen were akin to slaves, another to imagine that slaves were positioned like a Frenchwoman.

---

21. Hunt, *Inventing Human Rights,* 163; Sala-Molins, *Dark Side of the Light,* 8. The former argues that slavery was afforded more attention in the debates of the Constituent Assembly, the latter that the status of women was a more central concern.

Abolition and "Bourgeois Liberal Feminism" in Olympe de Gouges

One of the most remarkable things about Olympe de Gouges was that she managed to make a name for herself as a writer and political activist despite the fact that she was, in almost every respect, a social outsider. Not only was she a woman, but, unlike most other eighteenth-century women writers, she came from a modest social background and had not received an extensive education. Despite these apparent handicaps, Gouges became a vocal and prolific contributor to the social and political debates of the revolutionary period.[22] In theater, pamphlets, and other forms of writing she advocated an array of social reforms, including the recognition of women's political rights and, though her ideas on this subject were not straightforward, the abolition of slavery.

Scholars have characterized Gouges's commitment to abolition in contrasting ways. The contributors to *Translating Slavery* on the whole portray Gouges as a committed and passionate abolitionist, though as Marie-Pierre Le Hir notes in her essay "Feminism, Theater, Race," the dramatic works in which Gouges explores this question tend to "postpone the abolition of slavery to a not foreseeable future."[23] Contrastingly, in a book devoted to the social milieu of Parisian theater, Gregory Brown suggests that Gouges's antislavery stance was superficial if not utterly contrived, and interprets the fact that she rewrote her two principal antislavery pieces as the sign of a propensity for ambitious self-reinvention.[24] Synthesizing and responding to these contrasting perspectives, Christopher Miller presents a careful set of rereadings, and offers an appreciation that falls somewhere in between the somewhat idealized account of Gouges presented in *Translating Slavery* and the highly critical viewpoint of Brown (109–40).

I agree on a number of points with Miller's interpretation, but I want to take the discussion in a somewhat different direction. In the debate over Gouges's militancy, or lack thereof, what seems to have been largely overlooked is how Gouges's hesitant and contradictory stance compared with that of other contemporary antislavery writers. Miller draws a contrast between the complex and ambivalent perspective of Gouges, a woman writer, and the clear-cut militancy of a Saint-Lambert, a male writer. From my perspective this contrast is problematic because it overlooks the vagaries of the portrayal of slavery that we encounter in "Zimeo." I will argue that Gouges was neither more nor less ambivalent than most other contemporary antislavery writers, and that the

---

22. In November 1793 Gouges's outspoken political views led her to the guillotine. Though the official reason for her execution was that she had demonstrated "unpatriotic" support for ideas associated with the ousted Girondist faction, the fact that she was widely perceived as a woman who meddled in the affairs of men was unquestionably also an important factor. See Benoîte Groult's discussion of Gouges's execution in the introduction to *Olympe de Gouges, Oeuvres,* 58–59.

23. Le Hir, "Feminism, Theater, Race," 76.

24. Brown, *Field of Honor.*

complications of her position ought to be seen, not as symptoms of individual failure, but as reflections of the wider discursive framing of abolitionism in the 1780s and early 1790s. Correspondingly, I will argue that while Gouges's gender shaped some aspects of her presentation of the issues raised by slavery—notably her portrayal of black and enslaved women, and her depiction of relationships between men and women—it did not make her approach to slavery significantly different from that of Saint-Lambert, Butini, Dupont, or Condorcet. This is primarily because Gouges's feminist politics were informed by the same matrix of ideas about freedom, property, and individual rights that anchored liberal political economy.

Feminism was of course by no means incompatible with an abolitionist stance; however, these perspectives were perhaps not as seamlessly interwoven as the contributors to *Translating Slavery* seem to suggest. As in some other contexts, the presumption of symmetries and shared agendas here proves to be problematic. Thinking about race and gender as parallel sites of subjection, notably, gets in the way of thinking about them as sites of intersection, thereby obscuring the specific social experience of enslaved black women. By the 1980s and 1990s a number of black feminists had pointed to the historical blind spots of liberal feminism with regard to race and class, noting that white middle-class feminists had often ignored or excluded black women.[25] These tensions, however, are barely mentioned in *Translating Slavery*. In the case of Gouges, as we will see, the points of intersection between race and gender must be carefully examined, for while Gouges was clearly sympathetic to the predicament of the enslaved, she also tended to project a liberal socioeconomic philosophy inflected with feminist ideas onto the colonial context, without giving much consideration to the tensions and contradictions that this projection entailed.

Gouges first explored the question of slavery in a "drama" (i.e., a play with a serious subject matter but which was not a tragedy) entitled *Zamore et Mirza; ou, L'heureux naufrage* (*Zamore and Mirza; or, The Happy Shipwreck*).[26] The play was submitted to the Comédie française in 1784 and accepted by the theater's board of actors. Afterward, however, it was put on hold for several years. The causes of this deferral seem to come down to some combination of Gouges's propensity to become involved in impolitic quarrels and the troupe's rather dismissive attitude toward female authors. The obstacles to the play's performance further multiplied in the late 1780s when the debate between the Society of the Friends of Blacks and the colonial lobby or Club Massiac made Gouges's dramatization of slavery a highly controversial piece.[27] Since *Zamore*

25. See, for example, bell hooks, *Ain't I a Woman?*

26. *Zamore et Mirza, Oeuvres de Madame de Gouges*, vol. 3. Digital versions of the first editions of *Zamore et Mirza* (and the later *Esclavage des noirs*) can be downloaded from the Bibliothèque nationale's online catalog, *Gallica*.

27. See Groult, *Oeuvres de Madame de Gouges*, 23–27, and Blanc, *Marie-Olympe de Gouges*, 71–90.

and Mirza was never performed, many critics skip over it and focus on the reworked version that was performed in 1789 under the title *Black Slavery*. I (like both Brown and Miller) will discuss the earlier play at some length, both because the comparison helps illuminate Gouges's vision of the intersection of slavery and gender, and because it illustrates the evolution of Gouges's thinking in the 1780s, a decade in which slavery was becoming an increasingly prominent public issue.[28]

Though members of the colonial lobby opposed the staging of *Zamore and Mirza,* the play is not exactly an abolitionist polemic. While it represents slavery in a French colony, the colony in question is not, as one might anticipate, located in the French Caribbean. The play's front matter indicates that the action takes place on a deserted island and in a large city of the "Indes orientales" (East Indies) located nearby (2). The play's enslaved characters are called "indiens," a word that seems in the context to denote East Indians, but which in the eighteenth century, as today, could also refer to Amerindians.

Critical readings of *Zamore and Mirza* have responded to the indefiniteness of its setting in various ways. Miller suggests that Gouges may have had France's handful of trading posts in India in mind, or that she might have been thinking of the French colonies of Île de France and Île Bourbon in the Indian Ocean, but he acknowledges that the play does not include any references to specific Indian cities or places, and that (today's) Mauritius and La Réunion are closer to Africa than to India (122–24). Gouges's biographer, Olivier Blanc, suggests that the author chose a vague "Indian" setting in order to avoid controversy and censorship. The fact that Gouges inserted African and Antillean references into the later version of the play seems, however, to belie the idea that her goal was to avoid controversy (60).

Taking a more critical approach, Gregory Brown sees the fact that the play does not refer clearly to a specific colony as an indication that it is not really about slavery and race. This reading is, however, problematic, for although *Zamore and Mirza* does not contribute much on the subject of race—indeed, it more or less obscures the racial organization of the colonial order—slavery is a central theme. From my perspective the play's loosely Oriental setting is probably attributable to two factors: Gouges's ignorance of colonial geography—as noted earlier, she did not have an extensive education—and the prevalent cultural displacement of slavery on an axis running from West to East.[29]

The play opens on a desert island to which two slaves, Zamore and his fiancée Mirza, have fled after Zamore has killed the overseer of his owner's

28. Miller suggests that *Zamore and Mirza* and *Black Slavery* are so different that they should be treated as two different works (*French Atlantic Triangle*, 111). Since *Black Slavery* took shape as a revised version of *Zamore and Mirza*, I will approach it as such.

29. As Miller observes, Gouges's apparent ignorance of colonial geography was not necessarily excusable. Lack of familiarity with a practice that one is engaged in protesting can be seen to betoken a superficial form of radicalism (ibid., 128).

plantation. The presentation of events makes it clear that Zamore acted in self-defense and in order to protect Mirza from the unwanted advances of the overseer (4). This defense of Zamore is one of the more radical gestures of the play. Gouges effectively suggests that the killing of the overseer should be interpreted as an act mitigated by the circumstances in which it was performed, that is, in accordance with the principles of French law, rather than under the articles of the *Black Code,* according to which the murder of a colonist by a slave was automatically punishable by death.

Before long Zamore and Mirza are joined on the desert island by a young French couple, Sophie and Valere, who have been washed ashore in the aftermath of a shipwreck (8–11). Zamore and Mirza save their lives, and in return the French travelers promise to intercede with M. De Saint-Frémont, who is both Zamore's master and the governor of the colony from which he and Mirza have fled.

Sophie and Valere's readiness to help Zamore and Mirza is reinforced by their opposition to slavery. At several points in the play this stance is said to be representative of the wider views of the French people, and this claim in turn supports an opposition between the views of the virtuous and enlightened French characters—Sophie, Valere, and M. De Saint-Frémont and his wife (the latter are portrayed as metropolitans dispatched to a colonial outpost)—and the cruel and grasping "indiens" or "habitants" who make up the population of colonists/Creoles. This moral dichotomy lays the blame for slavery at the feet of the colonists, absolving France of any responsibility. In the unfolding of the plot, it is reinforced by the fact that M. De Saint-Frémont seems to be unable to either pardon or condemn Zamore and Mirza (e.g., 82). Since power over the slaves seems to reside with the "habitants" and not with the French, it proves impossible for him to exercise moral authority. A further aspect of the good French/bad Creole dynamic is that it separates the issue of slavery from that of colonization. The colony is depicted as French—at least it has a French governor—but slavery is represented as a system overseen by Creoles. Since M. De Saint-Frémont is portrayed as an enlightened and benevolent figure, it seems possible to draw the conclusion that without the Creoles and the system of slavery over which they preside, colonial rule by France would be a perfectly acceptable arrangement.

In the play's second act the action shifts from the desert island to the mainland, where Sophie and Mme De Saint-Frémont join forces to save the two condemned slaves (27). In the third and final act the plot comes to a climax when Zamore is about to be executed by the colonial militia. Though Sophie, Valere, and M. and Mme De Saint-Frémont all call for mercy, a hard-line judge insists that the law must be upheld. Just when all seems lost, an unforeseen revelation intervenes to save the day. It is discovered that Sophie is Saint-Frémont's long-lost daughter, the fruit of a youthful love affair, and in the aftermath of this revelation (it is not entirely clear how or why), sentiment prevails over law, and M. De Saint-Frémont, who had previously declared himself powerless to intervene, not only pardons them but also decrees their freedom (87–89). Though the play is not a tragedy, it nonetheless reaches its denouement through the tragic device of a peripeteia, a sudden reversal or change of fortune. In *Zamore and Mirza*, this reversal takes the form of a family romance (the father recognizes his illegitimate daughter), which also operates as a colonial family romance (the tensions within the colonial family are briskly resolved, and the image of France as benevolent father is kept intact).

Zamore and Mirza takes a critical perspective toward several aspects of colonial slavery. As we have seen, Gouges alludes to the brutality of overseers, a problem that the 1784 reforms to the *Black Code* attempted to address. The play also articulates a critique of the idea that race constitutes a basis for enslavement. When they are alone on the desert island in the play's first scene, the two enslaved protagonists discuss the causes of their servitude. Zamore explains to Mirza that slavery is based on skin color, and that it arises because art and knowledge have raised the *habitants* above nature, enabling them to seize the land of other peoples (6). He insists, however, that differences of skin color are merely superficial and do not constitute a legitimate reason for subjugating other people. But despite these gestures, it is not entirely clear whether the play advocates the abolition of slavery. Like Saint-Lambert, Gouges focuses more on the difference between good and bad forms of slave ownership than on slavery itself. For example, she portrays M. De Saint-Frémont as a good master who has presided over Zamore's education and treated him like a son. Correspondingly, when Zamore and Mirza are offered their freedom in the play's final scene, they both decline, stating that they prefer to stay with their benefactors (another echo of "Zimeo").

The published text of the play indicates that the performance was to be followed by a divertissement, or ballet, composed of two separate scenes, or tableaux (92–93). The first was to celebrate, not the slaves' pardon and emancipation (which, as we have seen, they appear to reject), but rather the consecration of their marriage. Though Gouges's decision to end the play with a wedding rather than a celebration of freedom and justice might seem rather surprising, it is consistent with the emphasis placed throughout the play on sentimental relations and conjugal bonds. As we have seen, the plot revolves around the interaction of three couples: Zamore and Mirza, Sophie and Valere, and the two Saint-Frémonts. It also includes a number of plot twists and subplots involving lost children (specifically lost daughters) and happy reunions. Gouges's representation of these family relationships certainly has much to do with her own biography. If she devised a plot that turns on a father's recognition of his illegitimate daughter, it was doubtless in part because she sought throughout her life to be recognized as the natural daughter of the playwright and academician, Jean-Jacques Lefranc de Pompignan, who for his part persistently refused to acknowledge her. Gouges's personal connection to the experience of illegitimacy also helped shape her outlook on women's social position. *Zamore and Mirza* includes implied criticism of the pressures that led men to disavow children born out of wedlock. This critique was developed further in the political pamphlets that Gouges authored in the late 1780s, many of which focus on the plight of illegitimate children and unmarried mothers.[30]

Gouges's feminist outlook is also manifest in other aspects of the play, such as the fact that two of the female protagonists, Sophie and Mme De Saint-Frémont, are portrayed as tireless activists who work harder than their husbands to secure the pardon of Zamore and Mirza. When Zamore and Mirza are on the verge of being executed in act 3, it is Sophie who bravely throws herself between the slaves and the firing squad, daring the judge and the militia to kill her too (74). But although Sophie and Mme de Saint-Frémont have a certain appeal as feminist figures, the emphasis placed on their heroism at times detracts from the play's engagement with the issue of slavery. As Miller, paraphrasing Gayatri Spivak observes, Sophie's self-sacrificing gesture can be seen to enact a scenario on which a white woman intervenes to save dark-skinned people from the white man.[31] In this dynamic the emphasis placed on gender dilutes rather than enriches the analysis of colonial relations because it displaces the focus of interest onto a different set of political concerns.

Above I suggested that the exploration of women's rights provided a discursive context for the representation of slavery, and that this framework shaped in significant ways the manner in which slavery and abolition were represented. *Zamore and Mirza* is a case in point. If the play's advocacy of abolition seems less than conclusive, it is in part because Gouges foregrounds other concerns, notably questions relating to gender, and these get in the way of a sustained exploration of the issue of slavery. In several scenes, as the example of Sophie's heroic intervention illustrates, the promotion of a white, liberal feminist agenda overshadows the case for abolition.

After waiting for several years for her play to be performed, Gouges decided to publish it. In 1788 it was printed along with a short postface, an essay titled *Réflexions sur les hommes nègres* (Reflections on Negroes).[32] Though this essay is largely a plea to the Comédie française to perform the play, and to be bold enough to perform it in blackface, it also contains some broader observations on the subject of race and slavery that are necessary to consider here.

Gouges begins the essay by explaining that she had been curious about black people since her childhood, and that it was because of this lifelong sympathy

---

30. In 1788–89 Gouges produced a series of brochures and articles calling for reforms including the right to civil divorce, state support for unmarried mothers, and recognition of the rights of illegitimate children. See Groult, *Oeuvres de Madame de Gouges,* 34–41.

31. Spivak, "Can the Subaltern Speak?" 92; Miller, *French Atlantic Triangle,* 130.

32. Both the French text of this essay and an English translation by Sylvie Molta are included in Kadish and Massardier-Kenney, *Translating Slavery.* References in the text are to this translation.

that she had devoted her first play to the subject of slavery (84).[33] Following these introductory remarks and a few quick statements to the effect that slavery is contrary to natural law, she turns to the main topic of the essay, which is the mistreatment of slaves by colonists (84–85). Though this commentary has been discussed less often than either the personal remarks with which the essay opens or Gouges's plea to the actors that her play be performed in blackface, it is an important passage from several perspectives. Here, as in the play itself, Gouges blurs the distinction between mistreatment and enslavement and, by extension, the difference between reform and abolition. Drawing a strong connection between bad slave management and *marronage* and insurrection, she suggests (like Diderot and Saint-Lambert before her), that slaves rebelled because they were subjected to harsh treatment rather than to throw off the shackles of bondage (85). She also argues that abuses were not in the colonists' interest, because they encouraged slaves to rebel, and even to try to poison their masters. Reforms were needed, she seems to imply, not only because slaves were suffering or because slavery was morally wrong, but also because of the dangers that colonists would otherwise face. Finally, anticipating that the "stick" might not be enough to get colonial planters to mend their ways, Gouges also tenders the "carrot." In a passage that attests to the influence of liberal economic theory, she claims that slaves would be much better workers if they were free. Freed slaves, she writes:

> Will be more exact and diligent in their work.... They will cultivate freely their own land like the farmers in Europe and will not leave their fields to go to foreign nations.... Their freedom will leave some Negroes to desert their country but much less than those who leave the French countryside. Young people hardly come of age... before they are on their way to Paris to take up the noble occupation of lackey or porter. There are a hundred servants for one position, whereas our fields lack farmers. (85–86)

In essence, Gouges appears to be saying here that if slavery were abolished, nothing would really change. Emancipated slaves would not depart for other countries; they would not, for example, immediately seek to return to Africa. Rather, they would remain in their fields, and as free workers they would be more productive than ever. In an afterthought with strong physiocratic overtones, Gouges wishes that French workers, too, would stay on their farms, rather than abandoning the countryside for the lure of work in Paris.

This passage resonates strongly with one that appears in the play itself. In an exchange with a confidante, Mme De Saint-Frémont contrasts her husband's

---

33. As Miller observes, Gouges's claim to have been interested in black people since her childhood may or may not have been true. What matters is not so much the veracity of the claim as Gouges's decision to portray her opposition to slavery as a matter of personal empathy (*French Atlantic Triangle*, 117–18).

benevolent treatment of his slaves with the harsh treatment meted out by the colonists. She explains that his approach was not only morally preferable but also more productive from an economic point of view: "My husband has remarked that if you treat them gently," she tells her companion, "you can do whatever you want with them" (32). Humane treatment is not only good in itself, it is also good for business.

I mentioned earlier that the divertissement with which Gouges wanted the play to end was to involve two episodes. The first, as described earlier, was to be a ballet celebrating Zamore and Mirza's marriage. The second, apparently unconnected scene was to be a dance evoking the discovery of America (92–93). Scholars have tended to view Gouges's decision to append a ballet depicting the arrival of Europeans in the Americas to a play nominally set in the East Indies as evidence of her ignorance of or indifference to colonial geography. But if we look closely at the content of the proposed ballet, another interpretation suggests itself.

Gouges's stage directions call for a group of "savages" who are alarmed by the approach of a European vessel to flee toward an inland forest. The foreign sailors disembark and pursue them as if meaning to attack, but then their general delivers a speech, described as a "moral lesson," and the savages, realizing that "he had come to the island to protect them," return to the shore (93). In this short sequence, a critique of Europeans' role as colonizers is juxtaposed with a celebration of their potential to act as liberators. I would like to suggest that this apposition replicates and in a sense clarifies the overall message of the play. In both play and ballet, criticism of slavery is juxtaposed with, and to some extent overshadowed by, a representation of the European capacity for benevolence. Reform slavery, Gouges seems to say, and colonial rule would be a desirable political arrangement.

Five years after Gouges submitted *Zamore and Mirza* to the Comédie française, a modified version of the play was staged under the revised title *L'esclavage des noirs; ou, L'heureux naufrage* (*Black Slavery; or, The Happy Shipwreck*). After only three performances the play was closed. The official explanation for this measure was that it had failed to bring in adequate receipts. A more accurate account would be that disruptions organized by supporters of the colonial lobby made its failure all but inevitable.[34] I now turn to this revised version of the play, a work (re)written and performed in the context of the heightened interest in colonial issues at the end of the 1780s.

The plot, cast of characters, and dialogue of *Black Slavery* are close to those of *Zamore and Mirza*, but as the new title suggests, the later version is more explicit about the fact that the enslaved population of the European colonies

---

34. On the circumstances of the play's performance and closure, see Blanc, *Marie-Olympe de Gouges*, 97; Le Hir, "Feminism, Theater, Race," especially 79–82; Miller, *French Atlantic Triangle*, 113–16.

was primarily of African descent. Though Zamor (spelled in the 1792 text without the final *e*) and Mirza are still represented as "Indian slaves," the word "East" is dropped from the stage directions, and the location of the action is given vaguely as the "Indies." The characters make a number of passing references to Africa or Africans. For example, in one exchange Valere calls Mirza a "jolie négresse" (pretty Negress) (95), and in another a slave named Azor mentions that he and his father had been abducted from the Guinea Coast (101). The later version of the play also includes a number of explicit calls for the emancipation of slaves. For example, in an exchange with the hardline judge who insists on Zamor's execution, M. De Saint-Frémont cries out: "I dare hope that before long there will no longer be any slaves. O Louis! O adored monarch! Would that I could this very moment put under your eyes the innocence of these condemned souls" (106). As this outcry suggests, *Black Slavery*, like *Zamore and Mirza*, represents abolition as a step that the French were eager to take, and basks patriotically in these enlightened values.

But while the play seems to explicitly call for emancipation, this message is attenuated by the incorporation of a more conservative subtext. The play's main characters emphasize the need to proceed cautiously, in ways that would preserve order and protect the colonial economy. For example, when he is about to be executed and the slaves are on the brink of revolt, Zamor delivers a speech in which he cautions the slaves that respect for law and order had to be placed before ideological concerns. He forbids the slaves to seek revenge for his execution or to start a revolt: "Fear especially this factious spirit," he warns them, "and never deliver yourselves into excess to escape slavery; fear breaking your irons with too much violence; time and divine justice are on your side" (116–17).

Similar admonishments are issued by other characters. When M. De Saint-Frémont rewards Zamor and Mirza with their freedom at the end of the play (in the 1792 version they appear to accept), he says that he wishes he could free all the colony's slaves (he doesn't explain why he can't). He nonetheless underscores that if the slaves' destiny should ever change, they would do well to keep the "public good" in mind and to place their hopes in a "benevolent and enlightened Government" (119). Ironically, though the slaves are not freed, they are asked to show respect and obedience at the time in the hypothetical future when the state decrees their freedom. The same injunction is voiced by an enslaved woman named Coraline (a new addition to the 1792 play, and Gouges's only black feminist character). Speaking before a gathering of slaves, Coraline says she has heard that in order to be good, you simply have to "cultivate your garden." The relevancy of *Candide*'s reference to "cultivation" for this colonial context is clarified when Coraline predicts that if and when the slaves were freed, they would remain at their stations and continue to perform their work (101). Here, as in the speech delivered by Saint-Frémont, slaves are reminded not of their right to freedom, but rather of their duty to keep the peace and maintain the status quo.

In 1792 Gouges arranged for *Black Slavery* to be printed, together with a short essay exploring issues related to the subject matter of the play. Just as the essay that accompanied *Zamore and Mirza* urged the Comédie française to perform the play, so the essay paired with *Black Slavery* defended its content in the wake of its tumultuous run. The two essays differ, however, to the extent that in the later piece Gouges clearly felt compelled to address the political circumstances of the day. By 1792 the French Revolution had radicalized, and the enslaved population of Saint-Domingue had risen up in revolt. Responding to developments on both sides of the Atlantic, Gouges delivers a message addressed not only to colonists but also to rebel slaves and radicals in metropolitan France.

In a first set of remarks, Gouges addresses the colonial lobby, which she accuses of conspiring to bring down her play. Yet rather than simply condemning the Club Massiac for its reactionary stance, Gouges attempts to justify her play on her enemies' terms by characterizing its message as "moral" but not "inflammatory" (3–4, 88). She claims, for instance, that she had been trying to help the colonists "preserve their properties and their most cherished interests" (88). These claims, as we have seen, are not entirely misplaced, for while the play advocates the abolition of slavery, it also strongly rejects violence and emphasizes the importance of respecting property and law.

In the second part of the essay Gouges turns her attention to the slaves. What is striking about this address is that rather than speaking to enslaved men and women in the language of rights and freedom, she confines herself to condemning the crimes they had committed in freedom's name. Instead of attacking slavery as a moral offense, Gouges embarks on a prolonged denunciation of violence, extremism, and disorder. Staying true to the outlook of *Zamore and Mirza,* Gouges reproaches the slaves for their failure to differentiate between good and bad masters in their blind pursuit of revenge. "Most of your Masters were humane and charitable, and in your blind rage you do not distinguish between innocent victims and your persecutors," she complains (88). As in *Zamore and Mirza,* and much like Saint-Lambert in "Zimeo," Gouges locates the fundamental problem of colonial slavery, not in the deprivation of liberty or in abduction from a native land, but in the ancillary problem of mistreatment. As a result (again like Saint-Lambert) she depicts masters who were not cruel as "innocent" victims, a portrayal that implies that their ownership of slaves did not raise any moral questions.

The passage ends with a contorted paraphrase of Rousseau, whom Gouges, like many other late eighteenth-century women writers, fervently admired. She writes that "men were not born in irons, and now you prove them necessary" (88). Instead of arguing that the chains of slavery should be broken, Gouges seems here to imply that if the slaves continued on their course of violence, their chains would actually be warranted. In words that echo the speeches of some of her characters, she urges the slaves of Saint-Domingue to let order and harmony, both "indispensable in the colonial commonweal" (88), prevail. The slaves' interests, she emphasizes, "consist only in social order," while their rights can reside only in the wisdom of law (88). Finally, she calls on slaves and people of color to prove to France, which she calls "an Enlightened Nation," that it had not been wrong in treating them as men or in granting them rights they would not have enjoyed in America (6, 89).

Though Gouges is categorical that freedom should emanate from the state and should not be achieved through acts of self-emancipation, she also has some negative things to say about the influence that French militants had exercised in the colony. The same men who had caused France's domestic politics to go astray, she argues, were responsible for the violence that had broken out in America. Since she does not name names, it is not entirely clear which radical figures she meant to attack. A little later in the preface she says something negative about Brissot, one of the founders of the Society of the Friends of Blacks, but this comes in the context of a more general discussion of nature and law, and it is not clear whether she intended to hold Brissot responsible for the escalating violence in France and the colonies.[35]

Gouges is usually characterized in political terms as a moderate "Girondist"—the name given to the loose-knit faction that dominated revolutionary politics from 1791 until its fall to the more radical "Montagnards" in March 1793—or as a "constitutional monarchist" who supported the Revolution but favored keeping the monarchy in place. The fact that she did not embrace the views of the most radical revolutionary element is sometimes given as an explanation for her reserved attitude toward abolition. Marie-Pierre Le Hir, for instance, suggests that Gouges favored reform in both metropolitan and colonial contexts, but that she also emphasized respect for law and political authority, and as a consequence held back from the most radical positions.[36] But while I would agree that Gouges placed order before rights, it seems problematic to suggest that her moderate, Girondist politics held her back from advocating emancipation in a more decisive way. The reformist, market-oriented, liberal politics of the Girondists were precisely those out of which the French abolitionist movement grew. Many if not most of the leading advocates of the rights of slaves in the early 1790s were at least loosely affiliated with this group, which was led by Brissot, the cofounder of the Society of the Friends of Blacks. In light of this, I propose that rather than viewing Gouges's apparent ambivalence toward abolition as a personal failing, it is historically more appropriate to see it as a reflection of the wider character of abolitionism among writers of Gouges's generation, and as a symptom of the complex conjunction between liberalism and attentiveness to questions of racial and social subordination.

35. According to Brissot's memoirs, Gouges attended some of the early meetings of the society. See Blanc, *Marie-Olympe de Gouges*, 91.
36. See, for example, Le Hir, "Feminism, Theater, Race," 76.

Today Gouges is remembered primarily as a writer who made the case for women's rights: as an advocate for women's social causes and a proponent of women's political equality. In turning her attention to the question of slavery, Gouges seems to have felt that there was a strong connection between this feminist agenda and the critical analysis of race and slavery. But as we have seen, her feminism often got in the way of her engagement with these issues. Her colonial plays feature displays of female virtue and draw attention to forms of injustice experienced by Frenchwomen, but they neglect the specific conditions of deprivation experienced by enslaved black women. Gouges's failures in this regard reflect a wider set of problems within the tradition of liberal feminism. As bell hooks and others have observed, the feminist movement has historically tended to neglect the circumstances of those who are most marginalized by existing power structures.[37] In the case of slavery, it may even have helped reinforce the status quo by suggesting that it could be ameliorated by targeted reforms and did not need to be subjected to a more extensive critique. This limitation is not, of course, unique to liberal feminism. Rather, as my wider discussions of liberal antislavery argument has suggested, it exemplifies the limitations of liberal political theory, with its emphasis on individualism and property rights.

Slaves into Subjects: Germaine de Staël's "Mirza"

The question of rights was not the only point of articulation between feminism and abolitionism in late eighteenth-century French fiction. Another important interface was the attempt to represent enslaved people as individuals with a rich inner life. Colonial fictions invited readers to identify with enslaved protagonists by portraying them as refined men and women who were capable of deep passions and acute emotional suffering. In portraying slaves in this light they tapped into the period's cult of emotional sensitivity, or *sensibilité,* a capacity for intense feeling and a predisposition for introspection. *Sensibilité* affected the representation of both male and female characters, but in the case of men it entailed a significant realignment of gender roles. Men were effectively feminized insofar as they were shown to be detached from the world of public affairs and endowed with the same capacity for passion and emotional disturbance that had previously been attributed to women alone. Because *sensibilité* was perceived as a feminine trait, it was often identified with women's writing. In fact, however, it owed much to the writing of Rousseau and was as prevalent in men's writing as in women's. This point is illustrated by the corpus of colonial fictions. The melancholic figure whom Léon-François Hoffmann has called the *nègre romantique* was as central to the antislavery writing of

37. See, for example, hooks, *Feminist Theory.*

Bernardin de Saint-Pierre, Saint-Lambert, and Victor Hugo as to that of Staël and Claire de Duras. But there were, all the same, some differences in the way that male and female writers channeled *sensibilité*. Whereas in colonial fictions authored by male writers the leading characters were invariably men, women writers also imagined *négresses romantiques,* imbuing their stance against slavery with a feminist orientation.[38]

Below I examine the workings of *sensibilité* in an antislavery fiction by a woman writer: Germaine de Staël's "Mirza; or, Letters of a Traveler," a work written before the outbreak of the Revolution, in around 1786, but not published until 1795, when it appeared in a volume titled *Recueil de morceaux détachés* (Collection of Assorted Pieces).[39] I consider how Staël channels the current of *sensibilité* to produce empathy for Africans and, correspondingly, to generate support for abolition. I also explore the place of gender in this strategy. Like Saint-Lambert's "Zimeo," "Mirza" counteracts the dominant stereotype of the African male by presenting a black hero who is refined and gentle. "Mirza," however, also conveys a feminist message to the extent that it features not only a black male protagonist but also a virtuous and intelligent black woman.

But although I will have a lot to say about the story's sentimental moorings, I also want to point to the presence of discursive currents that have generally been neglected by critics. In particular I will show that at the same time that she promotes psychological identification with Africans, Staël also rehearses the arguments of liberal economic theory, arguing for the abolition of slavery on pragmatic as well as moral grounds. As we shall shortly see, the entire first part of the story is taken up with economic questions, and it is only later in the narrative that feelings take center stage.

"Mirza" is narrated by a French traveler who recalls a visit that he has made to the small French outpost in Gorée Island: one of the principal hubs of the French slave trade in west Africa. He relates that during this stay he came across a new kind of entrepreneurial experiment: a sugar plantation located on African soil and manned by free workers. The plantation is managed by a former slave named Ximeo, a man who, having being freed by the colony's governor, had agreed to take on the running of the venture.

---

38. Victor Hugo's novel *Bug-Jargal* (1826) is based on the events of the slave revolt in Saint-Domingue.

39. Staël was a long-term supporter of abolition who participated both in the movement of the 1780s–90s and in the campaign to abolish the slave trade that took shape at the end of the Napoleonic Wars in 1814–15. In this later period she wrote two short essays calling for the immediate suppression of the slave trade: "Appel aux souverains" (An appeal to the Sovereigns) and "Préface pour la traduction d'un ouvrage de M. Wilberforce" (Preface for the Translation of a Work by Mr. Wilberforce). These essays are reproduced in Kadish and Massardier-Kenney, *Translating Slavery*, 157–62, 281–87.

In her description of this free, African plantation, Staël carefully balances moral and economic concerns. Through the intermediary of her narrator she emphasizes that the plantation was established for moral reasons, and that its primary purpose was to render the slave trade obsolete. Ximeo explains in this vein to the narrator: "When I realized that a product of our country, neglected by us, was the sole cause of the cruel suffering endured by these unfortunate Africans, I accepted the offer to give them the example of growing sugarcane" (149). At the same time, however, she underscores the economic merits of the project. The narrator notes that the land "yielded at least as much as a like surface farmed in Santo-Domingo by as many men, and the happy Blacks were not overwhelmed with work" (148–49).

Staël does not simply content herself with sketching a potential economic answer to an intractable moral problem; rather she inscribes this solution within a far-reaching vision of the future, a multifaceted program involving the transformation of colonial policy, the reform of global trade, and the agricultural "development" of Africa. When Ximeo explains the moral and economic rationale for the plantation, he thus not only states that Africans had "neglected" the cultivation of sugar but also emphasizes that this kind of neglect had to come to an end. Gesturing toward the beginning of a new era of African agriculture, he exclaims, "May my unfortunate compatriots renounce primitive life, devote themselves to work." In the course of this speech he calls for the replacement of the slave trade, which he characterizes as a legacy of the mercantile system, with a regime of free trade: "May free trade be established between the two parts of the world!" (149).

It is only after this introductory section, with its strong economic and political focus, that "Mirza" takes a sentimental turn. Recognizing the narrator as potentially sympathetic, Ximeo decides to explain why, despite his plantation's apparent success, he appears melancholy and preoccupied. He discloses that at an earlier time of his life he was torn between two women and two different kinds of love. Since his adolescence he had been betrothed to the beautiful Ourika, a woman of his own tribe. Shortly before they were to be married, however, he met and became enamored of Mirza, a member of the rival "Jolof" tribe, and a typically Staëlian heroine in the way she combines the qualities of both poet and muse. If Ourika's attractions are primarily physical, Mirza appeals to Ximeo's intellectual and spiritual side. Her refined intellect, however, is not entirely the product of her "native" intelligence. Rather, she has received extensive tutoring from a benevolent French mentor. Mirza speaks French and is conversant with French philosophical ideas. Convinced of the transformative value of the training that she has received, she undertakes to pass it on to her lover, Ximeo (149).

Several points can be made about this scenario of colonial education. One is that in her attempt to humanize her African characters, Staël effectively portrays them as French. Mirza and Ximeo speak perfect French and are conversant with French philosophical discourses. The knowledge they possess is French knowledge, and if they appear civilized, it is because they have been civilized by France. A second is that gender plays a central role in Staël's account of the transmission of knowledge. It is Mirza who educates Ximeo: the woman who teaches the man. And what Mirza opens up in Ximeo is not just knowledge but also feeling: a heightened emotional sensitivity that lends the hero a subtly feminine aura.[40] Just as the education of Africans is depicted as a European mission, so the sentimental education of men is represented as a feminine or perhaps feminist project.

After much soul searching, Ximeo decides to marry Ourika and renounce his love for Mirza. Soon afterward, however, he is wounded in battle and taken as a prisoner of war. In a narrative sequence that draws attention to the manner in which Europeans profited from the internal conflicts of Africa, Ximeo is slated to be sold to European traders. He is only saved from this fate when Mirza courageously intervenes and offers herself as a substitute for her wounded lover. Not to be outdone, Ximeo insists that he should be the one to board the slave ship bound for the Americas. Impressed by these heroic displays, the colonial governor declares both Mirza and Ximeo free.

The story nonetheless has a melancholy ending. Ximeo explains that although Mirza was freed from slavery, she could not break free of the past. Unable to live without Ximeo, or to live with the knowledge of his infidelity, she takes her own life. After this tragic event, Ximeo, Ourika, and the couple's young daughter begin their new life on the sugar plantation. Yet Ximeo, too, finds himself unable to shake off the past. He confides to the narrator that he goes every day to visit Mirza's tomb, which is apparently situated somewhere within the confines of the plantation. He also begs his new friend to remember his lover's name, asking him to speak it to his own children so that it might be preserved for posterity.

In its narrative chronology, "Mirza" travels from the present to the past: from Ximeo's peaceful existence on the orderly sugar plantation to an earlier period in which Africans were divided by warfare fomented by the slave trade, and in which Ximeo was torn between two women, one embodying his connection to Africa, the other symbolizing his relation to Europe. In its historical chronology, on the other hand, the narrative straddles the distance between 1786 and an incipient future. Though the slave trade and intertribal conflict were still very much alive in 1786, Staël's vision of a free plantation situated in Africa gestures toward a new colonial order emerging from the ruins of Atlantic slavery (or, in the figural language of the story, from its tomb). Structured around these two axes, the story manifests a complex, multidirectional temporality that can be read in several ways.

---

40. At one point the narrator describes him as being almost too slender for a man (148).

In emphasizing the sentimental register of the story, most critical readings also emphasize the reverberation of the past in the present, a perspective that aligns the political and cultural memory of slavery with the familiar Romantic idiom of loss and mourning. But I would argue that it is equally important to acknowledge how the story incorporates the present into a future that is beginning to take form. In this reading, the presence of Mirza's tomb in the vicinity of the plantation may be read as an allegory of how an Africa dotted with orderly plantations might one day grow out of the demise of the slave trade. Is it perhaps not incidental that at the time of the publication of "Mirza" in 1795, the Sierra Leone Company, founded two years earlier, was creating in west Africa a colony populated by former slaves.

We have seen that many colonial fictions gesture toward the possibility of self-emancipation but in the end represent freedom as a gift conferred by a European. "Mirza" is no exception. At the moment when the heroine offers to substitute herself for Ximeo, she delivers a stirring speech in which she informs the slave traders that although she consents to be a slave, she will never be enslaved by her condition: "I shall respect my masters' power," she says, "since I will have given it to them" (154). By eloquently reminding them that the human being is not defined by enslavement, her speech exerts significant moral pressure on the merchants and the governor. Yet it is a gesture of passive resistance rather than an overt act of rebellion, and as such the responsibility (if not the moral "right") of granting freedom falls to the colony's French governor. It is the governor who decrees the freedom of the two protagonists, and it is also he who comes up with the idea of growing sugarcane in Africa. Like the expatriate tutor who teaches Mirza "the knowledge that they [the French] misuse the philosophy whose lessons they follow so poorly," the governor embodies an ideal of enlightened French behavior that his compatriots, the slave traders, did not live up to.

But when we look closely at the governor's role in this affair, a number of questions arise. What does it mean for him to "free" Mirza and Ximeo before they have technically become slaves? And how does his standing as chief administrator of a slave-trading post correlate with his desire to bring an end to the slave trade? It may be recalled that similar questions arose with regard to Gouges's enlightened administrator, M. De Saint-Frémont, who magnanimously freed Zamor(e) and Mirza while at the same time claiming to be powerless to free the colony's other slaves.

It has been suggested that Staël based the figure of the governor of Gorée on the Chevalier de Boufflers, a writer and philosopher who served as governor of Senegal from 1785 to 1787, and with whom Staël had family ties.[41] Whether or not this was the case, it is interesting to note that Boufflers appears

---

41. Boufflers wrote about his experiences as governor of the French trading posts in Senegal in letters to his friend and later wife, the Comtesse de Sabran, a correspondence collected in *Lettres d'Afrique à Madame de Sabran*. In one letter Boufflers mentions that he had purchased a small

to have considered his role as governor to be quite separate from the activities of the Company of the Indies, which ran the colony's slave-trading operations. His correspondence suggests that far from seeing himself as slave trader in chief, he viewed himself as an enlightened administrator whose responsibilities lay in improving the colony's fortifications and system of communications. But while Boufflers may have spent his days taking notes on the colony's flora and fauna and devising ambitious agricultural schemes, his expenses were paid by the Company of the Indies, and his primary task as governor was to facilitate its operations.[42]

It is easy to understand why someone in Boufflers's position might have wanted to airbrush the facts, but why did writers whose ostensible purpose was to criticize slavery replicate these defenses in their portraits of enlightened colonial officials? The answer is presumably that their concern with attacking the foundations of slavery collided with their nationalistic inclination to portray France as the land of liberty and humanity. Thinking about this tension in relation to "Mirza," I suggest that the complex chronology of Staël's narrative—the representation of slavery as a past that haunts the present, but also as a present that will be transcended in an incipient future—can be read as an attempt to translate the insoluble contradictions of French colonial rule into a coherent temporal sequence. In this narrative the problematic past of slavery evolves into a future of free trade, free workers, and a benevolent French civilizing mission.

Does it matter that representations that elicited empathy with enslaved men and women on the basis of their common humanity were interwoven with arguments about the economic benefits of abolition? Did the overlay of these arguments dilute the moral perspective that the sentimental register cultivated? Did it support different visions of abolition, or of the future of the colonial system?

When sentimental representations were paired with economic arguments, the question of what was due to the individual became intertwined with the issue of what was necessary for the vitality and harmony of society or the state. In the liberal postulates that informed colonial fictions, economic and ethical prescriptions were broadly presumed to coincide. The freedom of the individual from enslavement, for example, was understood to contribute to the stability of society and to create potential for economic growth. But colonial fictions manifest a number of tendencies that reveal the problematic nature of these assumptions. Works that foreground the economic rationale for abolition tend also to represent the amelioration of living and working conditions as being more or less interchangeable with emancipation. The economic focus

African girl whom he planned to send as a gift to the Duchesse d'Orléans (60). This child later became the model for Ourika, the heroine of Claire de Duras's 1823 novella.

42. See Boufflers, *Lettres d'Afrique,* esp. 11–13, 125, 394–95.

also tended to preclude a genuine reflection on the overall legitimacy of colonial rule. Far from challenging the principle of colonization, late eighteenth-century antislavery fictions often depicted abolition as a point of departure for the initiation of new colonial ventures.

In the introduction to this book I argued that we have a "double ethical relation" to slavery. In contemplating the history of slavery, we have to confront not only the deprivation of liberty and physical and psychological asperities that slavery entailed but also the relative silence of contemporaries who observed, or at least were aware of, these practices, yet did nothing to intervene. I also observed that our moral relation to the silence of the "bystander" is, generally speaking, more immediate and more direct than our connection to the brutality of slavery itself. Last, I argue that because of the continued moral relevancy of this silence, when we think about the place of slavery in European history and culture, it is necessary to address patterns of nonrepresentation and displacement, and the ways in which opposition to slavery was framed when it finally coalesced. In concluding this examination I want to circle back to these ideas and attempt to draw a parallel.

Above I suggest that Lynn Hunt's account of the attribution of a right to freedom to slaves during the French Revolution is problematic because, in her effort to validate the Enlightenment's achievement in declaring human rights, Hunt oversteps the mark and forecloses the crucial gap between the principle of universal freedom from slavery and its implementation. As we saw earlier, Hunt draws a direct connection between the principle of abolition, to which many late eighteenth-century French thinkers subscribed, and the decree of abolition that was issued in 1794. It is very questionable, however, that the act of abolition was accomplished as the fulfillment of the principle. This narrative leaves out many details, not least the contribution of the rebel slaves of Saint-Domingue to the realization of their own emancipation. I want to argue that rather than closing the gaps that separated the declaration of rights from their extension to all human beings, or the declaration of rights from their immediate enactment, it is important to acknowledge and explore these intervals. In emphasizing the economic discourses in conjunction with which abolitionism took shape, what I am trying to do, in essence, is draw attention to the conditions, contingencies, and subtexts that accompanied the declaration of a universal human right to freedom from enslavement.

Returning to the question of continued moral relevancy that I raise in the introduction, I want to propose that the moral "lesson" of the Enlightenment with regard human rights lies not only in the invention of this powerful idea but also in the interval between principle and application. Having inherited the idea of human rights from the Enlightenment, we do not have to reinvent it. By contrast, like our late eighteenth-century forbears, we do have to contend with and respond to failures and refusals to implement rights long ago declared.

Conclusion
Slavery and Postcolonial Memory

In what ways does the colonial past shape or even determine the "post-colonial" landscape of the present? This question has been raised in many different ways and within the orbit of diverse disciplinary fields. To conclude this book I will draw on the historical perspective of the foregoing chapters in order to contribute a few specific points to this ongoing discussion. Building on some of my core arguments, I will point to several key respects in which, on the one hand the marginality of the colonies to eighteenth-century French culture, and on the other the economic structures and discourses of Old Regime colonialism, have continued to reverberate in contemporary relationships between France and its former colonies in the Caribbean and in the Indian Ocean, territories which since 1946 have been "overseas departments," or Départements d'Outre-Mer (DOM).

In the winter of 2009 rioting broke out in the overseas departments of Guadeloupe and Martinique. For several days in February protesters clashed with the police, vehicles were burned, businesses and public services were shut down, and the islands' leading industry—tourism—was effectively paralyzed. The crisis became so acute that, using language reminiscent of the era of colonial slavery, the socialist leader of Guadeloupe's Regional Council declared the island to be "on the verge of revolt."[1]

The riots had begun in Guadeloupe as a general strike over wages. Local unions demanded wage increases for low-income workers, pointing out that wages were generally lower in the DOM than in continental France, while

---

1. "Strike in Guadeloupe Escalates into Rioting," *International Herald Tribune,* Feb. 17, 2009.

prices were significantly higher. But as the strike continued and spread to Martinique, French Guiana, and La Réunion, other social and economic issues also came into focus. Protesters complained about price gouging by powerful local gas and utilities companies that enjoy virtual monopolies. They also drew attention to the race and class structure of French Caribbean society. In Martinique, for instance, wealth and property remain concentrated in the hands of a small white minority known as the *békés:* the descendants of colonial planters. Deep-Seated anger with this state of affairs boiled over after the French television channel Canal Plus aired a documentary about the wealth and power of the *békés* of Martinique. In one particularly inflammatory segment of this program, a prominent white businessman is heard expressing the view that racial mixing is pernicious, and that Martinique's whites are justified in trying to "preserve their race."[2] In the days after this broadcast protesters chanted anti-*béké* slogans, vocally proclaiming that "Martinique is ours, not theirs."[3]

This wave of civil unrest was interpreted, both in France and abroad, as an echo of the rioting that shook continental France in fall 2005. In both instances protesters complained about the disadvantages suffered by cultural/racial minorities and accused the government and social elites of indifference and contempt. And in both cases current socioeconomic issues were diagnosed as legacies of the colonial past. Militants and social scientists, for example, drew connections between the high levels of poverty and unemployment experienced by the descendants of immigrants and of the enslaved, and the hierarchy of the colonial order. Drawing on the historical perspective of this book I would like to comment in specific terms on what the French militant association Natives of the Republic has called the "colonial continuum."

The abolition of slavery in the French colonies in 1848 was not accompanied by a process of social and economic redistribution. Land and wealth largely remained in the hands of the white elite, and former slaves did not receive reparation for their years of unpaid labor. The enduring result of this dispensation is that the class structure of the DOM today remains closely aligned with the racial order of slavery.

Other features of the colonial socioeconomic order have also remained in place. Economic relationships between France and its overseas departments continue to a great extent to be governed by the mercantilist principles of eighteenth-century colonial administration. The elevated cost of living in the French Caribbean is linked to the fact that basic commodities are imported from, or at least via, France, with transportation costs being factored into prices. Moreover, a small number of French companies, including several run by *békés,* enjoy what basically amount to monopolies over important sectors

---

2. *Les derniers maîtres.*
3. "Blacks Slam Whites in Martinique Strike," *International Herald Tribune,* Feb. 13, 2009.

of commercial and economic life. Since they have a captive group of consumers, these businesses are able to control prices and manipulate the market. It is perhaps no surprise that the complaints voiced by the 2009 protesters echoed those articulated by eighteenth-century colonists. Then, as now, residents of the French Caribbean demanded a more competitive market and the elimination of monopolies, in other words, the relaxation of mercantilism and the decentralization of the relationship between colony—or postcolony—and metropole.

In the third section of this book, I show that although late-eighteenth-century liberal thinkers advocated the elimination of slavery and commercial monopolies, they did not call for a thoroughgoing transformation of the colonial social order. Writers such as Dupont de Nemours, Condorcet, Madame de Staël, and, at a later moment, Victor Schoelcher, envisaged that in the wake of emancipation plantation agriculture would continue much as before, with former slaves continuing to perform manual labor while former slave owners reprised their management role. They envisaged, in other words, the creation of a black agricultural underclass supervised by a small cohort of white proprietors. They did, of course, anticipate that free black workers would earn wages, and indeed they tried to win their compatriots over to abolition by predicting the creation of a strong new market for French goods. In nineteenth-century colonial rhetoric, freed slaves were imagined as a new *débouché* (outlet) for the products of French manufacturing industries.

As the complaints voiced during the 2009 protests in the DOM clarify, these liberal forecasts—this limited and Eurocentrist vision for the future of the colonies—have to a great extent been fulfilled. Though the Caribbean sugar industry collapsed with the rise of beet sugar, other forms of "monoculture" subsequently took its place. Today, as in the eighteenth century, the economies of Martinique and Guadeloupe are largely dependent on a single source of income. What sugar represented to the eighteenth-century colonies, tourism represents today. And like the Old Regime sugar business, tourism is by no means a neutral vehicle for economic development. Now, as in the heyday of mercantilism, the islands appear to exist for the benefit of visitors from the metropole: visitors who are generally more affluent than the local population, and who are also predominantly white.

Monocultural economies tend to be political traps. The rioting that took place the French Caribbean in 2009 led to an exodus of visitors and the cancellation of future vacation plans. But these disruptions affected not only tourists and the tourist industry but also the working-class residents who participated in the protests: people who are caught in a system that disadvantages them and that they would like to see dismantled, but which also represents their only viable current source of income. Since the French overseas departments have the highest unemployment rates in the European Union, they are places in which questions of employment and job security are particularly acute. Though I would certainly not want to draw a direct comparison between contemporary rioting and the slave insurgencies of the eighteenth century, in certain key respects the situation of contemporary *domiens* is akin to that of the rebel slaves who participated in the Haitian Revolution. In order to overthrow the regime of slavery, the enslaved of Saint-Domingue first found it necessary to disable the colonial plantocracy. Disrupting the production of sugar, however, meant dismantling the island's only established source of revenue. Caught in a vicious circle, Haiti achieved independence on the ruins of its economic base.

The demonstrations and riots of 2009 were tied to demands for specific changes, but they were also, in a broader sense, a plea to be heard. France's president, Nicolas Sarkozy, acknowledged as much when he said in a speech announcing new policy initiatives that while "Guadeloupe and Martinique are part of France," their inhabitants "have the sentiment that they are not always heard." He went on to suggest that France needed to "make a larger place for those who embody the diversity of France."[4] Sarkozy's speech highlighted the fact that although Antilleans and *Réunionnais* have been French citizens since 1848, an identity reinforced by "departmentalization" in 1946, they have generally felt marginal to and marginalized by the nation that claims them as citizens. Sarkozy rather allusively tied this sense of marginality to the issue of "diversity," a term that I take, in this context, to be a code word for race. Sarkozy concluded his speech with the promise that France would take new measures to stimulate the DOMs' stagnant economies. Echoing the arguments of eighteenth-century liberals, he suggested, notably, that greater market competition was an option that needed to be explored.

Over the last fifty years, lack of economic opportunity has led many *domiens* to leave the Caribbean for mainland France. Alongside Jamaicans, Puerto Ricans, Haitians, and other constituents of the African diaspora of the Americas, these contemporary migrants have participated in the formation of a new Caribbean diaspora in Europe and North America. Today, one in every four people born in Martinique or Guadeloupe lives in the metropole, a statistic that makes France, and more specifically the Parisian region, or "île de France," where most Antillean migration has been concentrated, a de facto "third island."[5] In many respects this movement has paralleled migration to France from the former colonies of the Maghreb. During the prosperous postwar years, when immigration from the Maghreb was actively encouraged, migration from the DOM was similarly promoted. Between 1963 and 1981, under the auspices of BUMI-DOM (Bureau pour le développement des migrations intéressant les départements d'outre-mer), Antilleans were recruited to occupy unskilled, low-paying jobs in France.[6] Whereas Maghrebian migrants usually took private-sector

4. Presidential communiqué, Feb. 13, 2009, http://www.elysee.fr/documents/index.
5. See Anselin, *L'émigration antillaise.*
6. See Tardieu, *Les Antillais à Paris,* 122.

industrial jobs, *domiens,* as French citizens, were directed toward large public concerns such as the postal services and mass transit. Like Maghrebians, they predominantly settled in working-class suburbs, and for many the only affordable option was public housing. To many Antillean observers, the BUMIDOM recruitment program was little more than a modern avatar of the Atlantic slave trade. In 1978, for example, the General Association of Guadeloupean Students provocatively characterized French government support for migration as a policy of "deportation serving the interests of French enterprise."[7] With similar acrimony the Martinican poet and political leader Aimé Césaire complained that France was draining the Antilles of their lifeblood.[8]

When France's economy slowed to a halt during the oil crisis of the 1970s, immigrants from the Maghreb were "invited" to return to their countries under the auspices of the policy of *aide au retour* (aid to return), and Antilleans were similarly encouraged to go back. But since economic conditions were worse in the Caribbean than in continental France, Antilleans, like Maghrebians, predominantly elected to remain. Though Antilleans are neither immigrants nor descendants of immigrants, as a community of migrants they have experienced many of the same forms of prejudice and marginalization as immigrants from the Maghreb. For example, they suffer from comparably high rates of youth unemployment and reside disproportionately in public housing.[9] According to sociologist Claude-Valentin Marie, over half the Antillean population of Île de France lives in public housing, versus 23 percent for the general population.[10] Given statistics such as these, it can scarcely be claimed that Antilleans who have relocated to the metropole have achieved seamless insertion. To the contrary, as the Martinican political scientist Fred Constant asserts, "In metropolitan France Antilleans have increasingly realized that color makes a French person of color a foreigner."[11]

But if internal migration from the DOM has paralleled immigration from the Maghreb in many respects, there is at least one way in which it has been markedly different, and this relates to the landscape of social and cultural representation.[12] Since the early 1980s immigration from the Maghreb has been a prominent political issue, a topic of sociological discourse, and a literary and cinematic theme. By contrast, the experience of Antillean migrants has remained largely invisible, generating little by way of public discussion, and relatively few self-representations in public media such as literature and film.

7. Constant, "Politique de la migration," 106.
8. Ibid., 112.
9. In 1990 unemployment among young Antilleans stood at 26 percent, a rate 10 percent higher than the national average but comparable to joblessness among young people of Maghrebian descent. See Marie, "Les Antillais de l'hexagone."
10. Marie, "Les populations des DOM-TOM."
11. Constant, "Politique de la migration," 110.
12. See my essay on the cultural invisibility of Antillean migration, Dobie, "Invisible Exodus."

Claude-Valentin Marie observed in an essay published in 1999 that the previous forty years of mass migration to the metropole had been "forty years in which it has been hard to count ourselves, forty years of feeling that we haven't counted,"[13] a formula that connects the cultural invisibility of Antillean migration to one of its underlying causes: the fact that French law does not permit the collection of statistics based on race or ethnicity, with the result that it is almost impossible to measure the specific experiences of "minority" groups that are not differentiated by foreign birth or nationality.

As I discuss in chapter 5, French social and political thought has historically defined diversity as something that exists outside rather than within the nation-state. Eighteenth-century French writers wrote extensively about Oriental despots and good (or bad) savages—about peoples perceived to embody geocultural difference—yet found little to say about enslaved Africans and their descendants, groups whose relation to France and to Africa was less easy to delineate. If, as several commentators have observed, the term immigration serves in contemporary France as a placeholder for an array of questions relating to diversity, discrimination, and disenfranchisement, it is partly because it ties the question of difference to foreign or external origins rather than to divisions that are internal to French society. And if the French descendants of Maghrebian immigrants, sometimes known as "beurs," have been represented as a distinct social group it is because they are perceived to have roots in another culture and to be victims of discrimination on the basis of these foreign origins. To consider Antillean migrants and their descendants as a distinct social group would be far more contentious because it would mean acknowledging that France is internally heterogeneous from the standpoint of race.

If the category of race has been subject to disavowal in French politics and social thought, it is not because race and racism have been absent or irrelevant from French history, but rather because there *has* been both racialization and racism, and these tendencies are perceived to be antithetical to republican political identity. French discomfort with racial thinking may betoken a legitimate perception that race is an artificial construct that projects rather than describes difference, but it is also unquestionably rooted in France's problematic history of racism, exemplified by colonial slavery. French disavowal of race is also, I contend, a disavowal of slavery: a forgetting or repression of a historical practice that controverts the nation's dominant republican narrative.

In this book I argue that colonial slavery posed, from its inception, a representational challenge. It contradicted Catholic universalism—hence the efforts expended on dispatching missionaries to convert slaves (or at least on using conversion as a pretext for enslavement)—and it also offended the principle that, having abolished feudal serfdom at the end of the Middle Ages, France

13. Tardieu, *Les antillais à Paris*, 102.

had established itself as a land of liberty. Unable to depict slavery with a clear conscience, French writers either avoided the subject or else projected it onto other geopolitical contexts.

These mechanisms of disavowal carried over into the postabolition era. As Catherine Reinhardt explains, after the abolition of slavery in 1848, Antilleans and their history were "deemed problematic by the state" and largely forgotten.[14] In socioeconomic terms colonial subjects were relegated to the status of second-class citizens, while on the level of public discourse their history was essentially "replaced by that of the French nation." In this dispensation, slavery was remembered only through the lens of abolition, as a reminder of republican generosity. It has only been in the last ten years that this selective remembering of the relationship between metropole and colony has been subject to a vigorous challenge.

An important point of departure for this reconsideration was the celebration of the 150th anniversary of abolition in 1998. To mark this anniversary the French government, under the presidency of Jacques Chirac, organized an extensive program of public ceremonies and cultural events. But in the eyes of many Antilleans, the entire emphasis of this commemoration was misplaced. From their point of view France was effectively congratulating itself for abolishing a system that it had previously established, leaving out both the contribution of the enslaved to their own emancipation and, even more fundamentally, the two-century history of slavery that preceded abolition. Seeing the anniversary as yet another French attempt to co-opt their history, many Antilleans chose to boycott the public events and organize their own forms of commemoration. Notably, on May 23, 1998, some forty thousand Antilleans marched in the streets of Paris, presenting what was an unprecedented display of community identity.

Their protests did not go unnoticed. Indeed, I think it would be fair to say that 1998 was a pivotal moment, not only in relation to the memory of slavery and colonial historiography, but also with regard to the articulation of a social discourse on race. In 2001, France's National Assembly passed a law proposed by a deputy from French Guiana recognizing slavery as a crime against humanity. It also convened a Committee for the Memory of Slavery, a body charged with, among other things, introducing the study of slavery into the school curriculum and establishing a yearly date for the commemoration of abolition. There have also been academic reverberations, including the publication of an unprecedented number of studies bearing on the history and culture of slavery, and on the place of race in contemporary French society. Finally, and just as important, there has been an acceleration of community activism. In the wake of the May 23 march, a group of Antilleans formed an association called the

14. Reinhardt, "Slavery and Commemoration."

Comité Marche du 23 mai (or CM 98), which is committed both to maintaining consciousness of the abolition of slavery and to uniting Antilleans in this goal. There has also been activism around the question of the specific experience of black French people. One significant piece of fallout from the rioting in 2005 was the creation of the CRAN (Conseil représentatif des associations noires), an umbrella organization that, breaking with the traditional French disavowal of racial categories, undertakes to represent the concerns and rights of France's black population. The CRAN's leadership asserts that since France is far from being color blind, it is legitimate and indeed necessary to consider blacks as a distinct social group.

If the events of 1998 served as an important catalyst for the heightened level of concern with race, racism, and the colonial continuum that is being manifested today in both metropolitan and Antillean French society, it is, I think, for reasons that have to do with the primary argument of this book. In order for these questions to come to the fore it proved necessary not only to remember France's historical involvement in slavery but also to acknowledge the consistent repression, displacement, and subordination of this history in favor of a redemptive republican narrative. For slavery and its various legacies to come into focus, in other words, it was first necessary to remember that they had repeatedly been forgotten.

Appendix

The Colonies and Slavery in Eighteenth-Century French Literature

This appendix surveys the representation and nonrepresentation of the colonial world in eighteenth-century French literature. It focuses primarily on writers viewed as leading exponents of Enlightenment social and political thought because it is in this group of texts that we perhaps most expect to discover an engagement with colonial slavery. This account is not intended to be exhaustive. It is rather an attempt to convey the overall standing of this set of questions in eighteenth-century French culture and to pinpoint key currents and tendencies. It also does not address scientific works devoted specifically to the topic of race because, as I note in the introduction, it is difficult to account for the relationship between racial thought and colonization and slavery without undertaking close readings of specific texts.

The Enlightenment figure most widely associated with the issue of slavery, both by eighteenth-century writers and by contemporary critics, is Montesquieu. In the words of Christopher Miller, "Montesquieu opened the door to a debate about slavery in France."[1] Yet Montesquieu's reputation in this regard rests primarily on the slender foundation of a single chapter in *Spirit of Law* (book 15, chapter 5). In this passage, as I discuss in chapter 1, Montesquieu quickly transposes the issue of Atlantic slavery onto an exploration of Oriental servitude. This process of orientalization was to be a key dimension of

1. Miller, *French Atlantic Triangle*, 66.

Montesquieu's influence on subsequent French writing about slavery. It could in fact be said that Montesquieu opened the door to writing about slavery as a predominantly Eastern phenomenon. In one passage of *Persian Letters,* Montesquieu's enlightened traveler, Usbek, observes that although Europe's princes loudly trumpeted their decision to put an end to serfdom—a decision that benefited them to the extent that it curtailed the power of the feudal nobility—they abandoned this principle when they conquered new lands and realized that it would be advantageous to have slaves to cultivate them. "Truth at one moment, error in another," Usbek concludes, passing a judgment that could equally be applied to Montesquieu's own rather uneven engagement with the practice of colonial slavery.[2] This brief allusion to colonial slavery in *Persian Letters* is overshadowed by the novel's much more well-developed reflection on slavery in the Orient. The novel examines several forms of Oriental servitude, including subordination to the power of a despotic ruler and the subjugation of women in the harem. In a suggestive passage, Usbek's deputy, the chief *black* eunuch, recalls how as an adolescent he was abducted from Africa, sold, and made into a eunuch so that he could serve in his master's harem (*Lettres persanes,* 84). But while his recollection evokes practices associated with colonial slavery, it quickly annexes them to a discussion of the trans-African/Arab slave trade, and thus to slavery in an Oriental context.

The Atlantic slave trade is addressed briefly as a moral and political issue in Claude-Adrien Helvétius's *De l'esprit* (On Mind) (1758), a highly controversial work that was condemned and publicly burned for its atheistic leanings.[3] Radicalizing Montesquieu's account of the interconnections between law, politics, and climate in *Spirit of Law,* Helvétius lays out a doctrine whereby virtue is held to be relative to the social and political conditions of the state. Morality, he contends, consists of serving the common good within a particular society, and as a result there can be no universal moral principles. Helvétius touches on the slave trade in the context of a meditation on international justice (discourse 3: chapter 4). He argues that people are motivated by their own interests, and that if, for the benefit of the public good, these interests are counteracted by laws, such restrictions must be backed up by a system of penalties and rewards. Helvétius argues that the situation is similar in the case of states, though the solution is more difficult to achieve. States attack and exploit less powerful groups, as the relationship between Europeans and Africans attests, and there is no international framework of punishments and rewards to keep this behavior in check.

Helvétius is lucid as to both the causes of the slave trade and their effects (he speaks about the destruction of the family and the propagation of warfare)

2. Montesquieu, *Lettres persanes,* letter 65, my translation. Margaret Mauldon, whose translation I cite elsewhere in this book, renders the French "Vérité dans un temps, erreur dans un autre" a little less directly as "Yesterday's truth is tomorrow's lie." *Persian Letters,* 103.

3. Helvétius, *De l'esprit.*

but his presentation of these issues constitutes an explanation rather than a condemnation of an existing state of affairs. This is consistent with Helvétius's overall method, which consists of relativizing cultural practices rather than declaring them good or bad. Moreover, since Helvétius conceptualizes utility in relation to individual states rather than as a transnational good, he also has no basis for offering a rationale for strengthening international legal protections.

If slavery in the Atlantic context is addressed by Helvétius only fleetingly, the same cannot be said for Oriental slavery. Like Montesquieu, Helvétius writes about Oriental despotism and the subjugation of Oriental peoples at great length. Several chapters of *On Mind* (discourse 3: chapters 16–21) explain why despotism does not correspond to the public good, and argue that it is a type of regime that is always, in the end, overthrown. In a chapter entitled "On Slavery and the Allegorical Genius of Orientals" (discourse 3: chapter 29), Helvétius goes so far as to reject Montesquieu's argument that slavery and subjugation are effects of climate and proposes instead in a more limited sense that they arise from a specific political regime, namely despotism, and that at a certain point in their history all governments tend toward despotism and by implication toward slavery (455–59). In other words, whereas Helvétius foresees no political solution to interregional (i.e., colonial) slavery, and indeed provides no moral basis for condemning it, he both condemns Oriental servitude and presages its political implosion.

Voltaire, in the eyes of Christopher Miller, is "the *philosophe* with by far the most vexed relation to the slave trade" (71). His oeuvre is of course so vast that it is impossible to summarize his writing on slavery with a few strokes of the pen. I will, however, touch on some of the principal works in which we can observe this vexed relationship. I will not discuss the numerous works by Voltaire, such as the philosophical tale *Zadig* (1747), in which slavery is shown as a feature of Oriental culture.

The history of European colonial expansion is addressed more concretely in *Essay on Universal History* than in most midcentury French texts (much more so than in *Spirit of Law*, for instance). Voltaire offers a brief history of each of the French colonies and discusses specific questions such as France's alliance with the Huron nation. He makes it clear that he thinks that France's most significant colonial possessions lay not in Canada, which he characterizes as a snowy wasteland, but in the Antilles, and to support this claim he presents figures on the growth and commercial importance of these settlements (2:375).[4] These figures include estimates for the enslaved and free populations of Saint-Domingue, details of the rise in the purchase price of slaves over the previous quarter century, and calculations of the revenue derived annually in France from trade in colonial goods. Voltaire shows, in essence, that though the

---

4. Voltaire, *Essai sur les mœurs.*

colonies might be mere "dots on the map," their demographic and commercial signification far surpassed their physical size (2:380).

But while Voltaire seems enthusiastic about certain aspects of colonization, his overall view is negative. He complains that the short-term gains reaped from the establishment of colonies all too often translated into serious long-term problems. Like Montesquieu in *Spirit of Law,* he associates colonization with depopulation and the global spread of diseases such as syphilis. He also blames the struggle between France and England for control of Canada for causing the outbreak of new wars in Europe (2:372–73), and argues that the wealth derived from the Antilles was of a fundamentally superficial and destructive nature (2:380).

This negative view of the consequences of colonization is given narrative form in the philosophical tale *Candide* (1759), which includes a brief indictment of the brutality of colonial slavery. Traveling through Surinam, Candide and his sidekick Cacambo encounter a "Negro" dressed in rags and missing both a hand and a leg.[5] The man explains that his hand had been severed when his finger became trapped in a sugar mill, and that his leg was cut off by his master after he tried to run away. Drawing the crucial connection between slavery and sugar, the slave observes that "it is at this price that you eat sugar in Europe." There is no question but that in this passage Voltaire evokes New World slavery in a vivid and morally lucid way. The only qualifying observation to be made here is that the passage evokes not a French colony but Surinam, the Dutch neighbor of French Guiana, a small but significant displacement that allows Voltaire to condemn colonial slavery without directly implicating France.

Voltaire's writing on colonization and slavery is marked by a central tension. In the passage just cited and in some sections of *Essay on Universal History,* Voltaire writes boldly and scathingly about the atrocities committed in the New World against indigenous people and enslaved Africans. Yet at the same time he represents indigenous Americans and Africans as both different from and inferior to Europeans. In *Candide,* for example, the chapter involving the mutilated slave is preceded by one in which the hero shoots what he thinks are some monkeys who are chasing a group of indigenous women, only to learn that the pursuers are the women's lovers (84–85). Though this episode is often read as an instance of cultural relativism, I suggest it indicates rather a predisposition to question, not the limit between the animal and the human, but rather, more narrowly, the boundary between "primitive" (i.e., African/Amerindian) peoples and primates.[6] A subscriber to polygenism, Voltaire argued that Africans, Amerindians, and Europeans have different origins and

5. Voltaire, *Candide,* translated by Burton Raffel, 101–2.
6. Speculation about the proximity between Africans and primates was by no means limited to Voltaire. Even Buffon, an adamant monogenist, pointed to resemblances between orangutans

display distinctive physical and intellectual traits. In some places he also draws a connection between these natural inequalities and the practice of slavery.

> Nature has annexed to this principle these different degrees of genius, and the characters of nations that are so rarely seen to change. It is for this reason that Negroes are the slaves of other men. They are bought on Africa's coasts like beasts, and the multitudes of these blacks, transplanted to our American colonies, serve a very small number of Europeans. (*Essay on Universal History,* 2:335)

Though Voltaire emphasizes in this passage that the slave trade was no credit to Europeans, his criticisms are mitigated by the fact that he views the inferiority of Africans as a secondary cause of slavery.

This bifurcation points to one of several factors that supported the neglect of colonization and slavery in eighteenth-century culture. Though many writers found slavery to be repugnant, their underlying perception that Africans were in essential respects different from or inferior to Europeans fostered a climate of ambivalence. One hypothesis that may be entertained in this regard is that if Voltaire wrote more concretely about the colonies and the slave trade than the other leading philosophers, it was perhaps because his moral aversion was attenuated by a particularly racist view of Africans.

One might expect references to colonial commerce and slavery to abound in Diderot and d'Alembert's *Encyclopédie (Encyclopedia)* (1751–65), the great compendium of Enlightenment thought. The work's full title, *Dictionnaire raisonné des sciences, des arts et des métiers* (Reasoned Dictionary of Sciences, Arts, and Trades), announces a concern with manufacture, and this focus is confirmed in d'Alembert's "Preliminary Discourse" (volume 1, 1751), which emphasizes the seriousness with which the editors approached everything relating to industry and modes of production. The colonial mode of production and the system of enslaved labor, however, occupy a fairly marginal place in the *Encyclopedia.*

Colonial slavery is evoked in a few articles that deal with aspects of colonial production and trade, for example "Sucrerie" (Sugar Refinery) (volume 15, 1765), and in some of the plates devoted to "Agriculture and Rustic Economy." In these entries slave labor is depicted as an integral facet of colonial production, and the moral and social dimensions of the practice are generally not brought into question.

There are also many articles in which one would expect to find a discussion of slavery but none is forthcoming. These include a number of agricultural/technical articles, including "Sugar" (volume 15, 1765), "Cotton" (volume 4, 1754), and "Tobacco" (volume 15, 1765). Another example is the article

---

and Hottentots, and even speculated on the possibility of sexual commerce between them. See "Nomenclatures des singes" (1766) in *Histoire naturelle,* Buffon, *Oeuvres.*

"Colony" (volume 3, 1753), which, having defined a colony as "the transport of a people, or of part of a people, from one country to another," makes no reference at all to the transportation of people to a colony from a third location such as Africa. Instead, most of the article is taken up with a rehearsal of the mercantilist theory of colonial trade.

Perhaps most surprisingly, the issue of colonial slavery is absent from the article "Slavery" (volume 5, published 1755). This text, one of the *Encyclopedia* articles that best represents the critical moral and political voice that is associated with the Enlightenment, strongly condemns slavery as an infraction of natural law. The examples of slavery that it examines, however, are drawn from the ancient world, medieval Europe, and the Orient. Almost no reference is made to what, in the circumstances, one would have to regard as the "elephant in the room": the booming contemporary business of Atlantic slavery. Colonial slavery is, by contrast, central to the article "Esclave" (Slave) (volume 5, 1755), a technical piece of writing that recites the articles of the *Black Code* but passes no moral comment whatsoever on the practices that it regulated. The slave trade and colonial slavery are also central to the series of texts devoted to the term "Nègre(s)" (Negro[es]) (volume 11, 1765), a convergence that demonstrates that, by the mid-eighteenth century, the term *nègre* had become virtually interchangeable with the figure of the colonial slave. While "slave" referred most often to the ancient world or to the Orient, colonial slavery was naturalized by its association with a specific racial group. "Nègres" were not so much enslaved as slaves by nature.

The *Encyclopedia* devotes three separate articles to the subject of "Negroes." The first, by Jean-Henri-Samuel Formey, considers blackness as a racial category through the lens of contemporary scientific discourse. As in other mid-century works, the question of race is linked with that of human reproduction. Like the scientific thinkers whose research he cites, Formey proposes that to understand the causes and significance of varieties in phenotype, one must understand how reproduction occurs and how characteristics are transmitted across generations. As in many other Enlightenment texts blackness as a question of race—that is, as a scientific question—is considered separately from (I might even go so far as to say it is divorced from) the issue of colonial slavery, which is addressed in two articles by Jean-Baptiste-Pierre Le Romain, who at one time was the chief engineer of the small French colony in Grenada. In the first piece, "Negroes (commerce)," Le Romain criticizes the barbarism and hypocrisy of the slave trade but, with a high degree of ambivalence, proceeds to blame Africans for its worst excesses and to recommend moderate (rather than either harsh or gentle) correction and punishment of the enslaved. In the second piece, "Negroes Considered as Slaves in the Colonies," all ambivalence vanishes, and indeed Le Romain claims that slaves lived in better conditions in the colonies than in Africa. He also discusses the work performed by slaves, lists the clauses of the *Black Code,* and provides anthropological information about the various African peoples of the Atlantic diaspora.

From the apparent discrepancy between these two articles it is possible to draw a broader conclusion about attitudes toward Atlantic slavery. What writers found most morally abhorrent was the act of enslaving free men and women, and transporting them far from their birth lands (in England, the campaign for abolition of the 1780s–early 1800s was waged almost exclusively over the banning of the slave trade.) By contrast, the use of slave labor in the colonies was legitimized by the perception that it was a necessary evil that enabled the production of valuable commodities.

The issue of colonial slavery is addressed from a more critical perspective in the article "Population," by Damilaville. This piece, which gives voice to the eighteenth-century obsession with depopulation, identifies colonial expansion and slavery, alongside several related phenomena—conquest, luxury, the valorization of commerce over agriculture—as major causes of depopulation in the modern world. Appearing in 1765 in volume 13, "Population" reflects the emergence of liberal economic discourse on the colonies, a perspective that advocated population growth and agricultural reform over luxury and trade.

The strongest moral indictment of colonial slavery articulated in the *Encyclopedia* is the article "Traite des nègres" (Black Slave Trade), published in volume 16 of the *Encyclopedia* in 1765. It was written by the Chevalier de Jaucourt, a prolific contributor to the *Encyclopedia* who also penned the article "Slavery." The distance between the two articles reflects a point made above— that the slave trade aroused more indignation than slavery itself—but it probably also reflects a discursive shift. "Black Slave Trade" appeared ten years after "Slavery" at a moment when slavery was beginning to emerge as an object of discussion and critique.

Denis Diderot, one of the two editors of the *Encyclopedia,* and one of the most radical political thinkers of the Enlightenment, did not devote significant attention to the question of colonization until the last decade of his life. In his *Encyclopedia* article "Humaine espèce" (Human Species) (volume 8, 1765), a text that argues, contra Voltaire, that all men belong to a single species and that physiological differences are a function of climate, he contributes a single sentence on the reduction of blacks to slavery by Europeans who claimed to be Christians. The fact that the article also contains some derogatory racial observations about the low intelligence of sub-Saharan Africans may explain why Diderot was not moved to press this point further. The article "Africa" (volume 1, 1751) is about Africa as a site of European commerce. Diderot shows no interest whatsoever in "indigenous" culture or history. Curiously, though, Diderot also says little about the slave trade, which is mentioned only briefly and in a neutral tone. In the article "Cotton" (volume 4, 1754) Diderot calls for the development of the French cotton industry and, correspondingly, for an increase in colonial production of cotton. He does not, however, reflect on the probable expansion of slavery that would be required to achieve this growth. As in many other Enlightenment texts, enthusiasm for colonial commodities overshadowed criticism of the colonial mode of production.

In the early 1770s Diderot's relative indifference to colonial questions was transformed into an ardent preoccupation with them. Having been invited to contribute to the second (1774) edition of Abbé Raynal's monumental *Histoire des deux Indes,* the first sustained attempt to write a history of the commercial and colonial expansion of modern Europe, Diderot became the driving force behind the work's dynamic third edition, published in 1780.[7] He also wrote *Supplement to Bougainville's Voyage* (1772), a meditation on cultural difference and the consequences of European expansion inspired by the navigator Bougainville's account of his voyage to newly discovered Tahiti. Finally, he revisited one of his early works, the *Bijoux indiscrets* (Indiscreet Jewels) (1748), adding two new chapters with decidedly colonial themes to this Oriental libertine novel. Diderot's intellectual journey from silence to discourse thus epitomizes the broader cultural trajectory of eighteenth-century French culture.

The famous statement that opens Rousseau's *On the Social Contract*—"Man was born free, and everywhere he is in chains"—might lead one to believe that Rousseau had a great deal to say about the most egregious contemporary case of bondage, the Atlantic slave trade. In fact, though Rousseau frequently uses the word *slavery* and ancillary terms such as *chains, yokes,* and *irons* in a metaphorical sense to denote social inequality and political subordination, he mentions colonial slavery directly in only one place, a passage of his novel *Julie; ou, La nouvelle Héloïse* (Julie; or, The New Heloise) (1761). While traveling the oceans of the world to overcome his doomed passion for Julie, the hero, St. Preux, witnesses with horror and chagrin the crimes committed against his fellow man on the coasts of Africa and Brazil. He writes to Julie's cousin and confidante Claire that, "I turned aside my eyes in contempt, horror, and pity, at seeing the fourth part of my fellow man turned into beasts for the service of others, I bemoaned being a man."[8] As Christopher Miller notes, Rousseau, like his protagonist, essentially turned his eyes away from this overwhelming spectacle of inequality and oppression (68).

If Rousseau's silence on the issue of colonial slavery seems particularly surprising, it is not only because of his critical approach to political authority but also because of the strong anthropological orientation of his philosophical writings. Rousseau was well versed in the travel literature on the Americas, and in *Second Discourse* (1755) based his arguments about primitive man on the Caribs of the Antilles. Like other thinkers of his generation, however,

---

7. Raynal, *Histoire philosophique* and *Histoire politique.*
8. Rousseau, *Julie,* translated by Philip Stewart and Jean Vaché, 6:340.

Rousseau was more interested in the profound contrast between the indigenous people of the Americas and members of advanced, European societies than in intermediate and diasporic figures such as transplanted African slaves, with the result that "native others" occupy a more important place in his oeuvre than displaced Africans.

Until the last three decades of the eighteenth century, colonization and slavery were, if anything, represented even less often in fictional forms such as the novel than in philosophical works that dealt in explicit terms with economic and political questions. Before 1769 there were hardly any fictional representations of French colonialism, though many tales and novels explored "adjacent" issues, such as slavery in the Oriental world and encounters between Europeans (particularly conquistadors) and indigenous Aztecs and Incas. The one major exception to this silence is the oeuvre of Abbé Prévost, who touches on French colonialism in two of his novels.

At the end of *History of Manon Lescaut and the Chevalier des Grieux,* the last and most famous volume of *Memoirs and Adventures of a Man of Quality* (1728–31), the two eponymous protagonists find themselves in France's fledgling Mississippi colony. Having been rounded up by the police, Manon is deported to New Orleans along with a cohort of other girls arrested for prostitution, and her doggedly faithful lover, the Chevalier de Grieux, decides to accompany her to the New World. Though the young couple attempts to make a fresh start in Louisiana, they rapidly discover that the colony is imbued with the same vices as the metropole. After a duel with the corrupt governor's nephew, the heroes flee into the wilderness where Manon, overcome with exhaustion, perishes. This denouement stands as one of the great tragic episodes of French literature. It is less often recognized as a story firmly grounded in French colonial history. After the founding of New Orleans in 1718, the monopoly trading company that controlled the colony attempted to accelerate the process of populating it by transporting vagrants, orphans, and other vulnerable members of French society across the Atlantic. They were particularly interested in single women who could be married off to colonists, and rounded up large numbers of young women, particularly prostitutes and orphans detained in public institutions. In an article devoted to representations of early colonial Louisiana, Pierre Berthiaume notes that these roundups began to create public alarm, and that accusations of summary deportations started to appear in the press.[9]

Prévost's subsequent novel, *Cleveland* (1731–39), which I discuss in chapter 4, evokes several different American colonies, including Spanish Cuba, French Martinique, and British outposts in Virginia and the Carolinas.

There were a number of reasons for Prévost's unusually acute awareness of colonial geography and history. Between 1746 and 1759 he edited the *Histoire*

9. Berthiaume, "Louisiana."

générale des voyages (General History of Voyages), an anthology of travel narratives previously printed in English that he translated for a French readership. These narratives provided the empirical template for the travels of his peripatetic characters, notably the globe-trotting Cleveland. A second important factor was that in the late 1720s–30s Prévost spent several long stretches in England, immersing himself in English literature, journalism, and political writing, and falling under its influence. His journal, *For and Against* (1733–40), a weekly social and political commentary, was modeled on Joseph Addison and Richard Steele's *The Spectator* (1711–14). Colonial affairs were more widely represented and debated in England than in France. There were more colonial planters in residence in London society, and there were also more enslaved/emancipated blacks imported from colonies to metropole to serve as domestics. This higher level of colonial consciousness, along with other aspects of the English literary scene, left its mark on Prévost.

In one issue of *For and Against* (1735), Prévost presents the "Harangue d'un chef nègre" (Harangue of a Black Leader), a text purporting to be the speech of a Maroon slave on the island of Jamaica, that had previously appeared in several English periodicals.[10] The speech of "Moses Bom-Saam" has been discussed by Michèle Duchet and Catherine Reinhardt as an example of the prevalence of the theme of marronage in eighteenth-century French writing on slavery. I agree that the "Harangue" influenced writing about slavery produced in the 1760s–80s.[11] Important texts such as Jean-François de Saint-Lambert's "Zimeo" (1769) and Louis-Sébastien Mercier's futuristic novel, *The Year Two Thousand Four Hundred and Forty* (1771) also broached the issue of Caribbean slavery through the figure of the runaway or rebel slave. At the same time, I would question Duchet's assertion that in the wake of Bom-Saam's speech the Maroon came to dominate the literary representation of black figures.[12] In 1735 Moses Bom-Saam was a very isolated figure in French literature: no characters remotely like him appeared until the 1760s.[13] Without Prévost's close connection to the English literary scene, slave speech probably would not have been represented in a mainstream French publication for another quarter century.

The forms of writing in which French colonialism was most widely represented between the 1630s and 1789 were empirically oriented genres such as travel writing. The best-known French literature of travel and exploration bearing on the Americas is the corpus of texts considering the Native American nations of New France. One reason for this wide diffusion was the

---

10. See Jameson, *Montesquieu et l'esclavage,* 211. According to Bruce D. Dickson, the speech was published in *The Prompter* in 1734, and in two other periodicals, the *London Magazine* and the *Gentleman's Magazine,* in 1735. *Origins of African-American Literature,* 27.

11. Reinhardt, *Claims to Memory,* 73.

12. Duchet, *Anthropologie et histoire,* 139.

13. Léon-François Hoffmann also makes this point, *Le nègre romantique,* 84.

synergy between writing on North America produced by the Jesuit fathers Lafitau (1724) and Charlevoix (1744), the Baron de Lahontan (1703), and the Dutch-born traveler, Cornelius De Pauw (1774), and the broader philosophical currents of the period.[14] Alongside the travel literature devoted to New France developed a less well-known but nonetheless significant corpus of writing on the Antilles. The major figures of this tradition were three Dominican priests, Fathers Raymond Breton (1666), Jean-Baptiste Du Tertre (1671), and Jean-Baptiste Labat (1722, 1742), all witnesses to and participants in the early development of the French Caribbean. To varying degrees each of these writers portrayed the Antilles as a terrain of encounter between Europeans and Amerindians.

Missionary accounts of the early Caribbean colonies dried up in the early eighteenth century and it was not until the last three decades of the century that secular eyewitness descriptions of the colonies began to appear. Whereas there was an almost continuous tradition of writing on New France, the representation of the Caribbean was marked by a hiatus. It fell off rapidly after there were no more "natives" to discover or convert, and it was only much later that slavery, métissage, and plantation society became significant topics of writing.

The colonial descriptions and reform proposals that started to appear in the late eighteenth century were mostly written by administrators and colonial magistrates, many of whom—for instance Michel René Hilliard d'Auberteuil (1777), Pierre Victor de Malouet (1788), and Médéric-Louis-Elie Moreau de Saint-Méry (1798)—were members of the white Creole elite. Their discussions of colonial administration and the management of slaves were reformist in tone but generally favorable toward slavery. The most richly descriptive work in this category is Moreau de Saint-Méry's *Topographic, Physical, Civil, Political, and Historical Description of the French Part of Saint-Domingue,* a work published in Philadelphia in 1797–98 at a time when Saint-Domingue was embroiled in revolutionary turmoil and the hierarchical universe that Moreau painstakingly describes had begun to collapse.

When considered collectively, seventeenth- and eighteenth-century French texts that touch on the colonial universe can be said to manifest a number of broad representational tendencies. In addition to the small overall volume of representation, and the displacements toward the Orient or toward encounters with indigenous people on which this book focuses, it is possible to point to a few further patterns. One is that the most abundant representations, and those richest in descriptive realism, appear in works produced by writers who had direct personal experience of the colonies. These writers were generally involved in some respect in the colonial system and had few reservations about the practice of slavery.

14. Lahontan, *Dialogues* and *Nouveaux voyages;* Lafitau, *Moeurs des sauvages amériquains;* Charlevoix, *Histoire et description générale;* De Pauw, *Recherches philosophiques sur les Américains.*

A second important tendency is the use of slavery as a metaphor for political oppression, somewhat at the expense of the literal meanings of the term, the most glaring example being that of Rousseau. Finally, in many eighteenth-century works the question of slavery stands in a relation of tension to attitudes toward race. Slavery is condemned as a moral offense, but this critique is undercut by statements bearing on the moral and intellectual inferiority of the people who are enslaved. This double-sidedness is discernable, for example, in writing by the earlier Diderot, as well as in the writings of Voltaire and Rousseau.[15]

~

In the late 1760s the colonial world belatedly became a subject of representation and moral debate. Colonial issues were represented in works of economic theory, as well as in a number of fictional texts. Ultimately, during the revolutionary period, the colonies became arenas of social activism and a focus of political activism.

The gradual transition from indifference to activism occurred for several reasons. An important factor was the loss of New France in 1763 by the terms of the Treaty of Paris. It is generally said that France agreed to hand over its remaining Canadian territories to England in order to secure the restoration of its more valuable Antillean possessions, Guadeloupe and Martinique. Though this account does not fully capture the complexity of events, what is clear is that the war, the peace treaty, and the cession of Canada drew attention to the colonial world, particularly the Antilles, the last bastion of French power in the Americas. Following the loss of New France, French writers and political figures began to contemplate new colonial ventures in other parts of the world, notably Africa and Asia, to envisage colonization without slavery, and to sketch out a new vision of colonial rule: conquest undertaken in the interests of humanity, and as an extension of the French Enlightenment.

Another contextual factor was the change in French political culture that occurred in the last three decades of the eighteenth century. In the 1770s and 1780s demands for social change and political reform became less abstract and more urgent. Reformers argued less for sweeping principles and more for targeted reforms. Ultimately, the abolition of slavery came to be included among these reforms.

In the 1770s and 1780s French writers produced two main kinds of writing on colonization and slavery. The first consisted of liberal economic and political treatises, works such as Mirabeau's *Friend of Mankind* (1757), Le Mercier de

---

15. See Voltaire, *Essai sur les mœurs*, 2:305–306; and Diderot's *Encyclopedia* article, "Human Species." On the scattered observations relating to Africans that appear in Rousseau's correspondence and published writings, see Cook, "Jean-Jacques Rousseau and the Negro."

la Rivière's *Natural and Essential Order of Political Societies* (1767), and Abbé Morellet's *Memoir on the Present Situation of the Company of the Indies* (1769). These works provided the conceptual context for the idea that tropical agriculture could be made profitable without slavery. Thinkers including Quesnay, Mirabeau, Turgot, Dupont de Nemours, and Condorcet—the French branch of the school of Adam Smith and Adam Ferguson—advocated a comprehensive rethinking of French economic policy. They called, in particular, for freedom of commerce (the termination of monopolies and the abolition of France's convoluted system of domestic tolls and tariffs), the liberalization of modes of production (the abolition of the medieval guild system and the end of colonial slavery), and for increased investment in agriculture. Most of the writing on colonization and slavery produced between 1763 and the French Revolution was shaped by the arguments of this school. So much so, in fact, that I argue that the flowering of liberal political economy was a cultural precondition for the emergence of colonization and slavery as significant cultural concerns.

The Abbé Raynal's monumental 1770 *History of the Two Indies* synthesized many of these ideas, and can to some extent be seen as an outgrowth of the thinking on colonization and commerce inaugurated during the previous decade. That Raynal undertook to produce a vast reference work on the history of European expansion indicates the growing interest generated by this topic. The fact that no less a figure than Denis Diderot came on board as an editor and writer for the 1774 and 1780 editions shows that the question of colonization was taking shape as an urgent philosophical issue.

The second principal genre of late eighteenth-century French writing on colonial society was sentimental fiction. Tales, novellas, and plays such as Gabriel Mailhol's *The Black Philosopher* (1764); Jean-François de Saint-Lambert's "Zimeo" (1769); Louis-Sébastien Mercier's *The Year Two Thousand Four Hundred and Forty;* (1771); Olympe de Gouges's *Black Slavery; or, The Happy Shipwreck* (1786); Joseph La Vallée's *The Negro as There Are Few Whites* (1789); Bernardin de Saint-Pierre's *Paul and Virginia* (1788) and *Empsaël and Zoraïde* (1792); and Germaine de Staël's "Mirza; or, Letters of a Traveler" (1795) all brought a sentimental dimension to the representation of slavery.[16] By portraying enslaved men and women as individuals, these texts made it possible for readers to envisage the impact of slavery in concrete, human terms.

Although these texts are heterogeneous, a few generalizations can be made about their dominant themes and about the ways in which they approach slavery. There is, first of all, significant overlap between the sentimental genre and the arguments made by economic thinkers, for instance, the claim that free labor was more productive than enslaved labor, and that sugar should be cultivated on "free" plantations in Africa. In *Empsaël and Zoraïde,* Bernardin

---

16. Bernardin de Saint-Pierre had previously touched on the issue of colonial slavery in his travel narrative, *Voyage to the Island of Mauritius.*

de Saint-Pierre's play about slavery, Antony Bénézet, a character based on the French-born Quaker abolitionist from Philadelphia, travels the coast of Africa arguing for the cultivation of sugar in Africa as a means of bringing an end to the slave trade, while Staël's short story "Mirza" is set in a sugar plantation in Senegal, an establishment founded by a former slave at the behest of an Enlightened French governor.

Several sentimental antislavery fictions contain episodes that explore the concern that abolition would spell both the end of a functioning colonial economy and the end of the rule of law. A number of others endeavor to show that, once emancipated, former slaves would remain at their stations, faithful to their masters, grateful for the gift of freedom.

In *The Black Philosopher*, a work that is part picaresque novel, part philosophical tale (it has been described as a parody of *Candide*), an African prince named Tintillo, having learned French and acquired French *lumières* from a traveler, is captured by a slave trader and shipped to Martinique. Conditions aboard the slave ship are bad, but the master to whom Tintillo is sold in Martinique is good (he puts his slave to work in a library!). As a result, when Maroons attack the colony, far from joining in their protest, he urges them to renounce violence and return to work. Voicing enlightened French colonial views, Tintillo argues that the slaves would have suffered worse fates in war-torn Africa; that Europeans had bought them legitimately; and that if they returned to work, they would be able to earn their freedom by legitimate means. The first French work of any length to have a protagonist of sub-Saharan African origin—there was no earlier French equivalent of *Othello* or *Oroonoko*—*The Black Philosopher* is also the fictional representation of colonial relations that comes closest to articulating a pro-slavery perspective. (Catherine Reinhardt has appropriately characterized it as an "assimilationist text.")[17] It is, however, far from being the only colonial fiction to suggest that freedom must be conferred from the outside, by France, or that Africans themselves bear the lion's share of responsibility for the slave trade. Several later works that take a more active stand on abolition approach the practice of slavery in a similarly nationalistic light.

A few late eighteenth-century colonial fictions represent what at first glance appears to be the opposite dynamic: slaves wresting their own freedom from their masters through acts of marronage.[18] An important precursor of these depictions, as we have seen, is the speech of Moses Bom-Saam in *For and Against*. Marronage also comes into play in *The Black Philosopher*, Olympe de Gouges's *Black Slavery*, and Saint-Lambert's "Zimeo."

In *The Year Two Thousand Four Hundred and Forty* (1771), Louis-Sébastien Mercier's narrator imagines waking up in the Paris of the future to discover a

---

17. Reinhardt, *Claims to Memory*, 75. See also Hoffmann, *Le nègre romantique*, 84–85.
18. On the figure of the Maroon, see Duchet, *Anthropologie*, 139; and Reinhardt, *Claims to Memory*, 59–86.

city cleansed of the social evils that plagued his own times. During a tour of the city he comes across various statues erected in honor of the great champions of world liberty. One statue represents a black man, the fragments of twenty scepters shattered at his feet. A dedicatory plaque identifies him as the "vengeur du nouveau monde!" (the avenger of the New World), and the narrator is told by his companions that this black leader "was the exterminating angel to whom the god of justice had lent his sword: he showed by example that sooner or later cruelty will be punished" (109).[19] Mercier's revolutionary/premonitory figure of the black avenger is revisited by Diderot in the 1774 and 1780 editions of *History of the Two Indies*.

As Catherine Reinhardt observes, the Maroon characters of eighteenth-century French fiction run the gamut from prototypes of the perceived violence and brutishness of Africans to eloquent mouthpieces for European values. In the majority of cases (Mercier's and Diderot's stand as exceptions), marronage does not secure liberty. Rather, liberty is conferred by France or its representatives, as a manifestation of the nation's principles. Yet despite what these fictions recount—that France, rather than Maroons, would enjoy the honor of according freedom—the presence of marronage as a theme in late eighteenth-century French fiction suggests that slave revolts in the colonies were beginning to have an impact, not only on the colonial elite but also on distant metropolitan observers. A galvanizing episode in this regard was the revolt of Makandal, which shook Saint-Domingue in the 1750s. Before he was captured and executed in 1758, Makandal was rumored to be plotting a mass poisoning of planters by an extended network of rebellious slaves. Even after his death he remained a powerful figure in Caribbean history, revered by blacks and feared by whites. When Saint-Domingue's enslaved population rose up in revolt en masse in 1791, Makandal served as a role model for Dutty Boukman and the rebellion's other early leaders.[20]

A last recurrent feature of late eighteenth-century colonial fictions of which I want to take note is the interweaving of the themes of slavery and gender. As I discuss in chapter 7, two women writers of the 1780s–90s, Staël and Gouges, authored fictional representations of slaves in which the "rights of woman" (as proclaimed by Olympe de Gouges) are interconnected with the rights of the enslaved. These authors empathized with the enslaved on the basis of a shared experience of subjection, but they also tended to overlook the specificities of slavery, projecting a liberal feminist agenda onto the colonial arena. It is also not insignificant that in the convergence of revolutionary feminism and

---

19. Mercier also wrote a more lighthearted work dealing with the relationship between France and her colonies, the drama *L'habitant de la Guadeloupe* (The Inhabitant of Guadeloupe) (1786). The play concerns a wealthy Creole who comes to Paris to choose an heir, and revolves around the differences between metropolitan and colonial perspectives on commerce, wealth, and hospitality. See Antoine, *Les écrivains français*, 114–15.

20. On Makandal, see Bénot, *La révolution française*, 139–40.

antislavery argument, as in the merger of economic theory and abolitionism, the issue of slavery was rendered visible within the framework of a discourse with resonance for the metropolitan context. Late eighteenth-century French writers tackled the issue of colonial slavery more directly and more often than any previous generation. But they generally explored slavery in conjunction with other social, political, and economic ideas, and not as a freestanding moral and political question. Understanding this economy of thought helps us understand why the abolition of slavery in 1793–94 lasted only eight years. Histories of slavery typically relate that "Napoleon Bonaparte restored colonial slavery" by a decree of May 1802.[21] But was the reality not more complex? Would it not be more accurate to say that the restoration of slavery reflected, not only the expansionist nationalism of Napoleon, but also the fundamental ambivalence of the revolutionary critique of slavery?

21. See, for example, Bénot, *La démence coloniale sous Napoléon,* which (in contradiction to much of Bénot's other work) represents Napoleon's decree as a negation of the revolutionary period's activism in relation to slavery. See also Hoffmann, *Le nègre romantique,* 10; and Kadish and Massardier-Kenney, *Translating Slavery,* 2.

Works Cited

Primary Sources

Addison, Joseph, and Richard Steele, eds. *The Spectator*. 4 vols. 1711–12, 1714. Reprint, New York: Dutton, 1945–46.

Alembert, Jean Le Rond de, and Denis Diderot, eds. *Encyclopédie; ou, Dictionnaire raisonné des sciences, des arts et des métiers*. Paris, 1751–72. (See below for a list of *Encyclopédie* articles cited in this work.)

Anquetil-Duperron, Abraham-Hyacinthe. *Législation orientale*. Amsterdam: M. M. Rey, 1778.

Barrère, Pierre. *Dissertation sur la cause physique de la couleur des nègres*. Paris, 1741.

———. *Nouvelle relation de la France equinoxale, contenant la description des côtes de la Guyane*. Paris: Piget, 1743.

Behn, Aphra. *Oroonoko; or, The Royal Slave: A True History*. London: William Canning, 1688.

Bernardin de Saint-Pierre, Jacques-Henri. *Empsaël et Zoraïde; ou, Les blancs esclaves des noirs au Maroc*. 1792. Reprint, Exeter: University of Exeter Press, 1995.

———. *Études de la nature*. 3 vols. Paris: P.-F. Didot le jeune, 1784.

———. *Études de la nature*. Vol. 5, *Paul et Virginie*. Brussels: B. Le Francq, 1788–89.

———. *Voeux d'un solitaire, pour servir de suite aux "Études de la nature," Suite des Voeux d'un solitaire, pour servir de complément au 5e volume des Études de la nature*. 2 vols. Paris: P.-F. Didot le jeune, 1789–92.

———. *Voyage à l'Île de France, à l'Île de Bourbon, au Cap de Bonne-Espérance, etc. Avec des observations nouvelles sur la nature et sur les hommes, par un officier du roi* (1773), in *Oeuvres posthumes de Jacques Bernardin de Saint-Pierre*. 2 vols. (Paris: Le Dentu, 1840).

Bessner, Charles-Alexandre de. *De l'esclavage des nègres*. 1774. Aix-en-Provence: Centre des Archives d'Outre-Mer, Guiane: Démographie de la Guyane française archive, DFC 221.

Bonaparte, Lucien. *La tribu indienne; ou, Edouard et Stellina*. 2 vols. Paris: Imprimerie de Honnert, 1798.

Boufflers, Stanislas-Jean de. *Lettres d'Afrique à Madame de Sabran*. Arles: Actes Sud, 1998.

Bougainville, Louis-Antoine de. *Voyage autour du monde par la frégate du roi "La Boudeuse" et la flûte l'Étoile en 1766, 1767, 1768 et 1769.* Paris: Nyon, 1771.

Breton, Raymond. *Dictionnaire caraïbe-français mêlé de quantité de remarques historiques pour l'éclaircissement de la langue.* Auxerre: Gilles Bouquet, 1666.

——. *Petit catéchisme.* Auxerre: Gilles Bouquet, 1664.

Brissot de Warville, Jacques-Pierre. *Discours sur la nécessité d'établir à Paris une société pour concourir, avec celle de Londres, à l'abolition de la traite et de l'esclavage des nègres.* Paris, 1788.

——. *Examen critique des voyages dans l'Amérique septentrionale, de M. le Marquis de Chastellux.* London, 1786.

——. *Mémoire sur les noirs de l'Amérique septentrionale.* Paris: 1789.

Buffon, Georges Louis Leclerc, Comte de. *Oeuvres.* Paris: Gallimard, 2007.

Butini, Jean-François. *Lettres africaines.* London, 1771.

——. *Othello, drame en cinq actes et en vers, imité de Shakespeare.* Geneva, 1785.

——. *Traité du luxe.* Geneva: Bardin, 1774.

Chambon, M. *Le commerce de l'Amérique par Marseille ou explication des lettres-patentes du roi, portant règlement pour le commerce qui se fait de Marseille aux Isles Françoises de l'Amérique.* 2 vols. Amsterdam: M.-M. Rey, 1783.

Chamfort, Sébastien. *Oeuvres de Chamfort.* 4 vols. Paris: Imprimerie des Sciences et des Arts, 1794.

Charlevoix, Pierre-François-Xavier de. *Histoire de l'Île espagnole ou de Saint-Domingue.* 2 vols. Paris: H.-L. Guérin, 1730–31.

——. *Histoire et description générale de la Nouvelle France.* 3 vols. Paris: Nyon fils, 1744.

Chastellux, François-Jean de. *Voyages de M. le Marquis de Chastellux dans l'Amérique septentrionale, dans les années 1780, 1781 et 1782.* Paris, 1786.

Chateaubriand, François-René de. *Atala; ou, Les amours de deux sauvages dans le désert.* Paris: Migneret, 1801.

——. *Atala; René.* 1801. Translated by Irving Putter. Berkeley: University of California Press, 1980.

——. *Génie du christianisme; ou, Beautés de la religion chrétienne.* 5 vols. Paris: Migneret, 1802.

——. *Mémoires d'outre-tombe.* 1848–50. Reprint, Paris: Gallimard, 1997.

——. *Oeuvres complètes de M. le Vicomte de Chateaubriand.* 18 vols. Paris: Ladvocat, 1826–31.

——. *Voyage en Amérique.* 2 vols. 1827. Reprint, Paris: M. Didier, 1964.

Choderlos de Laclos, Pierre-Ambroise-François. *Dangerous Liaisons.* 1782. Translated by Douglas Parmée. New York and Oxford: Oxford University Press, 1995.

Code noir. Paris, 1742.

Condorcet, Marie-Jean-Antoine-Nicolas Caritat, Marquis de. *Lettres sur le commerce des grains.* Paris: Couturier, 1774.

——. *Réflexions sur le commerce des blés.* London, 1776.

——. *Réflexions sur l'esclavage des noirs et autres textes abolitionnistes.* 1781. Reprint, Paris: L'Harmattan, 2003.

——. *Vie de M. Turgot.* London, 1786.

Coréal, François (Francisco). *Voyages de François Coréal aux Indes occidentales contenant ce qu'il a vu de plus remarquable pendant son séjour depuis 1666 jusqu'en 1697.* 2 vols. Paris: A. Cailleau, 1722.

Crébillon, Claude-Prosper Jolyot de. *Le Sopha, conte moral.* 1742. Reprint. Paris: Le Divan, 1930.

Cugoano, Ottobah. *Narrative of the Enslavement of Ottobah Cugoano, a Native of Africa.* London, 1787.

De Lamet, Adrien Augustin de Bussy, and Germain Fromageau. "Règles sur le commerce des esclaves en général, et des nègres en particulier." *Dictionnaire des cas de conscience.* Paris, J. B. Coignard, 1733.

De Pauw, Cornelius. *Recherches philosophiques sur les Américains; ou, Mémoires intéressants pour servir à l'histoire de l'espèce humaine.* 3 vols. Berlin, 1768–70.

Defoe, Daniel. *Roxana; or, The Fortunate Mistress.* London, 1724.

Diderot, Denis. *Les bijoux indiscrets.* 1748. In *Oeuvres de Diderot.* 5 vols. Paris: Robert Laffont, 1994–97.

——. *Supplement to Bougainville's Voyage, Rameau's Nephew and Other Works.* Translated by Jacques Barzun and Ralph H. Bowen. Indianapolis: Bobbs-Merrill, 1964.

Dorat, Claude-Joseph. *Lettres en vers et oeuvres mêlées.* 2 vols. Paris: Delalain, 1792.

Dumont, P. J. *Histoire de l'esclavage en Afrique (pendant trente-quatre ans).* Paris: Pillet ainé, 1819.

Dupont de Nemours, Pierre-Samuel. *Journal de commerce.* April 1759.

Du Tertre, Jean-Baptiste. *Histoire générale des Antilles habitées par les Français.* 4 vols. Paris: Thomas Jolly, 1667–71.

——. *Histoire générale des isles de St. Christophe, de la Guadeloupe, de la Martinique et autres. . . .* Paris: Jacques and Emmanuel Langlois, 1654.

Éphémérides du citoyen. Paris: N. A. Delalain, 1765–72.

Equiano, Olaudah. *The Interesting Narrative of the Life of Olaudah Equiano or Gustavus Vassa, the African.* 1791. Reprint, New York: W. W. Norton, 2001.

Forbonnais, François Véron Duverger de. *Éléments du commerce.* Paris: Briasson, 1754.

——. *Recherches et considérations sur les finances de France depuis l'année 1595 jusqu'à l'année 1721.* Basel: Cramer, 1758.

Fraisse, Jean-Antoine. *Livre de dessins chinois tirés d'après les originaux de Perse, des Indes, de la Chine et du Japon.* 1735.

Fromaget, Nicolas. *Eighteenth-Century French Romances.* Vol. 6, *The Prophet's Cousin.* 1742. Translated by Eric Sutton. London: Chapman and Hall, 1926.

——. *Le cousin de Mahomet et la folie salutaire.* 1742. Toulouse: Anacharsis, 2007.

Gouges, Olympe de. *Black Slavery; or, the Happy Shipwreck.* 1792. Translated by Maryann DeJulio. In Kadish and Massardier-Kenney, eds., *Translating Slavery,* 87–119.

——. *L'esclavage des noirs ou l'heureux naufrage.* Paris, 1792.

——. *Oeuvres.* Edited by Benoîte Groult. Paris: Mercure de France, 1986.

——. "Reflections on Negroes." 1788. Translated by Sylvie Molta. In Kadish and Massardier-Kenney, eds., *Translating Slavery,* 84–86.

——. "Réflexions sur les hommes nègres." 1788. In Kadish and Massardier-Kenney, eds., *Translating Slavery,* 229–31.

——. *Zamore et Mirza,* vol. 3 of *Oeuvres de Madame de Gouges.* Paris: Cailleau, 1788.

Graffigny, Françoise de. *Lettres d'une Péruvienne.* 1747. Reprint, Oxford: Voltaire Foundation, 2002.

Grégoire, Henri. *De la littérature des nègres; ou, Recherches sur leurs facultés intellectuelles, leurs qualités morales et leur littérature.* Paris: Maradan, 1808.

Grotius, Hugo. *The Rights of War and Peace.* 1625. Translated by A. C. Campbell. Westport, CT: Hyperion, 1993.

Gueullette, Thomas-Simon. *Mille et une heure [sic], contes péruviens.* 2 vols. Amsterdam, 1734.

Helvétius, Claude-Adrien. *De l'esprit.* Paris: Durand, 1758.

Hilliard d'Auberteuil, Michel René. *Considérations sur l'état présent de la colonie française de Saint-Domingue, ouvrage politique et législatif.* 2 vols. Paris: Grangé, 1775–76.

Hobbes, Thomas. *Leviathan.* London: Andrew Crooke, 1651.

Hugo, Victor. *Bug-Jargal.* Geneva: Famot, 1973.

Hume, David. "Of National Characters." In *Essays Moral and Political.* London: A. Millar, 1748, 267–88.

Inventaire et mise en possession de l'habitation Valette, September 27, 1792. Musée du nouveau monde, La Rochelle, 87-4-2.

Journal de Commerce. Brussels: Van den Bergen, 1759–62.

Journal de Guyenne, 1785–91. Archives Régionales de la Gironde (ARG) 4L 1370.

Kolb, Peter. *Description du Cap de Bonne-Espérance: où, L'on trouve tout ce qui concerne l'histoire-naturelle du pays, la religion, les moeurs et les usages des Hottentots.* Amsterdam: J. Cauffe, 1741.

Labat, Jean-Baptiste. *Nouveau voyage aux isles de l'Amérique contenant l'histoire naturelle de ces pays, l'origine, les moeurs, la religion & le gouvernement des habitans anciens & modernes.* 6 vols. Paris: G. Cavelier, 1722.

——. *Nouveau voyage aux isles de l'Amérique.* 8 vols. Paris: Théodore le Gras, 1742.

——. *Voyage aux îles d'Amérique: Exposition organisée par la Direction des Archives de France.* Paris: Archives nationales, 1992.

Lafitau, Joseph-François. *Moeurs des sauvages amériquains comparées aux moeurs des premiers temps.* 2 vols. Paris: Saugrain l'aîné, 1724.

Lahontan, Louis Armand de Lom d'Arce, Baron de. *Dialogues de Monsieur le Baron de Lahontan et d'un sauvage dans l'Amérique contenant une description exacte des moeurs et des coutumes de ces peuples sauvages.* Amsterdam: Veuve de Boetman, 1704.

——. *New Voyages to North America....*2 vols. London: H. Bonwicke, T. Goodwin, M. Wotton, B. Tooke, and S. Manship, 1703.

——. *Nouveaux voyages en Amérique septentrionale.* The Hague: Frères l'Honoré, 1703.

La Morlière, Charles-Jacques-Louis-Auguste Rochette de. *Angola, histoire indienne.* Paris, 1741.

Landolphe, Jean-François. *Mémoires du Capitaine Landolphe contenant l'histoire de ses voyages pendant trente-six ans aux côtes d'Afrique et aux deux Amériques, rédigés sur son manuscript par J. S. Quesné.* 2 vols. 1823. Reprint, Paris: Hachette, 1975.

Lavallée, Joseph. *Le nègre comme il y a peu de blancs.* Paris: Buisson, 1789.

Lecointe-Marsillac, *Le More-Lack; ou, Essai sur les moyens les plus doux et les plus équitables d'abolir la traite et l'esclavage des nègres d'Afrique, en conservant aux colonies tous les avantages d'une population agricole.* Paris: Prault, 1789.

Le Mercier de la Rivière, Pierre-Paul-François. *Le Mercier de la Rivière 1719–1801.* Edited by Louis-Philippe May. 2 vols. Paris: CNRS, 1975–78.

——. *L'ordre naturel et essentiel des sociétés politiques.* Paris: Desaint, 1767.

Le Page du Pratz, Antoine-Simon. *Histoire de la Louisiane.* 3 vols. Paris: de Bure, 1758.

Lesage, Alain-René. *Histoire de Gil Blas de Santillane.* Paris: Pierre Ribou, 1715–35.

Ligon, Richard. *A True and Exact History of the Island of Barbados.* London: Humphrey Mosely, 1657.

Long, Edward. *History of Jamaica; or, General Survey of the Ancient and Modern State of the Island: With Reflections on Its Situation, Settlements, Inhabitants, Climates, Products, Commerce, Laws and Governments.* 2 vols. London: T. Lowndes, 1774.

Mailhol, Gabriel. *Le philosophe nègre.* London and Frankfurt, 1764.

Malouet, Victor de. *Mémoire sur l'esclavage des nègres.* Neufchâtel, 1788.

Marat, Jean-Paul. *Chains of Slavery: A Work wherein the Clandestine and Villainous Attempts of Princes to Ruin Liberty are Pointed out.* London: T. Becket, T. Payne, J. Almon, and Richardson and Urquhart, 1774.

Marivaux, Pierre Carlet Chamblain de. *Le paysan parvenu: or, The Fortunate Peasant; Being Memoirs of the Life of Mr.——.* London: John Brindley, 1735.

Marmontel, Jean-François. *Les Incas; ou, La destruction de l'empire du Pérou.* Paris: Lacombe, 1777.

Maubert de Gouvest, Jean-Henri. *Lettres iroquoises.* Lausanne, 1752.

Melon, Jean-François. *Mahmoud le Gasnévide, histoire orientale: Fragment traduit de l'arabe.* Rotterdam: G. Hofhoudt, 1729.

——. *Essai politique sur le commerce.* n.p., 1734.

Mercier, Louis-Sébastien. *L'an deux mille quatre cent quarante.* London, 1774.

——. *L'habitant de la Guadeloupe.* Paris: Poincot, 1785.

——. *Tableau de Paris.* 2 vols. 1783–88. Reprint, Paris: Mercure de France, 1994.

Mirabeau, Victor de Riquetti, Marquis de. *L'ami des hommes, ou traité de la population.* 1757. 3 vols. Reprint, Avignon, 1758–59.

Mocquet, Jean. *Voyages en Afrique, Asie, Indes occidentales et orientales.* 1617. Reprint, Rouen: David Berthelin, 1665.

Molière, *Le bourgeois gentilhomme.* Paris: Robert Ballard, 1670.

——. *The Bourgeois Gentleman*. 1670. Translated by Bernard Sahlins. Chicago: I. R. Dee, 2000.

Montaigne, Michel de. *Essais*. 1595. Reprint, Paris: Pochothèque, 2001.

Montesquieu, Charles-Louis de Secondat, Baron de la Brède et de. *De l'esprit des lois*. 2 vols. 1748. Reprint, Paris: Flammarion, 1979.

——. *Lettres persanes*. 1721. Paris: Garnier-Flammarion, 1964.

——. *Oeuvres complètes*. Vol. 2, *Considérations sur les richesses de l'Espagne*. Paris: Gallimard, 1949–51.

——. *Persian Letters*. 1721. Translated by Margaret Mauldon. Oxford: Oxford University Press, 2008.

——. *The Spirit of the Laws*. 1748. Translated by Anne M. Cohler, Basia C. Miller, and Harold S. Stone. Cambridge: Cambridge University Press, 1989.

Moreau de Saint-Méry, Médéric-Louis-Élie. *Description topographique, physique, civile, politique et historique de la partie française de l'isle Saint-Domingue*. 2 vols. Philadelphia, 1797.

Morellet, André. *Mémoire sur la situation actuelle de la Compagnie des Indes*. Paris: Desaint, 1769.

——. *Réflexions sur les avantages de la libre fabrication et de l'usage des toiles peintes en France*. Geneva, 1758.

Petit, Émilien. *Traité sur le gouvernement des esclaves*. 2 vols. Paris: Knapen, 1777.

Poivre, Pierre. *Travels of a Philosopher, Being Observations on the Customs, Manners, Arts of Several Nations in Asia and Africa*. London: J. Davidson, 1769.

——. *Voyages d'un philosophe; ou, Observations sur les moeurs et les arts des peuples de l'Afrique, de l'Asie, et de l'Amérique*. Yverdon: Société Nationale de Typographie, 1768.

Pomet, Pierre. *Histoire générale des drogues*. Paris: J.-B. Loyson and A. Pillon, 1694.

——. *A Compleat History of Druggs*. London: R. Bonwicke, 1712.

Prévost, Antoine François. *Histoire générale des voyages; ou, Nouvelle collection de toutes les relations de voyages par mer et par terre*. 15 vols. Paris: Didot and other publishers, 1746–59.

——. *Le philosophe anglais; ou, Histoire de Monsieur Cleveland, fils naturel de Cromwell, écrite par lui-même, et traduite de l'anglais*. 8 vols. Utrecht: Étienne Neaulme, 1731–39.

——. *Le pour et contre*. 20 vols. Paris: Didot, 1733–40.

——. *Mémoires et aventures d'un homme de qualité qui s'est retiré du monde*. 7 vols. Paris, 1731.

Pufendorf, Samuel. *De officio hominis et civis*. London, 1673.

Quesnay, François. *Oeuvres économiques complètes et autres textes*. Edited by Christine Théré, Loïc Charles, and Jean-Claude Perrot. Paris: INED, 2005.

——. "Remarques sur l'opinion de l'auteur de *l'esprit des lois* concernant les colonies." 1766. In *François Quesnay et la physiocratie*, 2:781–90. Paris: INED, 1958.

——. *Tableau économique*. Versailles, 1758.

Raynal, Guillaume-Thomas. *Histoire philosophique et politique des établissements et du commerce des Européens dans les deux Indes*. 7 vols. Paris: Lacombe, 1778.

——. *Histoire politique et philosophique des établissements et du commerce des Européens dans les deux Indes*. 10 vols. Geneva: J. L. Pellet, 1780.

Roubo, André. *L'art du menuisier*. 4 vols. Paris: Saillant et Nyon, 1769–75.

Rousseau, Jean-Jacques. *The Collected Writings of Rousseau*. Vol. 6, *Julie; or, The New Héloïse*. 1761. Translated by Philip Stewart and Jean Vaché. Hanover, NH: University Press of New England, 1997.

——. *The Discourses and Other Early Political Writings*. Translated by Victor Gourevitch. Cambridge and New York: Cambridge University Press, 1997.

——. *Discours sur les sciences et les arts*. Geneva: Barillot et fils, 1750–51.

——. *Discours sur l'origine et les fondements de l'inégalité parmi les hommes*. Amsterdam: M. M. Rey, 1755.

——. *Du contrat social; ou, Des principes du droit politique*. Amsterdam: M. M. Rey, 1762.

——. *Emile; or, On Education*. 1762. Translated by Allan Bloom. New York: Basic Books, 1979.

——. *Émile; ou, De l'éducation*. 1762. Reprint, Paris: Garnier-Flammarion, 1966.

——. *Lettre à M. D'Alembert sur les spectacles*. Geneva: Droz, 1948.

——. *On the Social Contract, Rousseau's Political Writings*. 1762. Translated by Frederick Watkins. London: Thomas Nelson, 1953.

——. *Politics and the Arts: Letter to M. D'Alembert on the Theatre*. 1758. Translated by Allan Bloom. Ithaca, NY: Cornell University Press, 1968.

Saint-Lambert, Jean-François de. *Les saisons, poème*. Amsterdam, 1769.

——. "Zimeo." 1769. In Charara, *Les fictions coloniales du dix-huitième siècle*, 50–78. Paris: L'Harmattan, 2005.

Savary des Brûlons, Jacques. *Dictionnaire universel de commerce*. 3 vols. Paris, 1723–30.

Say, Jean-Baptiste. *Traité d'économie politique; ou, Simple exposition de la manière dont se forment, se distribuent, et se consomment les richesses*. Paris: Imprimerie de Crapelet, 1803.

Schoelcher, Victor. *Esclavage et colonisation*. Edited by Émile Tersen. Paris: PUF, 2007.

Seymour, Frances. *A New Miscellany: Being a Collection of Pieces of Poetry from Bath, Tunbridge, Oxford…in the Year 1725*. London, 1726.

Staël, Germaine de. "Mirza; or, Letters of a Traveler". Translated by Françoise Massardier-Kenney. In Kadish and Massardier-Kenney, eds., *Translating Slavery*, 146–57.

——. *Mirza; ou, Lettres d'un voyageur, Recueil de morceaux détachés*. 1795. In Kadish and Massardier-Kenney, *Translating Slavery*, 271–81.

Thiery de Menonville, Nicolas-Joseph. *Traité de la culture du nopal et de l'éducation de la cochenille dans les colonies françaises de l'Amérique*. Cap-Français: Veuve Herbault; Paris: Delalain, 1787.

Tocqueville, Alexis de. *De la démocratie en Amérique*. 2 vols. 1835 and 1840. Reprint, Paris: Garnier-Flammarion, 1981.

——. *Democracy in America*. 1835 and 1840. Translated by George Lawrence. New York: Anchor Books, 1969.

——. *Voyage au Lac Onéida: Quinze jours dans le désert*. 1860. In *Oeuvres de Tocqueville*. 2 vols. Paris: Pléïade, 1991.

Turgot, Anne-Robert-Jacques. *Oeuvres de Turgot et documents le concernant*. Edited by Gustav Schelle. 5 vols. Paris: F. Alcan, 1913–23.

——. *Réflexions sur la formation et la distribution des richesses*. 1769–70. Reprint, n.p., 1788.

Vanmour, Jean-Baptiste. *Recueil de cent estampes représentant différentes nations du Levant tirées sur les tableaux peints d'après nature en 1707 et 1708*. Paris: Le Hay, 1714.

Voltaire. *Alzire; ou, Les Américains*. Paris: Jean-Baptiste-Claude Bauche, 1737.

——. *Candide; or, Optimism*. 1759. Translated by Burton Raffel. New Haven, CT: Yale University Press, 2005.

——. *Complete Works of Voltaire* (in progress). Vol. 100, *Correspondence*. Oxford: Voltaire Foundation, 2001.

——. *Dictionnaire philosophique*. 1764. Reprint, Paris: Garnier, 1967.

——. *Essai sur les mœurs et l'esprit des nations et sur les principaux faits de l'histoire depuis Charlemagne jusqu'à Louis XIII*. 2 vols. 1756, 1771. Reprint, Paris: Bordas, 1990.

——. *L'homme aux quarante écus*. Paris: Compagnie des Libraires Associés, 1768.

——. *L'ingénu, histoire véritable, tirée des manuscrits du Père Quesnel*. London, 1767.

——. *The Ingenu; or, The Sincere Huron; A True History*. London: S. Bladon, 1768.

——. *Zadig; ou, La destinée. Histoire orientale*. 2 vols. 1747. Reprint, Paris: Hachette, 1929.

Articles in d'Alembert and Diderot, Encyclopédie

Alembert, Jean Le Rond de. "Eulogy of Montesquieu." Vol. 5, 1755.

——. "Preliminary Discourse." Vol. 1, 1751.

Boucher d'Argis, Antoine Gaspard. "Slave." Vol. 5, 1755.
Condorcet, Marie-Jean-Antoine-Nicolas Caritat, Marquis de. "Monopolist." Vol. 10, 1765.
——. "Monopoly." Vol. 10, 1765.
Damilaville, Étienne Noël. "Population." Vol. 12, 1765.
Diderot, Denis. "Africa." Vol. 1, 1751.
——. "Cotton." Vol. 4, 1754.
——. "Human Species." Vol. 8, 1765.
——. "Prospectus." Advertisement to potential subscribers. Paris, 1750.
Forbonnais, François Véron Duverger de. "Colony." Vol. 3, 1753.
——. "Commerce." Vol. 3, 1753.
Formey, Jean-Henri-Samuel. "Negro (natural history)." Vol. 11, 1765.
Jaucourt, Louis de. "Black Slave Trade." Vol. 16, 1765.
——. "Despotism." Vol. 4, 1754.
——. "Slavery." Vol. 5, 1755.
——. "Tobacco." Vol. 15, 1765.
Le Romain, Jean-Baptiste-Pierre. "Indigo." Vol. 8, 1765.
——. "Negroes (commerce)." Vol. 11, 1765.
——. "Negroes, Considered as Slaves in the Colonies of the Americas." Vol. 11, 1765.
——. "Sugar Refinery." Vol. 15, 1765.
Quesnay, François. "Farmers." Vol. 6, 1756.
Rousseau, Jean-Jacques. "Economy." Vol. 5, 1755.
Saint-Lambert, Jean-François de. "Luxury." Vol. 9, 1765.

Secondary Sources

Adorno, Theodor, and Max Horkheimer. *Dialectic of Enlightenment.* Translated by John Cumming. New York: Seabury, 1972.
Agnani, Sunil. "Doux Commerce, Douce Colonisation: Diderot and the Two Indies of the French Enlightenment." In *The Anthropology of the Enlightenment,* edited by Larry Wolff and Marco Cipolloni, 65–84. Stanford: Stanford University Press, 2007.
Allemagne, Henry-René de. *La toile imprimée et les indiennes de traite.* Paris: Gründ, 1942.
Altman, Janet Gurkin. "Graffigny's Epistemology and the Emergence of Third-World Ideology." In *Writing the Female Voice: Essays on Epistolary Literature,* edited by Elizabeth Goldsmith, 172–202. Boston: Northeastern University Press, 1989.
——. "Making Room for 'Peru': Graffigny's Novel Reconsidered." In *Dilemmes du roman: Essays in Honor of Georges May,* edited by Catherine Lafarge, 33–46. Stanford: Anma Libri, 1989.
——. "A Woman's Place in the Enlightenment Sun: The Case of Françoise de Graffigny." *Romance Quarterly* 38, no. 3 (1991): 261–72.
Anselin, Alain. *L'émigration antillaise en France: La troisième île.* Paris: Karthala, 1990.
Antoine, Régis. *Les écrivains français et les Antilles, des premiers pères blancs aux surréalistes noirs.* Paris: Maisonneuve et Larose, 1978.
Appadurai, Arjun, ed. *The Social Life of Things: Commodities in Cultural Perspective.* Cambridge: Cambridge University Press, 1986.
Aravamudan, Srinivas. *Tropicopolitans: Colonialism and Agency, 1688–1804.* Durham, NC: Duke University Press, 1999.
Aubert, Guillaume. "'The Blood of France': Race and Purity of Blood in the French Atlantic World." *William and Mary Quarterly* 61, no. 3 (2004): 439–78.
Bailyn, Bernard. *Atlantic History: Concept and Contours.* Cambridge, MA: Harvard University Press, 2005.
Baker, Keith Michael. *Inventing the French Revolution: Essays on French Political Culture in the Eighteenth Century.* Cambridge: Cambridge University Press, 1990.

Balibar, Étienne. "Is There a Neo-Racism?" In *Race, Nation, Class: Ambiguous Identities,* edited by Étienne Balibar and Immanuel Wallerstein, 17–28. New York: Verso, 1991.

Banks, Kenneth J. *Chasing Empire across the Sea: Communications and the State in the French Atlantic, 1713–1763.* Montreal: McGill University Press, 2002.

Behdad, Ali. *Belated Travelers: Orientalism in the Age of Colonial Dissolution.* Durham, NC: Duke University Press, 1994.

Bénot, Yves. "Condorcet journaliste et le combat anti-esclavagiste." In *Condorcet, mathématicien, économiste, philosophe, homme politique,* edited by Pierre Crépel and Christian Gilain, 376–84. Paris: Minerve, 1989.

——. "Deleyre de *l'Histoire des voyages* (t. XIX) à *l'Histoire des deux Indes.*" *Dix-huitième siècle* 25 (1993): 369–86.

——. *La démence coloniale sous Napoléon.* Paris: La Découverte, 1992.

——. *Diderot: de l'athéisme à l'anticolonialisme.* Paris: Maspéro, 1970.

——. "La question coloniale en 1789 ou l'année des déceptions et des contradictions." In *Les lumières, l'esclavage, la colonisation,* edited by Roland Desné and Marcel Dorigny, 199–209. Paris: La Découverte, 2005.

——. *La Révolution française et la fin des colonies.* Paris: La Découverte, 1989.

Berg, Maxine. *Luxury and Pleasure in Eighteenth-Century Britain.* Oxford: Oxford University Press, 2005.

Berg, Maxine, and Elizabeth Eger, eds. *Luxury in the Eighteenth Century: Debates, Desires, Delectable Goods.* Basingstoke: Palgrave Macmillan, 2002.

Berlin, Ira, and Philip D. Morgan, eds. *The Slaves' Economy: Independent Production by Slaves in the Americas.* London: Frank Cass, 1991.

Berry, Christopher J. *The Idea of Luxury: A Conceptual and Historical Investigation.* Cambridge: Cambridge University Press, 1994.

Berthiaume, Pierre. "Abaquis et Nopandes, ou l'herméneutique inversée du *Philosophe anglais* de Prévost." *Tangence* 72 (2003): 93–107.

——. *L'aventure américaine au XVIIIe siècle: Du voyage à l'écriture.* Ottawa: Presse de l'Université d'Ottawa, 1990.

——. "Louisiana, or the Shadow Cast by French Colonial Myth." *Dalhousie French Studies* 58 (2002): 10–25.

Bhabha, Homi. "Of Mimicry and Man: The Ambivalence of Colonial Discourse." In *The Location of Culture,* 85–92. New York: Routledge, 1994.

Biehn, Michel. *En jupon piqué et robe d'indienne: Costumes provençaux.* Marseille: Éditions Jeanne Lafitte, 1987.

Blackburn, Robin. *The Making of New World Slavery: From the Baroque to the Modern, 1492–1800.* London: Verso, 1997.

——. *Overthrow of Colonial Slavery, 1776–1848.* London: Verso, 1988.

Blanc, Olivier. *Marie-Olympe de Gouges: Une humaniste à la fin du XVIIIè siècle.* Cahors: René Viénet, 2003.

Blum, Carol. *Strength in Numbers: Population, Reproduction, and Power in Eighteenth-Century France.* Baltimore: Johns Hopkins University Press, 2002.

Borges, Jorge Luis. "The Dread Redeemer Lazarus Morell." In *A Universal History of Infamy,* 17–29. Translated by Norman Thomas di Giovanni. New York: E. P. Dutton, 1972.

Boucher, Philip. *Cannibal Encounters: Europeans and Island Caribs, 1492–1763.* Baltimore: Johns Hopkins University Press, 1992.

Boulle, Pierre H. *Race et esclavage dans la France de l'ancien régime.* Paris: Perrin, 2007.

Brac, Virginie, and Myriam Cottias. *Tropiques amers.* Television program. Paris: France, May 3, 2007.

Braidwood, Stephen J. *Black Poor and White Philanthropists: London's Blacks and the Sierra Leone Settlement.* Liverpool: University of Liverpool Press, 1994.

Braudel, Fernand. *La Méditerranée et le monde méditerranéen a l'époque de Philippe II.* 3 vols. Paris: Armand Colin, 1949.

Brown, Gregory S. *A Field of Honor: Writers, Court Culture and Public Theater in French Literary Life from Racine to the Revolution*. New York: Columbia University Press, 2002.

Buckridge, Steeve O. *The Language of Dress: Resistance and Accommodation in Jamaica, 1760–1890*. Kingston: University of the West Indies Press, 2004.

Burnard, Joyce. *Chintz and Cotton: India's Textile Gift to the World*. Kenthurst, Australia: Kangaroo Press, 1994.

Cauna, Jacques de. *Au temps des îles à sucre: Histoire d'une plantation de Saint-Domingue au XVIIIè siècle*. Paris: Karthala, 1987.

Césaire, Aimé. *Discourse on Colonialism*. 1955. Translated by John Pinkham. New York: Monthly Review Press, 2000.

Charara, Youmna, ed. *Les fictions coloniales du dix-huitième siècle*. Paris: L'Harmattan, 2005.

Chassagne, Serge. *Le coton et ses patrons: France, 1760–1840*. Paris: Éditions de l'École des Hautes Études en Sciences Sociales, 1991.

Chaussat, Dominique, and Florence Chaussat, eds. *Les meubles du Port Rochelais*. La Rochelle: Éditions Être et Connaitre, 2000.

Chérel, Albert. *De Télemaque à Candide*. Paris: Del Duca, 1958.

Cixous, Hélène. *"Coming to Writing" and Other Essays*. Cambridge, MA: Harvard University Press, 1991.

Cohen, William B. *The French Encounter with Africans: White Responses to Blacks, 1530–1880*. Bloomington: Indiana University Press, 1980.

Colley, Linda. *Captives: Britain, Empire and the World, 1600–1850*. New York: Knopf, 2004.

Constant, Fred. "Politique de la migration: Essai d'évaluation." In *1946–1996: Cinquante ans de départementalisation d'outre-mer*, edited by Fred Constant and Justin Daniel, 97–132. Paris: L'Harmattan, 1997.

Cook, Mercer. "Jean-Jacques Rousseau and the Negro." *Journal of Negro History* 21, no. 3 (1936): 294–303.

Cooper, Frederick. *Colonialism in Question: Theory, Knowledge, History*. Berkeley and London: University of California Press, 2005.

Cottias, Myriam. *La question noire: Histoire d'une construction coloniale*. Paris: Bayard, 2007.

Cottias, Myriam, and Arlette Farge, eds. *De la nécessité d'adopter l'esclavage en France*. Paris: Bayard, 2007.

Crawford, M. D. C. *The Heritage of Cotton: The Fibre of Two Worlds and Many Ages*. New York and London: G. P. Putnam's Sons, 1931.

Crowston, Clare Haru. *Fabricating Women: The Seamstresses of Old Regime France, 1675–1791*. Durham, NC and London: Duke University Press, 2001.

Curran, Andrew. "Rethinking Race History: The Role of the Albino in the French Enlightenment Life Sciences." *History and Theory* 48 (2009): 151–79.

Dabydeen, David. *Hogarth's Blacks: Images of Blacks in Eighteenth Century English Art*. Athens: University of Georgia Press, 1987.

Darnton, Robert. *The Forbidden Best-Sellers of Pre-Revolutionary France*. New York and London: W. W. Norton, 1996.

Davis, David Brion. "Constructing Race: A Reflection." In *The Image of God: Religion, Moral Values, and Our Heritage of Slavery*, 307–22. New Haven, CT: Yale University Press, 2001.

——. *The Problem of Slavery in Western Culture*. 1966. Reprint, Oxford: Oxford University Press, 1988.

Davis, Robert C. *Christian Slaves, Muslim Masters: White Slavery in the Mediterranean, the Barbary Coast and Italy, 1500–1800*. London: Palgrave-Macmillan, 2003.

Dayan, Joan. *Haiti, History, and the Gods*. Berkeley: University of California Press, 1995.

Debien, Gabriel. *Esclaves aux Antilles françaises, XVIIe–XVIIIe siècles*. Basse-Terre, Guadeloupe: Société d'histoire de la Guadeloupe, 1974.

———. *Les engagés pour les Antilles (1634–1715)*. Paris: Société de l'histoire des colonies françaises, 1952.

———. *Une indigoterie à Saint-Domingue à la fin du XVIIIe siècle*. Cairo: Revue d'Histoire des Colonies, 1946.

DeJean, Joan. *The Essence of Style: How the French Invented High Fashion, Fine Food, Chic Cafés, Style, Sophistication and Glamour*. New York: Free Press, 2005.

Delesalle, Simone, and Lucette Valensi. "Le mot 'nègre' dans les dictionnaires français d'ancien régime: Histoire et lexicographie." *Langue française* 15 (1972): 79–104.

Delon, Michel. "L'appel au lecteur dans *l'Histoire des deux Indes*." In *Lectures de Raynal: L'histoire des deux Indes en Europe et en Amérique au XVIIIe siècle*. Edited by Hans-Jürgen Lüsebrink and Manfred Tietz, 53–66. *Studies on Voltaire and the Eighteenth Century* 286. Oxford: Voltaire Foundation, 1991.

De Man, Paul. "Metaphor (Second Discourse)." In *Allegories of Reading: Figural Language in Rousseau, Nietzsche, Rilke, and Proust*, 135–59. New Haven, CT: Yale University Press, 1979.

Depitre, Édgard. *La toile peinte en France aux XVIIè et XVIIIè siècles*. Paris: Marcel Rivière, 1912.

Derrida, Jacques. *On Grammatology*. Translated by Gayatri Chakravorty Spivak. Baltimore: Johns Hopkins University Press, 1976.

Dessalles, Adrien. *Histoire générale des Antilles*. 5 vols. Paris: Libraire-éditeur, 1847–48.

Dickson, Bruce D. *The Origins of African-American Literature, 1680–1865*. Charlottesville: University of Virginia Press, 2001.

Dobie, Madeleine. "Exotic Economies and Colonial History in the *Esprit des Lois*." *Studies on Voltaire and the Eighteenth Century* 362 (1998): 145–67.

———. *Foreign Bodies: Gender, Language, and Culture in French Orientalism*. Stanford: Stanford University Press, 2001.

———. "Graffigny's Writing Subject: Language and Identity in the *Lettres d'une Péruvienne*." *Eighteenth Century: Theory and Interpretation* 38, no. 2 (1997): 99–117.

———. "Invisible Exodus: The Cultural Effacement of Antillean Migration." *Diaspora* 13, no. 2/3 (2004): 149–83.

Dockès, Pierre. "Le paradigme sucrier (XIe–XIXe siècle)." In *L'économie de l'esclavage colonial: Enquête et bilan du XVIIe au XIXè siècle*, edited by Fred Célimène and André Legris, 109–26. Paris: C. N. R. S., 2002.

Dorigny, Marcel, ed. *Les abolitions de l'esclavage: De L. F. Sonthonax à V. Schoelcher: 1793–1794–1848*. Paris: UNESCO, 1995.

Dorigny, Marcel, and Bernard Gainot, eds. *La Société des amis des noirs, 1788–1799*. Paris: UNESCO, 1998.

Dorlin, Elsa. *La matrice de la race: Généalogie sexuelle et coloniale de la nation française*. Paris: La Découverte, 2006.

Douthwaite, Julia. "Relocating the Exotic Other in Graffigny's *Lettres d'une Péruvienne*." *Romanic Review* 82, no. 4 (1991): 456–71.

Dubois, Laurent. *Avengers of the New World: The Story of the Haitian Revolution*. Cambridge, MA: Belknap Press of Harvard University Press, 2004.

———. *A Colony of Citizens: Revolution and Slave Emancipation in the French Caribbean, 1787–1804*. Chapel Hill: University of North Carolina Press, 2004.

———. "La république métissée: Citizenship, Colonialism, and the Borders of French History." *Cultural Studies* 14 (2000): 15–34.

Duchet, Michèle. *Anthropologie et histoire au siècle des lumières*. Paris: Maspéro, 1971.

———. *Diderot et l'Histoire des deux Indes; ou, L'écriture fragmentaire*. Paris: Nizet, 1978.

Dufrenoy, Marie-Louise. *L'Orient romanesque en France, 1704–1789*. 3 vols. Montreal: Beauchemin, 1946–47.

Du Pasquier, Jacqueline. *Bordeaux Musée des arts décoratifs: Mobilier bordelais et parisien*. Paris: Éditions de la Réunion des Musées Nationaux, 1997.

Durkheim, Émile. *Montesquieu and Rousseau, Forerunners of Sociology.* Translated by Ralph Manheim. Ann Arbor: Michigan University Press, 1960.

Ehrard, Jean. "*L'Encyclopédie et* l'esclavage colonial." In *La Période révolutionnaire aux Antilles,* 229–39. Fort-de-France: Faculté des lettres et sciences humaines, Université des Antilles et de la Guyane, 1988.

——. "L'esclavage devant la conscience des lumières françaises: Indifférence, gêne, révolte." In Dorigny, ed., *Les abolitions de l'esclavage,* 143–52.

Elisabeth, Léo. *La société martiniquaise aux XVIIe et XVIIIè siècles, 1664–1789.* Paris: Karthala, 2003.

Estève, Laurent. *Montesquieu, Rousseau, Diderot: Du genre humain au bois d'ébène.* Paris: Unesco, 2002.

Evers, Sandra T. J., and Vinesh Y. Hookoomsing, eds. *Globalization and the South-West Indian Ocean.* Réduit, Mauritius: University of Mauritius Press, 2000.

Fabella, Yvonne. "'An Empire Founded on Libertinage': The *Mulâtresse* and Colonial Anxiety in Saint Domingue." In *Gender, Race and Religion in the Colonization of the Americas,* edited by Nora E. Jaffary, *109–123.* Aldershot: Ashgate, 2007.

Fassin, Didier, and Eric Fassin, eds., *De la question sociale à la question raciale? Représenter la société française.* Paris: La Découverte, 2006.

Felsenstein, Frank. *English Trader, Indian Maid: Representing Gender, Race, and Slavery in the New World: An Inkle and Yarico Reader.* Baltimore: Johns Hopkins University Press, 1999.

Figeac, Michel. *La douceur des lumières: Noblesse et art de vivre en Guyenne au XVIIIème siècle.* Paris: Mollat, 2001.

Flaubert, Gustave. *Madame Bovary.* 1857. Translated by Gerard Hopkins. Oxford: Oxford University Press, 1998.

Foster, Helen B. *New Raiments of Self: African American Clothing in the Antebellum South.* Oxford and New York: Berg, 1997.

Foucault, Michel. *Les mots et les choses: Une archéologie des sciences humaines.* Paris: Gallimard, 1966.

Fredrickson, George. *Racism: A Short History.* Princeton, NJ: Princeton University Press, 2002.

Freud, Sigmund. *The Standard Edition of the Complete Psychological Works of Sigmund Freud.* Translated by James Strachey. Vols. 4–5, *The Interpretation of Dreams.* 1900. London: Hogarth Press, 1953–74.

Garraway, Doris. *The Libertine Colony: Creolization in the Early French Caribbean.* Durham, NC: Duke University Press, New York, 2005.

Geggus, David. *Haitian Revolutionary Studies.* Bloomington: Indiana University Press, 2002.

——, ed. *The Impact of the Haitian Revolution in the Atlantic World.* Columbia: University of South Carolina Press, 2001.

Genette, Gérard. *Figures III.* Paris: Seuil, 1972.

Georgel, Chantal, Françoise Vergès, and Alain Vivien, eds. *L'abolition de l'esclavage: Un combat pour les droits de l'homme.* Brussels: Éditions Complexes, 1998.

Ghachem, Malick. "The Age of the Code Noir in French Political Economy." In *A Vast and Useful Art: The Gustave Gimon Collection on French Political Economy,* edited by M. J. Parrine, 66–76. Stanford: Stanford University Libraries, 2004.

Gilroy, Beryl. *Inkle and Yarico.* Leeds: Peepal Tree, 1996.

Gilroy, Paul. *The Black Atlantic: Modernity and Double Consciousness.* London and New York: Verso, 1993.

Girardet, Raoul, ed. *Le nationalisme français, 1870–1914.* Paris: Seuil, 1983.

Goggi, Gianluigi. *Diderot: Contributions à l'histoire des deux Indes.* Siena: University of Siena Press, 1976–77.

——. "La collaboration de Diderot à la première édition de *l'Histoire des deux Indes.*" In *Lectures de Raynal: "L'histoire des deux Indes" en Europe et en Amérique au XVIIIe siècle.*

Edited by Hans-Jürgen Lüsebrink and Manfred Tietz, 17–52. *Studies on Voltaire and the Eighteenth Century* 286. Oxford: Voltaire Foundation, 1991.

Goodman, Dena, and Kathryn Norberg, eds. *Furnishing the Eighteenth Century: What Furniture Can Tell Us about the European and American Past.* New York: Taylor and Francis, 2007.

Goveia, Elsa V. *The West Indian Slave Laws of the Eighteenth Century.* Barbados: Caribbean Universities Press, 1970.

Grosrichard, Alain. *Structure du sérail: La fiction du despotisme asiatique dans l'occident classique.* Paris: Seuil, 1978.

Grove, Richard H. *Green Imperialism: Colonial Expansion, Tropical Edens and the Origins of Environmentalism, 1600–1800.* Cambridge: Cambridge University Press, 1995.

Guénif-Souilamas, Nacira. "La république aristocratique et la nouvelle société de cour." In *La république mise à nu par son immigration,* edited by Nacira Guénif-Souilamas, 7–27. Paris: Fabrique, 2006.

Guillaumin, Colette. *L'idéologie raciste: Genèse et langage actuel.* Paris: Gallimard, 2002.

Hale, Dana. "French Images of Race on Product Trademarks during the Third Republic." In *The Color of Liberty: Histories of Race in France,* edited by Sue Peabody and Tyler Stovall, 131–47. Durham, NC: Duke University Press, 2003.

Haudrère, Philippe, Gérard Le Bouëdec, and Louis Mézin, eds. *Les Compagnies des Indes.* Rennes: Ouest-France, 2001.

Hayot, Émile. *Les gens de couleur libres du Fort-Royal de 1679 à 1823. Revue française d'histoire d'outre-mer 16,* nos. 202–203. 1969.

Hearn, Lafcadio. *Two Years in the French West Indies.* New York: Harter and Bros., 1890.

Henderson, W. O. "The Anglo-French Commercial Treaty of 1786." *Economic History Review* 10, no. 1 (1957): 104–12.

Hirschman, Albert O. *The Passions and the Interests: Political Arguments for Capitalism before Its Triumph.* Princeton, NJ: Princeton University Press, 1977.

Hoffmann, Léon-François. *Le nègre romantique: Personnage littéraire et obsession collective.* Paris: Payot, 1973.

hooks, bell. *Ain't I a Woman? Black Women and Feminism.* Boston: South End Press, 1981.

———. *Feminist Theory from Margin to Center.* London: Pluto Press, 2000.

Hughes, Clair. *Dressed in Fiction.* New York: Berg, 2006.

Hulme, Peter. *Colonial Encounters: Europe and the Native Caribbean, 1492–1797.* London and New York: Methuen, 1986.

Hunt, Lynn. *Inventing Human Rights: A History.* New York: W. W. Norton, 2007.

International Herald Tribune. Paris, 1967–.

Jaenen, Cornelius J., "Problems of Assimilation in New France, 1603–1645." *French Historical Studies* 4, no. 3 (1966): 265–89.

James, C. L. R. *The Black Jacobins: Toussaint L'Ouverture and the San Domingo Revolution.* New York: Vintage, 1963.

Jameson, Russell P. *Montesquieu et l'esclavage: Étude sur les origines de l'opinion antiesclavagiste en France au XVIIIè siècle.* Paris: Hachette, 1911.

Janneau, Guillaume. *Le meuble de l'ébénisterie.* Paris: Éditions de l'Amateur, 1989.

Jarry, Madeleine. *Chinoiseries: Le rayonnement du goût chinois sur les arts décoratifs des XVIIe et XVIIIe siècles.* Paris: Vilo, 1981; Fribourg: Office du Livre, 1981.

Jennings, Jeremy. "The Debate about Luxury in Eighteenth- and Nineteenth-Century French Political Thought." *Journal of the History of Ideas* 68, no. 1 (2007): 79–105.

Jennings, Lawrence. *French Anti-Slavery: The Movement for the Abolition of Slavery in France, 1802–1848.* Cambridge: Cambridge University Press, 2000.

Jullien, Dominique. *Récits du Nouveau monde: Les voyageurs français en Amérique de Chateaubriand à nos jours.* Paris: Nathan, 1992.

Jurt, Joseph. "Condorcet: L'idée de progrès et l'opposition à l'esclavage." In *Condorcet, mathématicien, économiste, philosophe, homme politique,* edited by Pierre Crépel and Christian Gilain, 384–95. Paris: Minerve, 1989.

Kadish, Doris, and Françoise Massardier-Kenney, eds. *Translating Slavery: Gender and Race in French Women's Writing, 1783–1823.* Kent, OH: Kent State University Press, 1994.

Kopytoff, Igor. "The Cultural Biography of Things." In Appadurai, ed., *The Social Life of Things,* 64–94.

Koselleck, Reinhart. *Critique and Crisis: Enlightenment and the Pathogenesis of Modern Society.* Cambridge, MA: MIT Press, 1988.

Labrouquère, André. "Les idées coloniales des physiocrates." Doctoral thesis, Université de Paris, 1927.

Lafontant, Julien. *Montesquieu et le problème de l'esclavage dans "l'esprit des lois."* Sherbrooke, Quebec: Naaman, 1979.

Larrère, Catherine. *L'invention de l'économie au XVIIIème siècle.* Paris: PUF, 1992.

Le Hir, Marie-Pierre. "Feminism, Theater, Race: *L'esclavage des noirs.*" In Kadish and Massardier-Kenney, *Translating Slavery,* 65–83.

Lemire, Beverly. *Fashion's Favourite: The Cotton Trade and the Consumer in Britain, 1660–1800.* Oxford: Oxford University Press, 1991.

Leroux, Émilienne. *Histoire d'une ville et de ses habitants: Nantes.* Nantes: Editions ACL, 1984.

Les derniers maîtres de la Martinique. Television documentary. Paris: Canal Plus, January 30, 2009.

Lévi-Strauss, Claude. *Anthropologie structurale.* Paris: Plon, 1958.

——. *Tristes tropiques.* Paris: Plon, 1955.

Liauzu, Claude, ed. *Dictionnaire de la colonisation française.* Paris: Larousse, 2007.

Longino, Michele. *Orientalism in French Classical Drama.* Cambridge: Cambridge University Press, 2002.

Lowe, Lisa. *Critical Terrains: French and British Orientalisms.* Ithaca, NY: Cornell University Press, 1991.

Lüsebrink, Hans-Jurgen, and Anthony Strugnell, eds. *L'histoire des deux Indes: Réécriture et polygraphie. Studies on Voltaire and the Eighteenth Century* 333. Oxford: Voltaire Foundation, 1995.

Marie, Claude-Valentin. "Les Antillais de l'hexagone." In *Immigration et intégration: L'état des savoirs,* edited by Philippe Dewitte, 99–105. Paris: La Découverte, 1999.

——. "Les populations des DOM-TOM en France métropolitaine." *Espaces-Population-Sociétés* 2 (1986): 197–206.

Massardier-Kenney, Françoise. "Staël, Translation, and Race." In Kadish and Massardier-Kenney, *Translating Slavery,* 135–45.

Matar, Nabil. *Piracy, Slavery and Redemption.* New York: Columbia University Press, 2001.

Mauss, Marcel. Essai sur le don: forme et raison de l'échange dans les sociétés archaïques. *L'Année sociologique,* 2nd series 1, 1923–24.

——. *The Gift: The Form and Reason for Exchange in Archaic Societies.* London: Routledge, 2001.

May, Louis-Philippe. *Histoire économique de la Martinique, 1635–1763.* Paris: Presses Modernes, 1930.

McClellan, James E. *Colonialism and Science: Saint-Domingue in the Old Regime.* Baltimore: Johns Hopkins University Press, 1992.

Meinig, D. W. *The Shaping of America: A Geographical Perspective on Five Hundred Years of History.* 4 vols. New Haven, CT: Yale University Press, 1986–2004.

Melzer, Sara E. "Magic and the Conversion of 'Outsiders' into 'Insiders' in the French Empire." In *The Meanings of Magic from the Bible to Buffalo Bill,* edited by Amy Wygant, 178–210. Oxford: Berghahn Books, 2006.

——. "Une 'seconde France'? Re-penser le paradigme 'classique' à partir de l'histoire oubliée de la colonisation française." In *La littérature, le XVIIe siècle et nous: dialogue transatlantique,* edited by Hélène Merlin-Kajman, 75–84. Paris: Presse Sorbonne Nouvelle, 2008.

Mercier, Roger. *L'Afrique noire dans la littérature française: Les premières images, XVIIe–XVIIIe siècles.* Dakar: Université de Dakar, 1962.

Midlo Hall, Gwendolyn. *Africans in Colonial Louisiana: The Development of Afro-Creole Culture in the Eighteenth Century.* Baton Rouge: Louisiana State Press, 1992.

Miller, Christopher L. *French Atlantic Triangle: Literature and Culture of the Slave Trade.* Durham, NC: Duke University Press, 2007.

Mobilier créole. Cahiers du patrimoine 15–16 (1997).

Muthu, Sankar. *Enlightenment against Empire.* Princeton, NJ: Princeton University Press, 2003.

Ndiaye, Pap. *La condition noire: Essai sur une minorité française.* Paris: Calmann-Lévy, 2008.

Noël, Erick. *Être noir en France au dix-huitième siècle.* Paris: Tallandier, 2006.

Offen, Karen. "How (and Why) the Analogy of Marriage with Slavery Provided the Springboard for Women's Rights Demands in France, 1640–1848." In *Women's Rights and Transatlantic Antislavery in the Era of Emancipation*, edited by Kathryn Kish Sklar and James Brewer Stewart, 57–81. New Haven, CT: Yale University Press, 2007.

Ogle, Gene. "'The Eternal Power of Reason' and 'The Superiority of Whites': Hilliard d'Auberteuil's Colonial Enlightenment." *French Colonial History* 3 (2003): 35–50.

O'Hagan, Timothy. "Rousseau: Conservative or Revolutionary? A Critique of Lévi-Strauss." *Critique of Anthropology* 11 (1978): 19–38.

Pagden, Anthony. *European Encounters with the New World: From Renaissance to Romanticism.* New Haven, CT: Yale University Press, 1993.

Peabody, Sue. "'A Dangerous Zeal': Catholic Missions to Slaves in the French Caribbean, 1635–1800." *French Historical Studies* 25, no. 1 (January 2002): 58–76.

——. "'A Nation Born to Slavery': Missionaries and Racial Discourse in Seventeenth-Century French Antilles." *Journal of Social History* 38, no. 1 (2004): 113–26.

——. *"There Are No Slaves in France": The Political Culture of Race and Slavery in the Ancien Régime.* New York: Oxford University Press, 1996.

Peabody, Sue, and Tyler Stovall, eds. *The Color of Liberty: Histories of Race in France.* Durham, NC and London: Duke University Press, 2003.

Pétré-Grenouilleau, Olivier. *L'argent de la traite: Milieu négrier, capitalisme et développement; Un modèle.* Paris: Aubier, 1996.

Pioffet, Marie-Christine. "L'espace américain comme figure du désenchantement." *Études francophones* 17, no. 1 (2002): 77–92.

Piroux, Lorraine. "The Encyclopedist and the Peruvian Princess: The Poetics of Illegibility in French Enlightenment Book Culture." *PMLA* 121, no. 1 (2006): 107–23.

Pitts, Jennifer. *A Turn to Empire: The Rise of Liberal Imperialism in Britain and France.* Princeton, NJ: Princeton University Press, 2005.

Pluchon, Pierre. *La route des esclaves: Négriers et bois d'ébène au XVIIIe siècle.* Paris: Hachette, 1980.

Porter, Dennis. *Haunted Journeys: Desire and Transgression in European Travel Writing.* Princeton, NJ: Princeton University Press, 1991.

Prakash, Gyan. "After Colonialism." In *After Colonialism: Imperial Histories and Postcolonial Displacements*, edited by Gyan Prakash, 3–19. Princeton, NJ: Princeton University Press, 1995.

Pratt, Mary-Louise. *Imperial Eyes: Travel Writing and Transculturation.* New York and London: Routledge, 1992.

Price, Lawrence Marsden. *Inkle and Yarico Album.* Berkeley: University of California Press, 1937.

Pucci, Suzanne R. "Letters from the Harem: Veiled Figures of Writing in Montesquieu's *Lettres persanes.*" In *Writing the Female Voice: Essays on Epistolary Literature*, edited by Elizabeth Goldsmith, 114–34. Boston: Northeastern University Press, 1989.

Quicherat, Émile. *Histoire du costume en France depuis les temps les plus reculés jusqu'à la fin du XVIIIème siècle.* Paris: Hachette, 1875.

Racault, Jean-Michel. "L'effet exotique dans L'histoire des deux Indes et la mise en scène du monde colonial dans l'Océan Indien." In *L'histoire des deux Indes, réécriture et polygraphie,* edited by Gaston Rambert, 119–32. *Studies on Voltaire and the Eighteenth Century* 333. Oxford: Voltaire Foundation, 1995.

Rambert, Gaston, ed. *L'histoire du commerce de Marseille.* 7 vols. Paris: Plon, 1949–66.

Ramond, Pierre. *Marquetry.* Translated by Jacqueline Derenne et al. Los Angeles: J. Paul Getty Museum, 2002.

Reddy, William M. *The Rise of Market Culture: The Textile Trade and French Society, 1750–1900.* Cambridge: Cambridge University Press, 1984.

——. "The Structure of a Cultural Crisis: Thinking about Cloth in France before and after the Revolution." In Appadurai, ed., *The Social Life of Things,* 261–84.

Reinhardt, Catherine A. *Claims to Memory: Beyond Slavery and Emancipation in the French Caribbean.* New York and Oxford: Bergahn Books, 2006.

——. "Slavery and Commemoration: Remembering the French Abolitionary Decree, 150 Years Later." In *Memory, Empire and Postcolonialism,* edited by Alec G. Hargreaves, 11–36. Lanham, MD: Lexington, 2005.

Resnick, Daniel P. "The *Société des amis des noirs* and the Abolition of Slavery." *French Historical Studies* 7, no. 4 (1972): 558–69.

Ribeiro, Aileen. *Dress in Eighteenth-Century Europe, 1715–1789.* New Haven and London: Yale University Press, 2002.

——. *Fashion in the French Revolution.* New York: Holmes and Meier, 1988.

Roach, Joseph R. *Cities of the Dead: Circum-Atlantic Performance.* New York: Columbia University Press, 1996.

Roche, Daniel. *La culture des apparences.* Paris: Fayard, 1989.

Roger, Philippe. *L'ennemi américain: Généalogie de l'antiaméricanisme français.* Paris: Seuil, 2002.

Rothschild, Emma. *Economic Sentiments: Adam Smith, Condorcet, and the Enlightenment.* Cambridge, MA: Harvard University Press, 2001.

Rousso, Henry. *Le syndrome de Vichy: De 1944 à nos jours.* Paris: Seuil, 1987.

——. "Les raisins verts de la guerre d'Algérie." In *La guerre d'Algérie, 1954–1962,* edited by Yves Michaud, 127–51. Paris: Odile Jacob, 2004.

Said, Edward. *Orientalism.* New York: Vintage, 1979.

Sala-Molins, Louis. *Dark Side of the Light.* Translated by John Conteh-Morgan. Minneapolis: University of Minnesota Press, 2006.

——. *Le code noir ou le calvaire de Canaan.* Paris: PUF, 1987.

——. *Misères des lumières: Sous la raison, l'outrage.* Paris: Robert Laffont, 1992.

Salverte, François de. *Les ébénistes du dix-huitième siècle, leurs oeuvres et leurs marques.* Paris and Brussels: G. Vancrest, 1923.

Saugera, Eric. *Bordeaux, port négrier: Chronologie, économie, idéologie, XVIIe–XIXe siècles.* Paris: Karthala, 1995.

Schmidt, Nelly. *L'abolition de l'esclavage: Cinq siècles de combats (XVIe–XXe siècle).* Paris: Fayard, 2005.

Seeber, Edward W. *Anti-Slavery Opinion in France during the Second Half of the Eighteenth Century.* Baltimore: Johns Hopkins University Press, 1937.

Sepinwall, Alyssa Goldstein. *The Abbé Grégoire and the French Revolution: The Making of Modern Universalism.* Berkeley: University of California Press, 2005.

Shohat, Ella. "Rupture and Return: Zionist Discourse and the Study of Arab Jews." *Social Text* 75, 21, no. 2 (2003): 49–75.

Shovlin, John. *The Political Economy of Virtue: Luxury, Patriotism, and the Origins of the French Revolution.* Ithaca, NY: Cornell University Press, 2006.

Sollors, Werner. *Neither White nor Black yet Both.* New York: Oxford University Press, 1997.

Spivak, Gayatri Chakravorty. "Can the Subaltern Speak?" In *Marxism and the Interpretation of Culture,* edited by Cary Nelson and Lawrence Grossberg, 271–313. Urbana: University of Illinois Press, 1988.

Stein, Robert Louis. *The French Slave Trade in the Eighteenth Century: An Old Regime Business.* Madison: University of Wisconsin Press, 1979.

——. *The French Sugar Business in the Eighteenth Century.* Baton Rouge: Louisiana State University Press, 1988.

Steiner, Philippe. "L'esclavage chez les économistes français (1750–1803)." In Dorigny, ed., *Les abolitions de l'esclavage,* 165–78.

Stewart, Philip. "L'Amérique de l'Abbé Prévost: Aspects documentaires de 'Cleveland.'" *French Review* 49, no. 6 (1976): 868–82.

Tardieu, Marc. *Les Antillais à Paris: D'hier à aujourd'hui.* Paris: Karthala, 2006.

Tarrade, Jean. *Le commerce colonial de la France à la fin de l'Ancien Régime.* 2 vols. Paris: PUF, 1972.

Taussig, Michael. *Mimesis and Alterity: A Particular History of the Senses.* New York: Routledge, 1993.

Terjanian, Anoush. "'Doux commerce' and Its Discontents: Slavery, Piracy, and Monopoly in Eighteenth-Century France." Ph.D. diss., Johns Hopkins University, 2005.

Théré, Christine. "L'édition économique et ses auteurs en 1789." In *La pensée économique pendant la Révolution française,* edited by Gilbert Faccarello and Philippe Steiner, 59–65. Grenoble: Presses Universitaires de Grenoble, 1990.

Todorov, Tzvetan. *The Conquest of America: The Question of the Other.* Translated by Richard Howard. New York: Harper and Row, 1984.

——. *La conquête de l'Amérique: La question de l'autre.* Paris: Seuil, 1982.

Trouillot, Michel-Rolph. *Silencing the Past: Power and the Production of History.* Boston: Beacon Press, 1995.

Undank, Jack. "Graffigny's Room of Her Own." *French Forum* 13 (1988): 297–318.

Van den Abbeele, Georges. *Travel as Metaphor: From Montaigne to Rousseau.* Minneapolis: University of Minnesota Press, 1992.

Vaughan, Megan. *Creating the Creole Island: Slavery in Eighteenth-Century Mauritius.* Durham, NC and London: Duke University Press, 2005.

Vergès, Françoise. *Abolir l'esclavage: Une utopie coloniale, les ambiguïtés d'une politique humanitaire.* Paris: A. Michel, 2001.

——. *Monsters and Revolutionaries: Colonial Family Romance and Metissage.* Durham, NC and London: Duke University Press, 1999.

Vrignaud, Gilberte. *Vêture et parure en France au dix-huitième siècle.* Paris: Editions Messene, 1995.

Wallerstein, Immanuel. *Mercantilism and the Consolidation of the European World Economy, 1600–1750.* 3 vols. New York: Academic Press, 1980.

Weber, Caroline. *Queen of Fashion: What Marie-Antoinette Wore to the Revolution.* New York: Henry Holt, 2006.

Weber, Jacques, ed. *Compagnies et comptoirs: l'Inde des Français XVII–XVIIIè siècle.* Paris: Société Francaise d'Outre-Mer, 1991.

Weiss, Gillian. "Barbary Captivity and the French Idea of Freedom." *French Historical Studies* 28, no. 2 (2005): 231–64.

Williams, David. *Condorcet and Modernity.* Cambridge and New York: Cambridge University Press, 2004.

Williams, Eric. *Capitalism and Slavery.* London: Andre Deutsch, 1944.

Wolvesperges, Thibaut. *Le meuble français en laque.* Paris: Éditions de l'Amateur, 2000.

Young, Robert. *Colonial Desire: Hybridity in Theory, Culture and Race.* New York: Routledge, 1995.

Zantop, Susanne. *Colonial Fantasies: Conquest, Family, and Nation in Precolonial Germany, 1770–1870.* Durham, NC: Duke University Press, 1997.

Index

Note: Page numbers in *italics* indicate illustrations.